THE ROLLER BLADE SEVEN

PRESENTED BY SCOTT SHAW

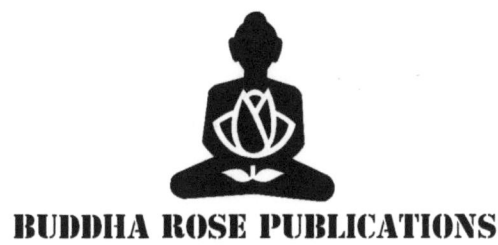

BUDDHA ROSE PUBLICATIONS

The Roller Blade Seven
Copyright © 2015 By Scott Shaw
www.scottshaw.com
All Rights Reserved

This book contains material protected under International and Federal Copyright Laws
and Treaties. Any unauthorized reprint or use of this material is prohibited.
No part of this book may be reproduced or transmitted in any form or by any means,
electronic or mechanical, including photocopying, recording, or by any information storage
and retrieval system without express written permission from the author or the publishing Company.

First Edition 2015

ISBN 10: 1-87779287-X
ISBN 13: 978-1-877792-87-8

Library of Congress Control Number: 2015956158

Printed in the United States of America

10 9 8 7 6 5 4 3 2 1

THE ROLLER BLADE SEVEN
A PHOTOGRAPHIC EXPLORATION

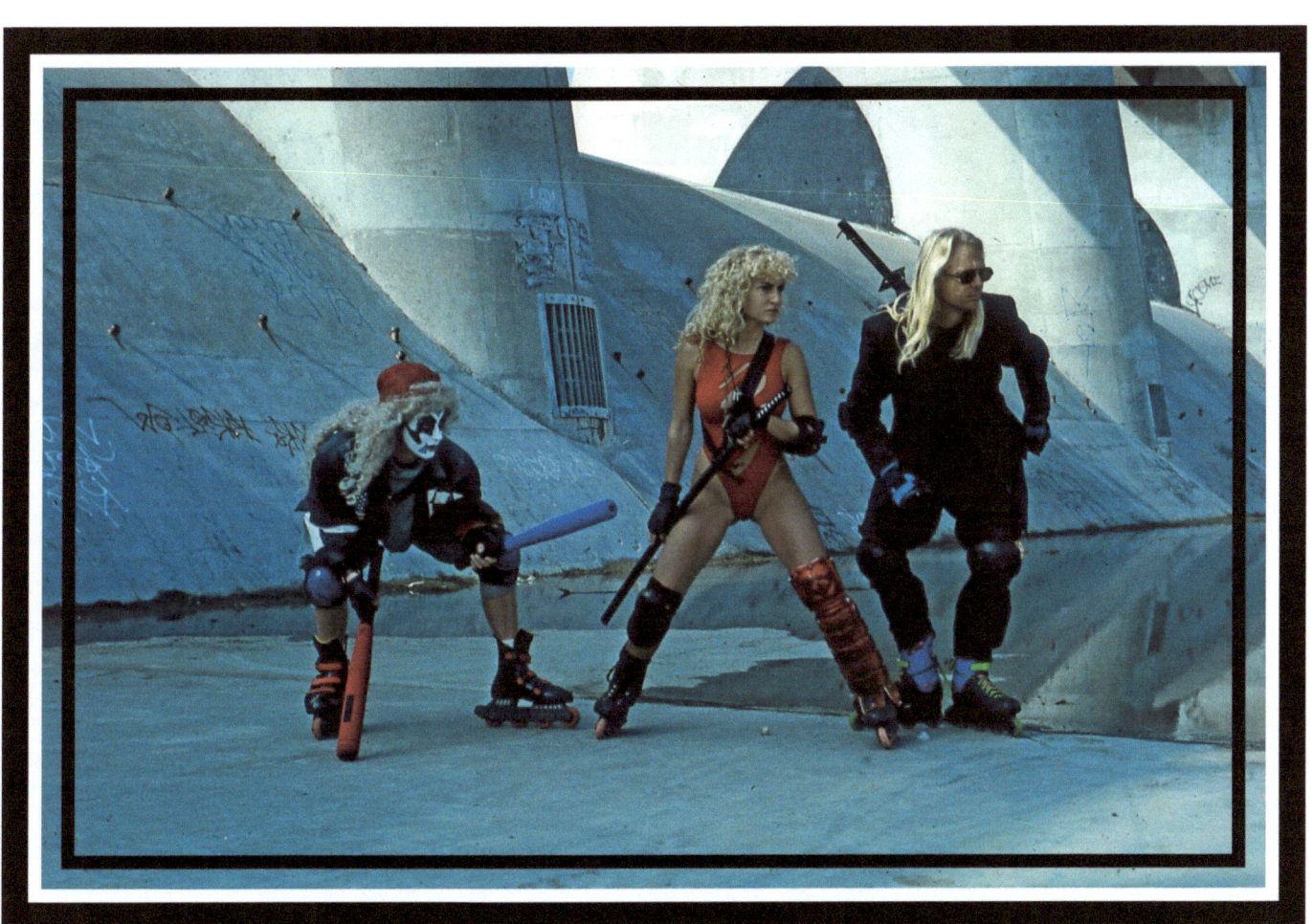

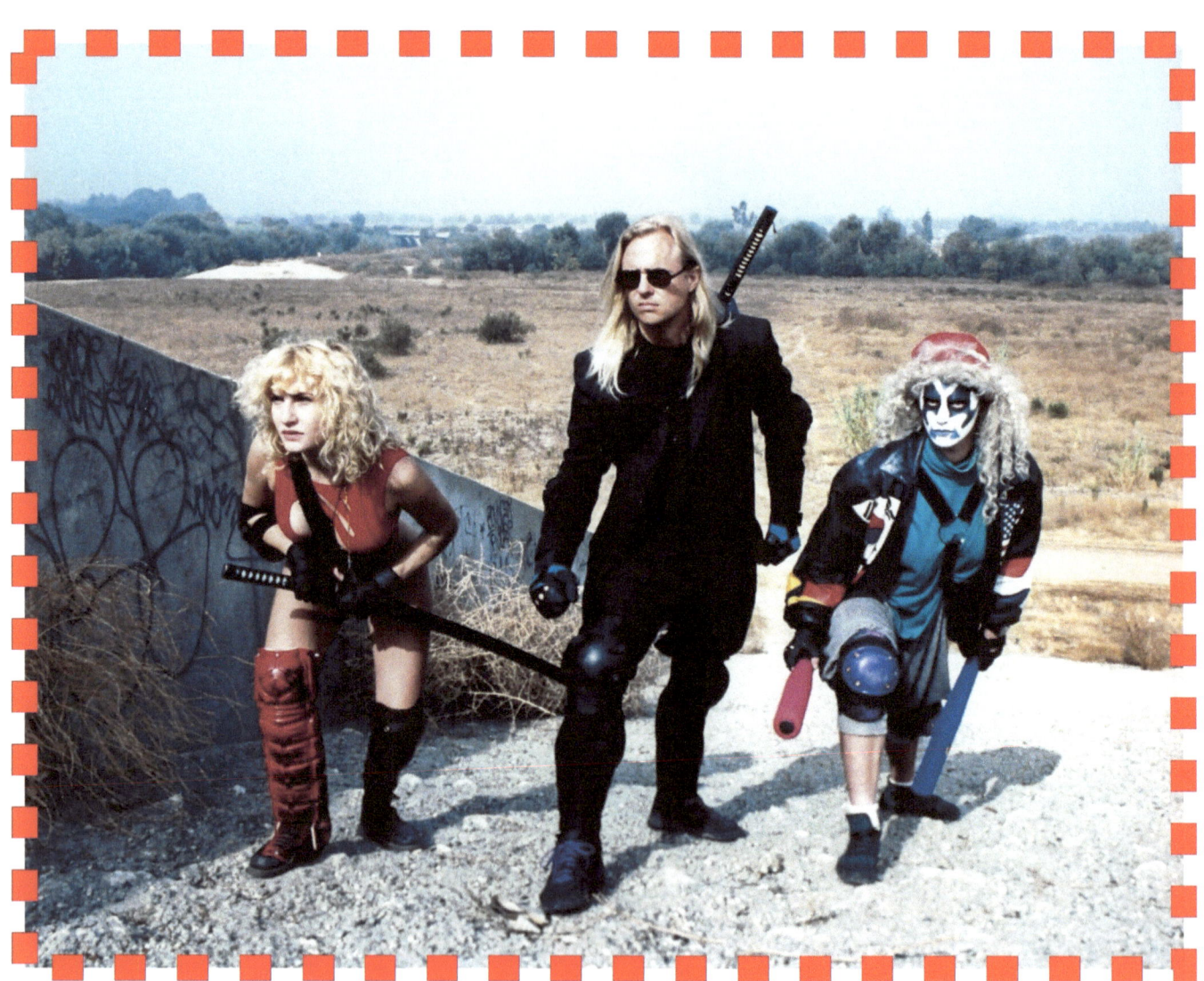

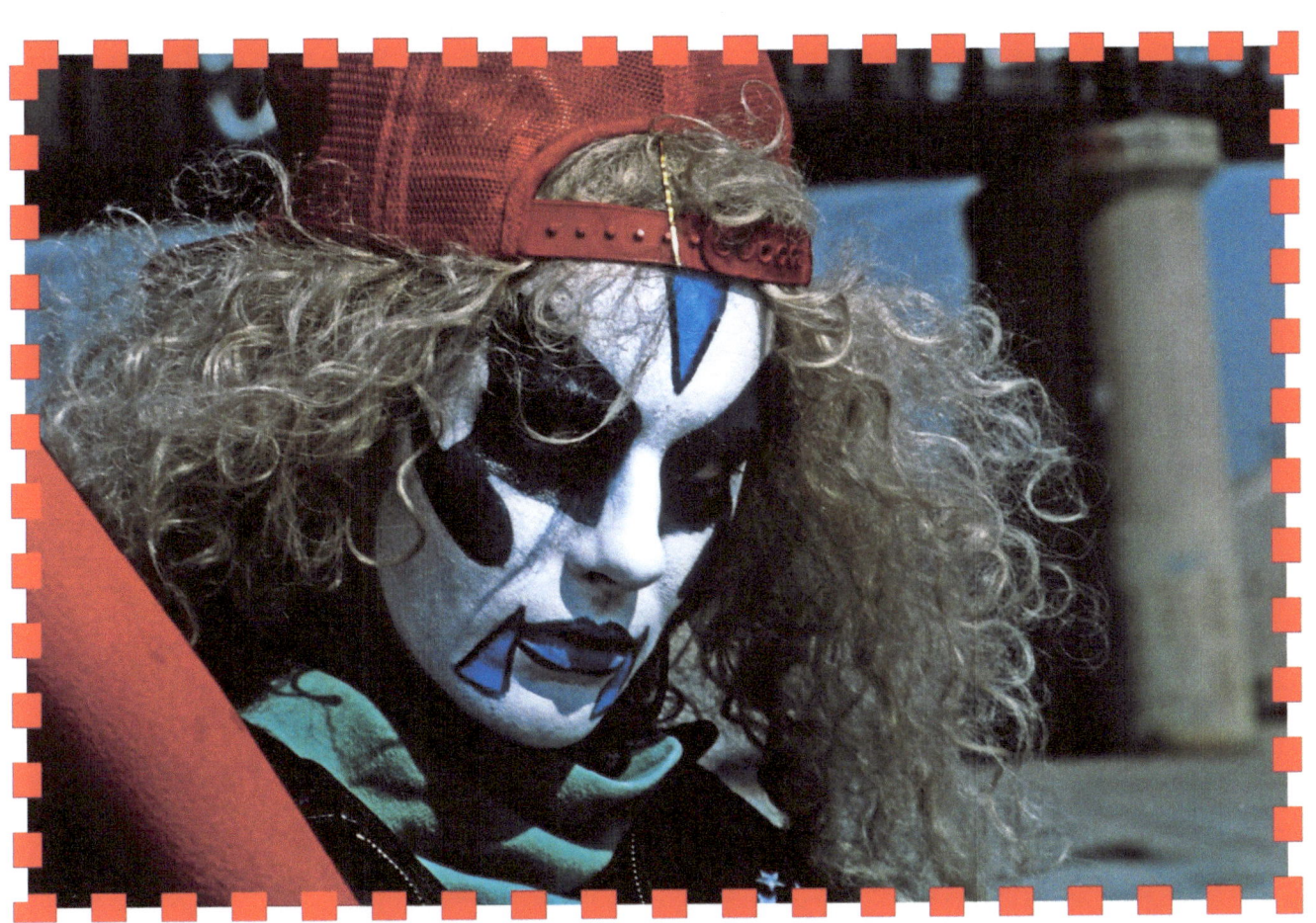

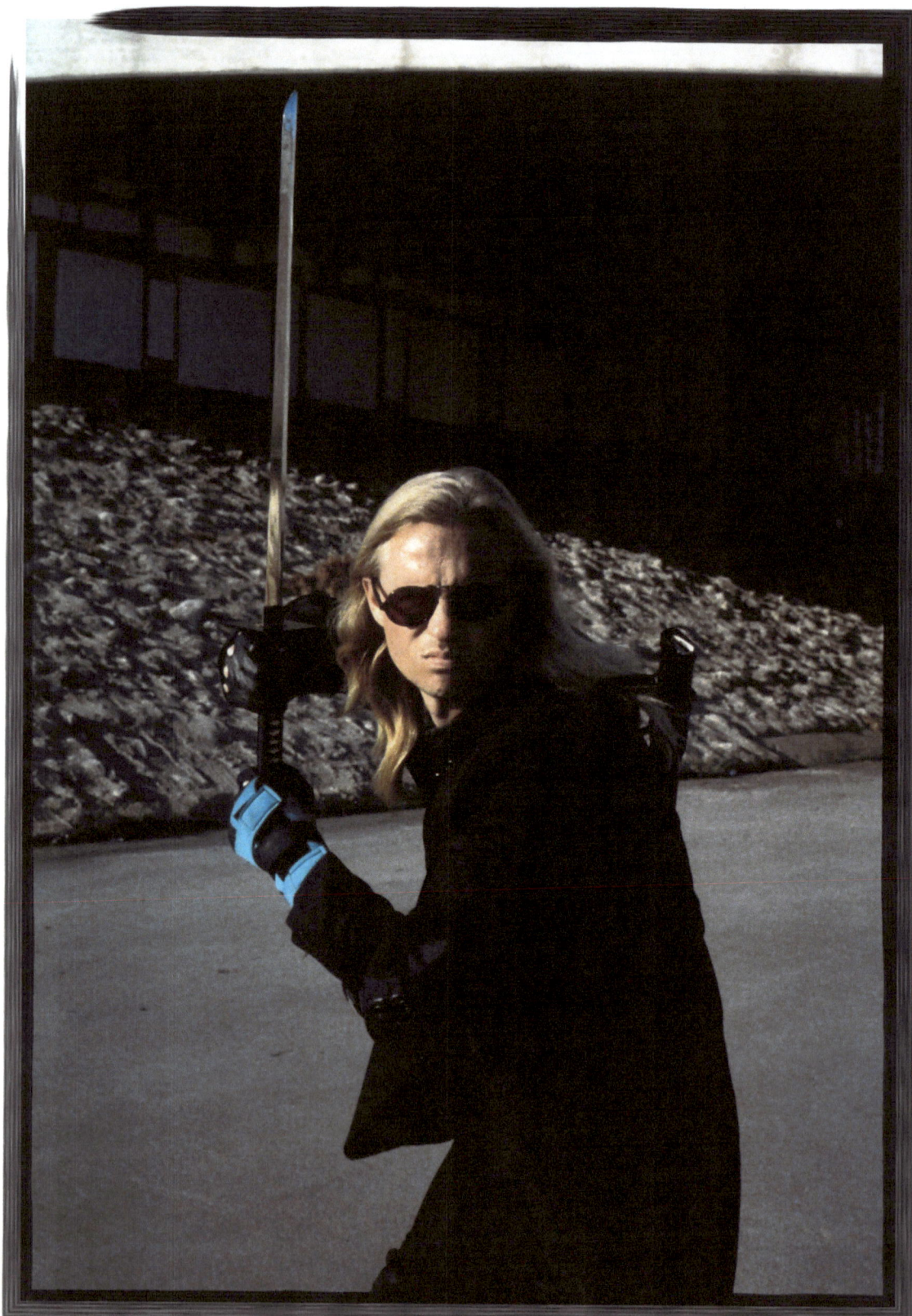

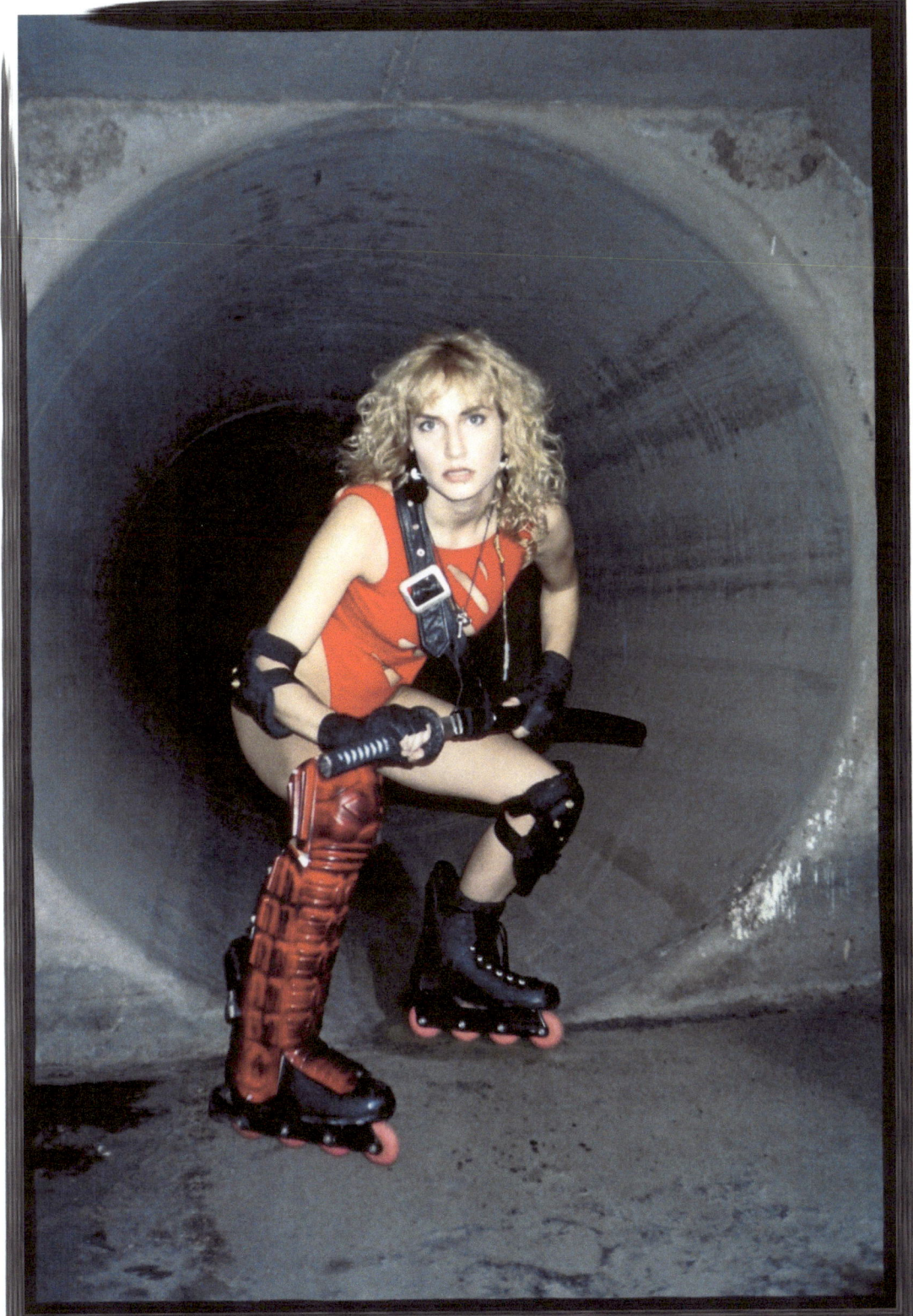

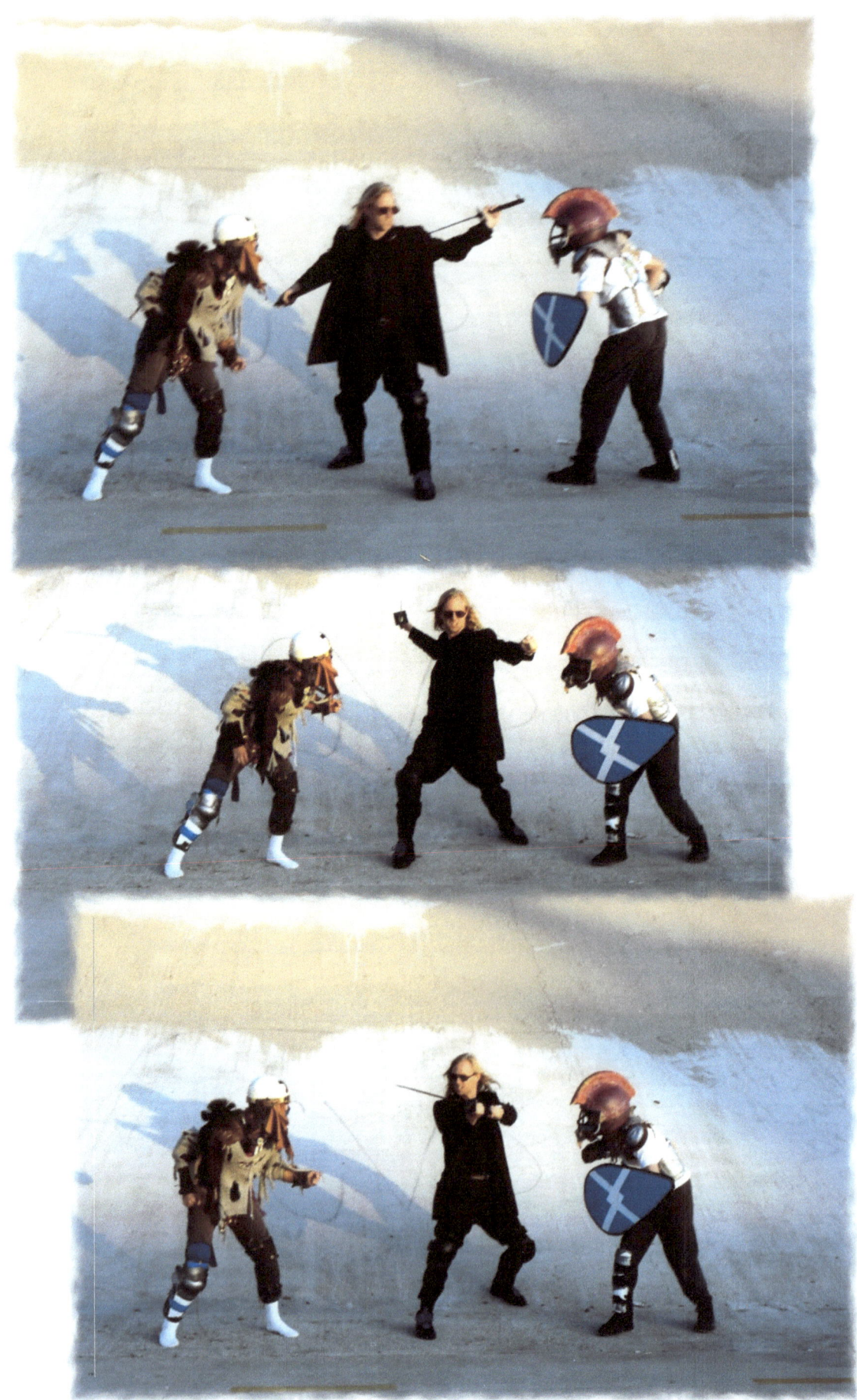

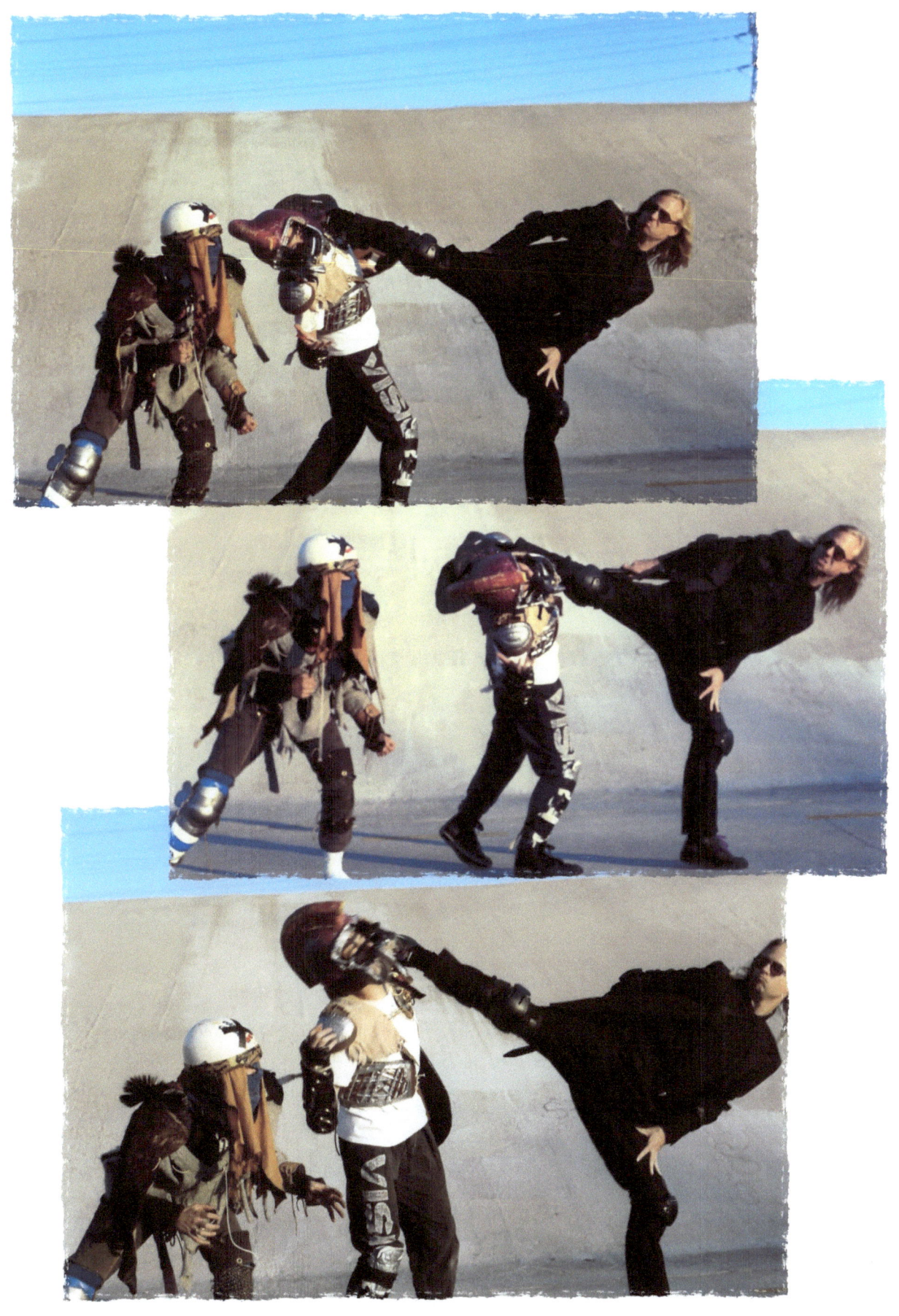

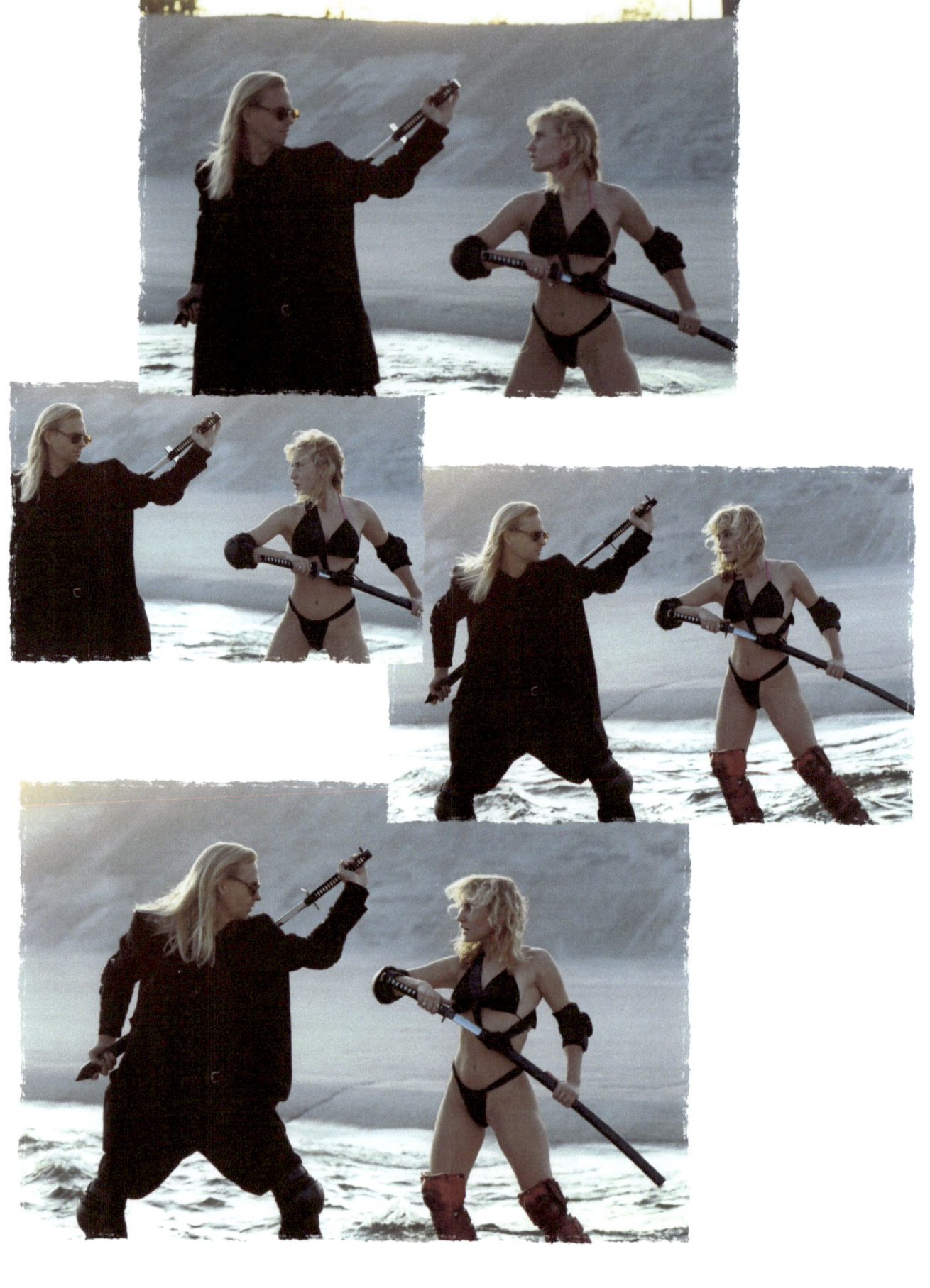

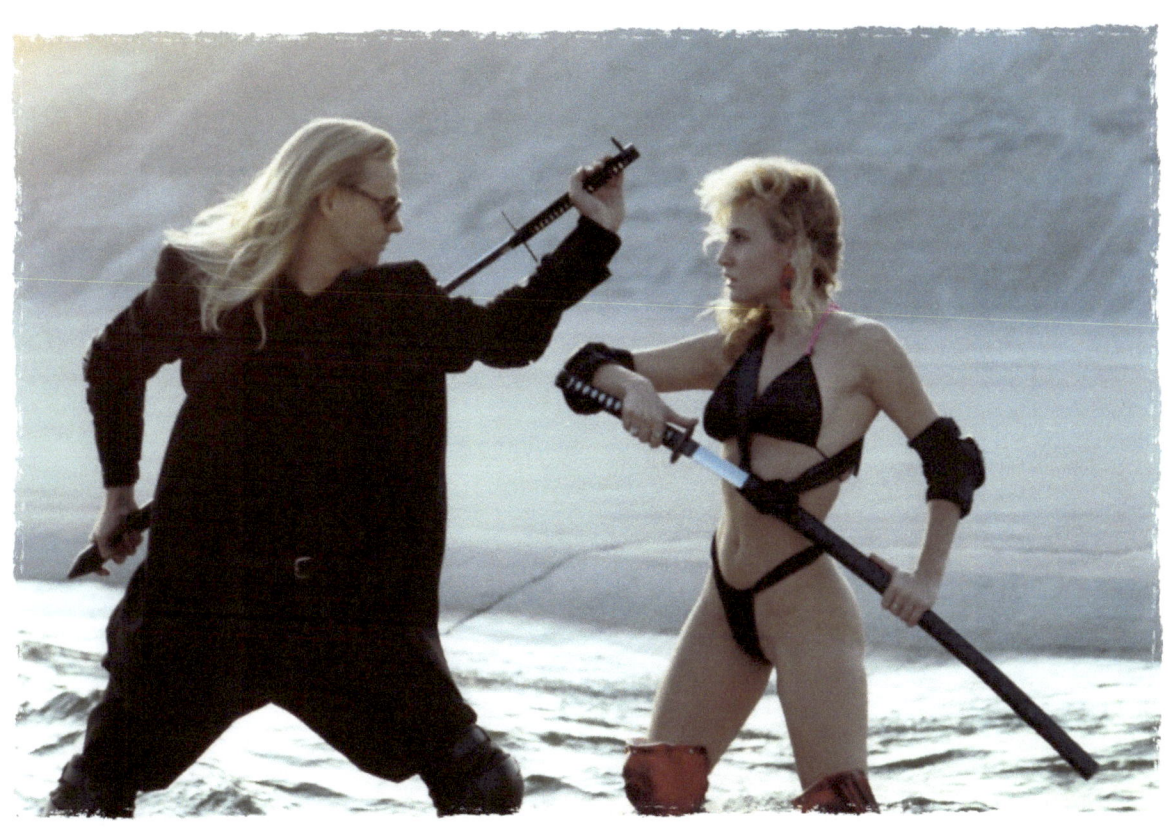
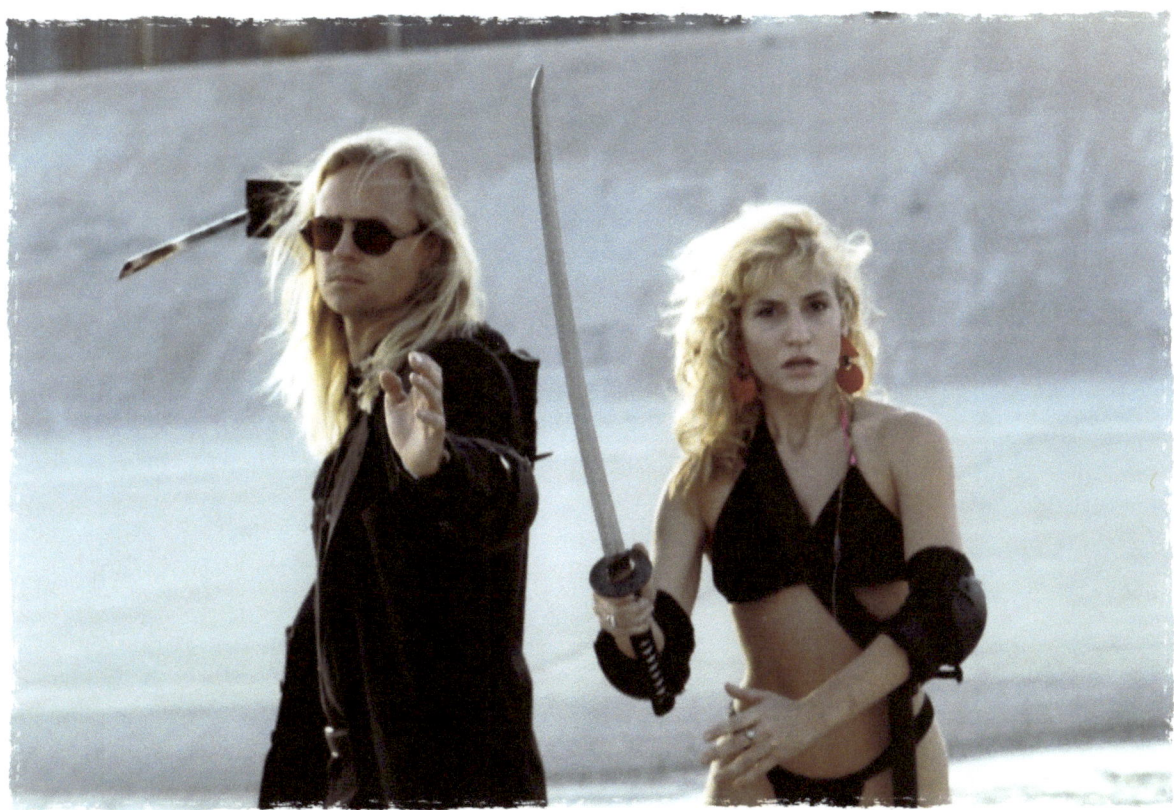

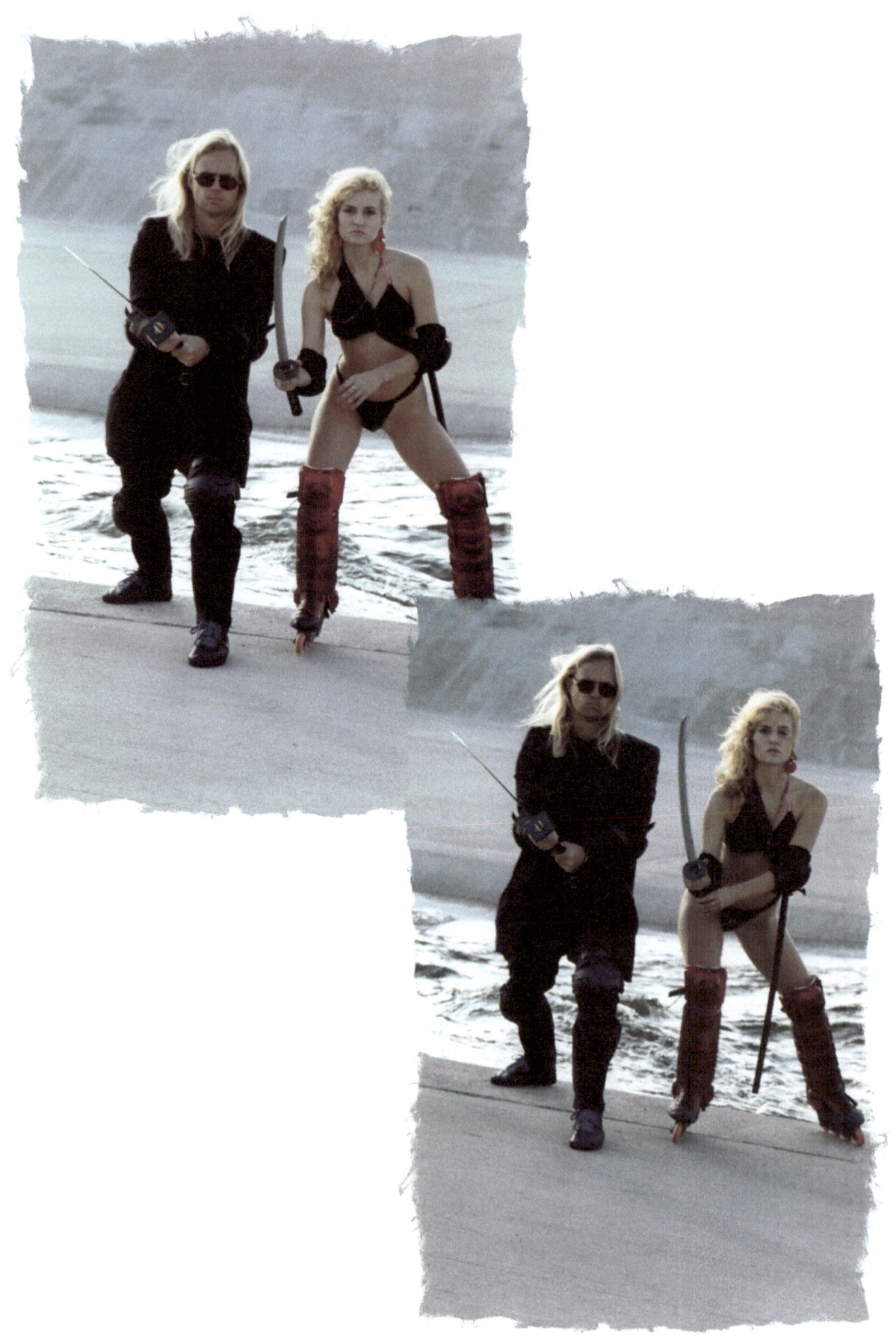

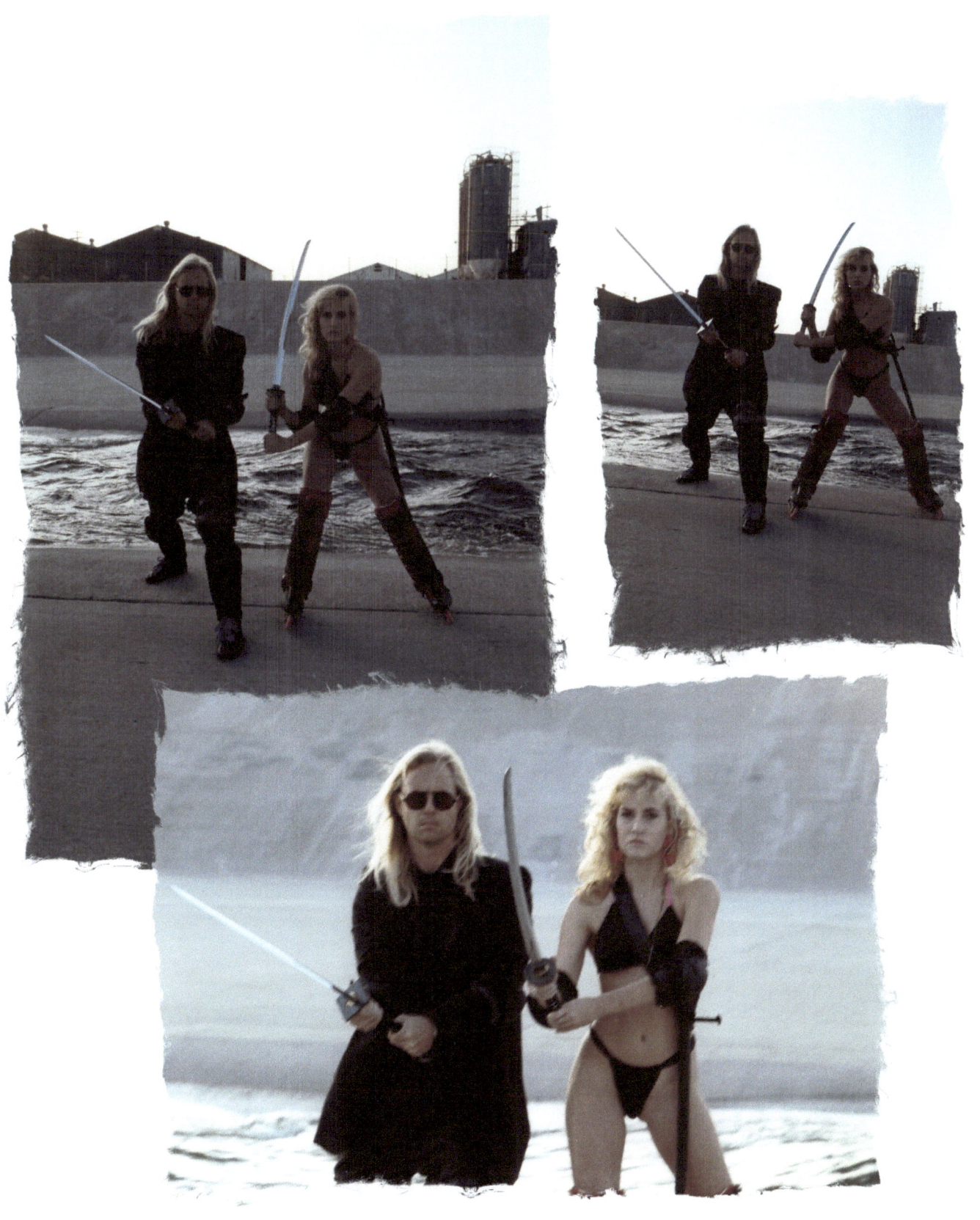

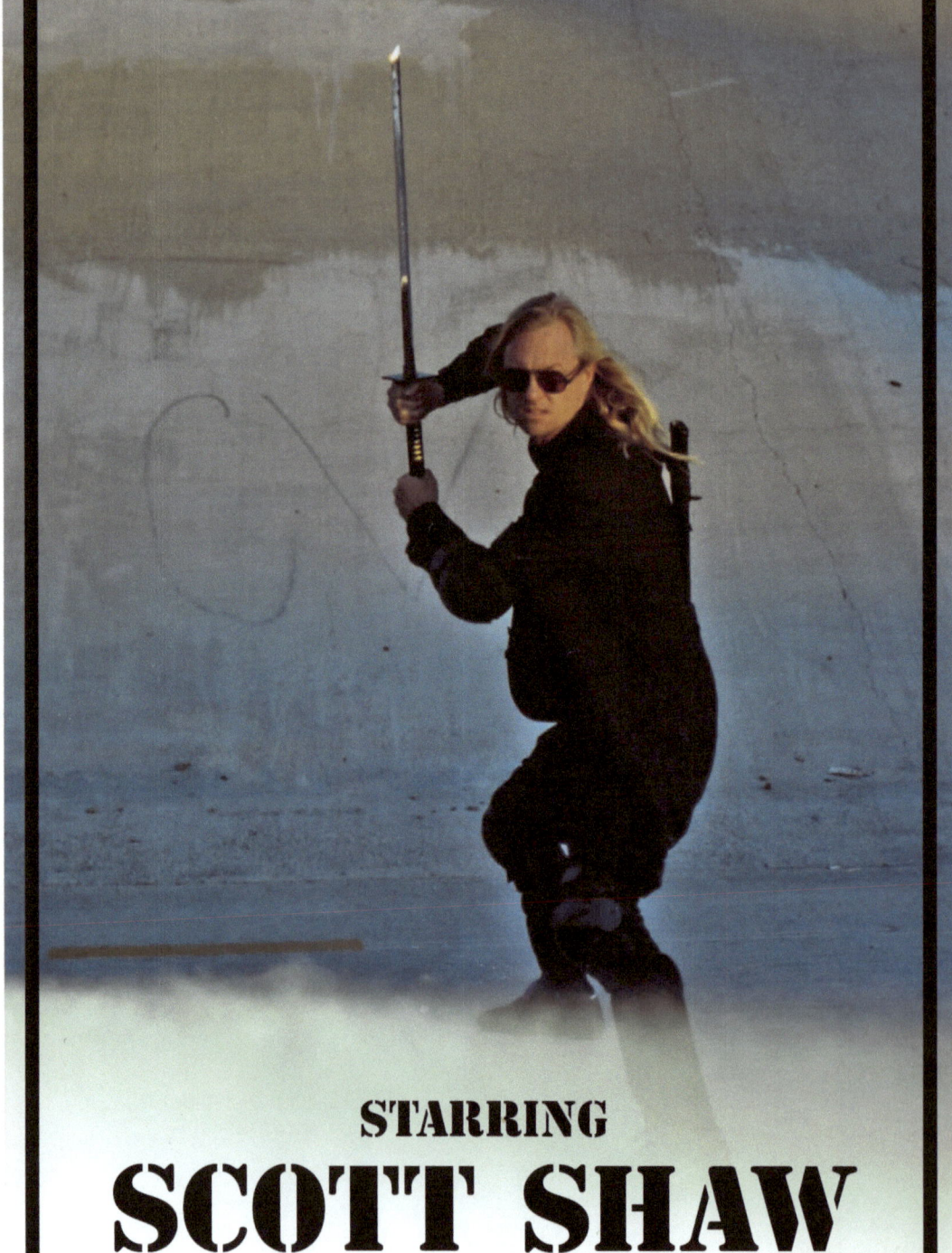

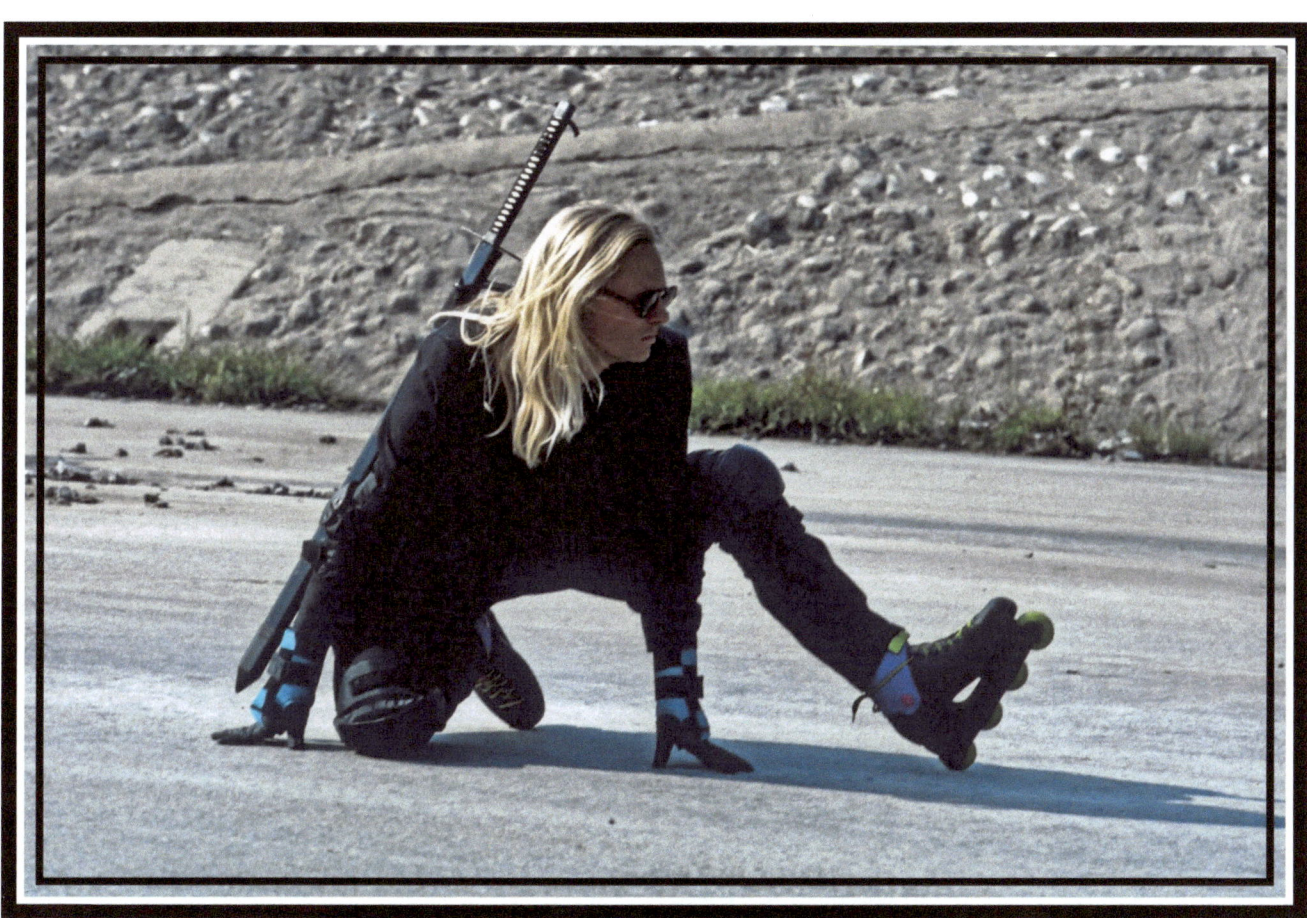

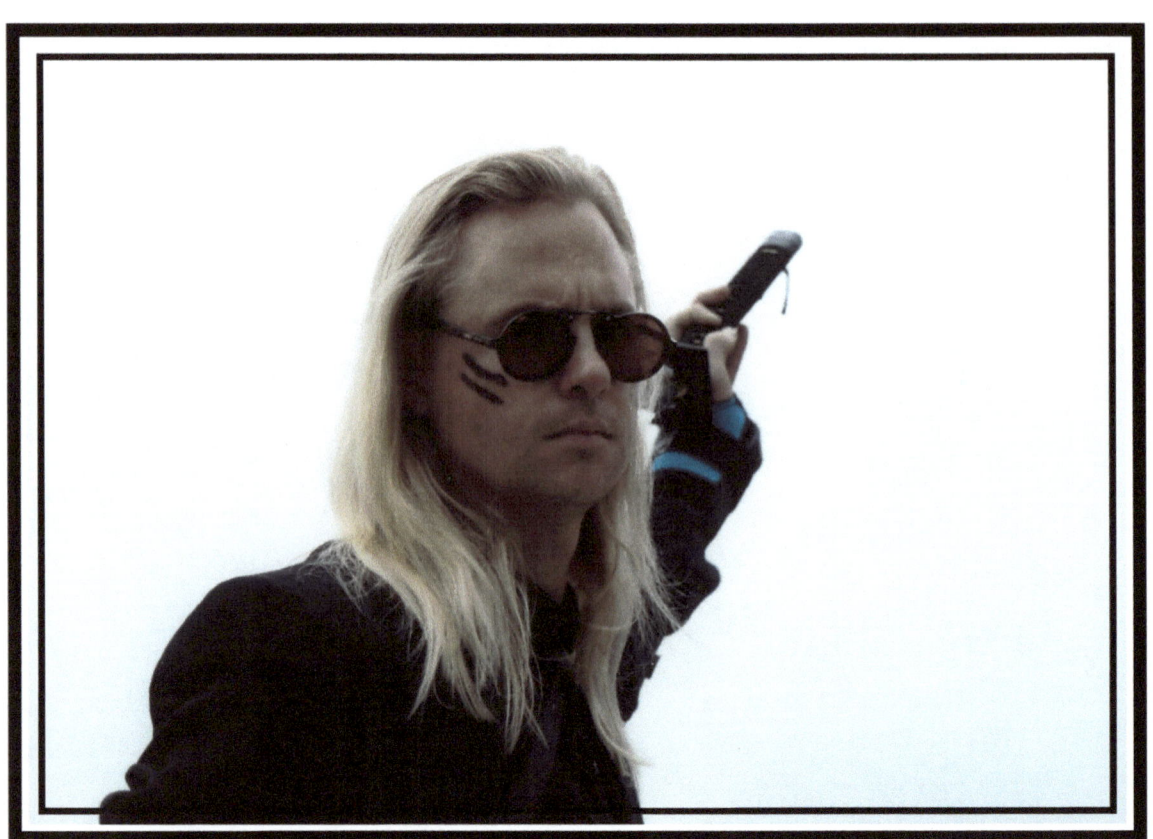
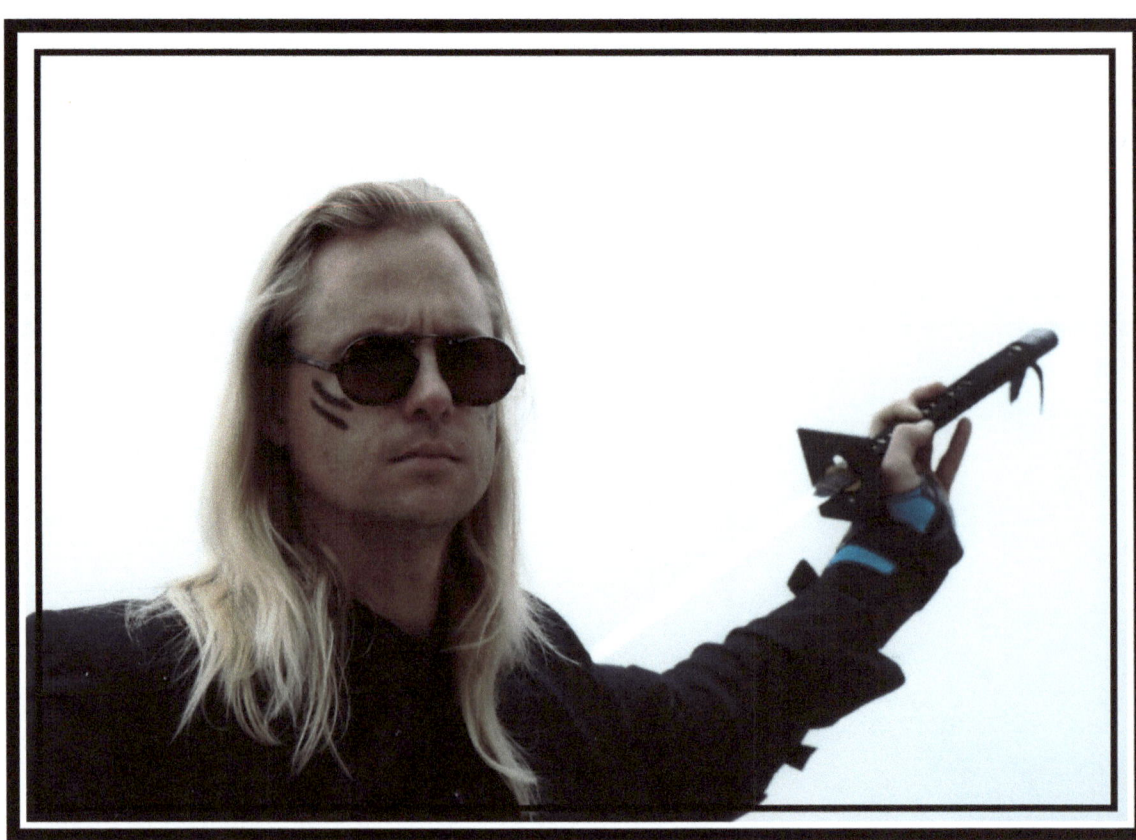

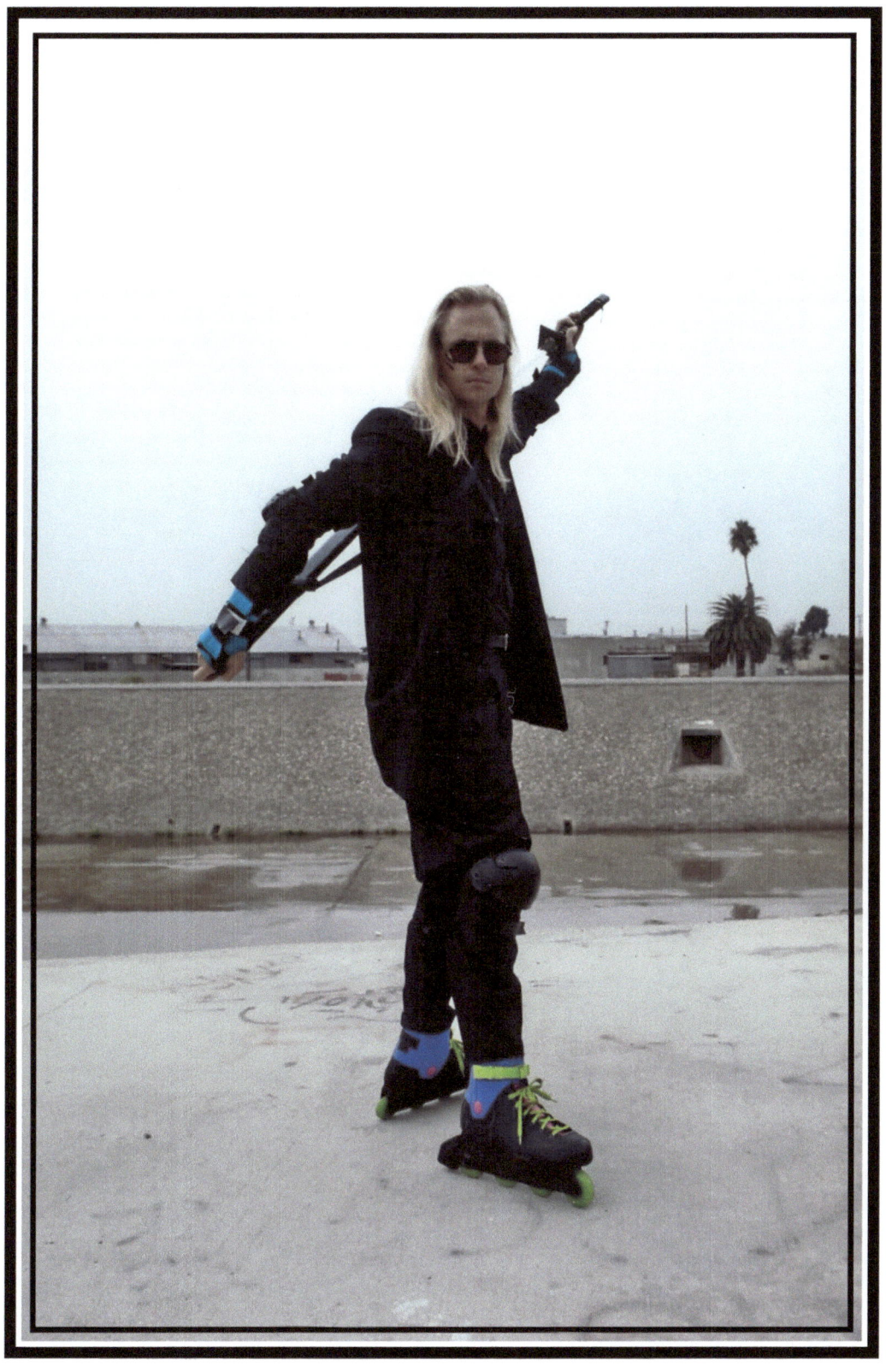

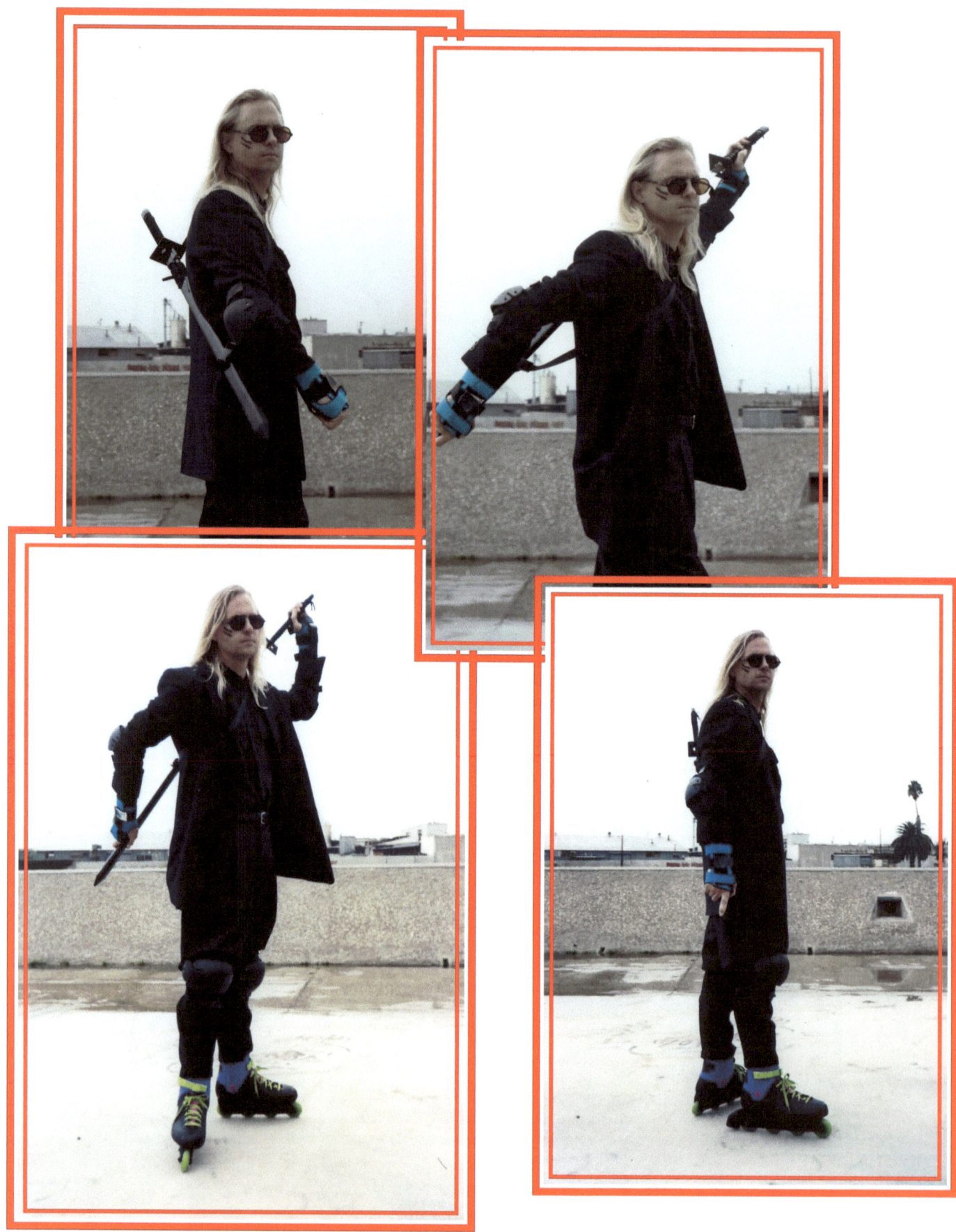

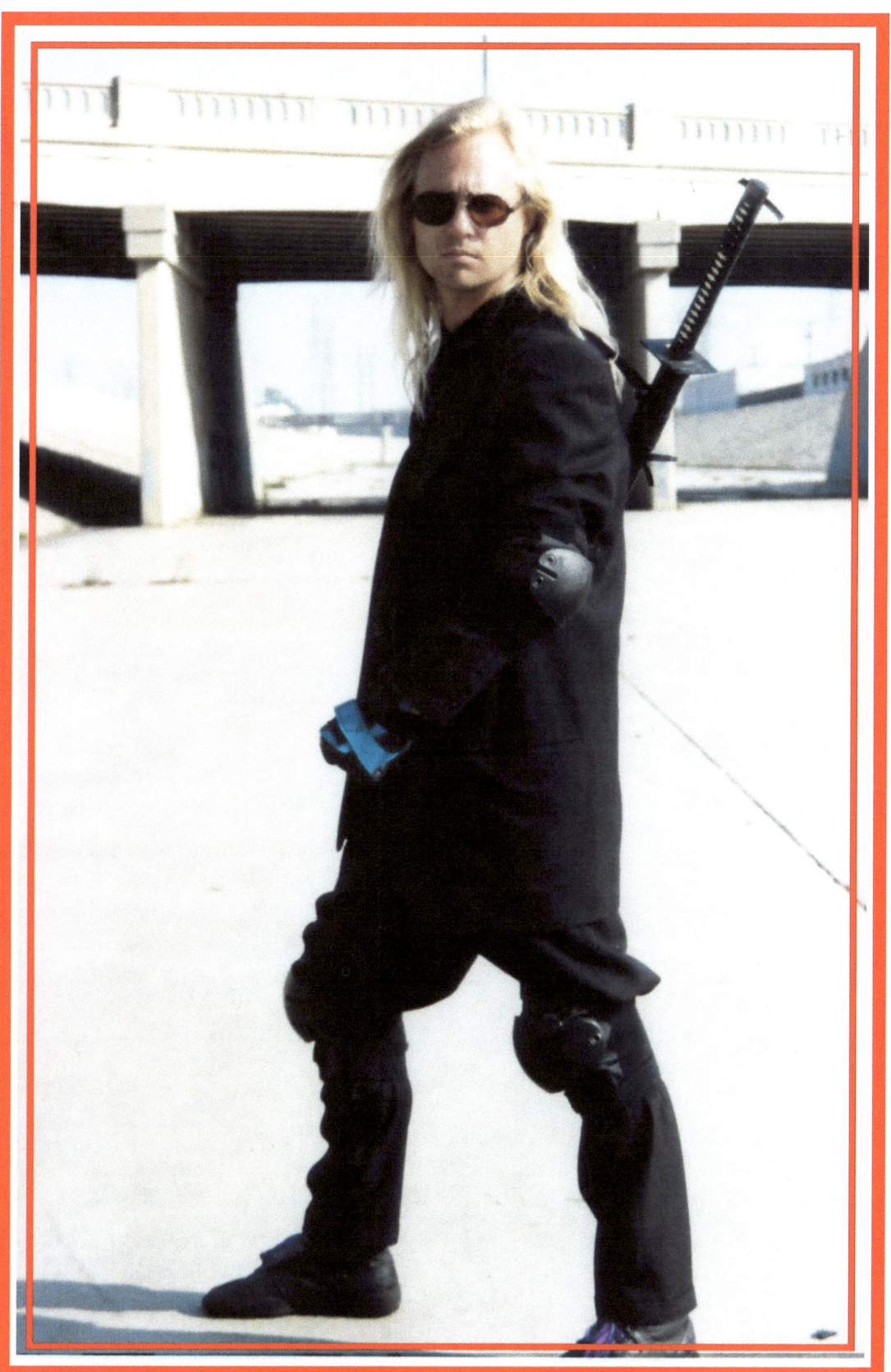

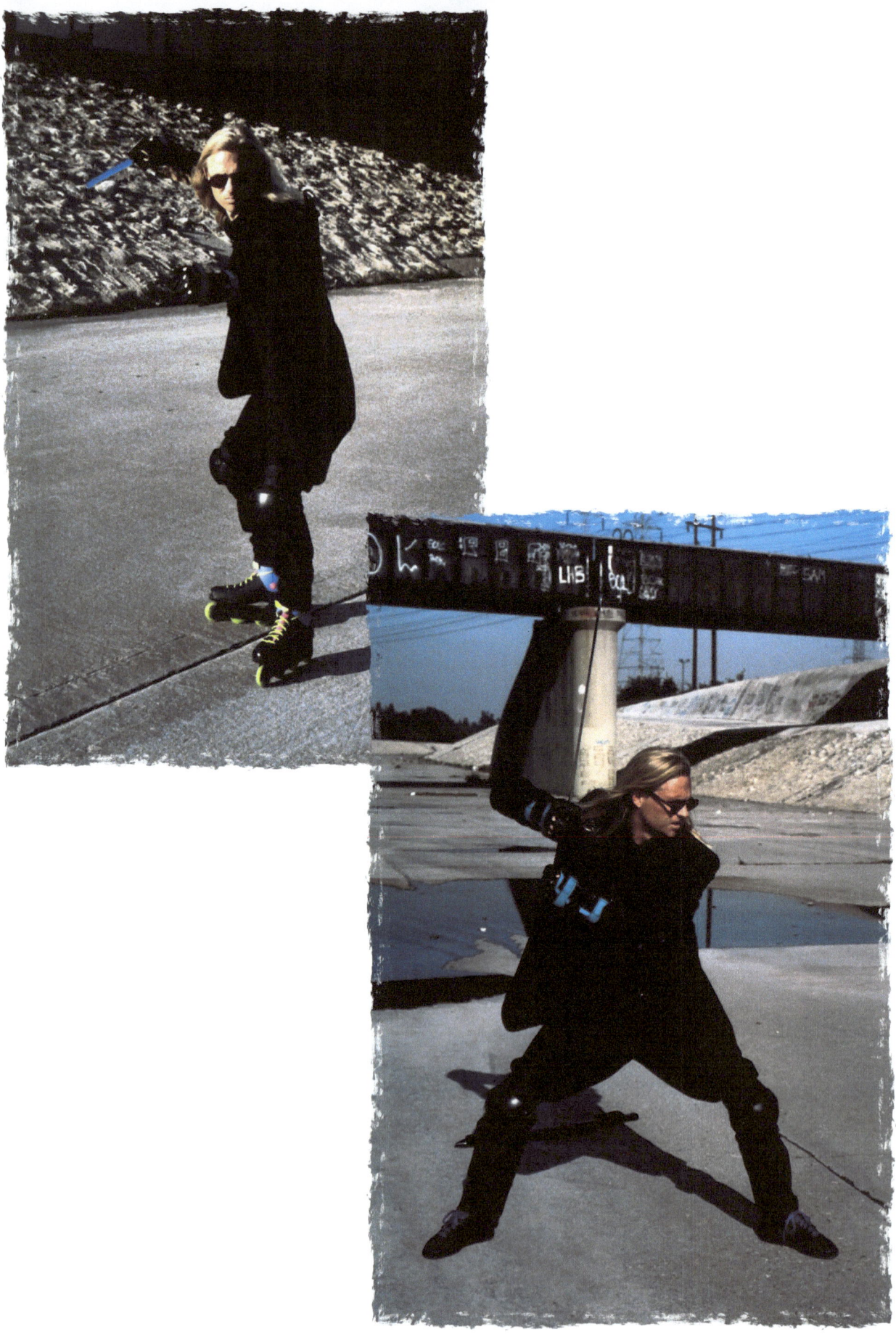

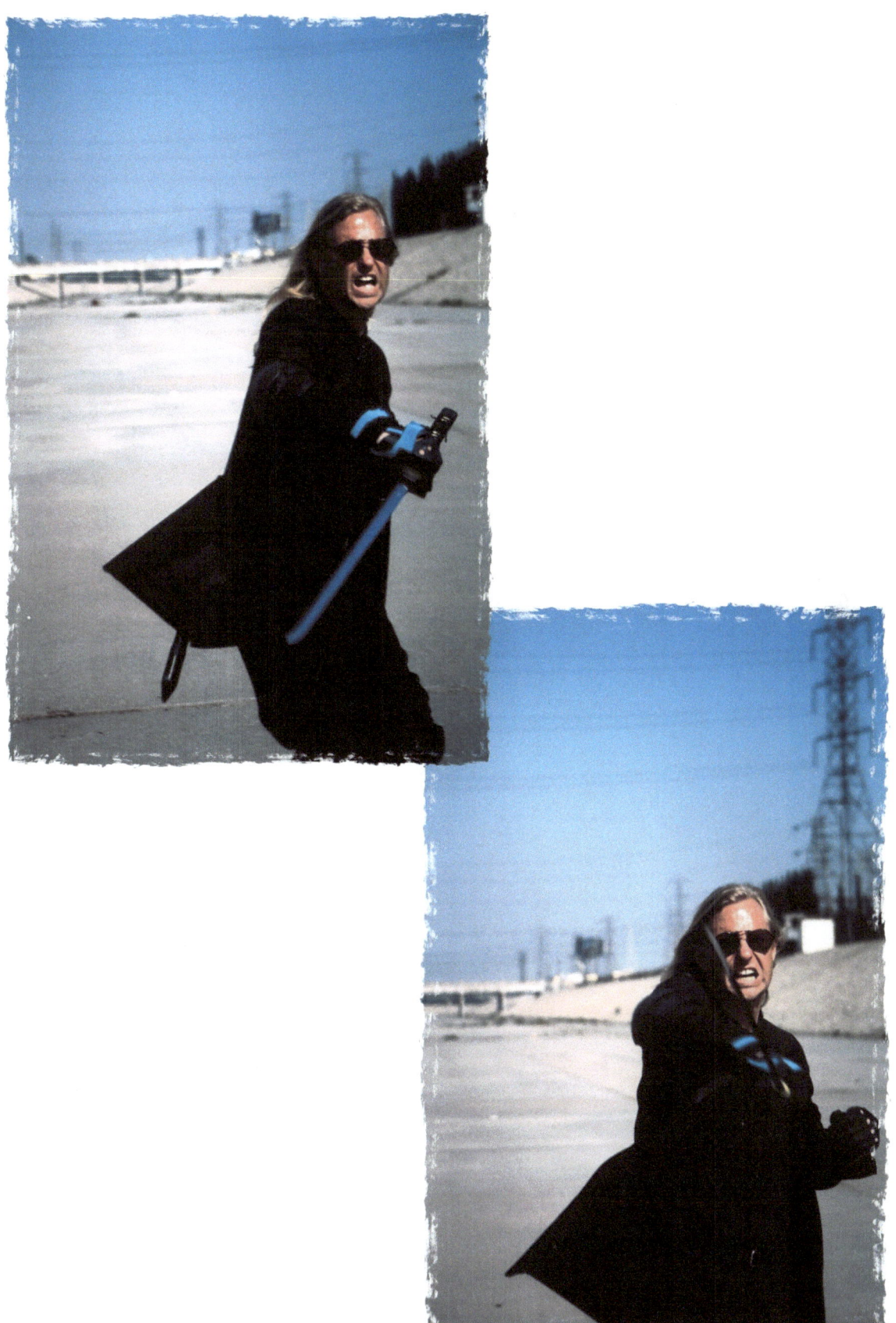

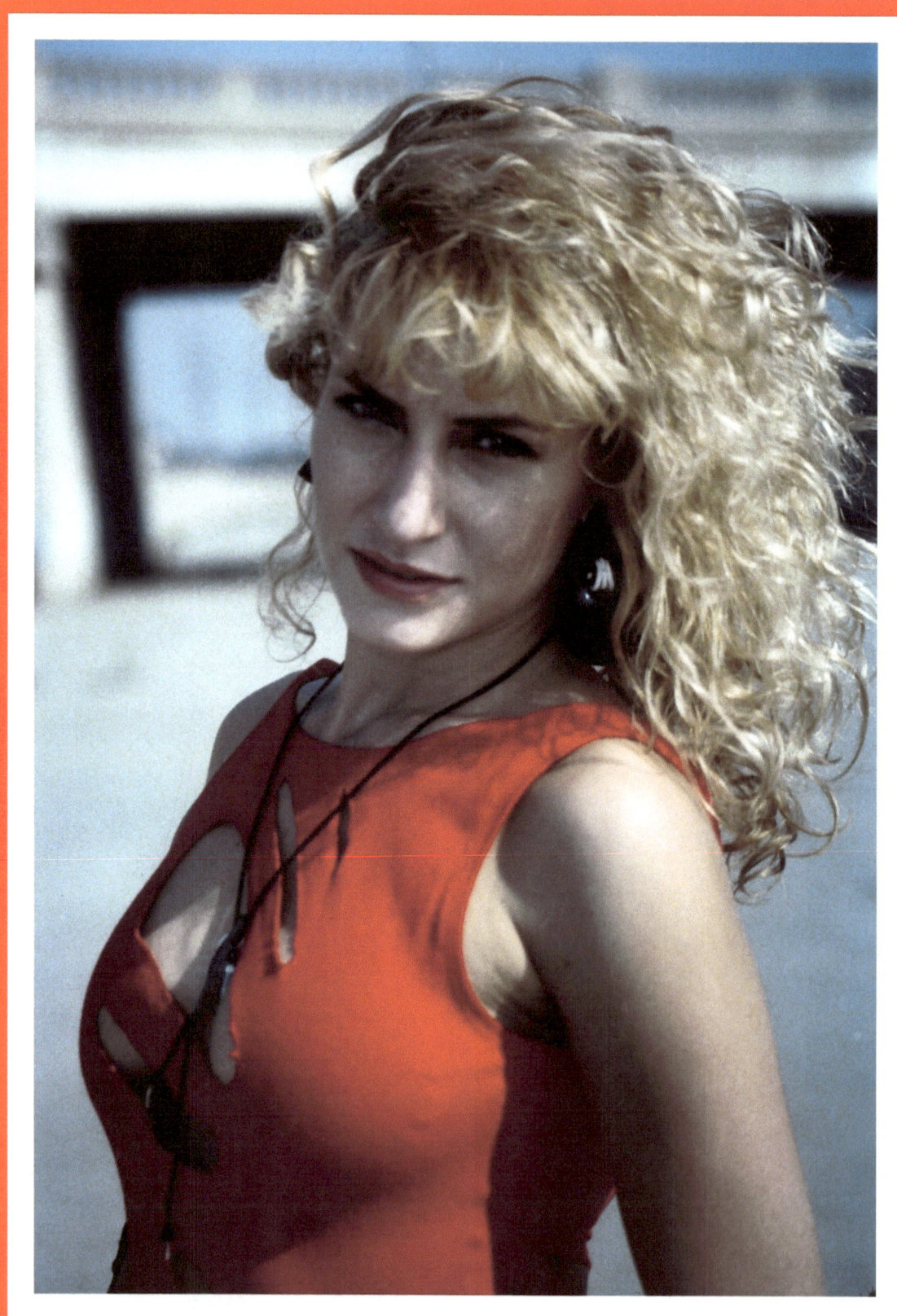

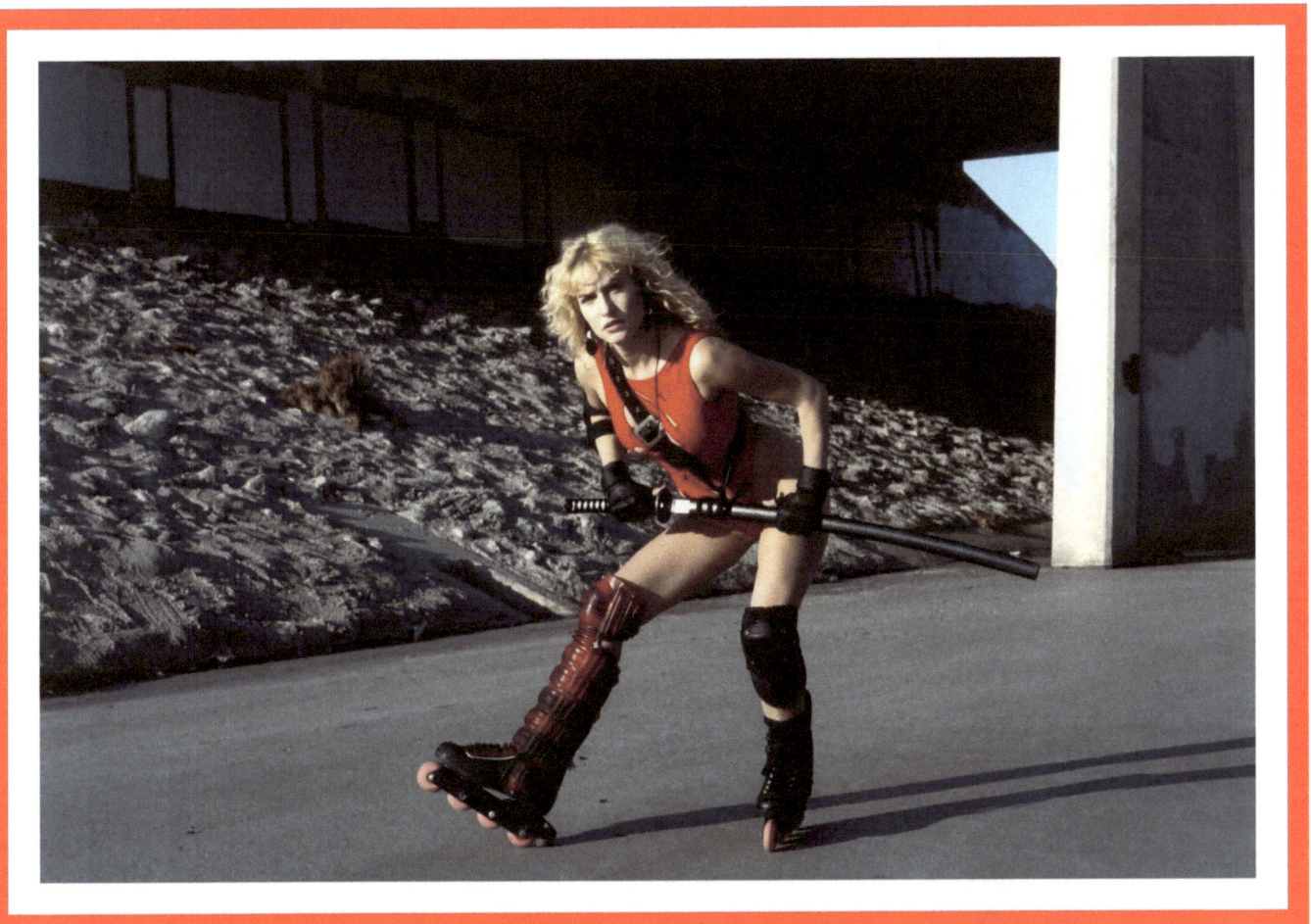

ALLISON CHASE
AS STELLA SPEED

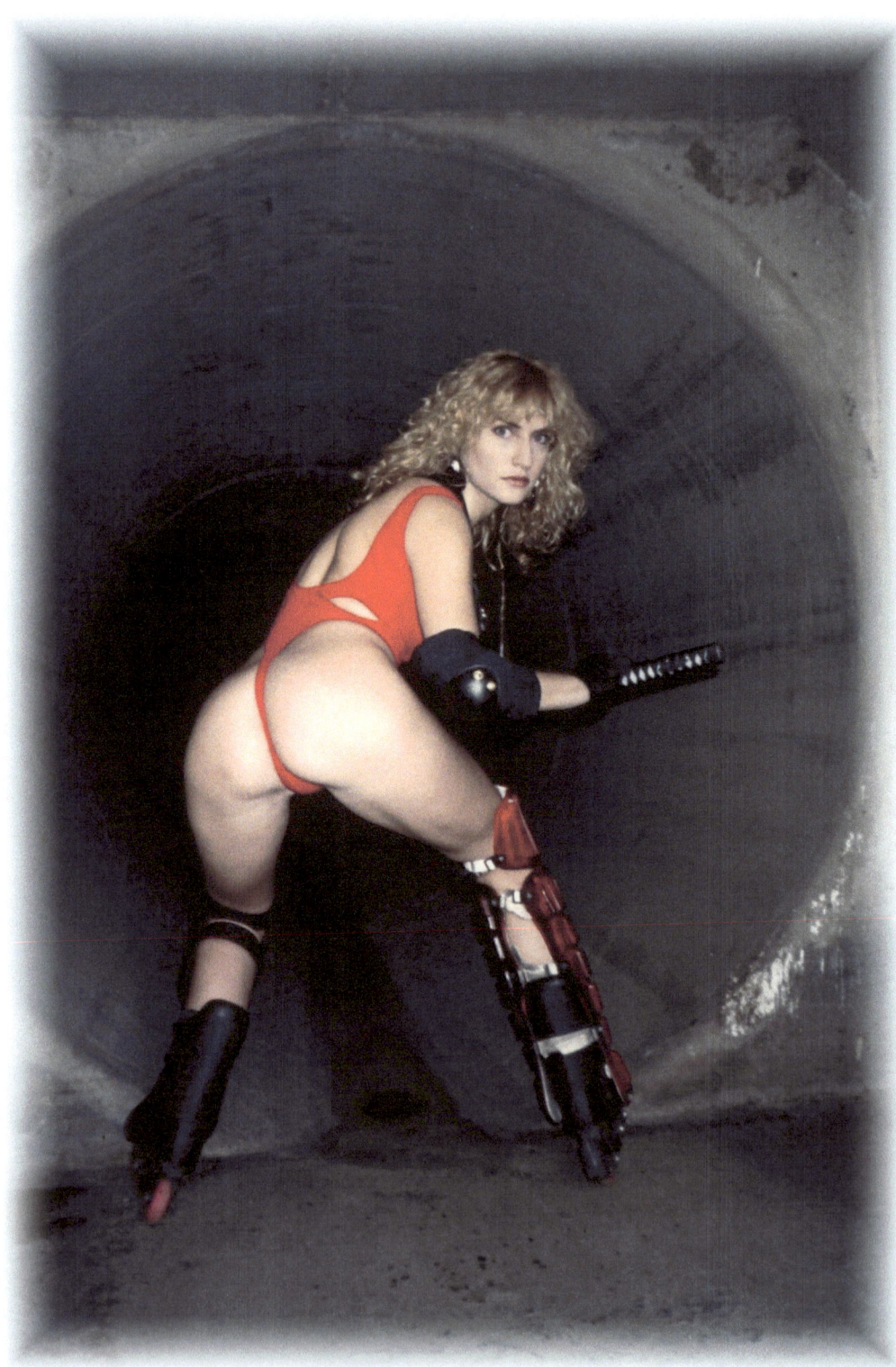

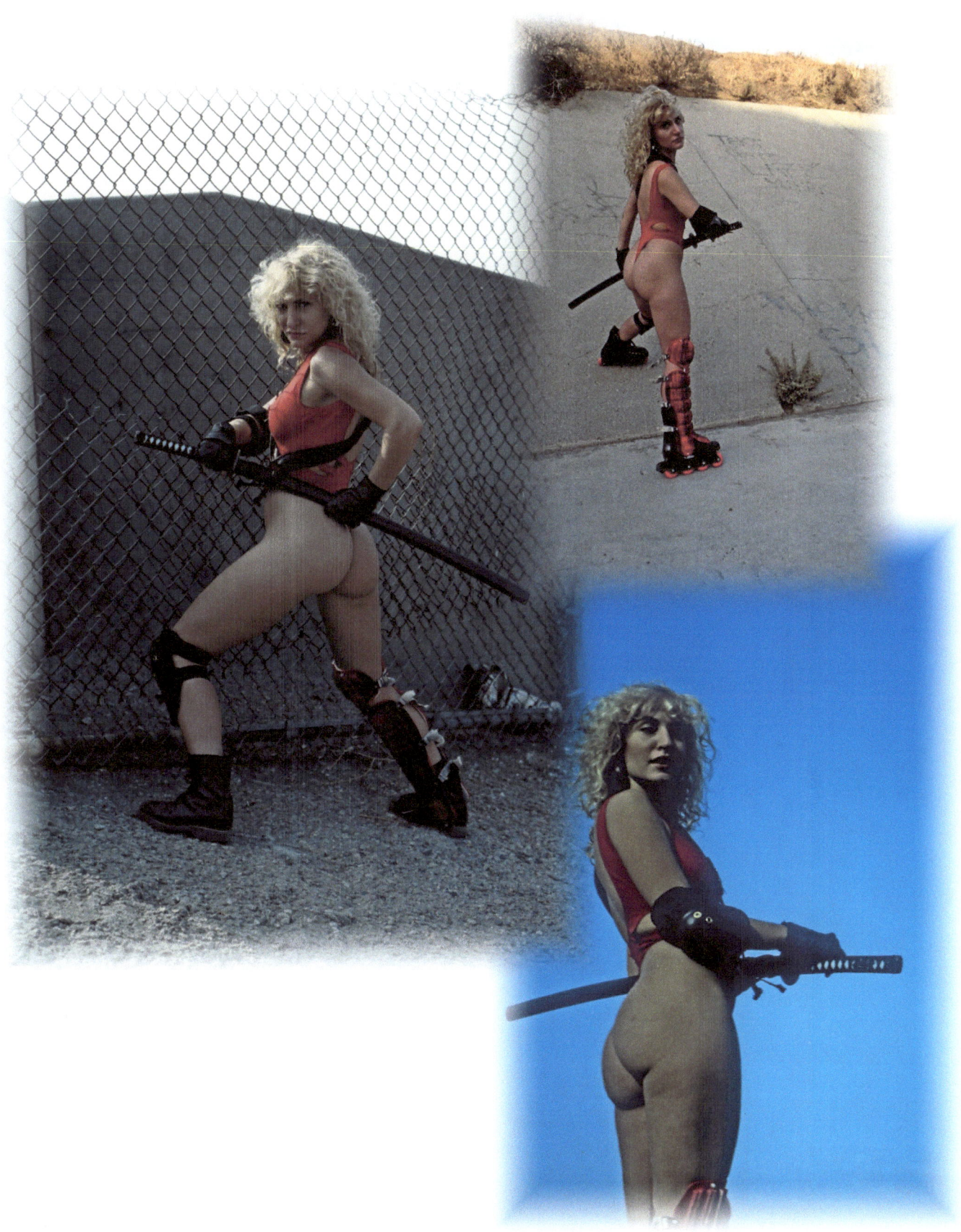

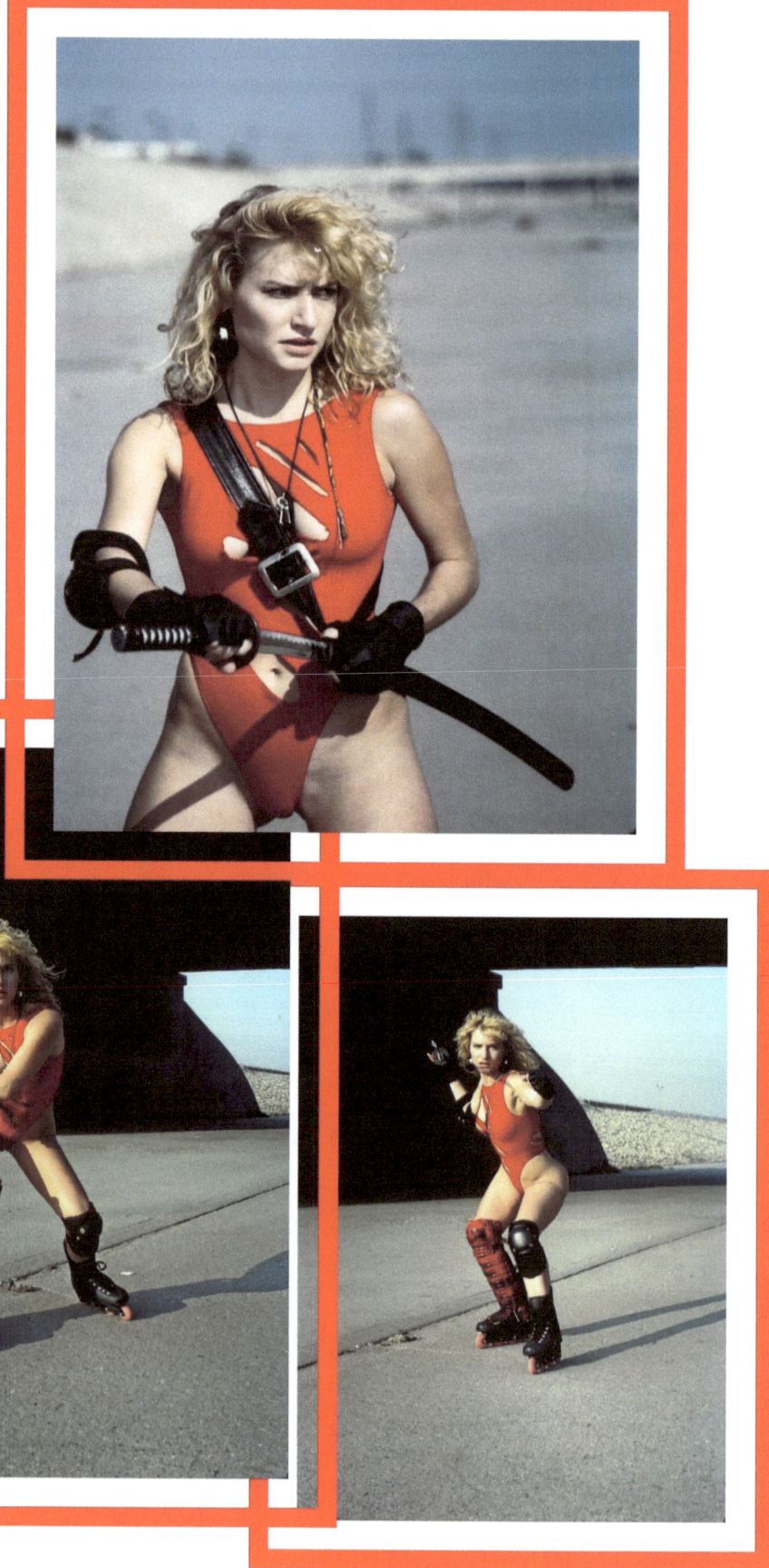

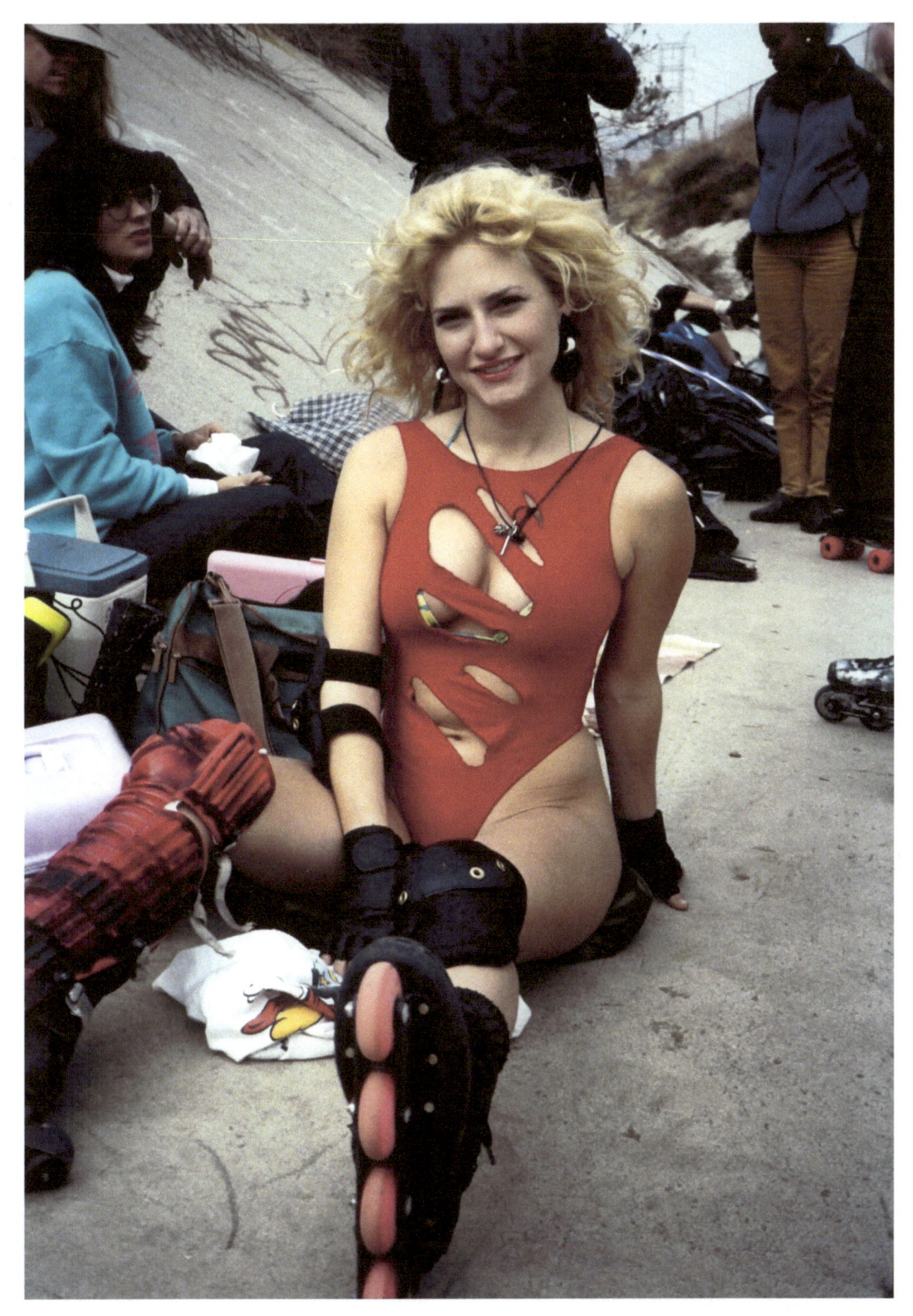

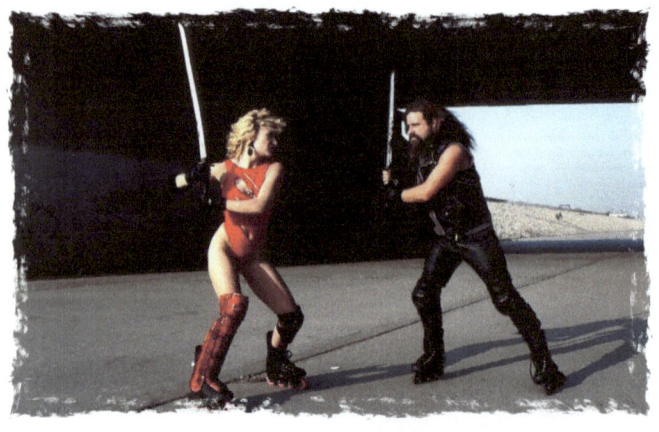
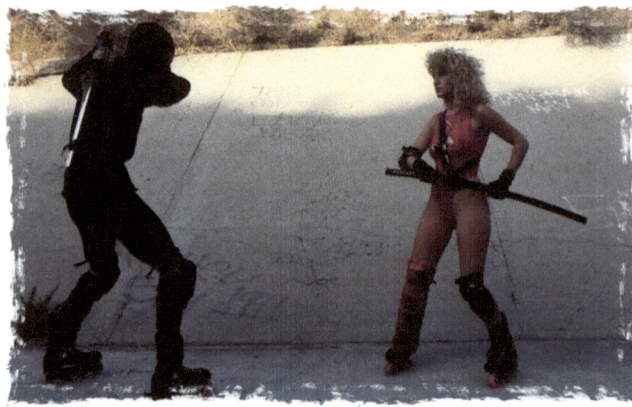
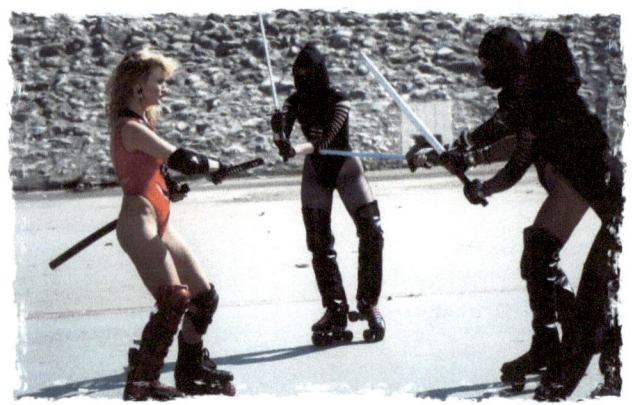
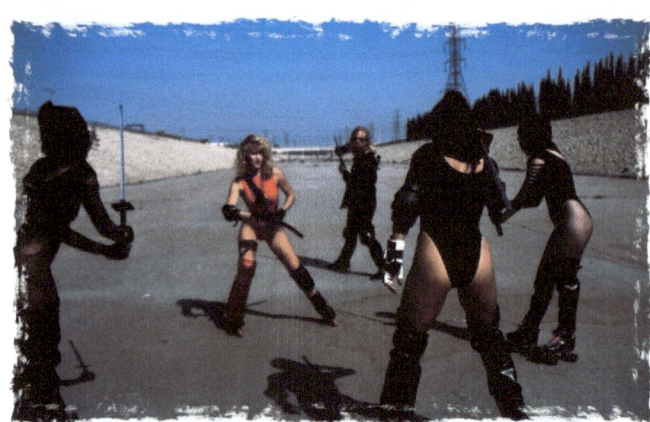
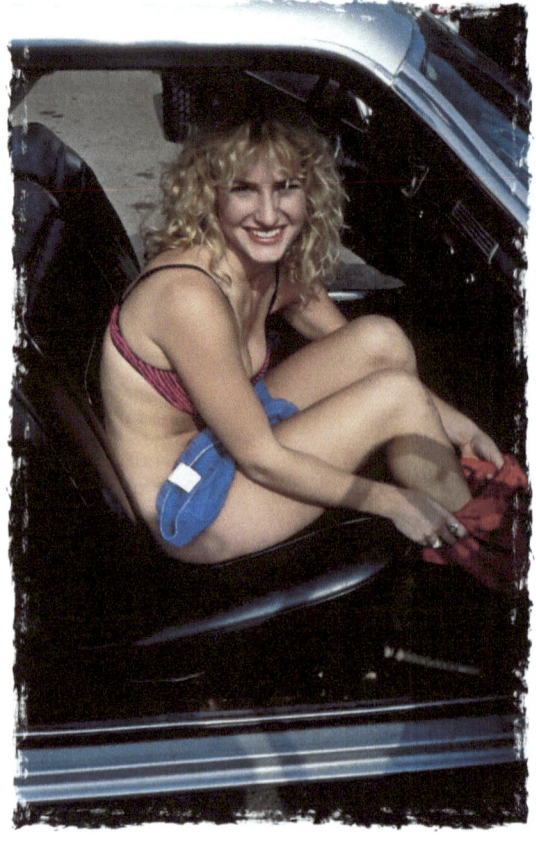
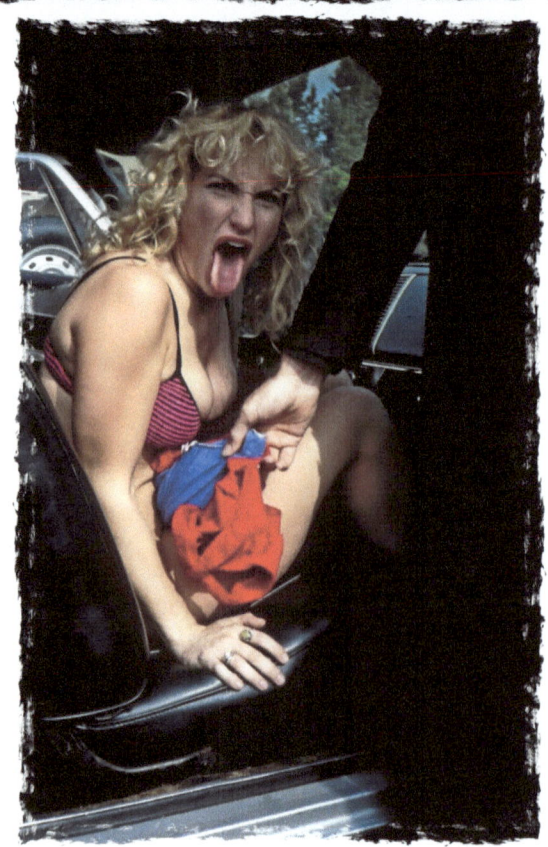

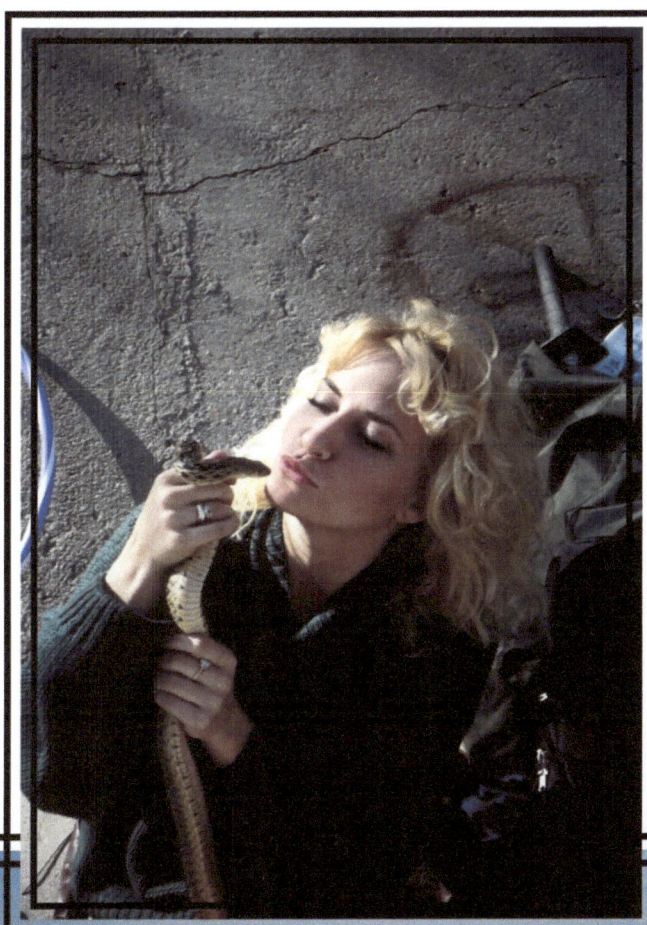

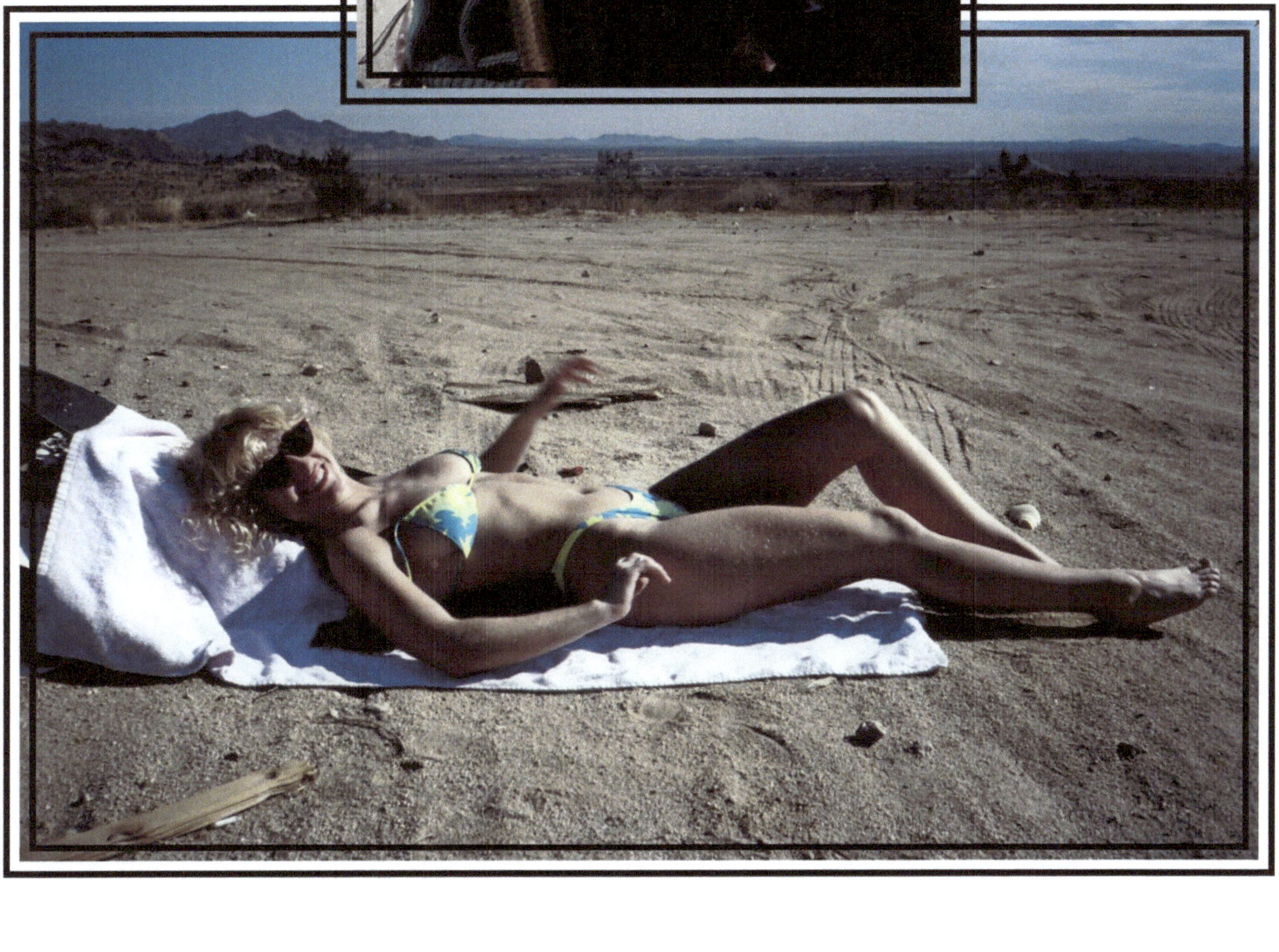

DONALD G. JACKSON

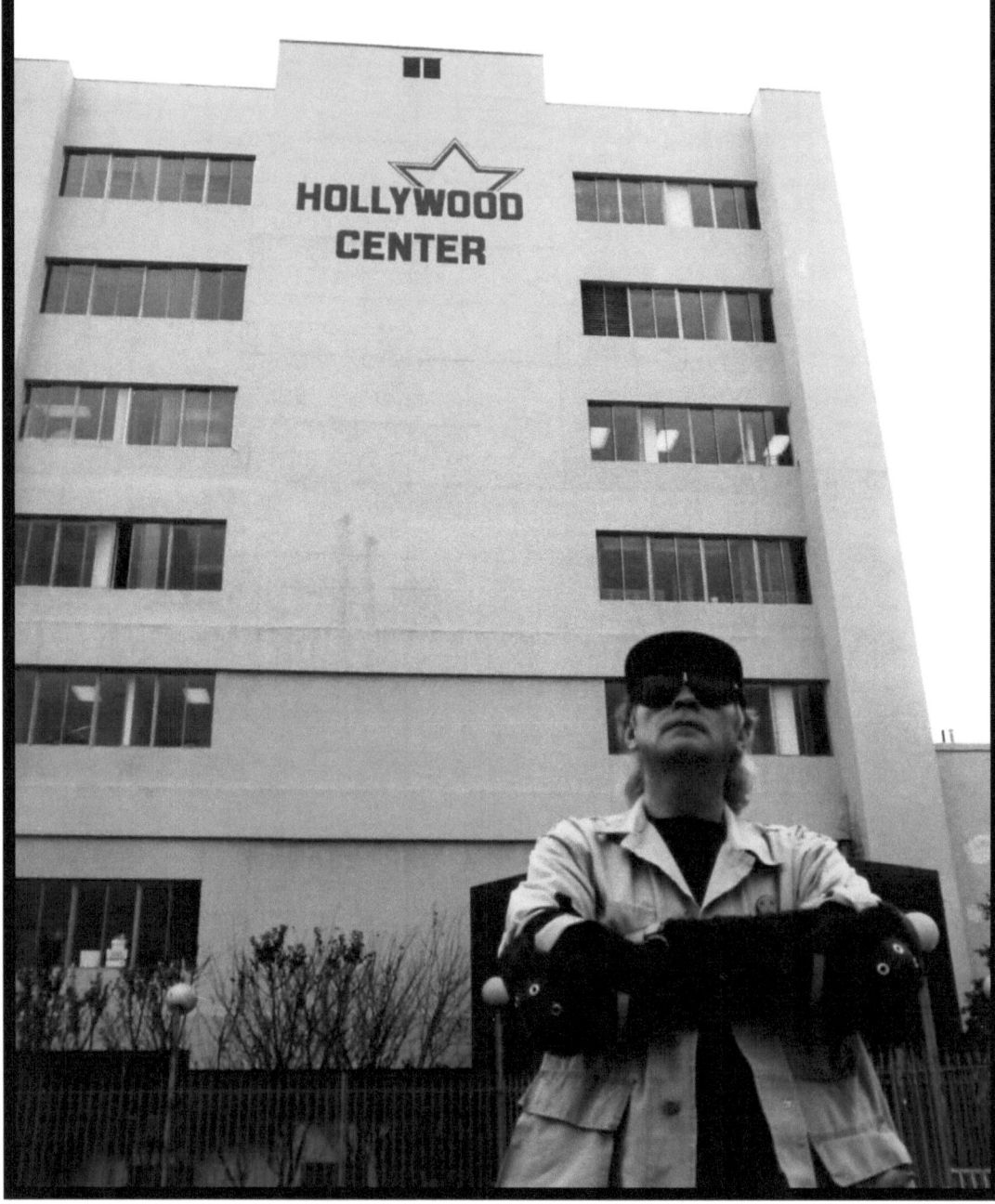

ROLLER BLADE SEVEN PRODUCTION OFFICES

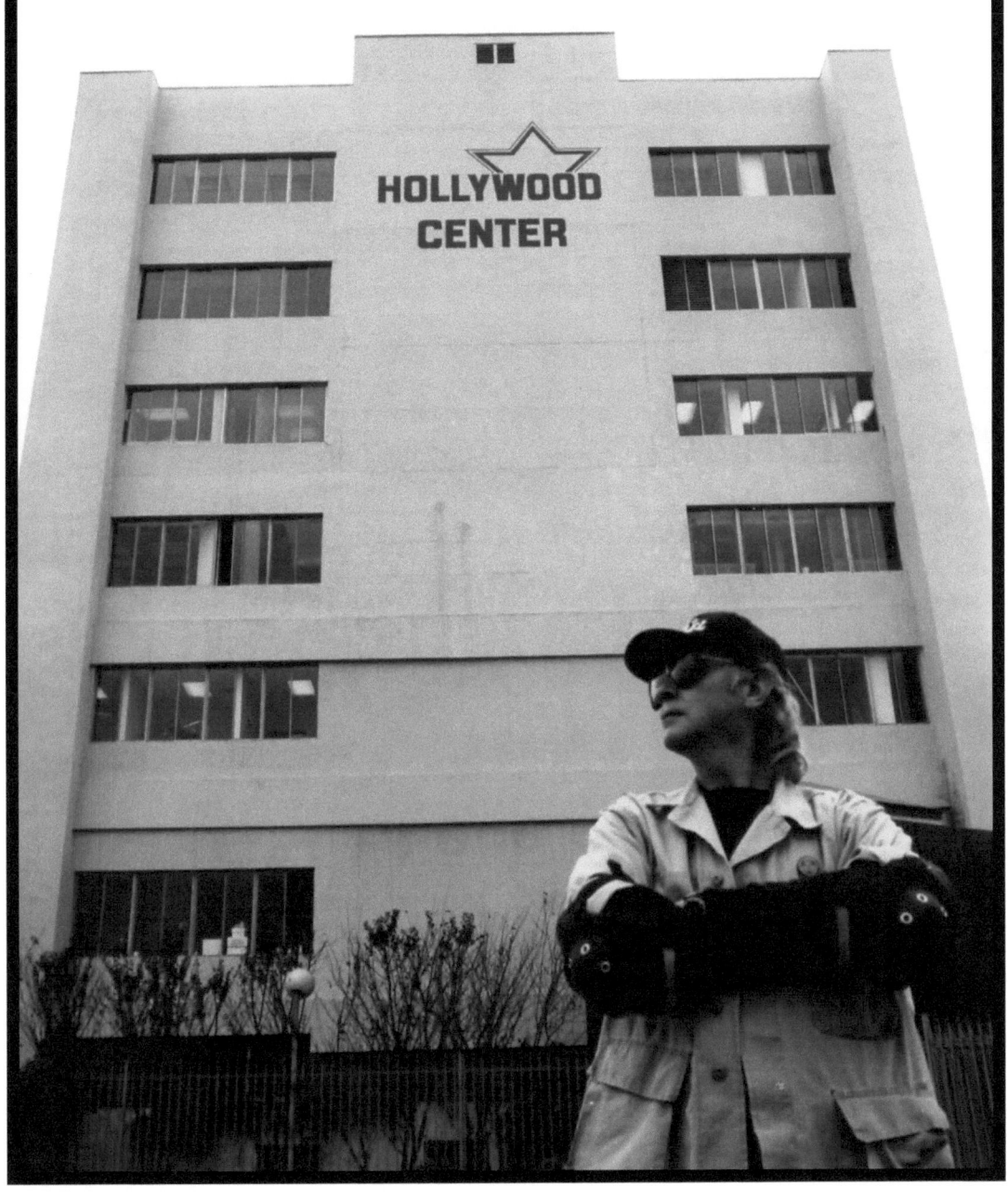

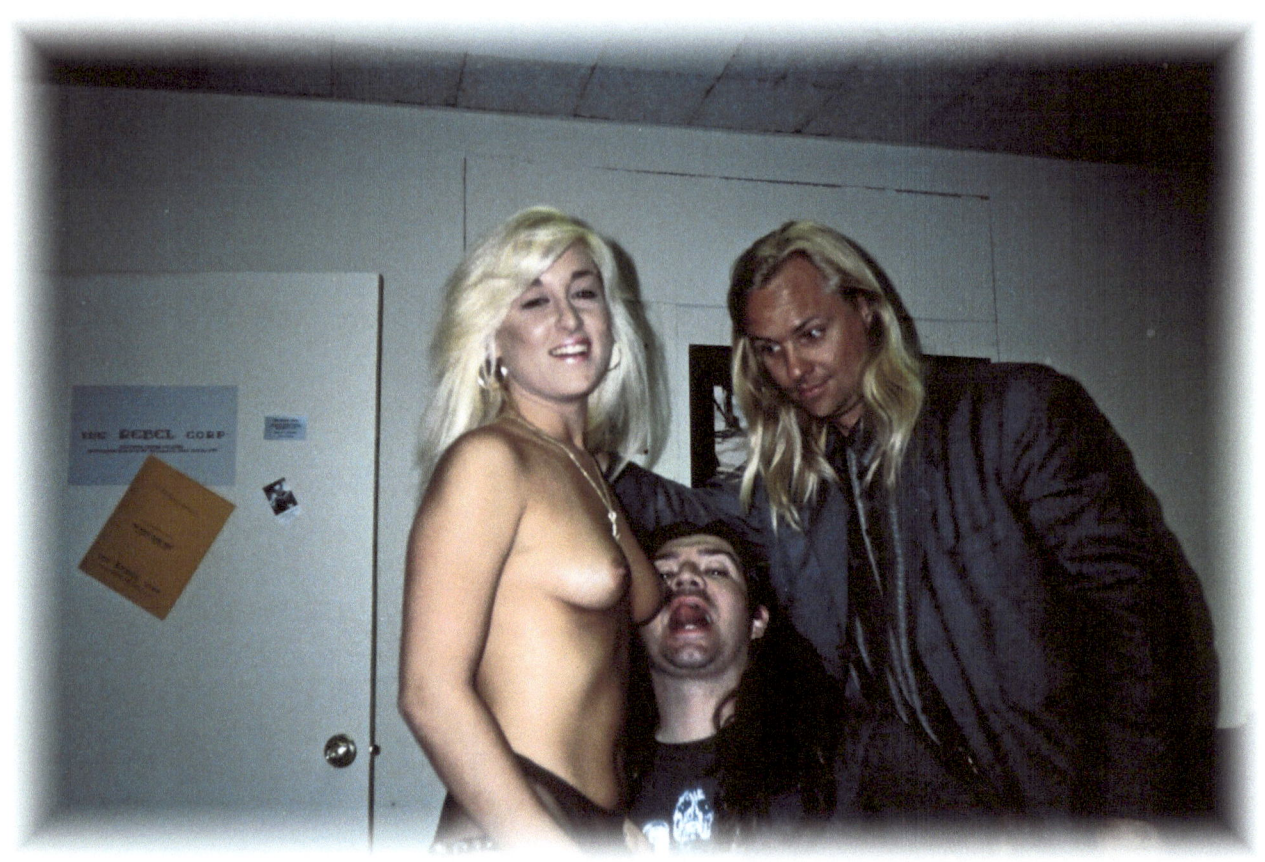

PRODUCTION OFFICE SHENANIGANS

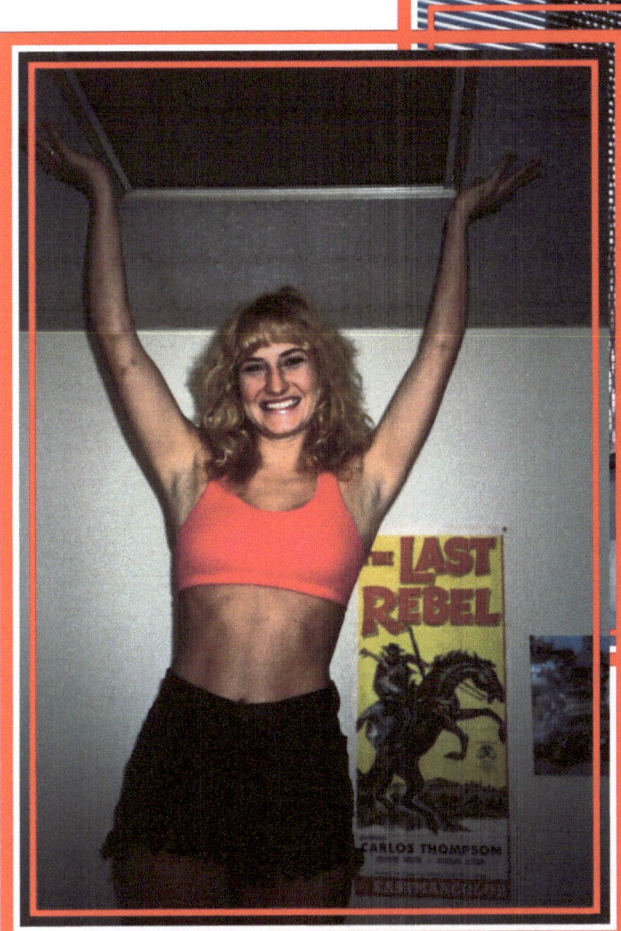
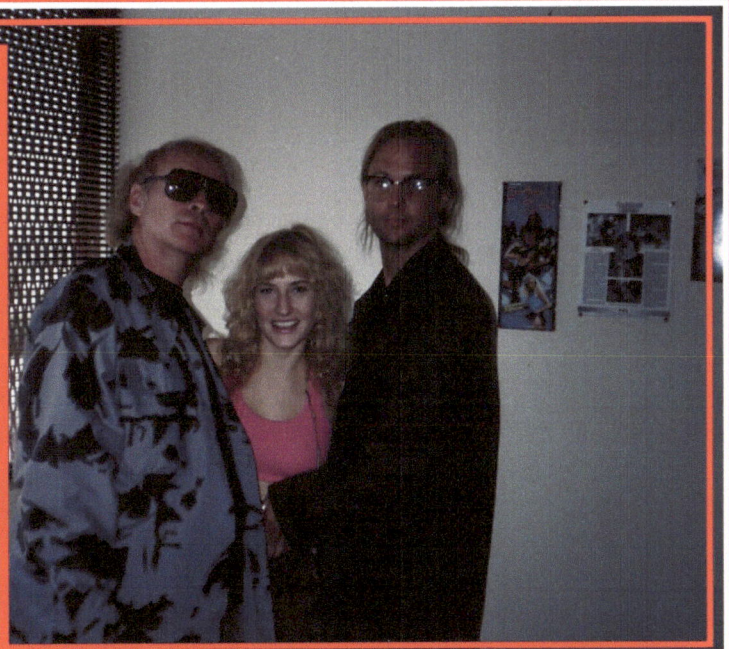
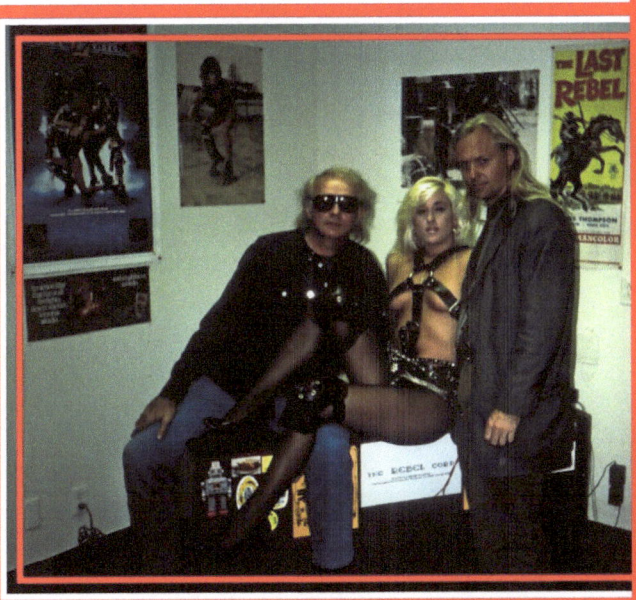
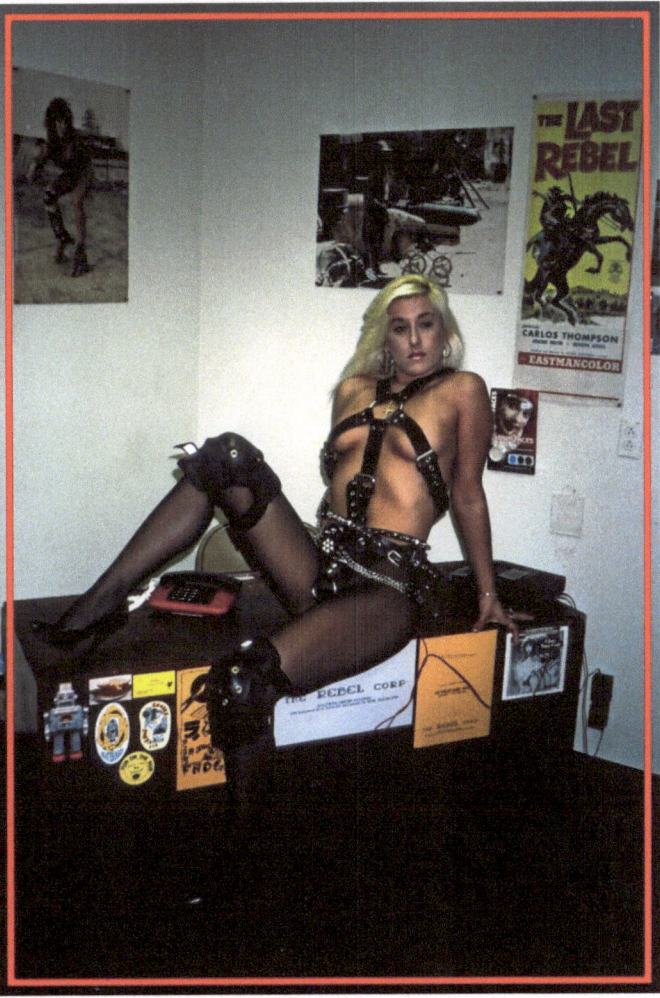

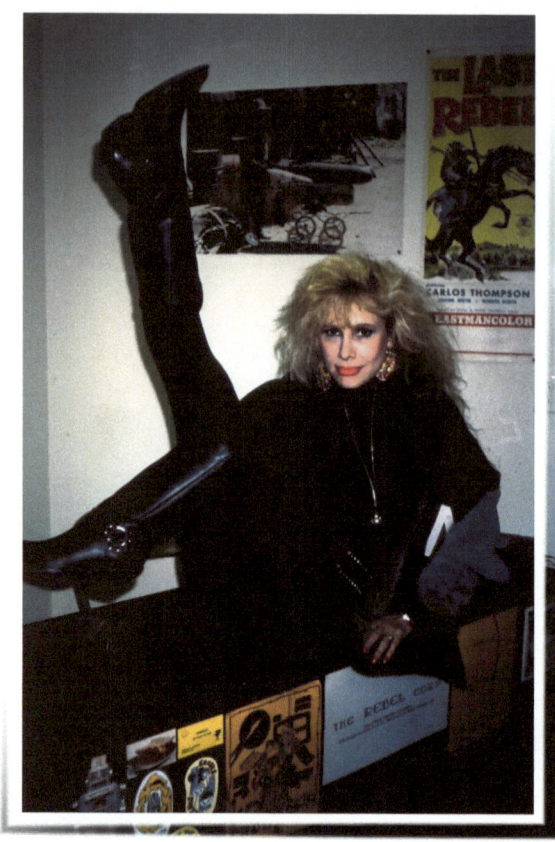
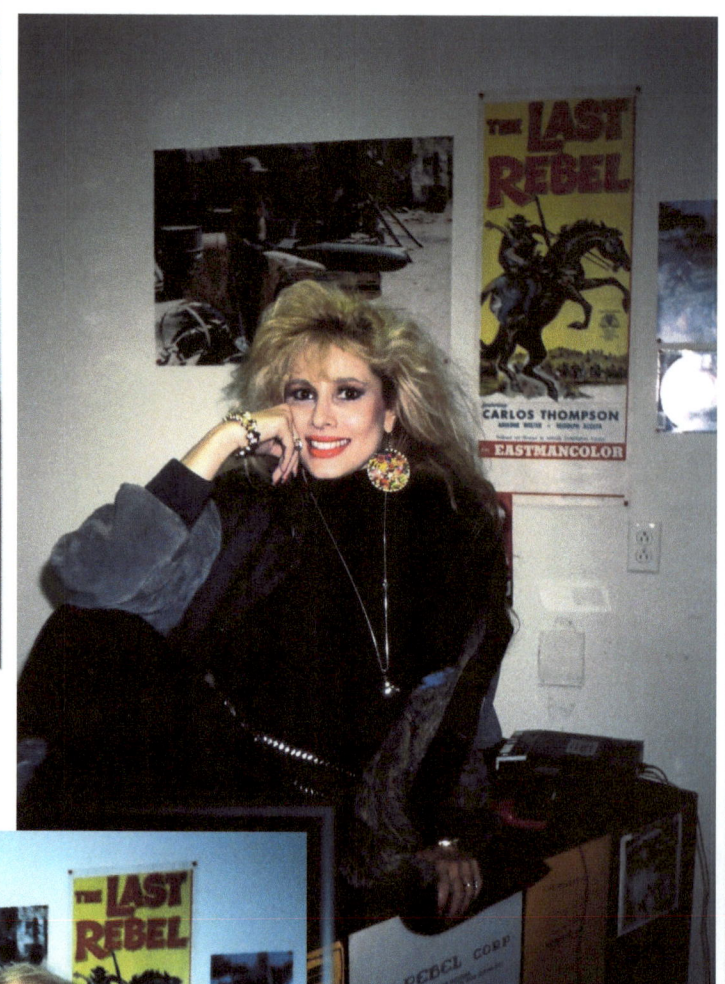
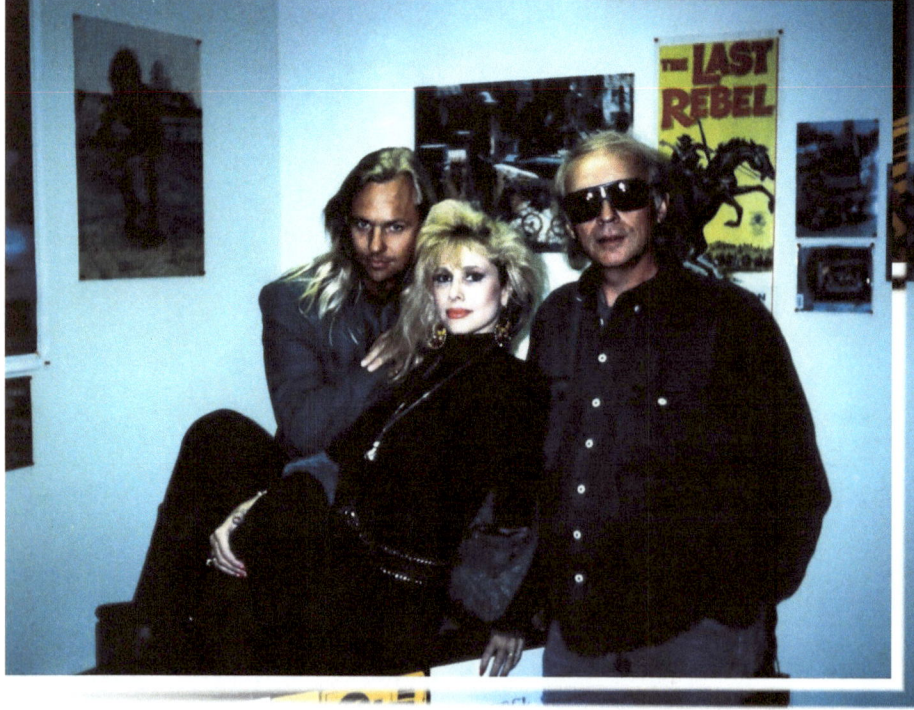

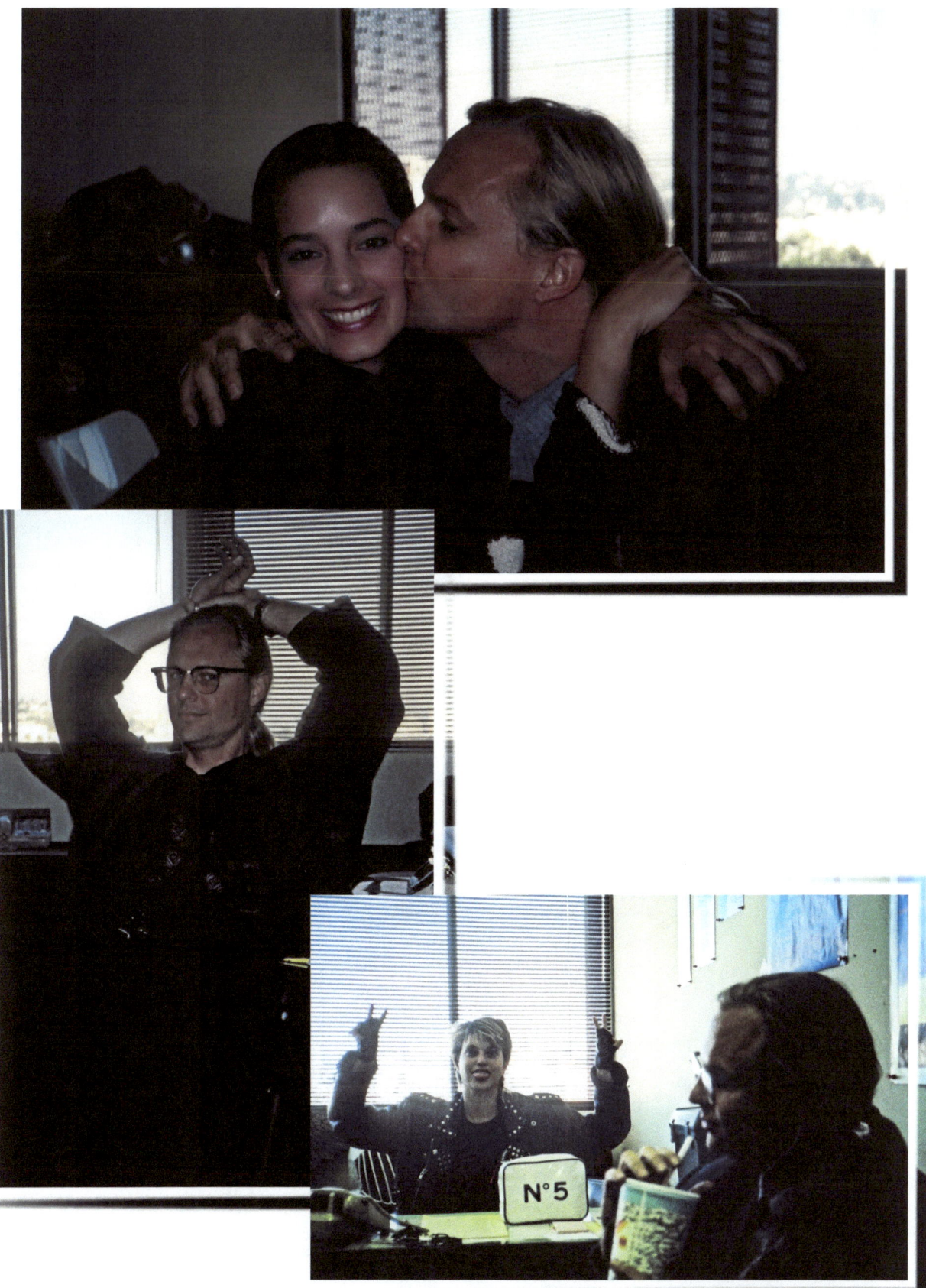

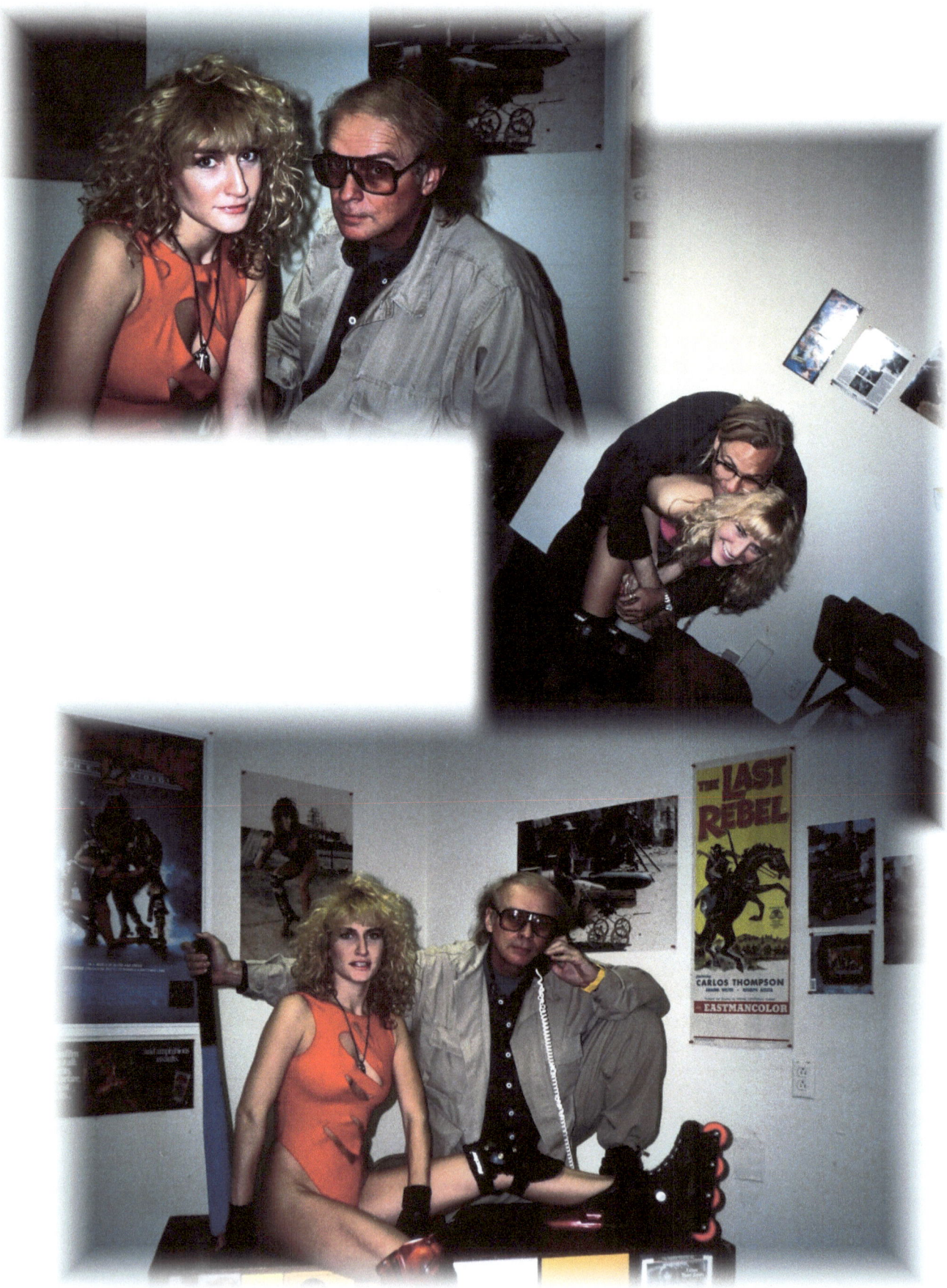

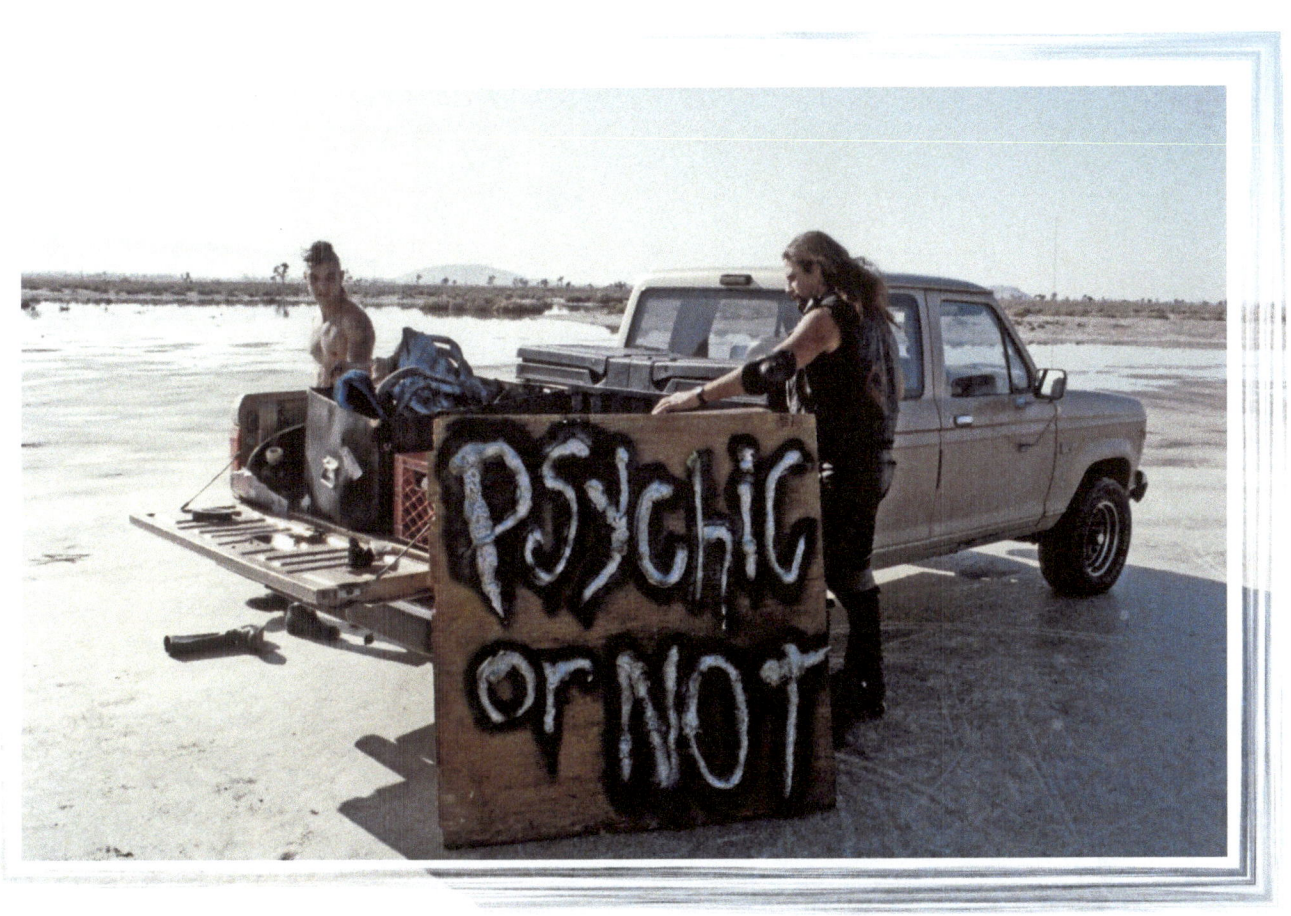

THE CHARACTERS

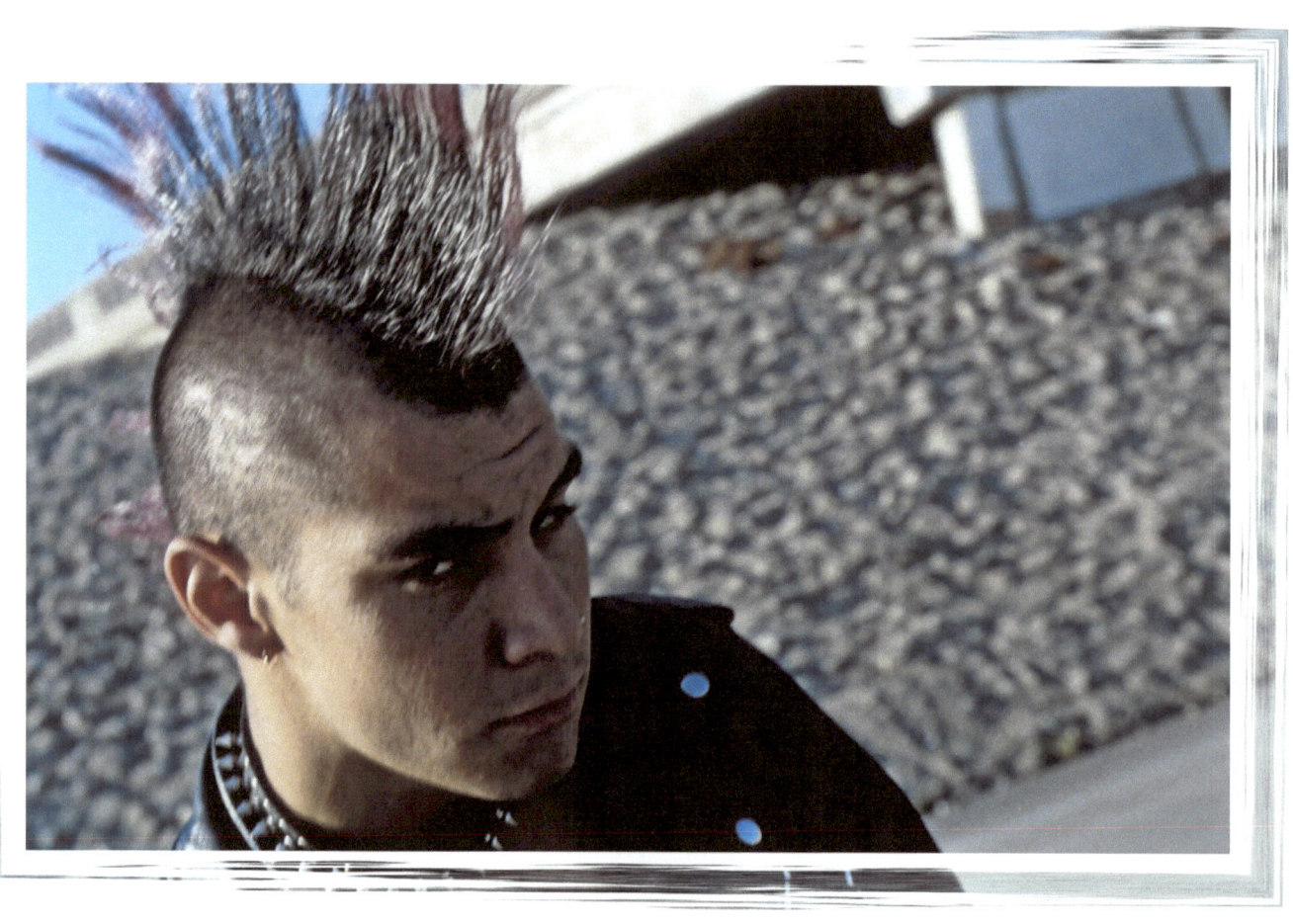

MOHAWK

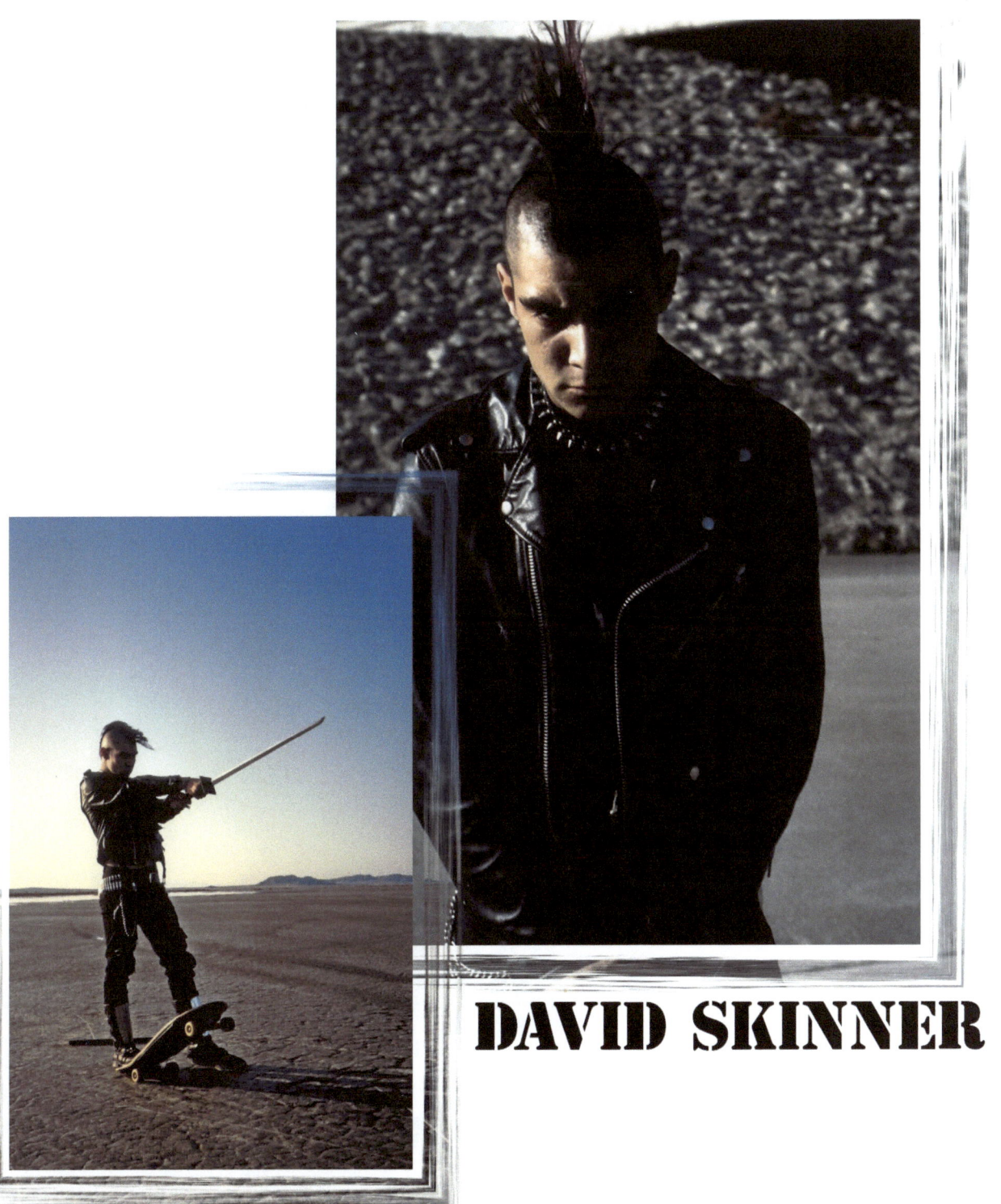

DAVID SKINNER

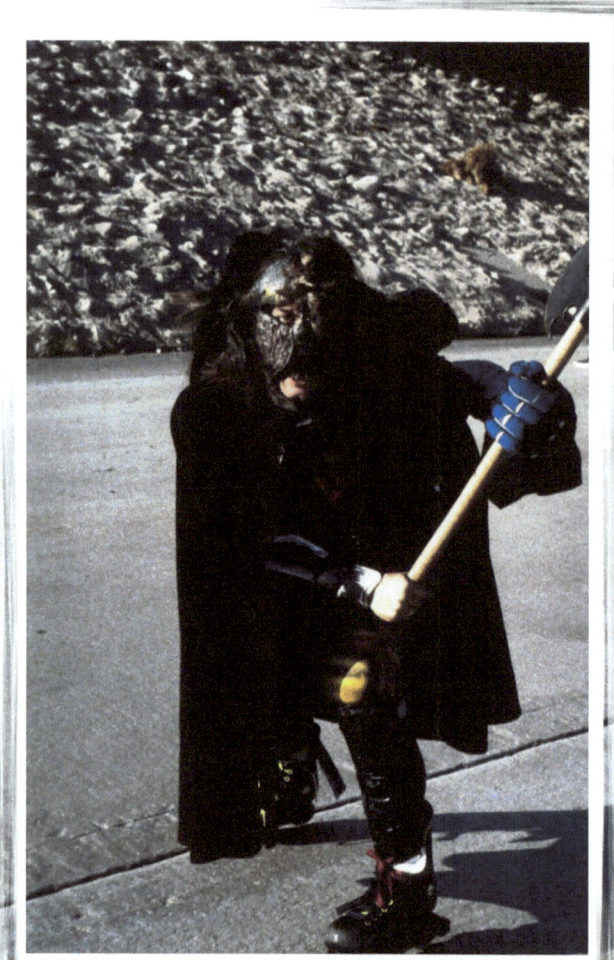

ROCKIN' RON

LITTLE STEVE

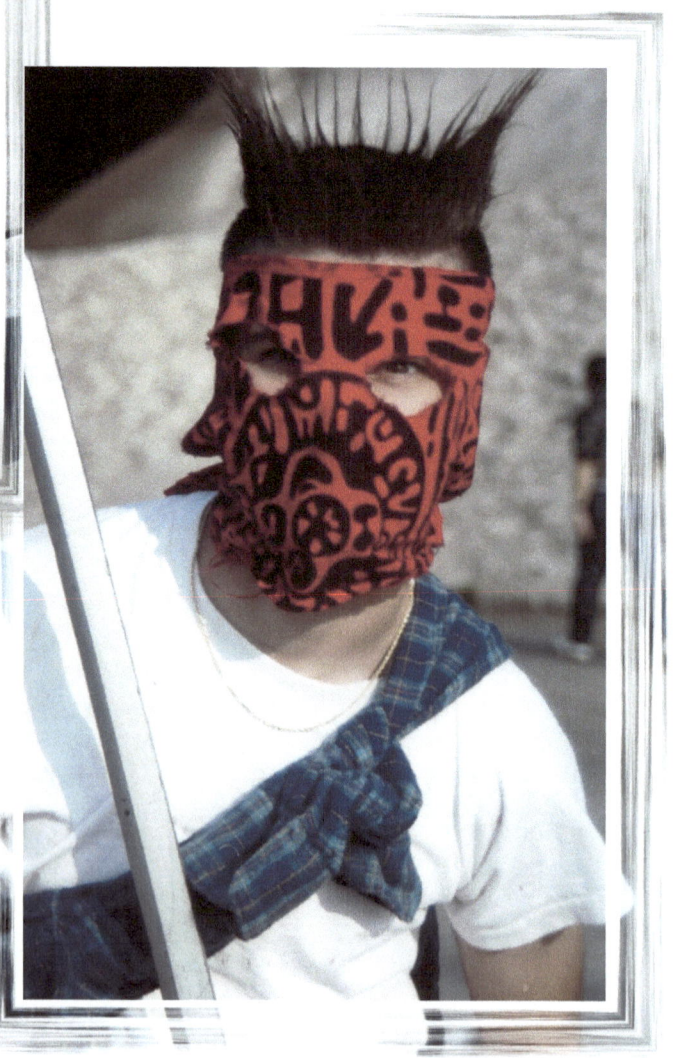

WHEELZONE WARRIORS

CHOPPER
MARK RICHARDSON

STEALTH
ROGER ELLIS

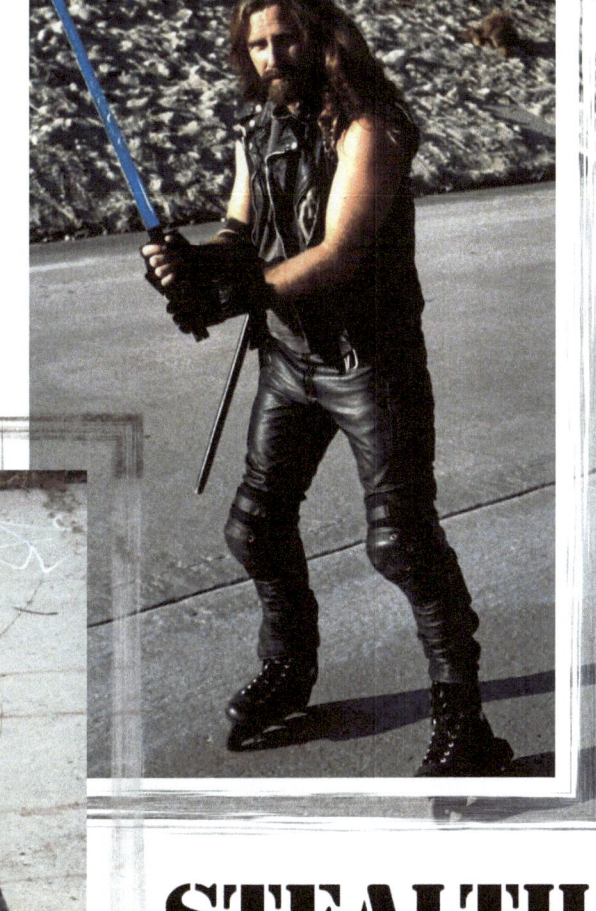

KABUKI

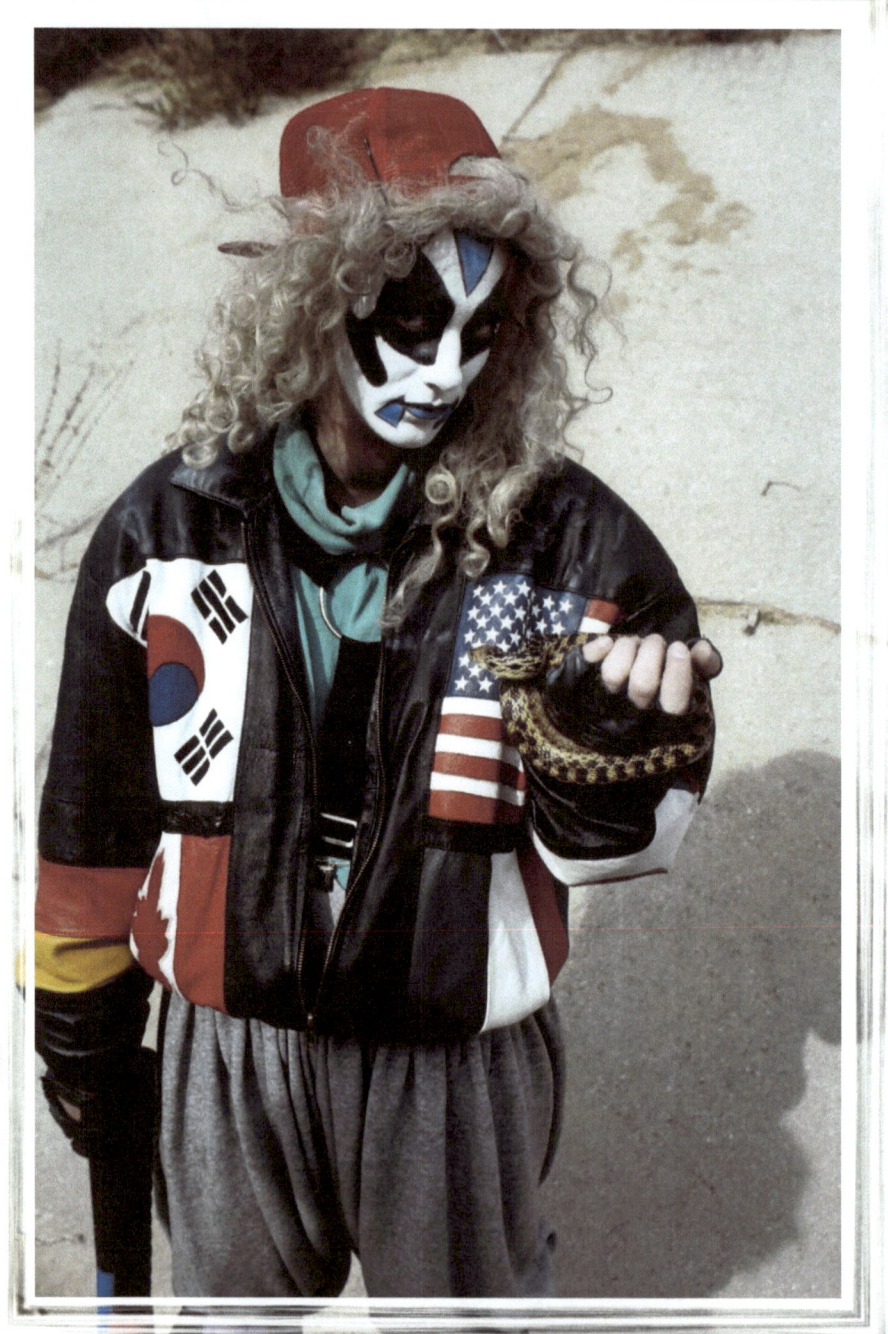

CLAUDIA SCHOLTZ

JAY BECHTOL

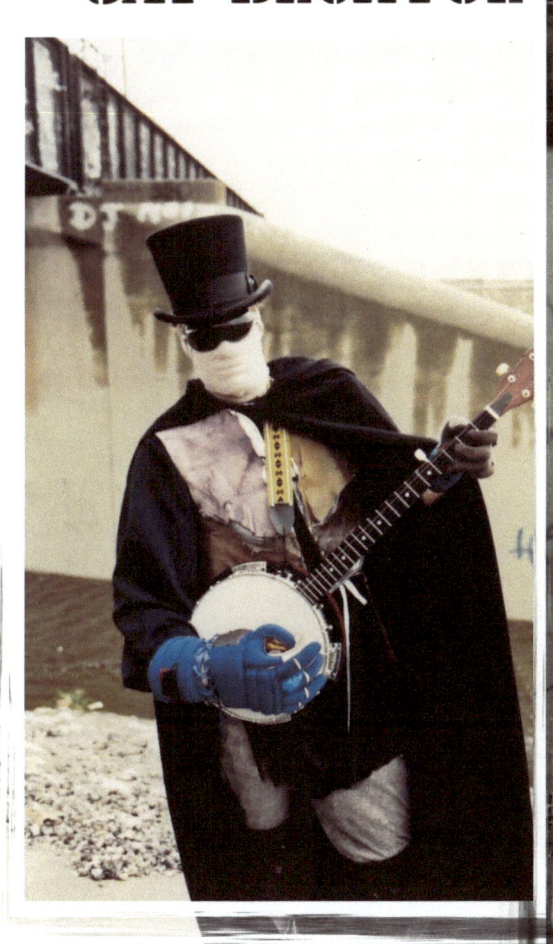
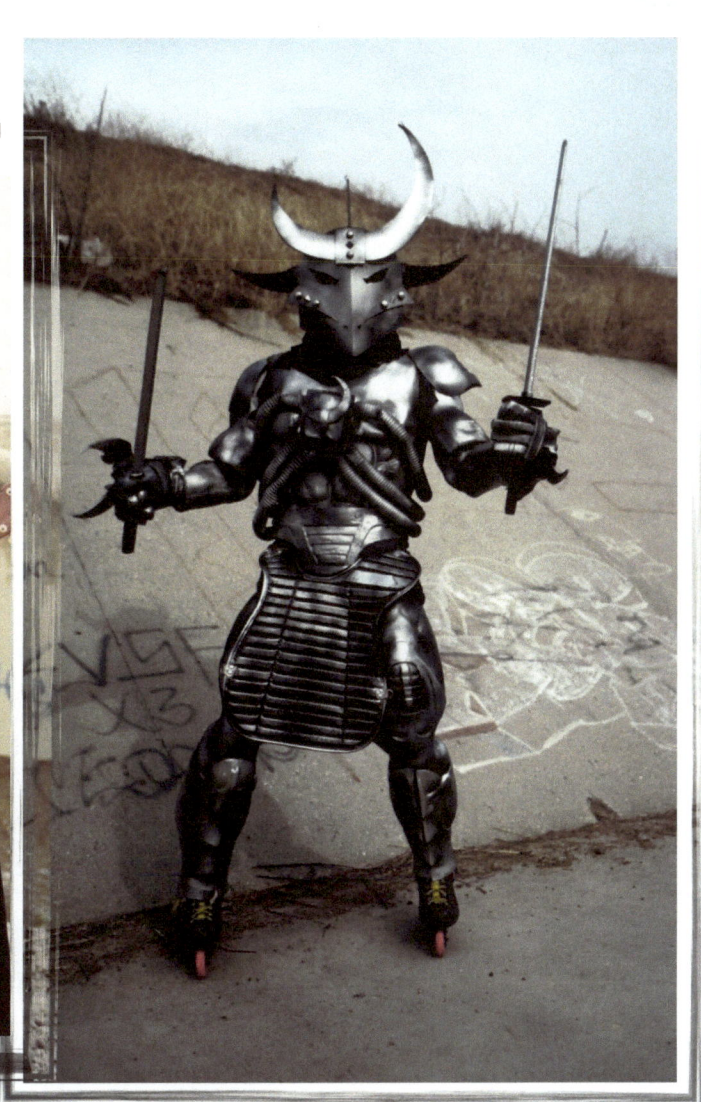

FUKASAI NINJA
BANJO MAN
WHEELZONE WARRIOR

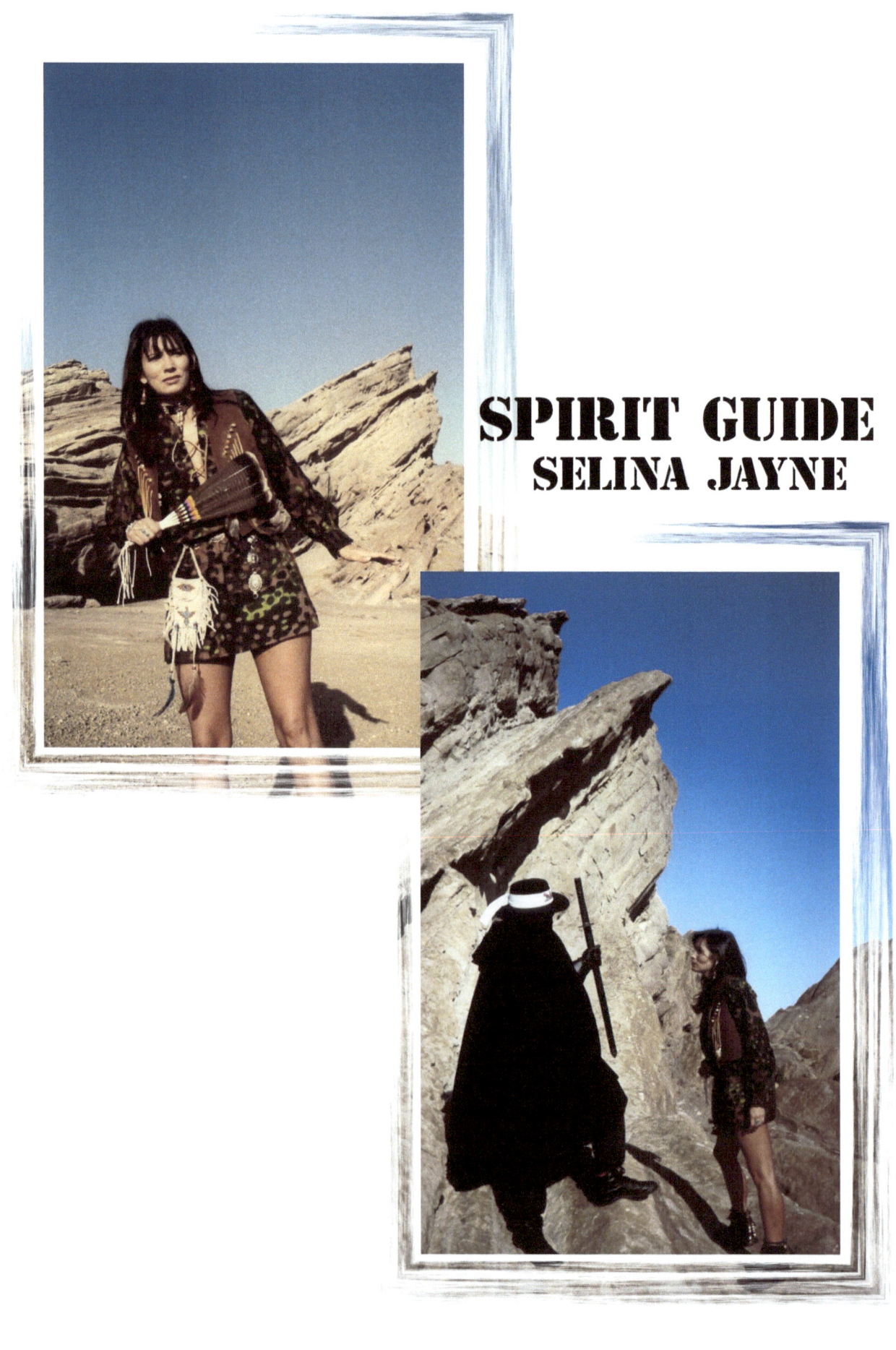

SPIRIT GUIDE
SELINA JAYNE

UTILITY NINJA KENNETH H. KIM

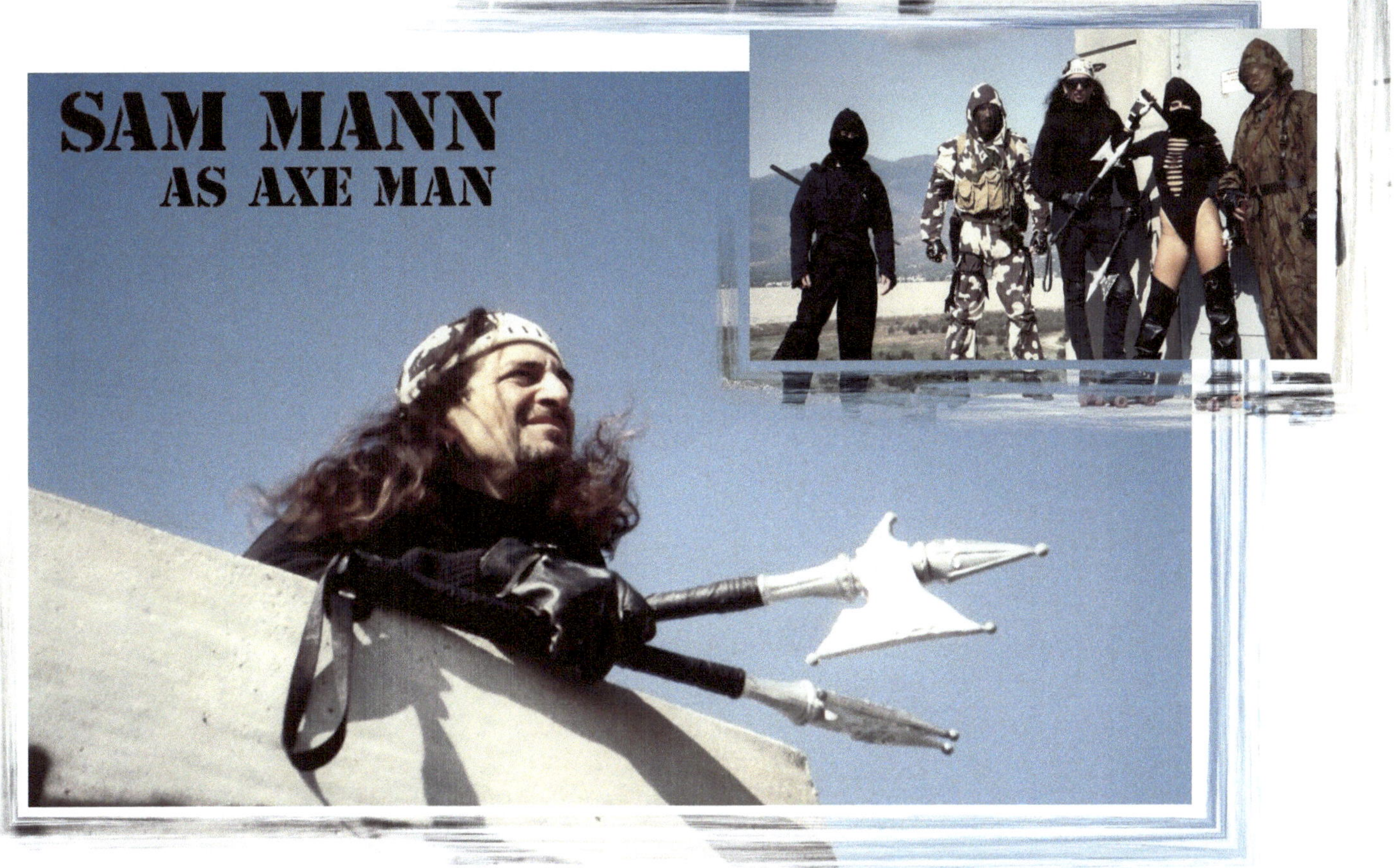

SAM MANN
AS AXE MAN

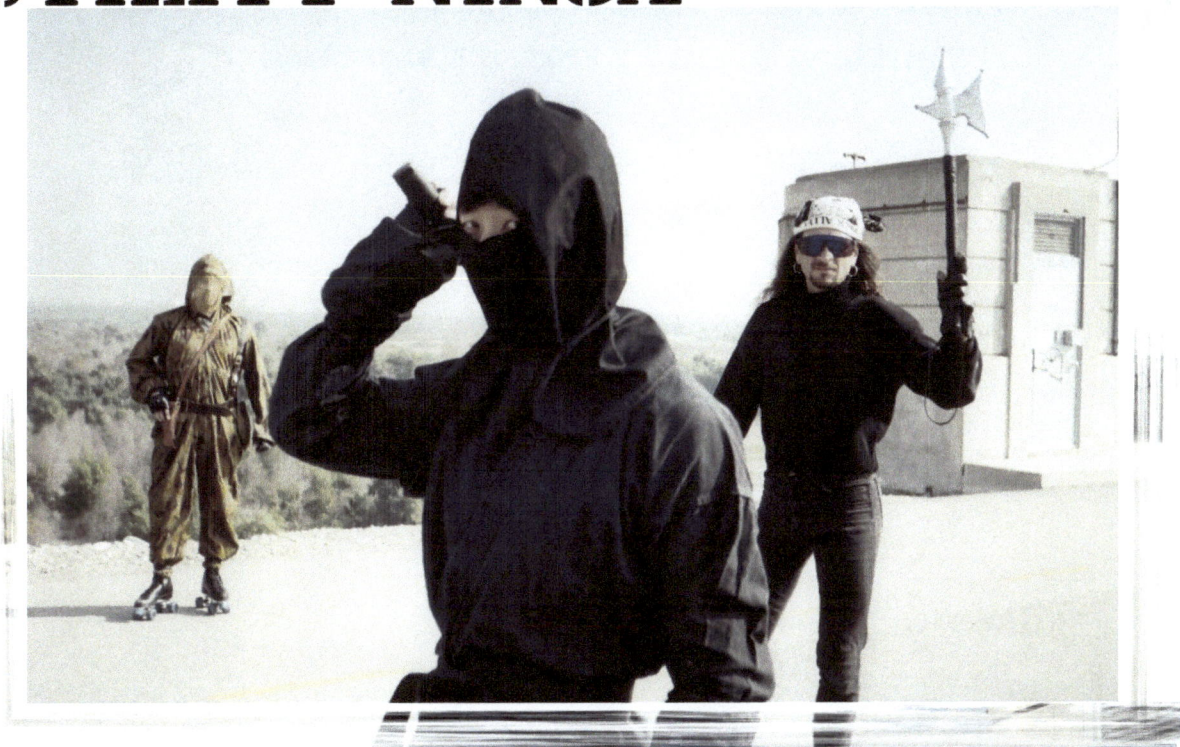

SISTER SPARROW

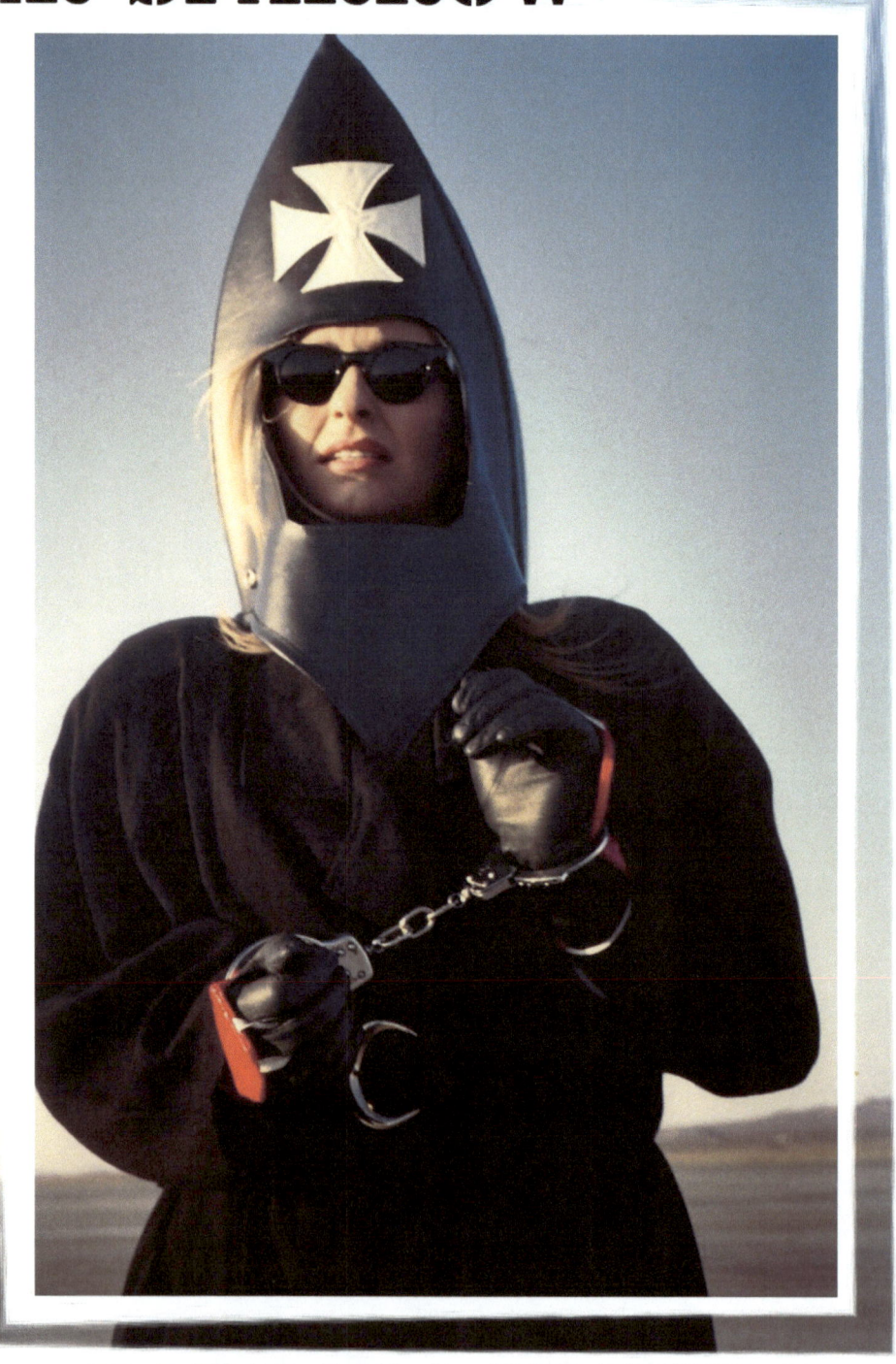

BARBARA NICKELL

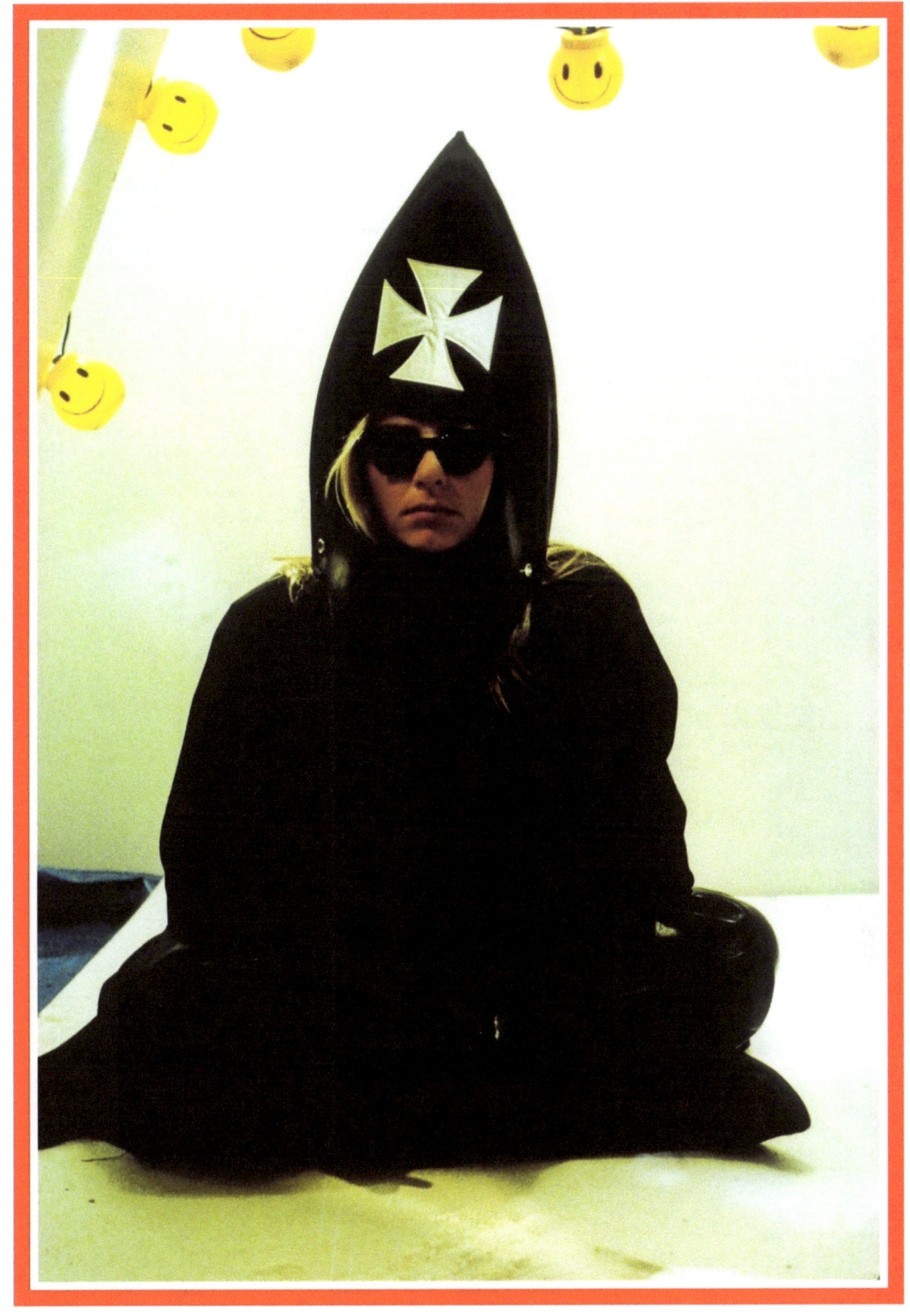

"You mean my sister that became your sister?"
"Yes, our sister – sister."

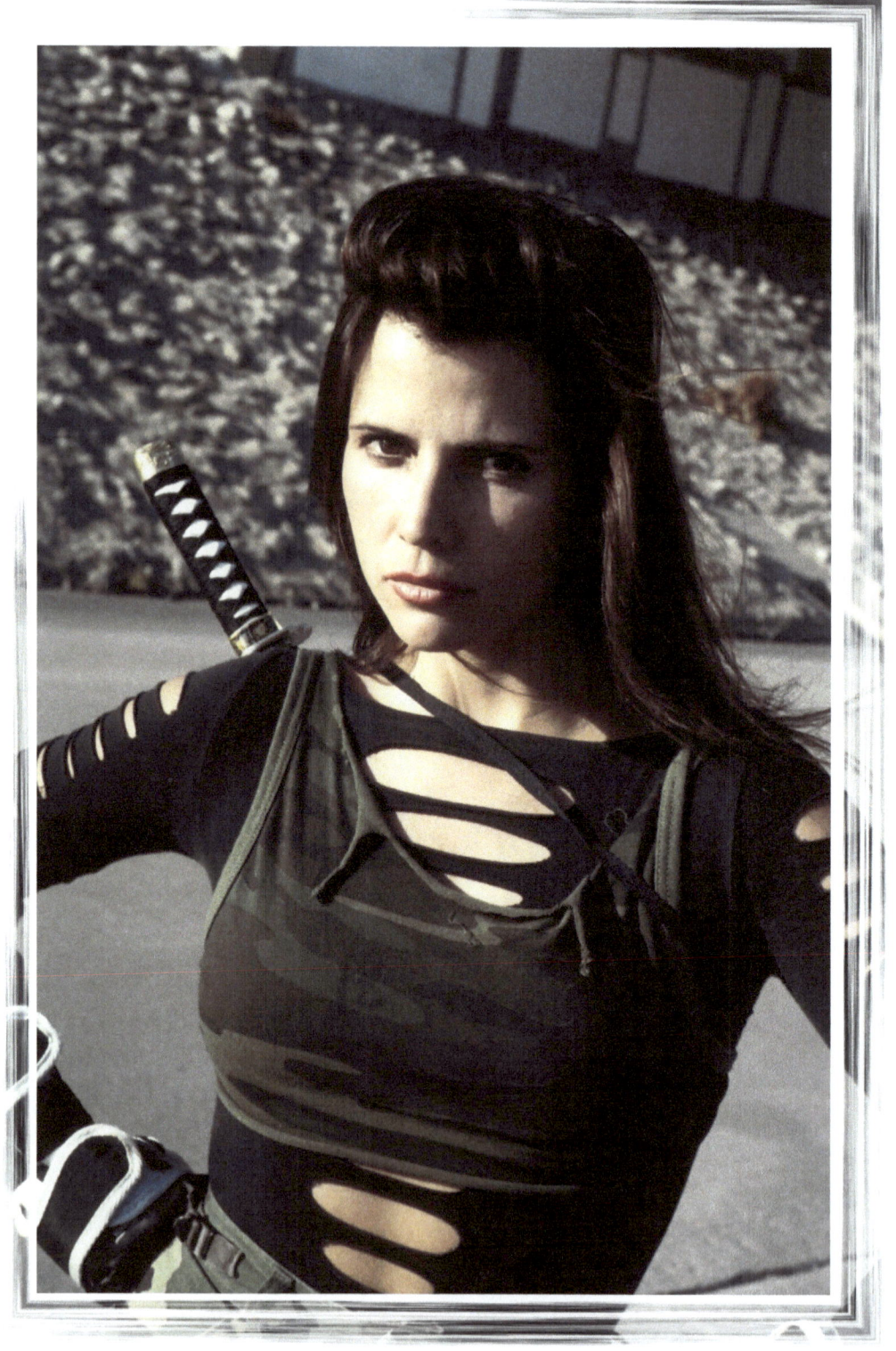

DIANA CUEVAS

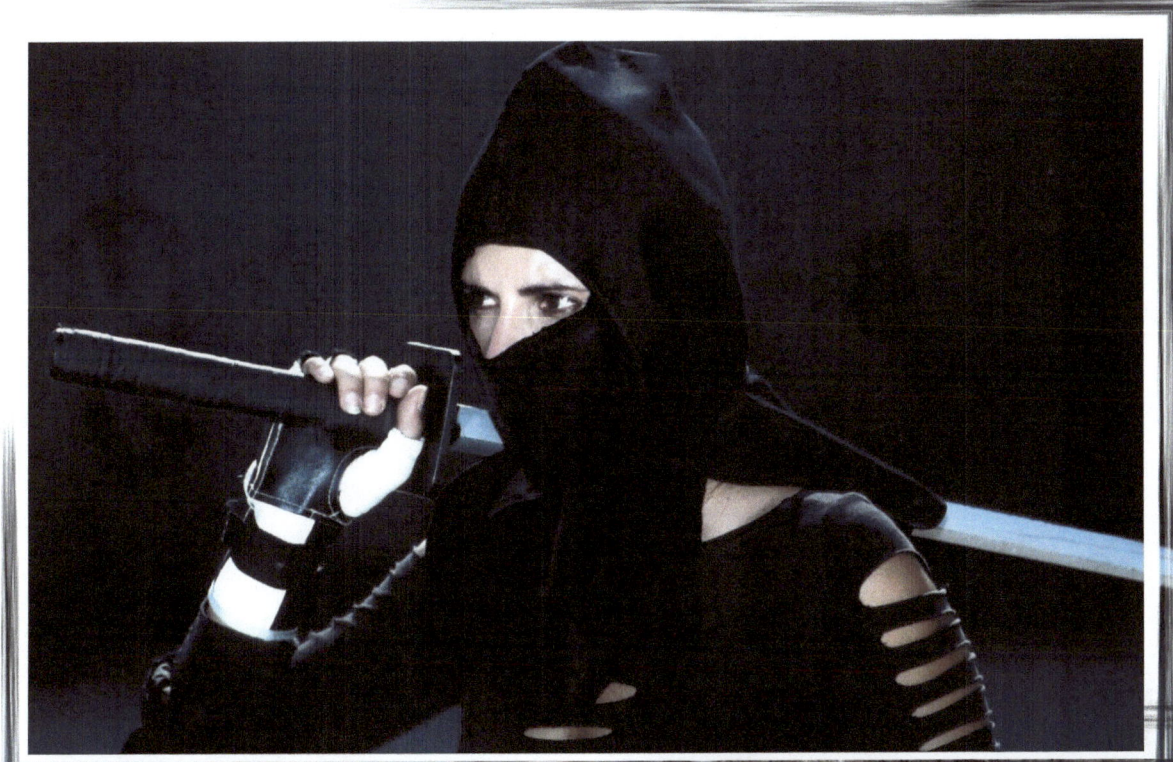

**NINJA
WHIP METAL
WHEELZONE WARRIOR**

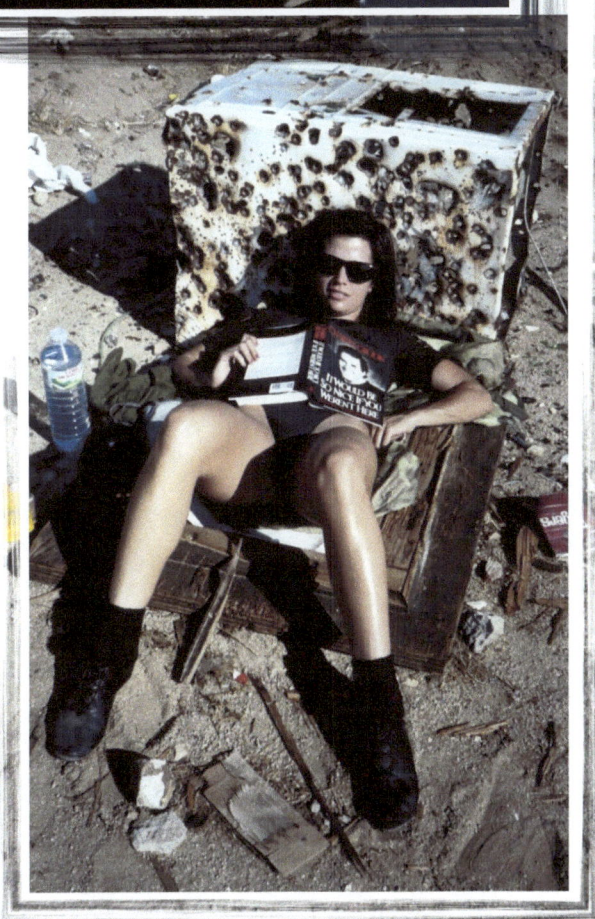

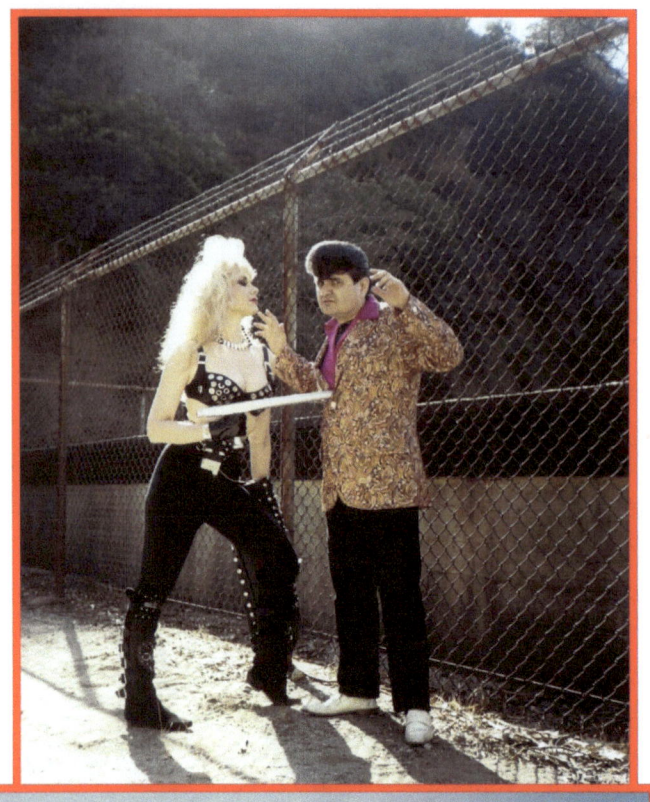

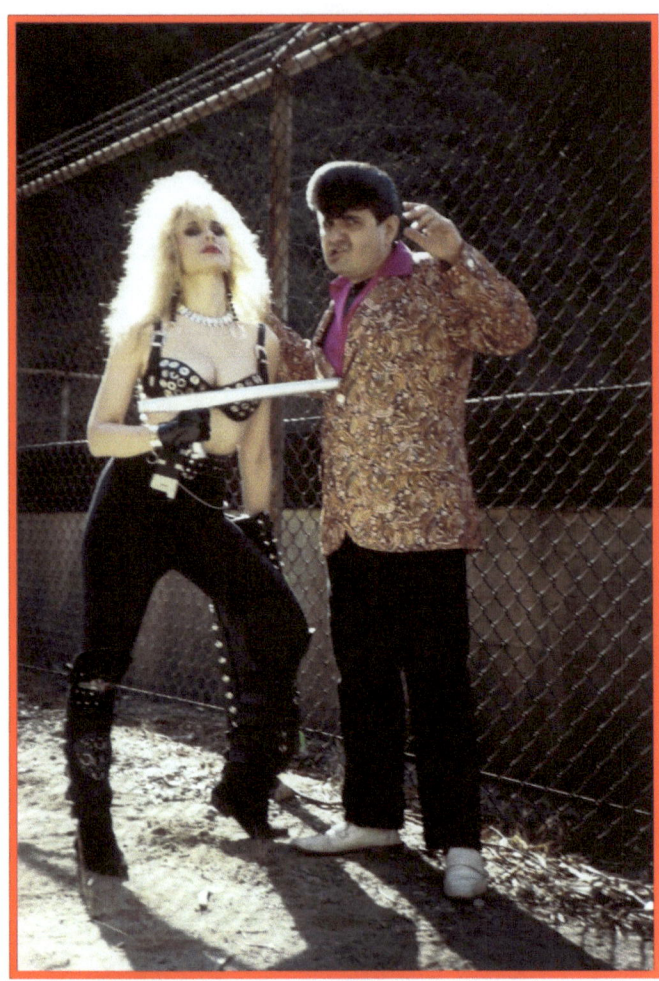

RHONDA SHEAR
AS OFFICER DARYL SKATES

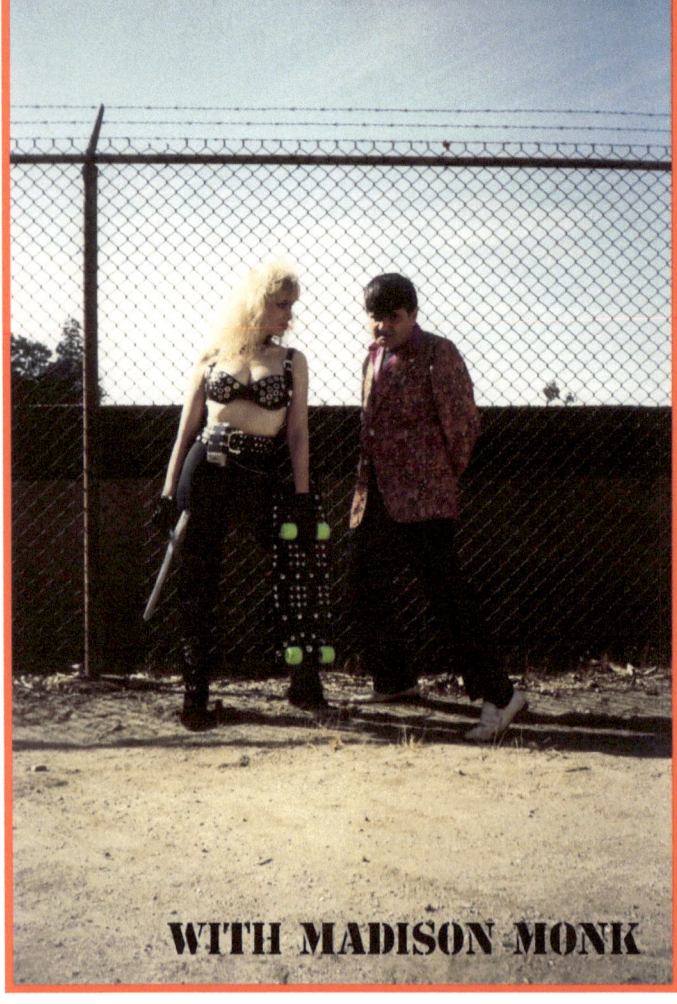

WITH MADISON MONK

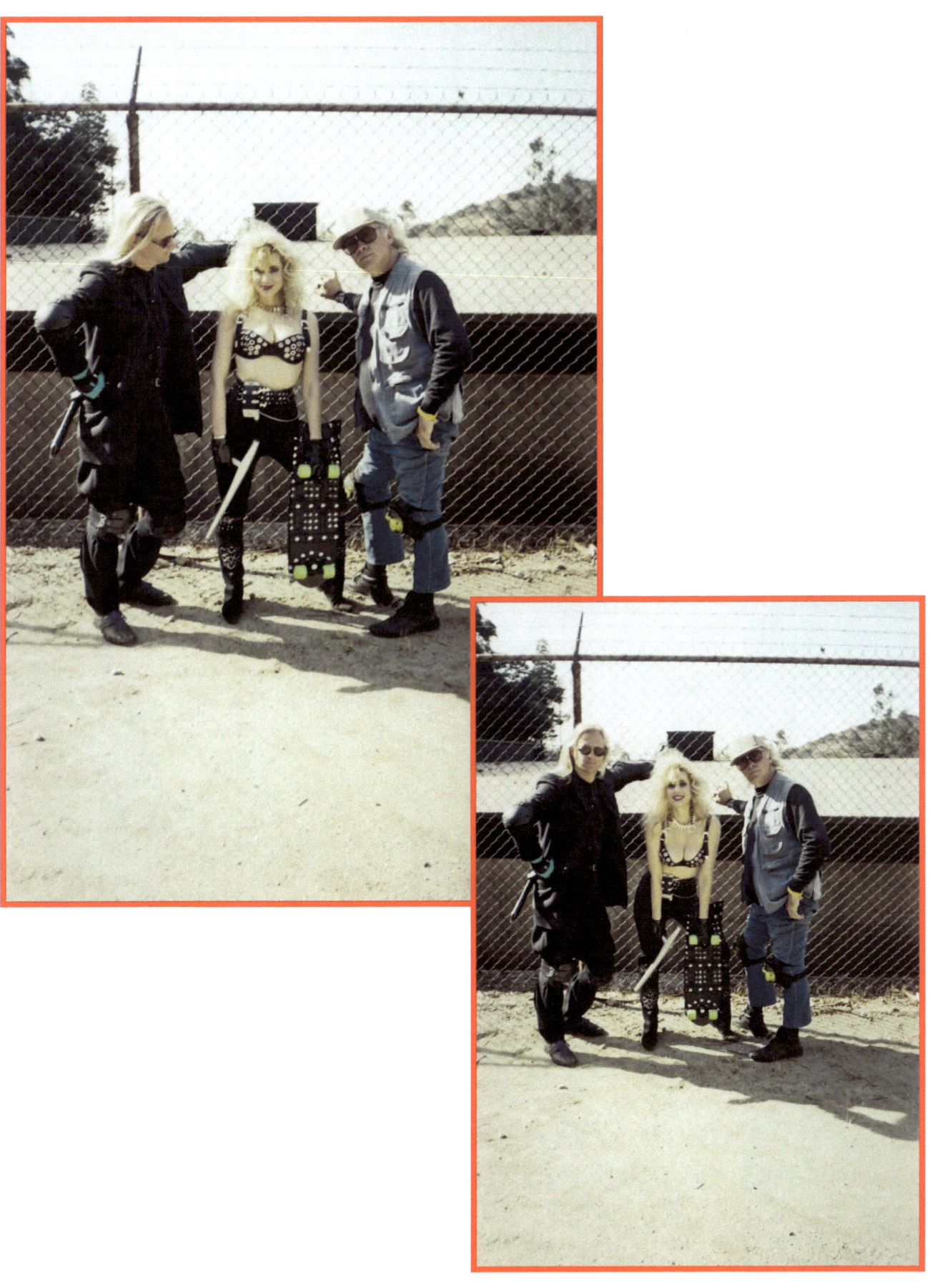

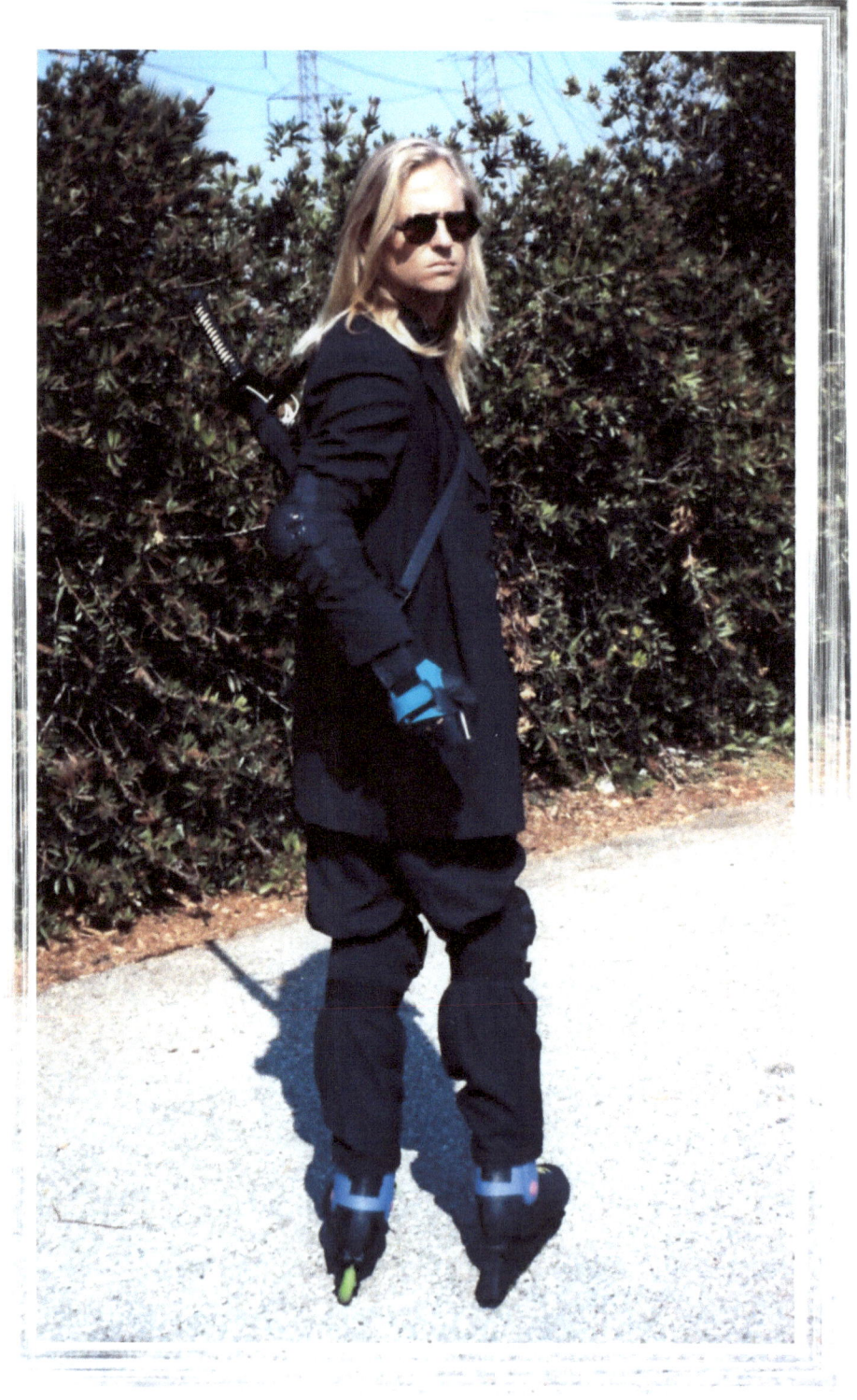

**WARDROBE STILLS
DAY ONE OF PRODUCTION**

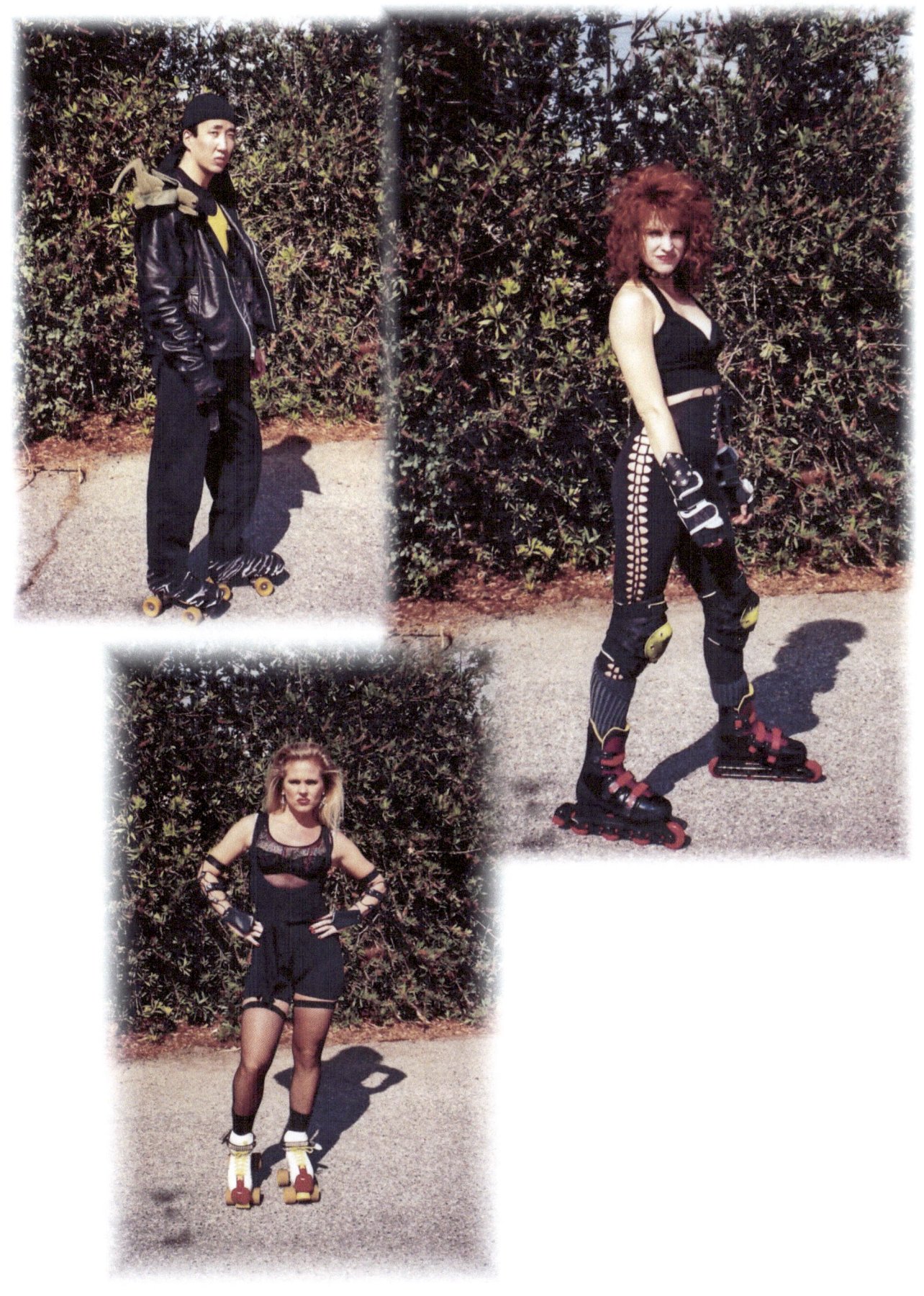

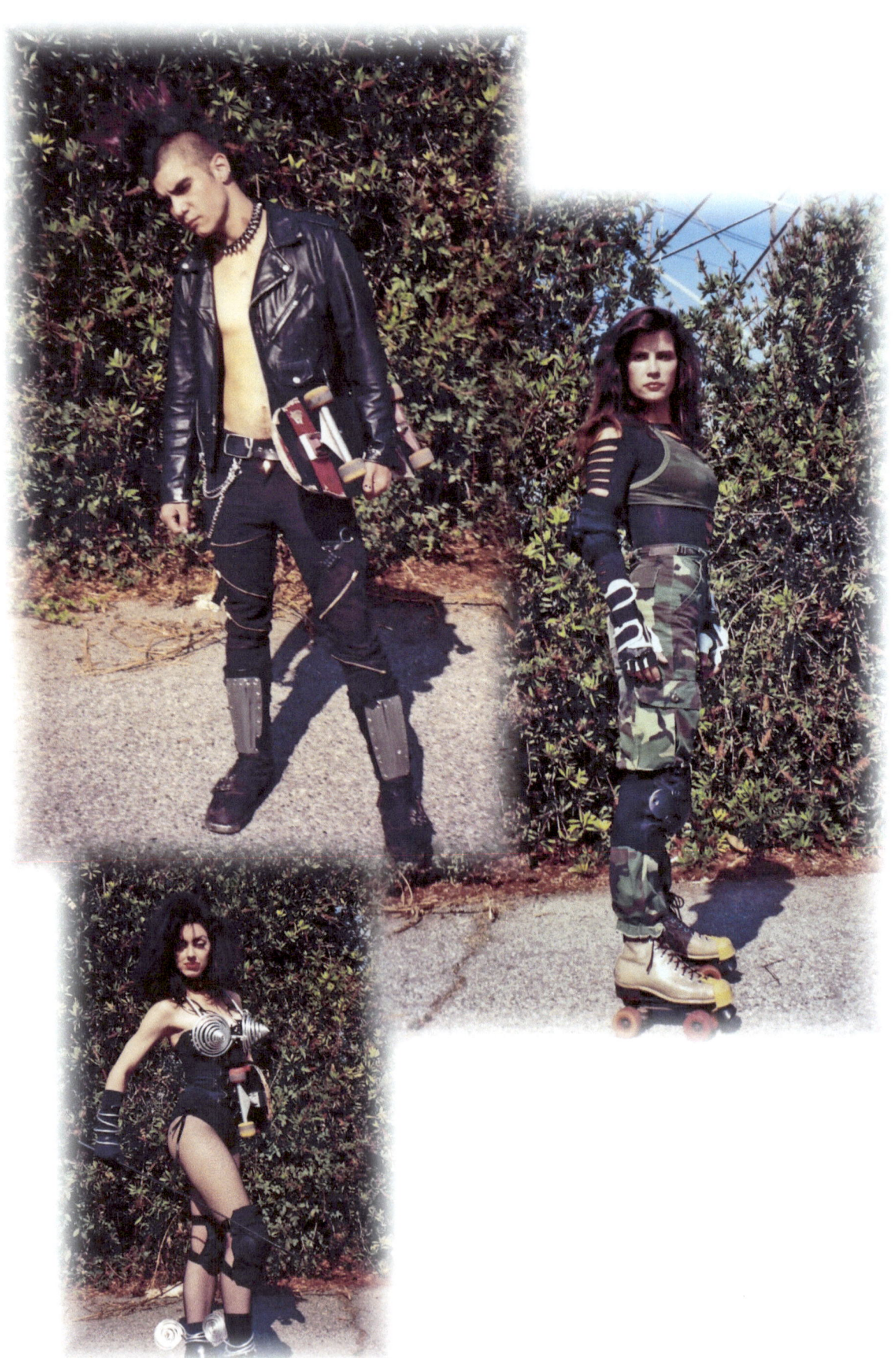

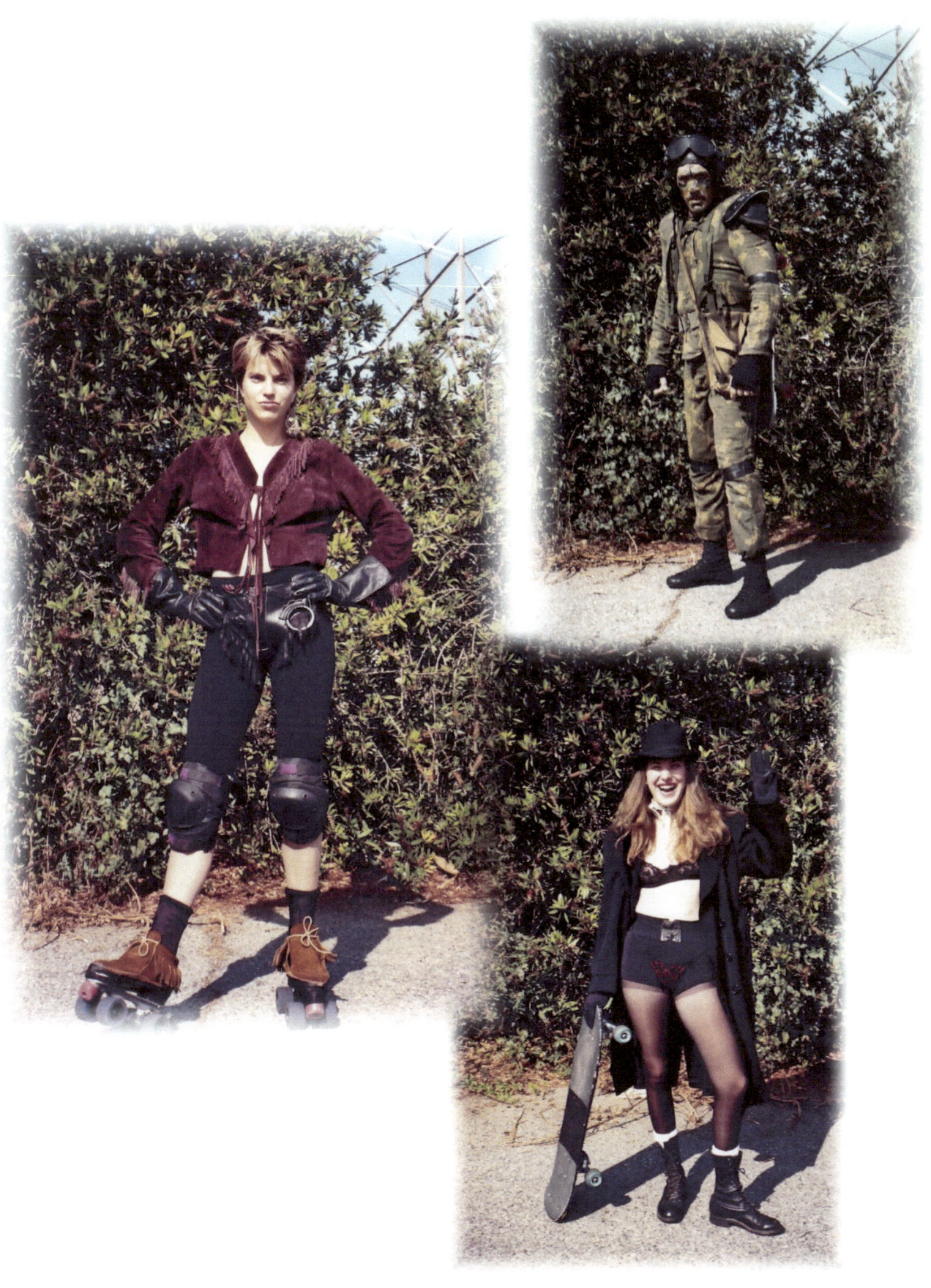

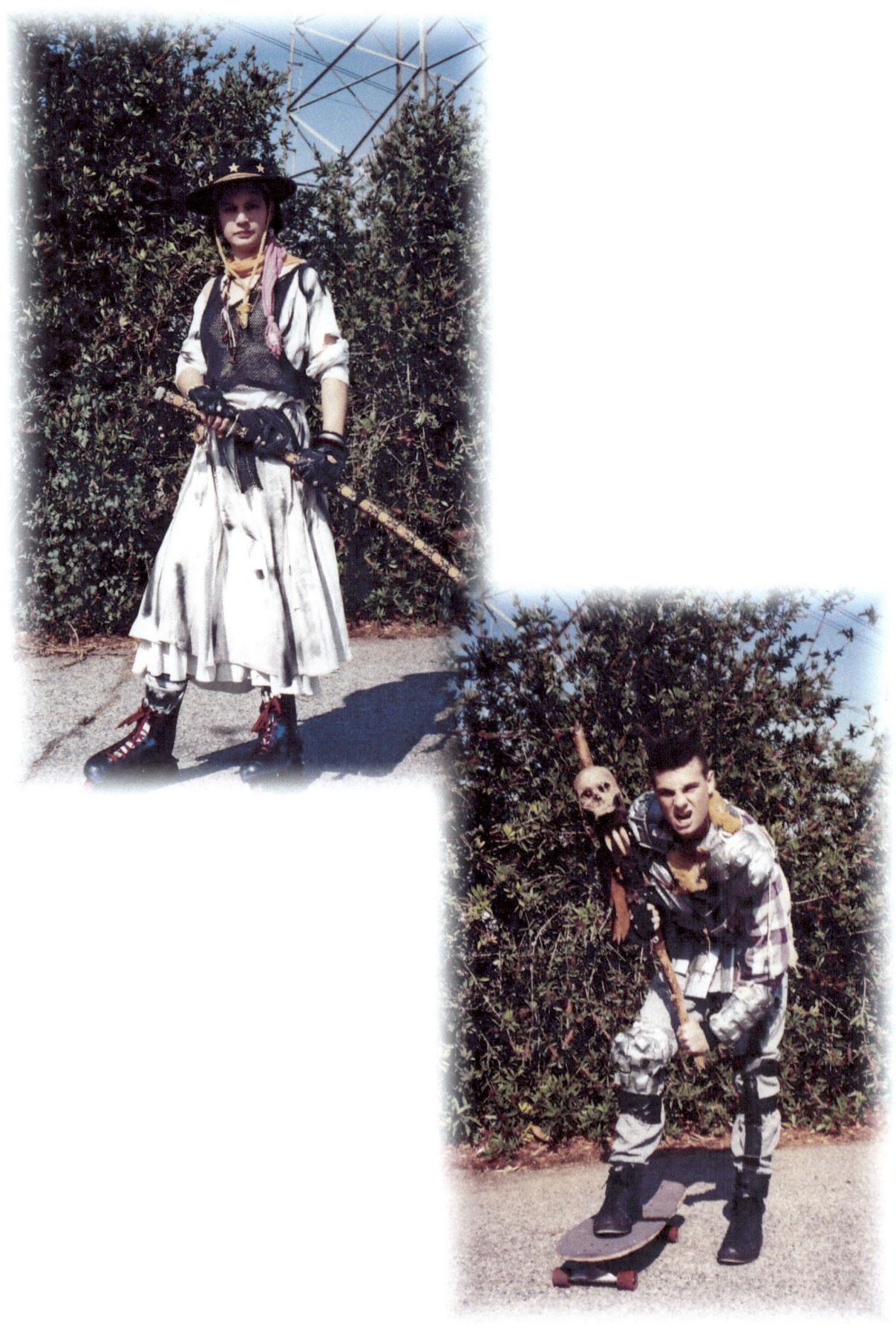

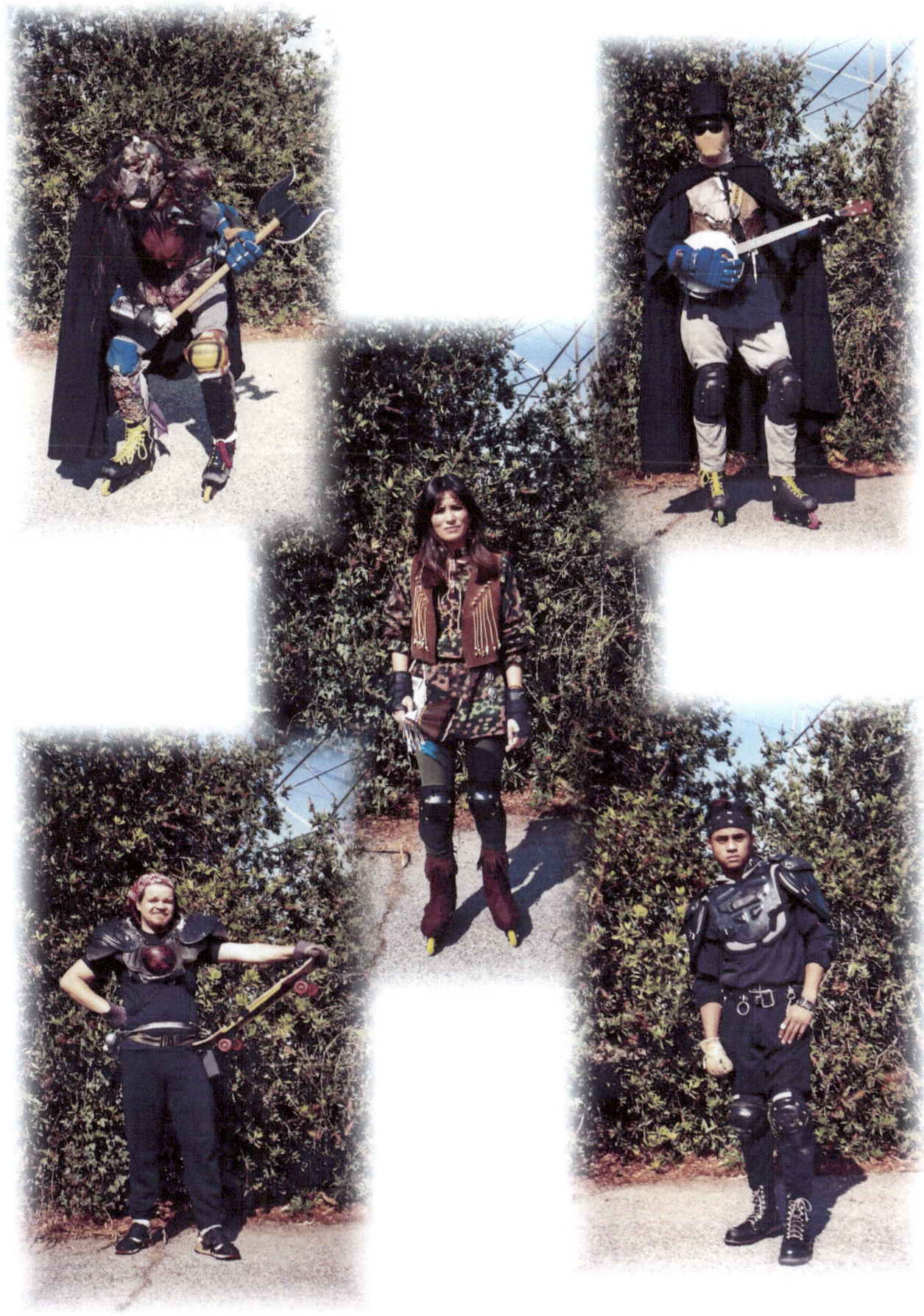

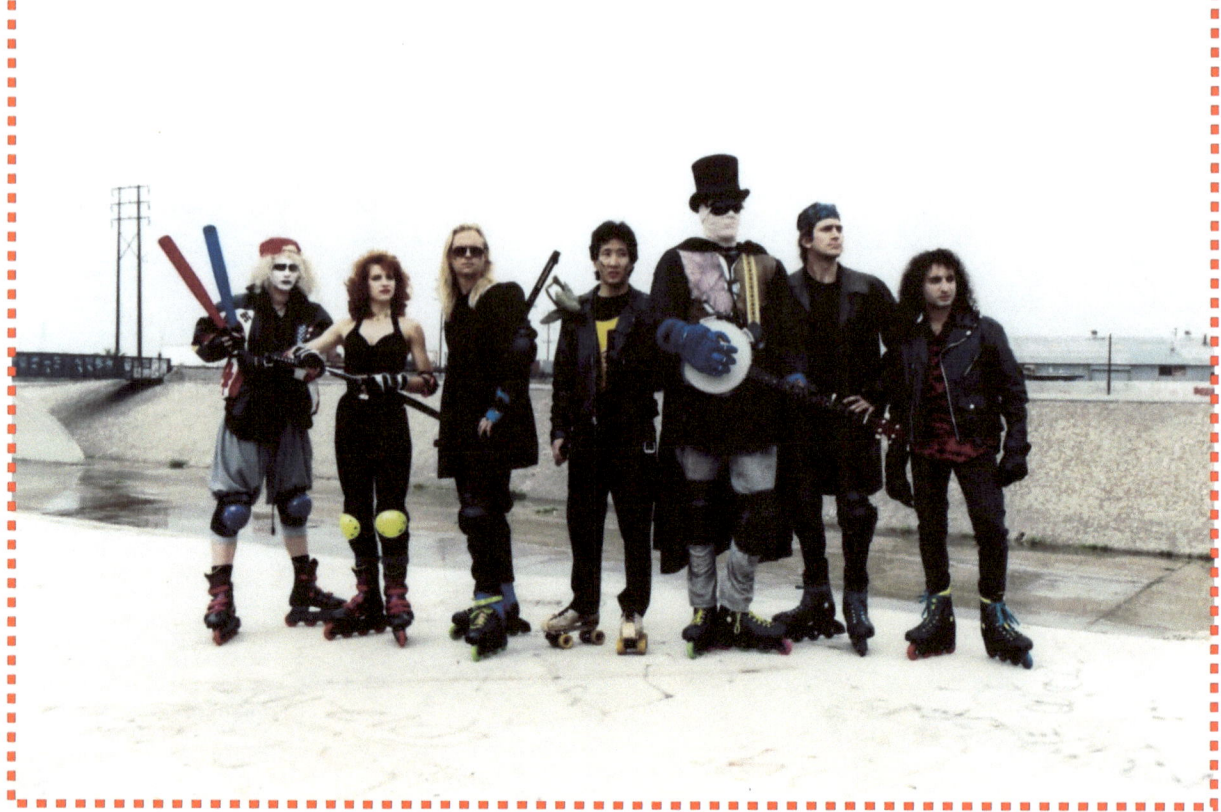

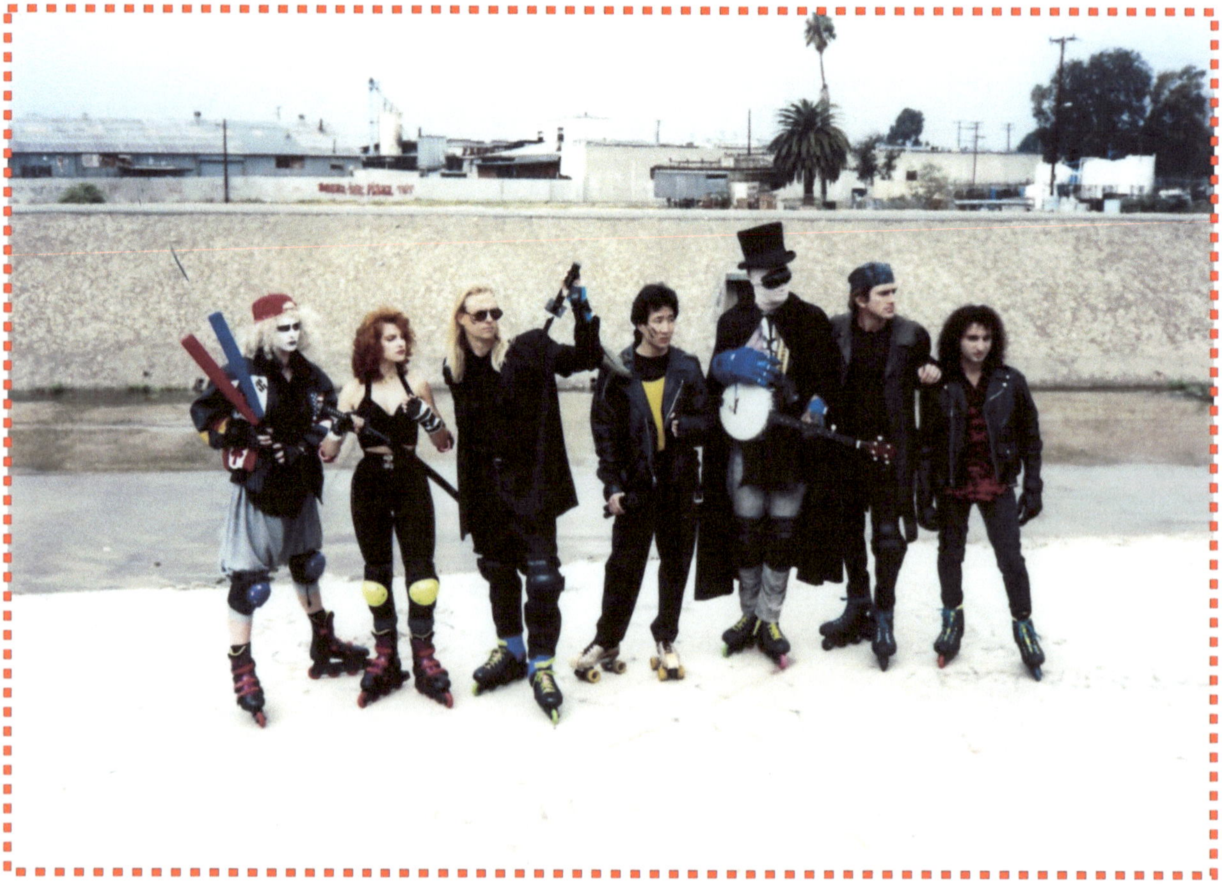

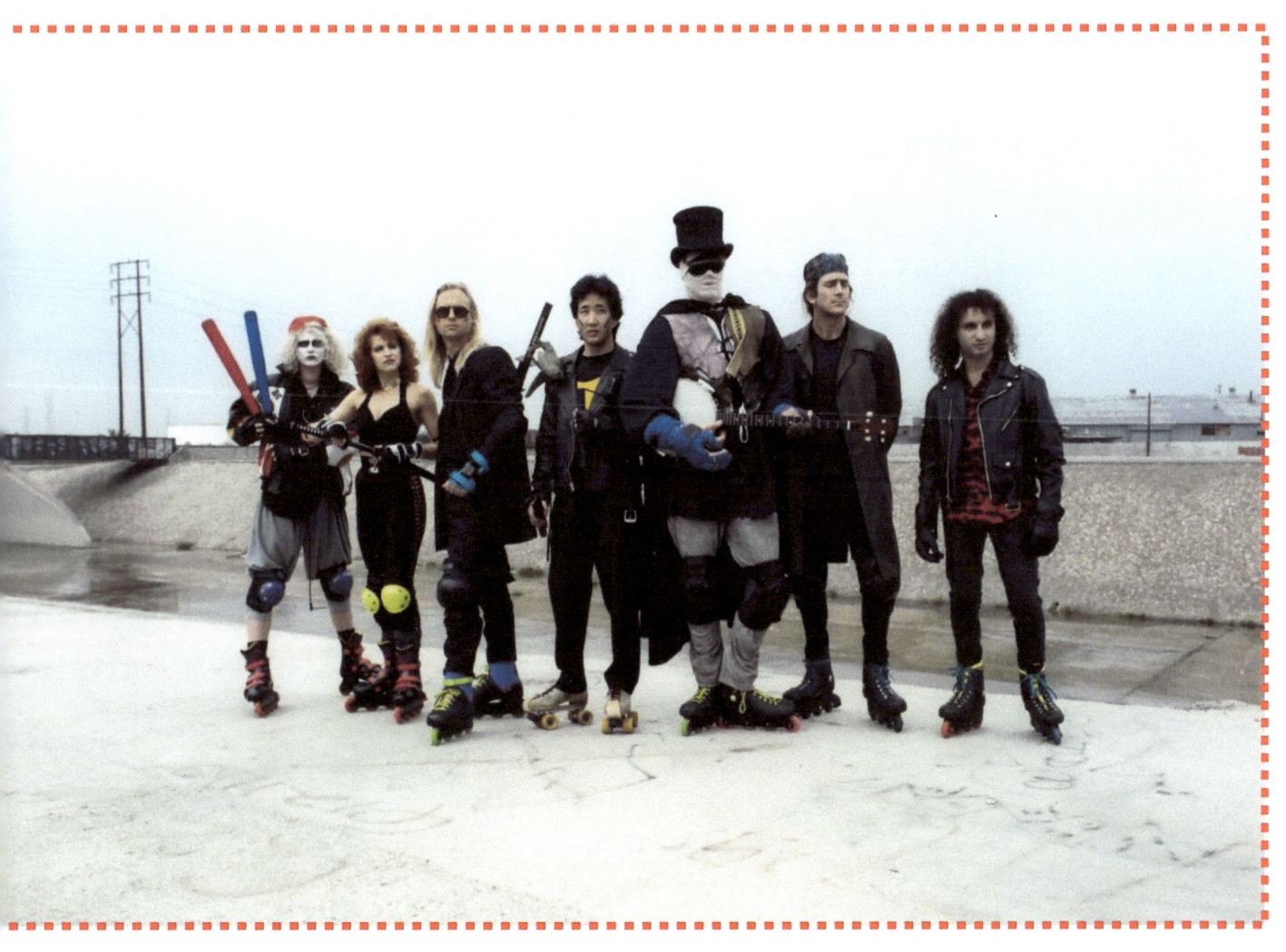

THE ORIGINAL ROLLER BLADE SEVEN

Yes, there was actually seven....

KABUKI
ON DAY ONE OF PRODUCTION.
My–my... How people change.

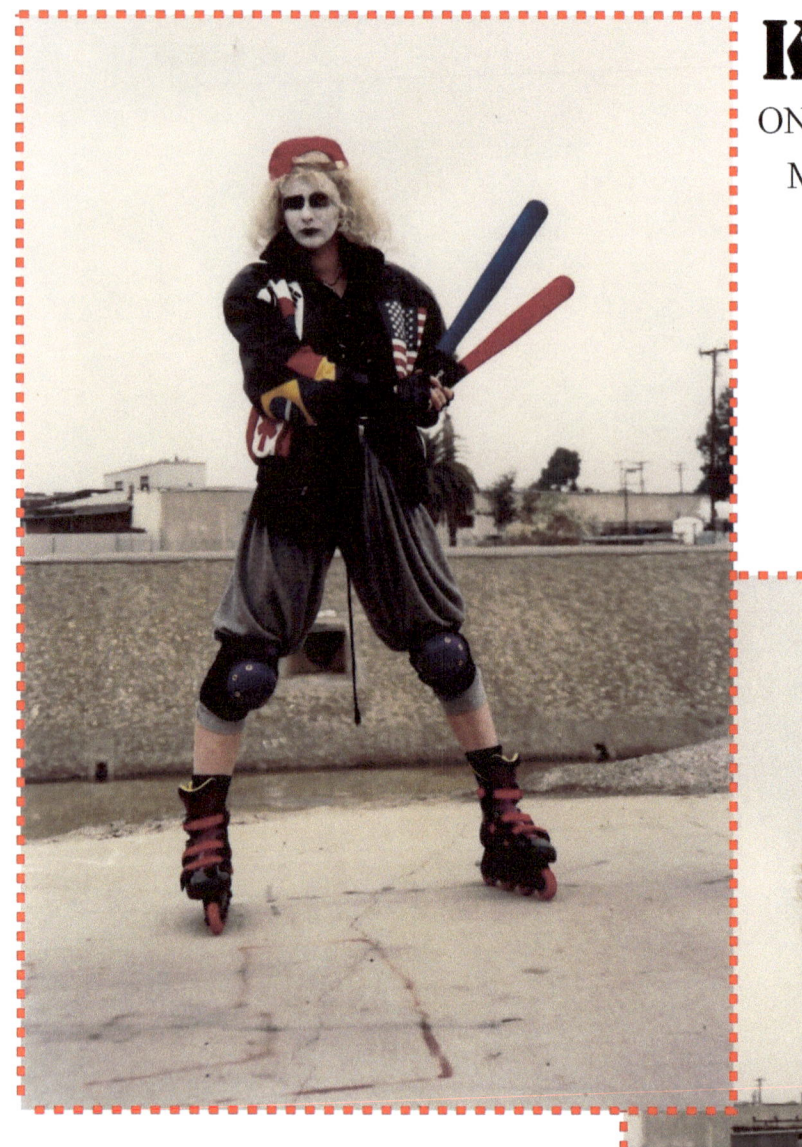

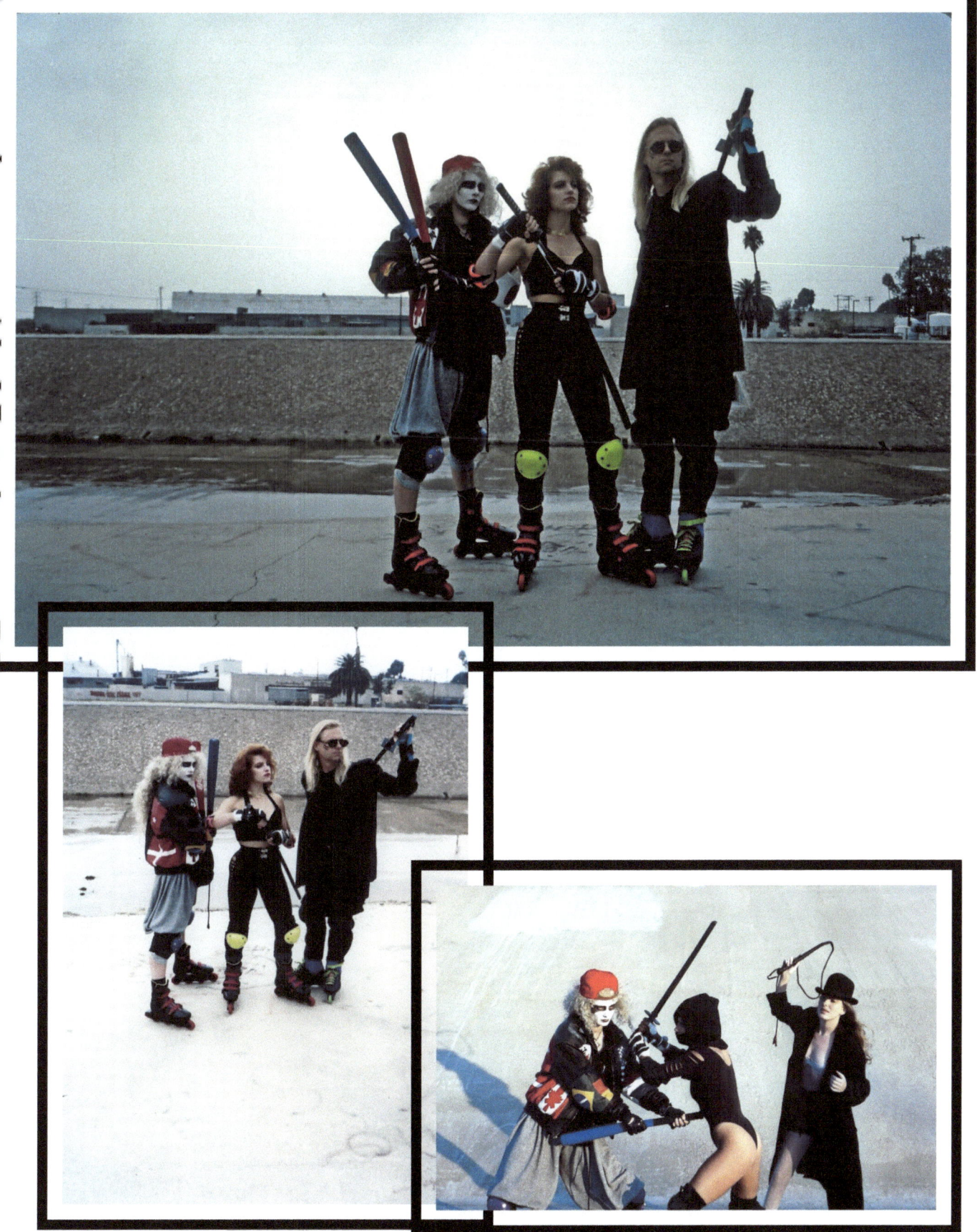

ON THE SET

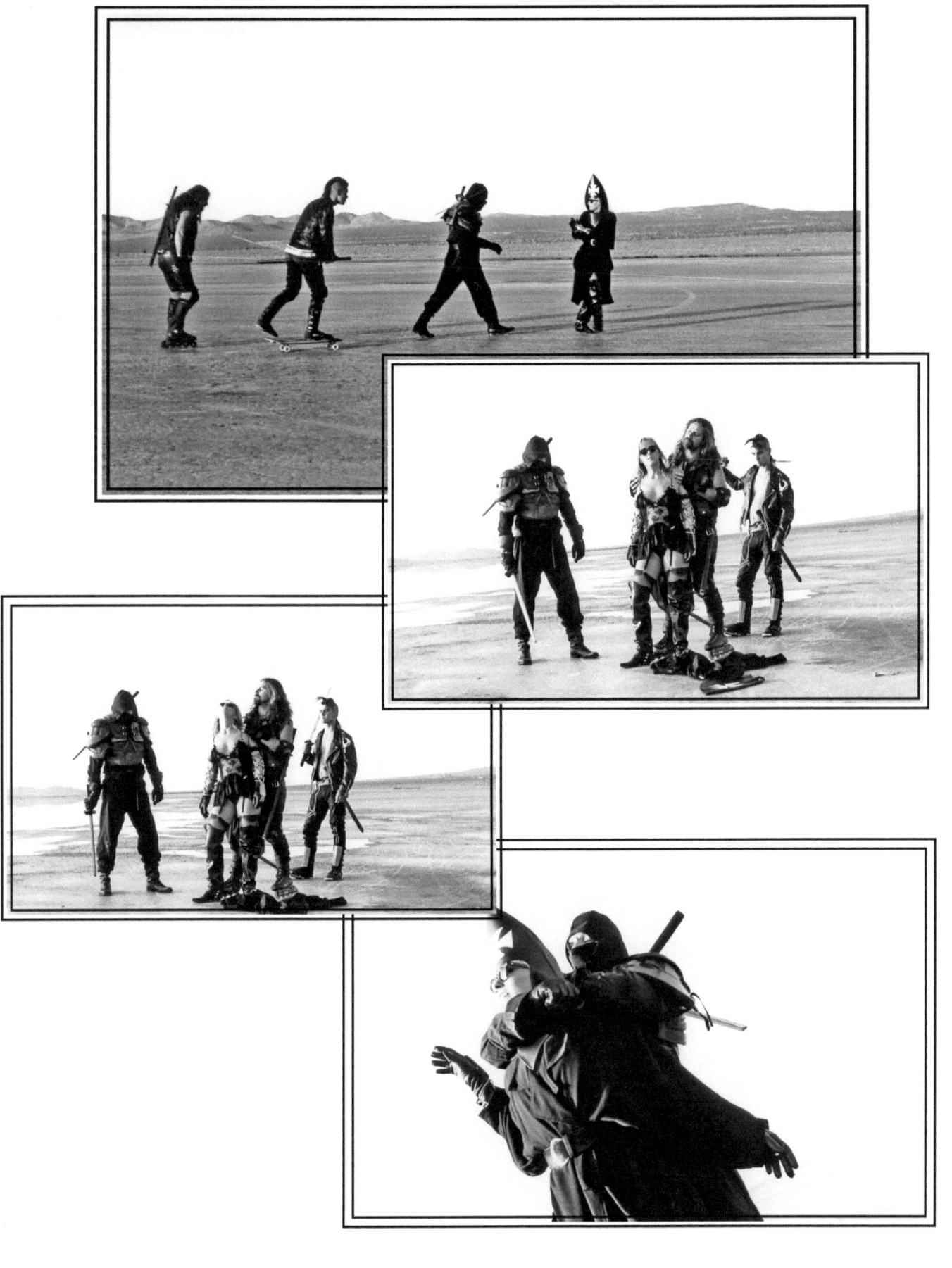

WHEELZONE WARRIORS

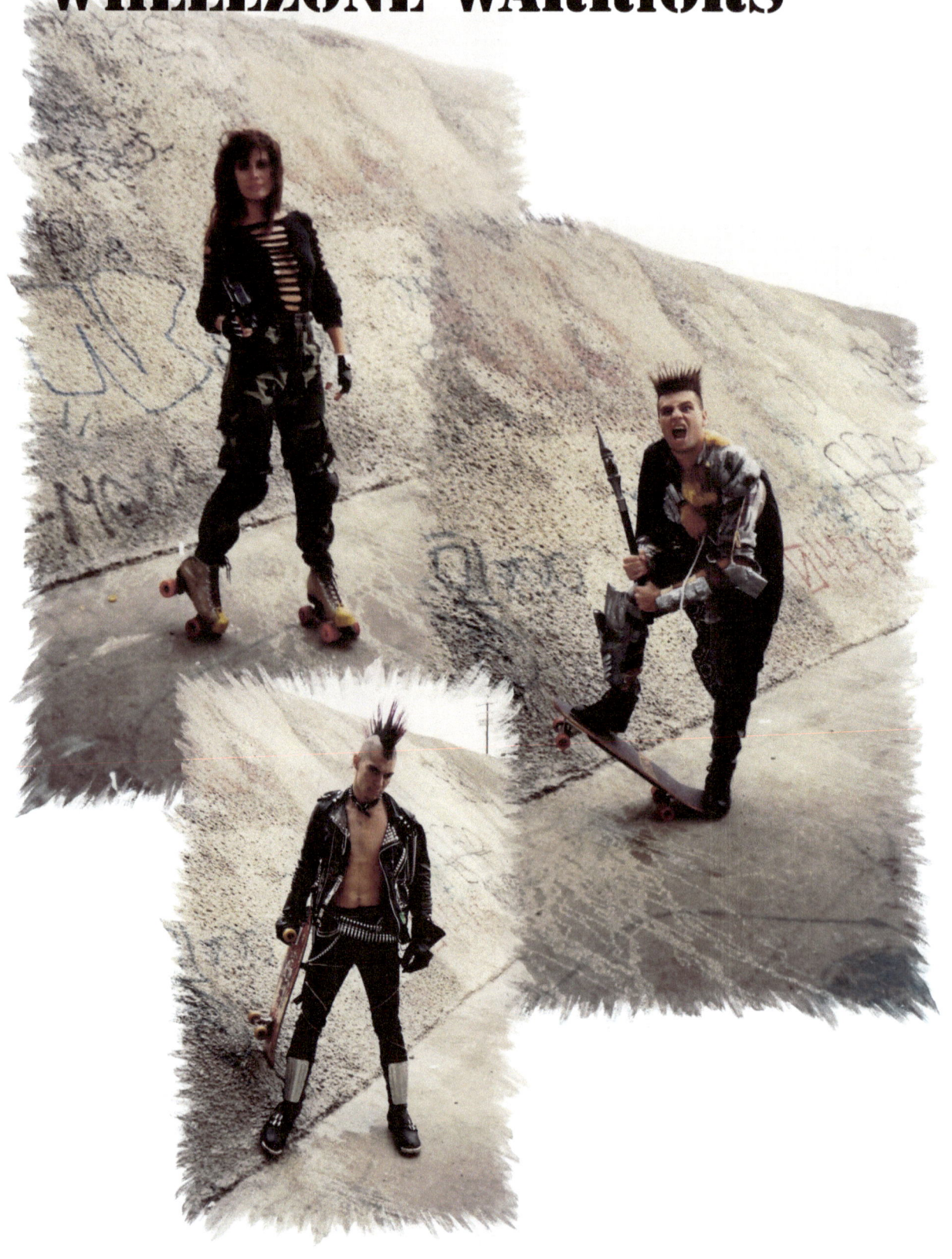

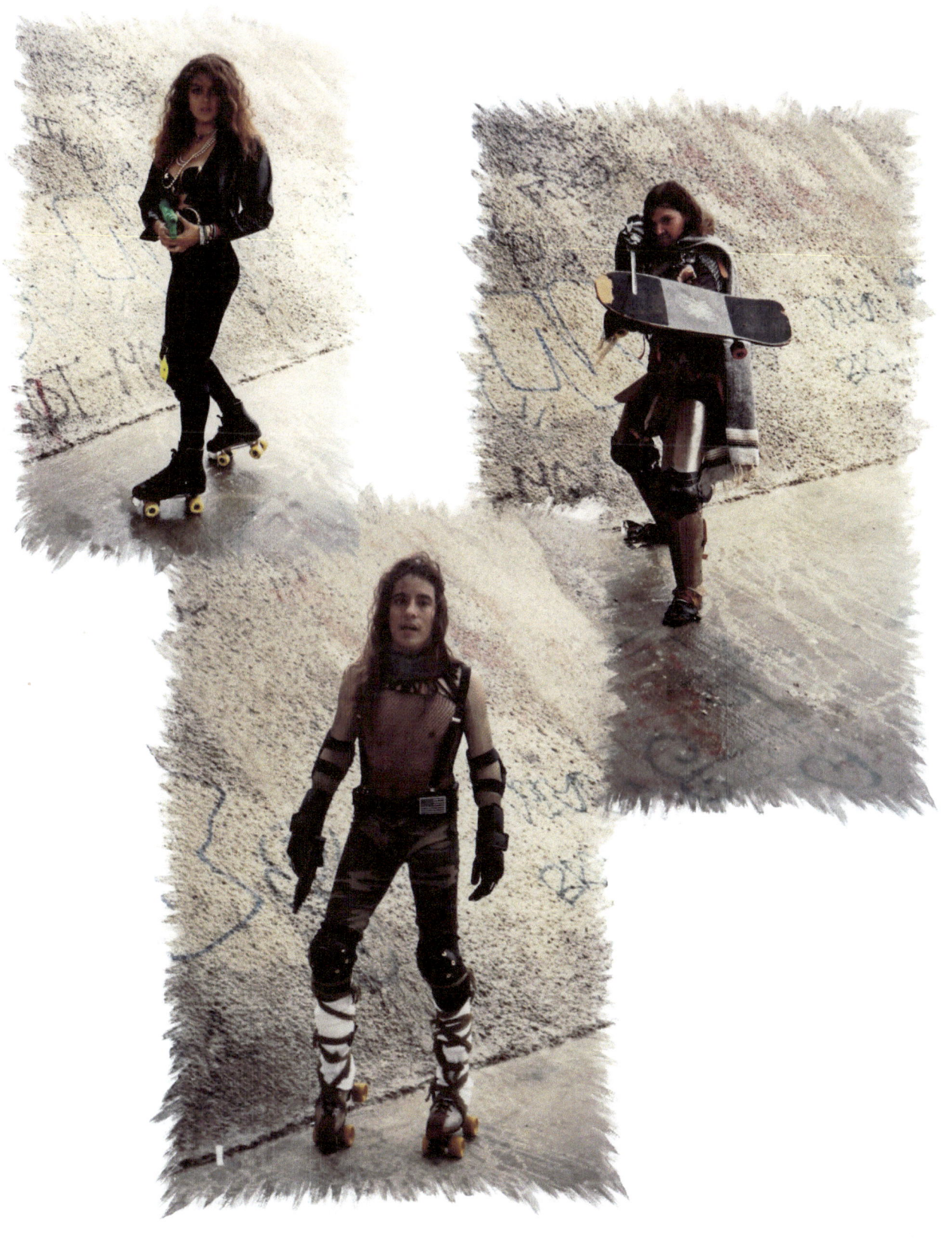

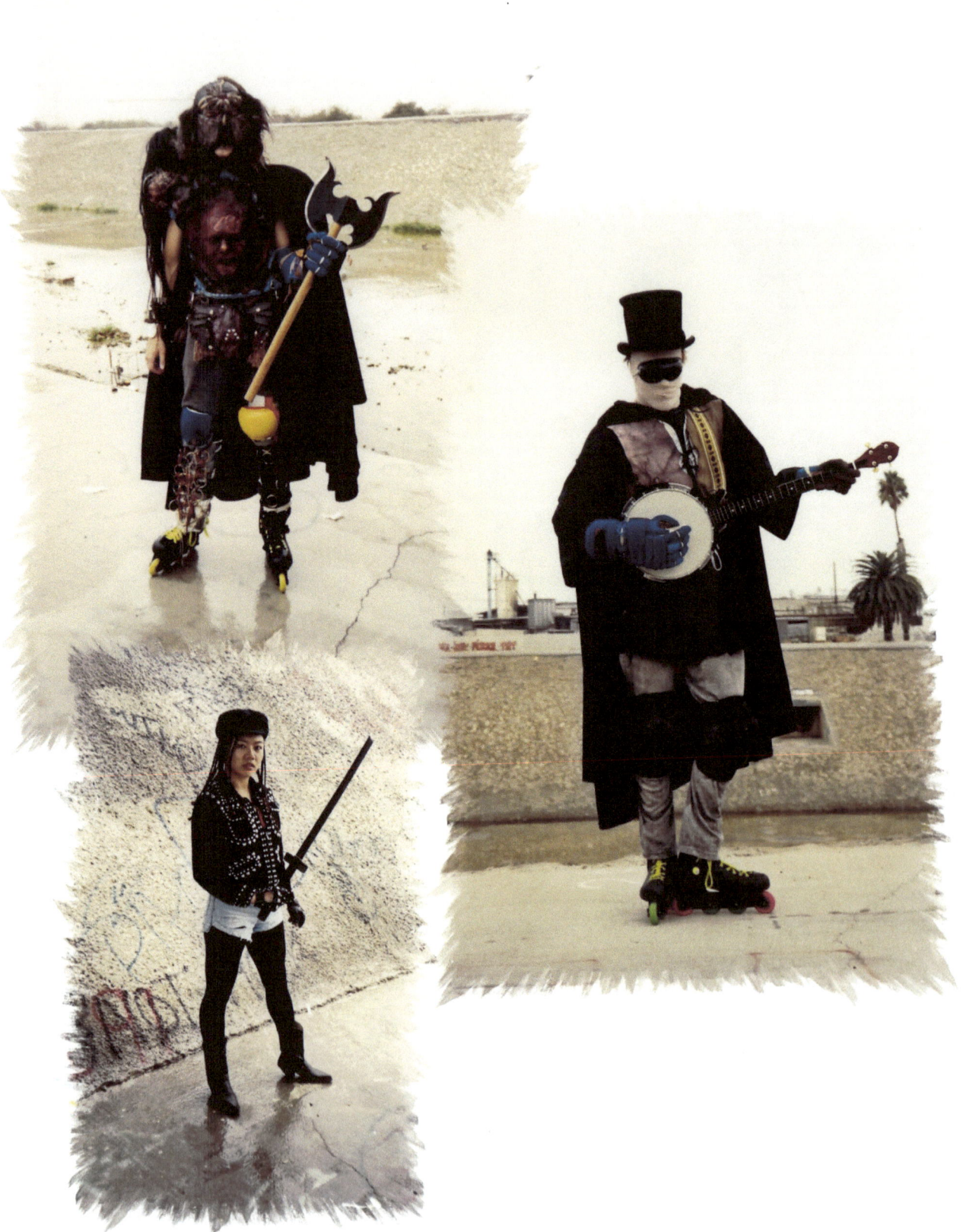

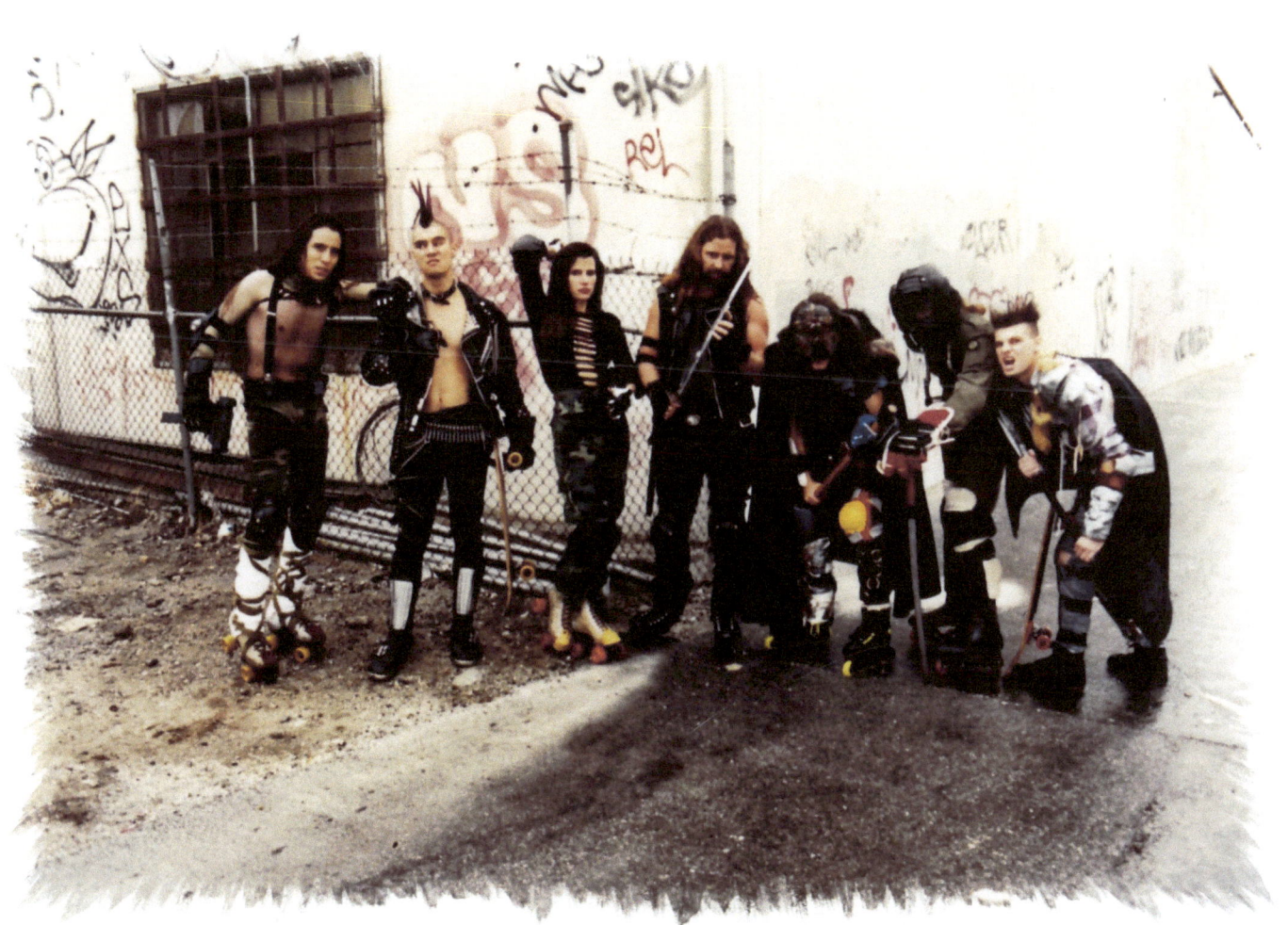

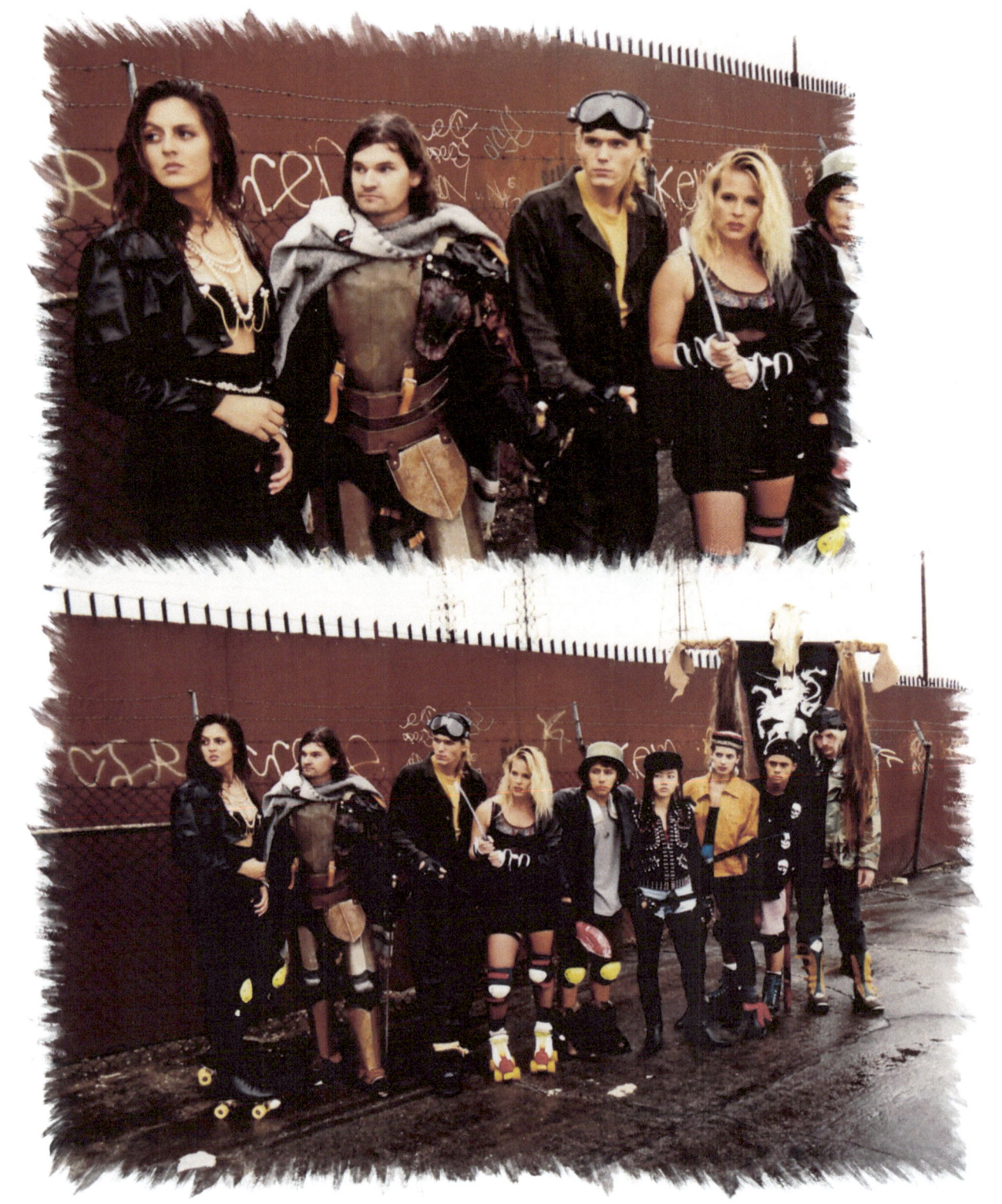

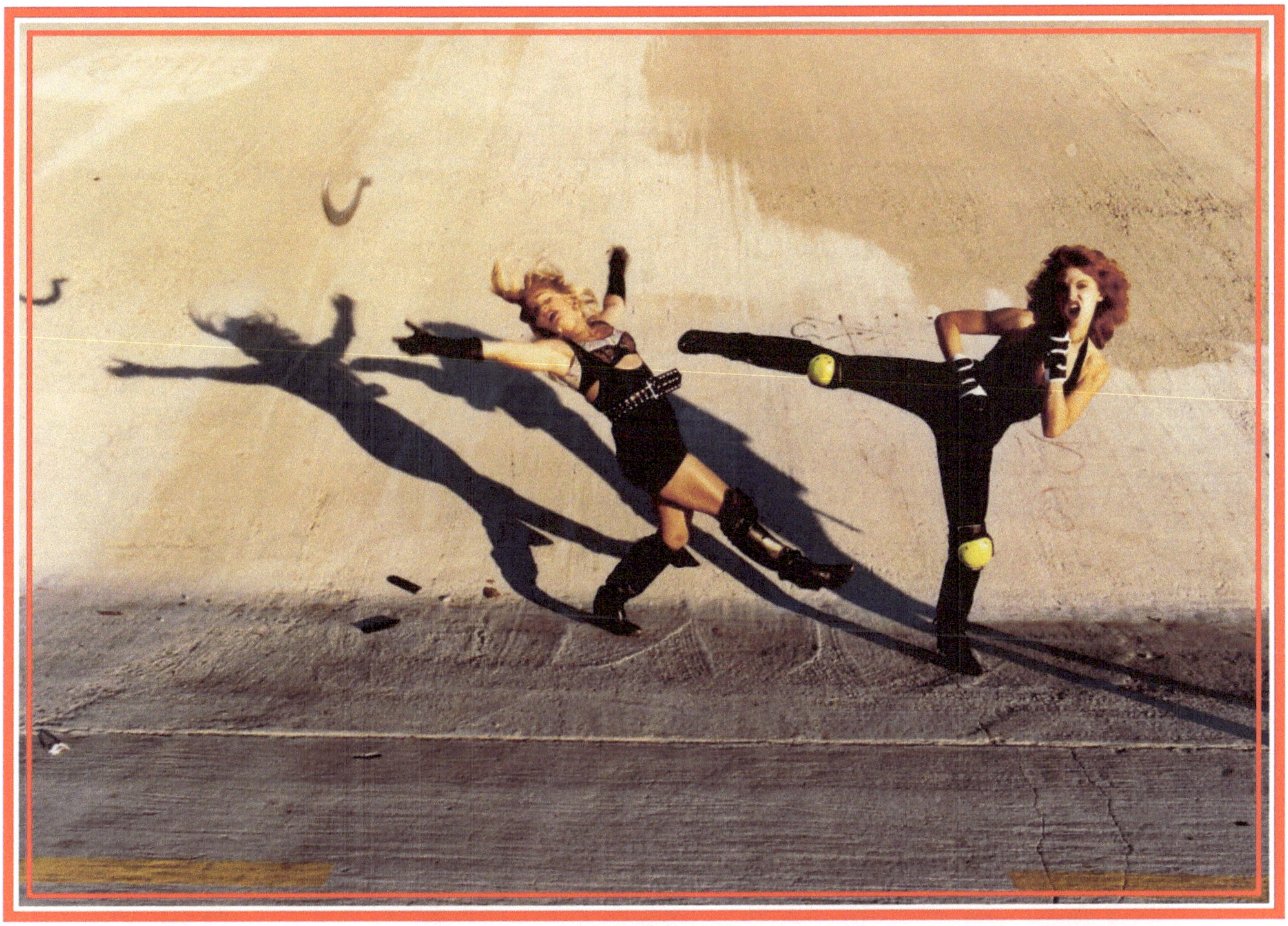

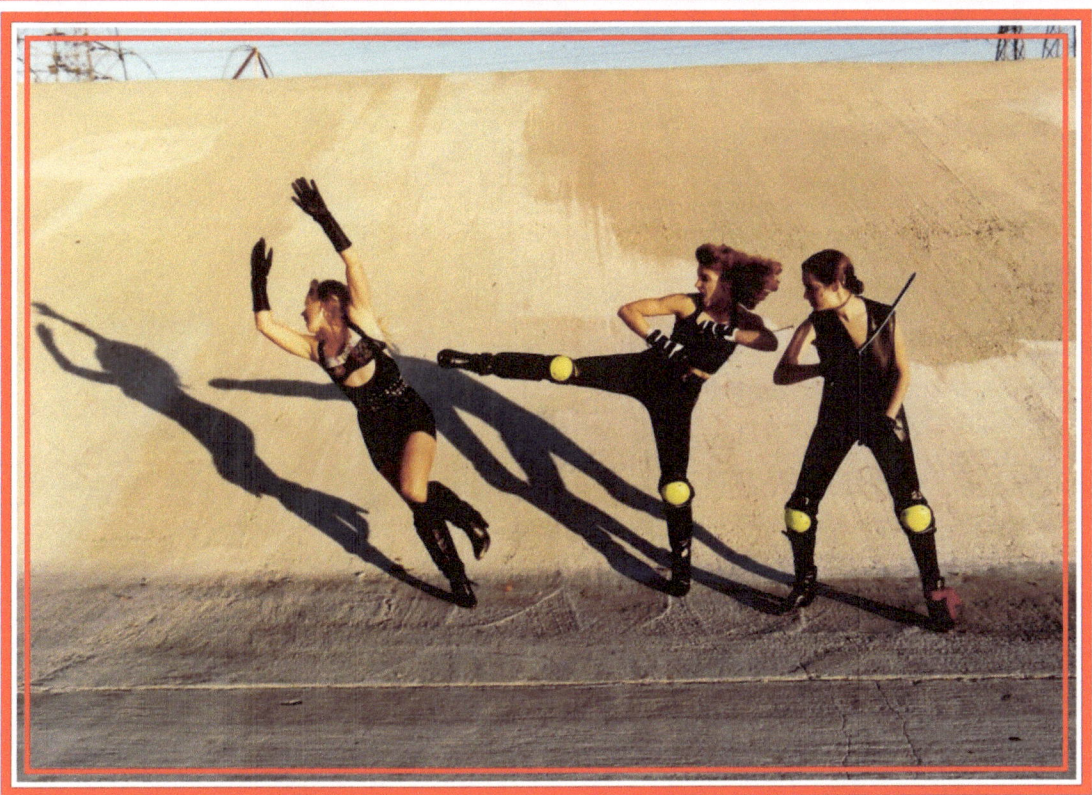

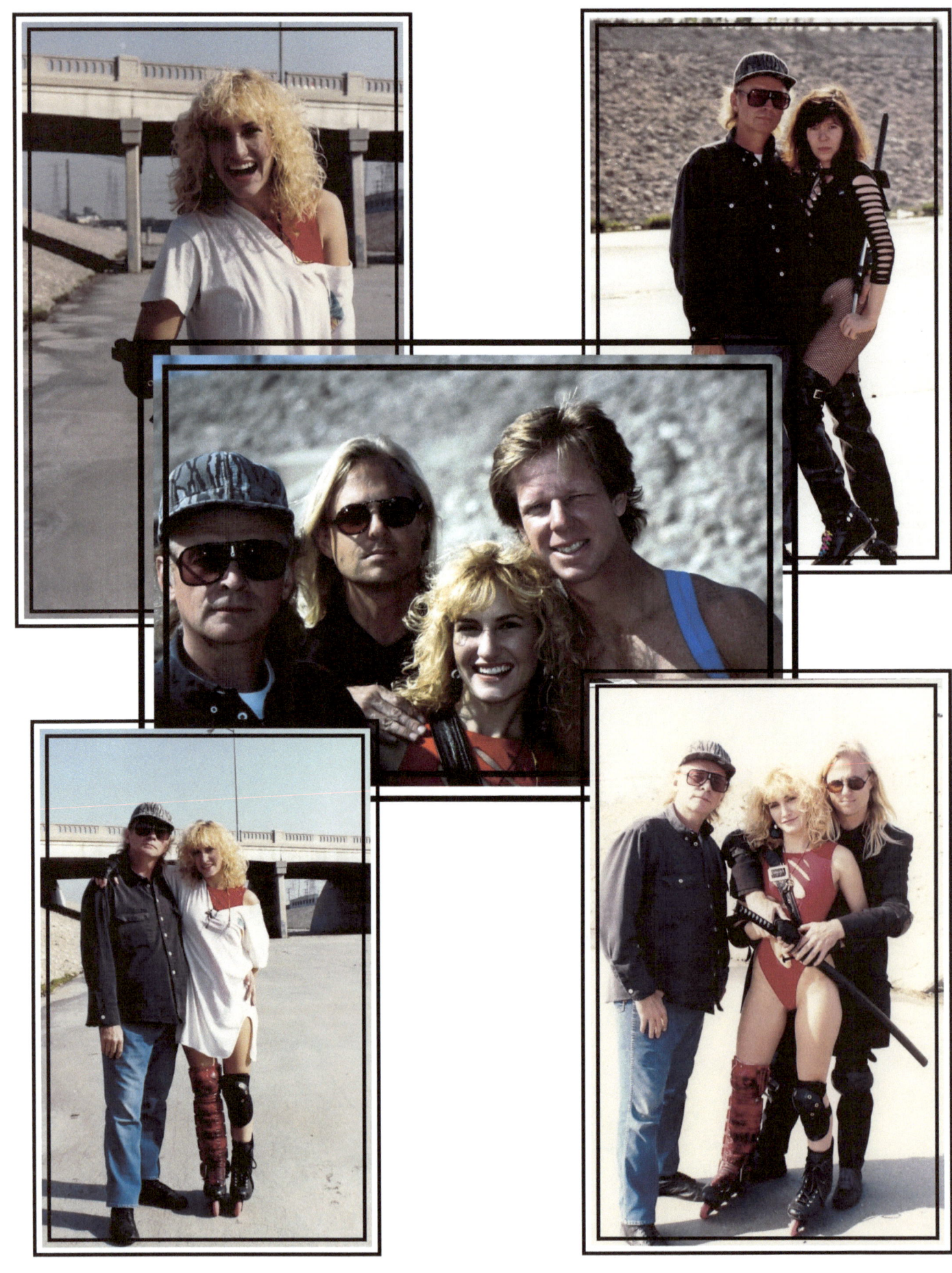

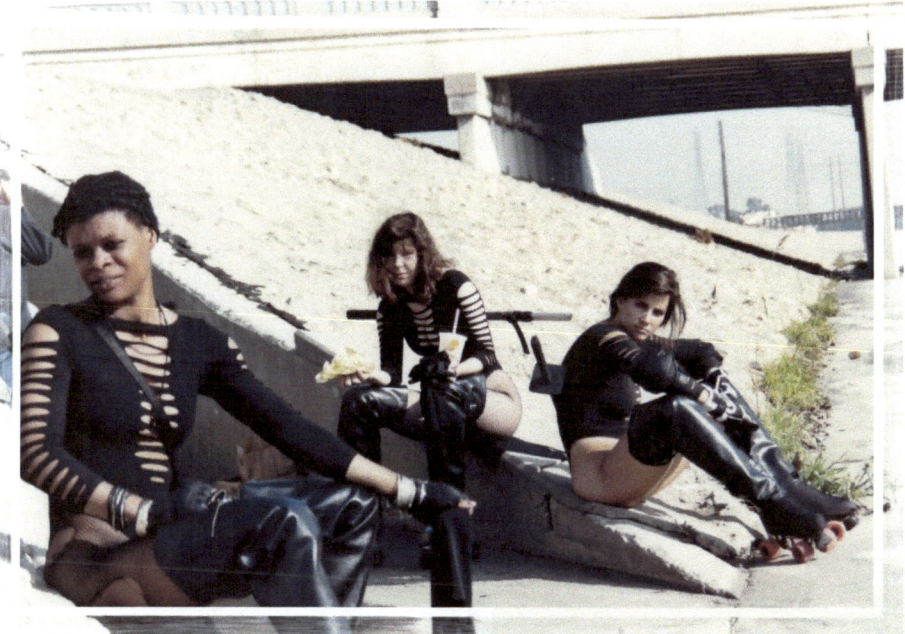

THE NINJA GIRLS

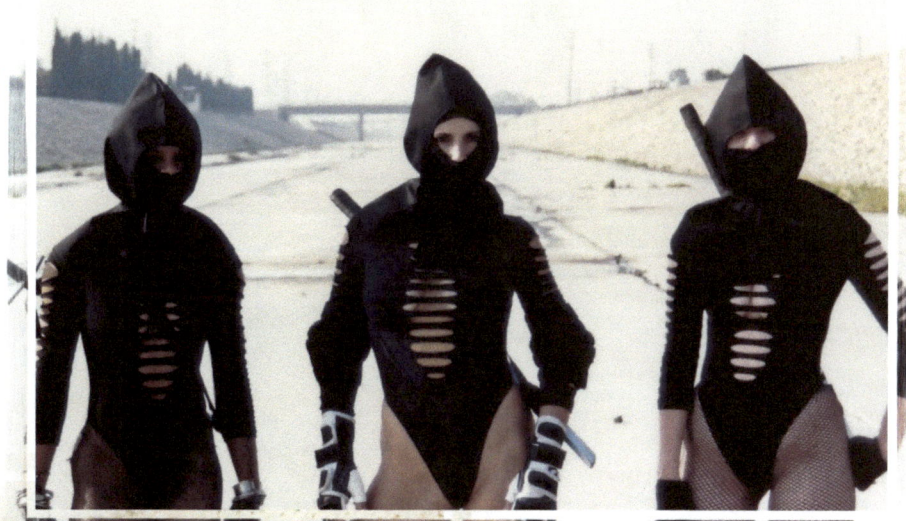

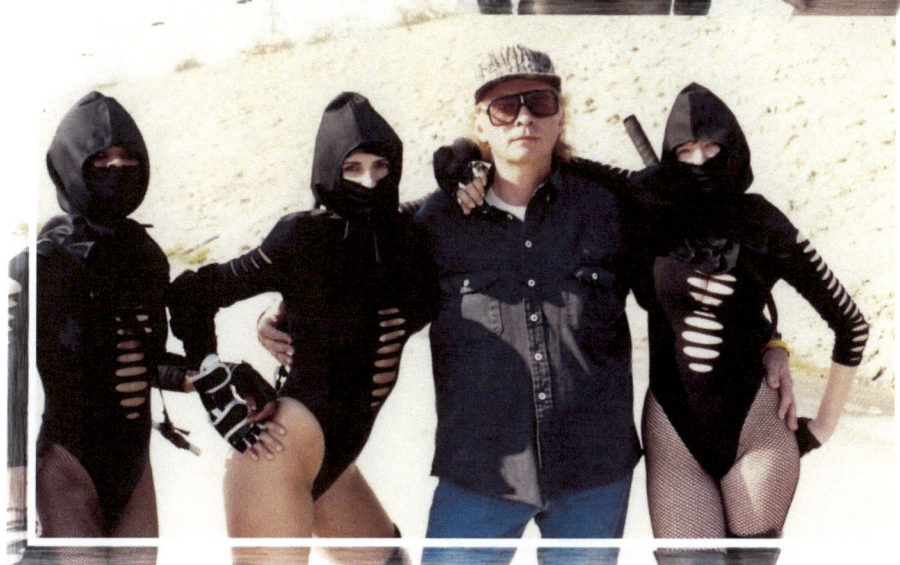

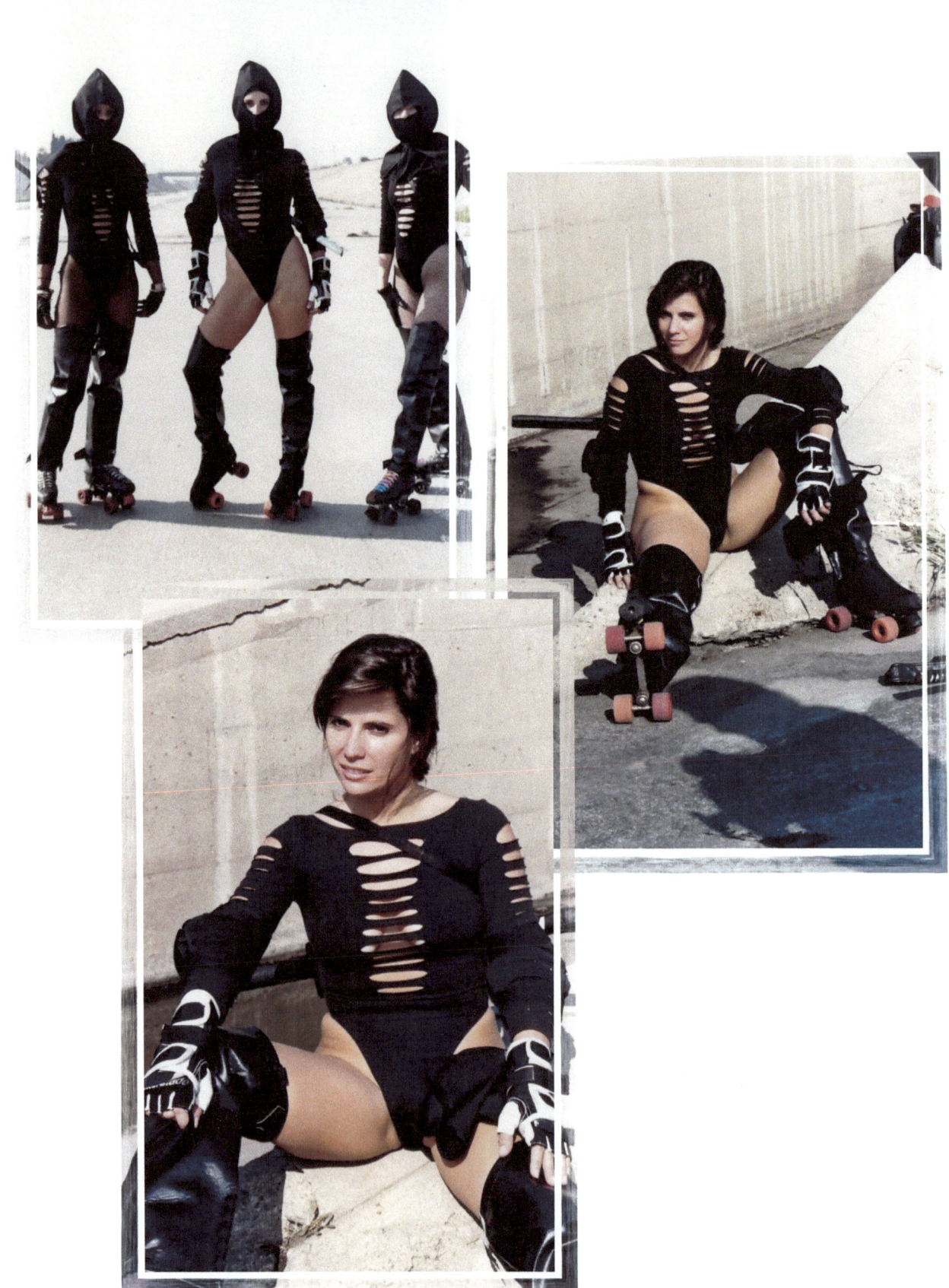

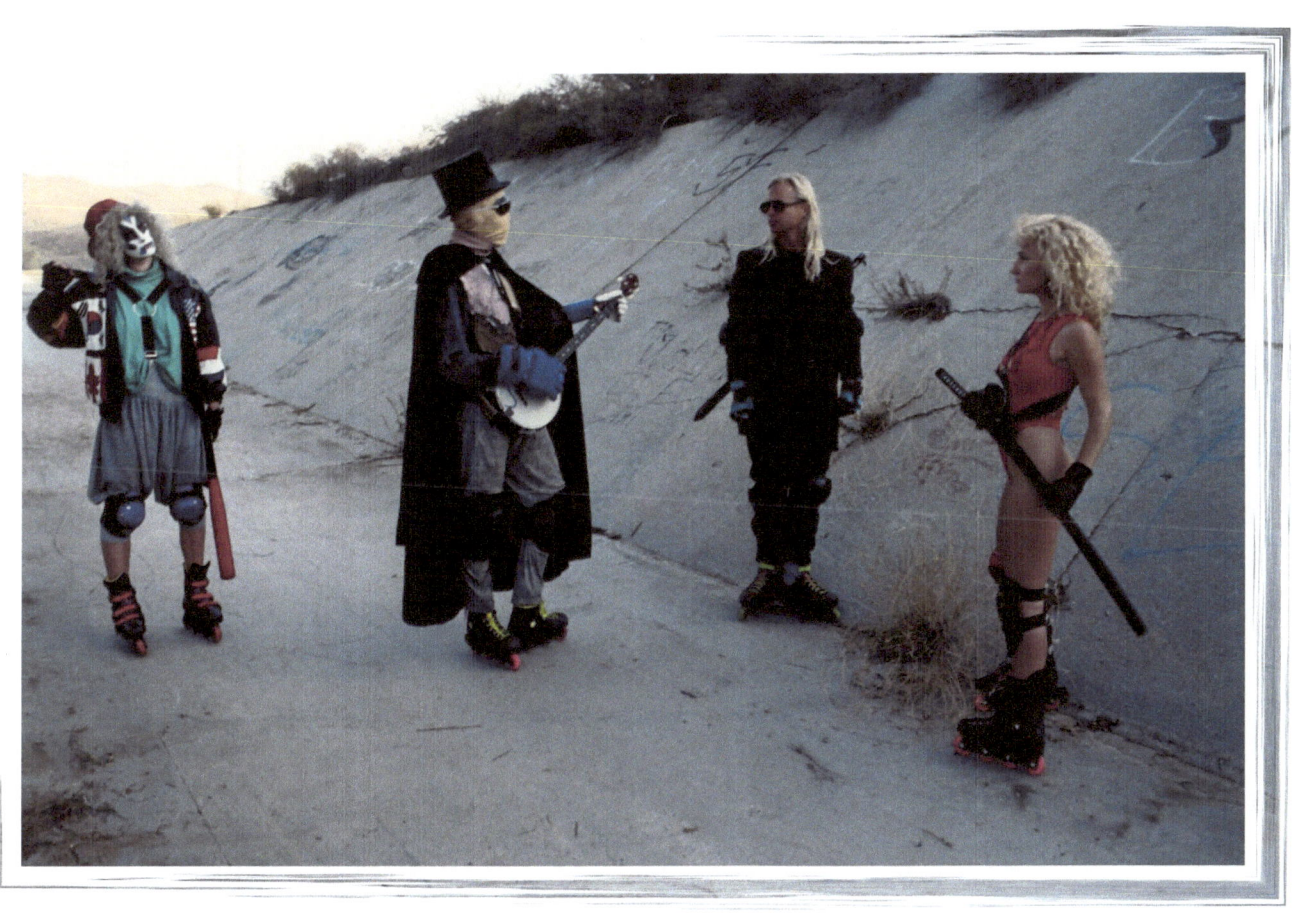

"I hate banjos."

JILL KELLY
AS SEX METAL

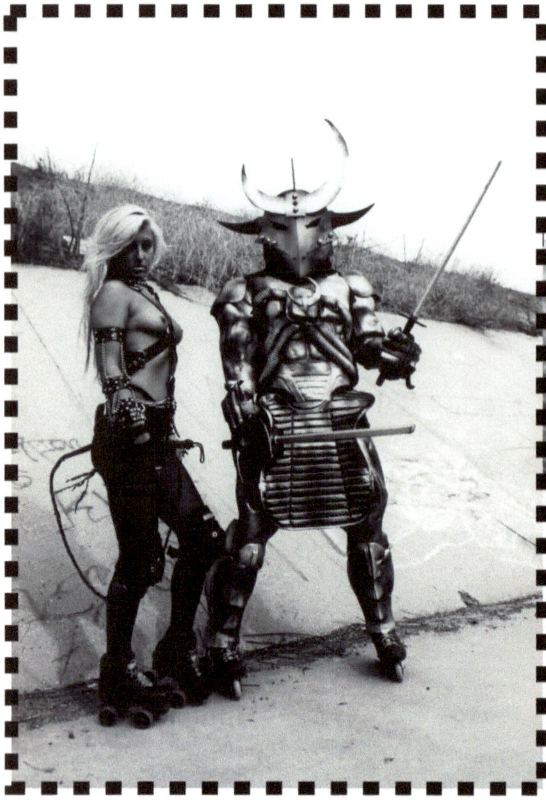

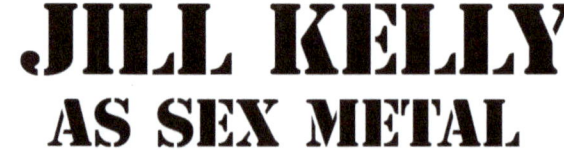

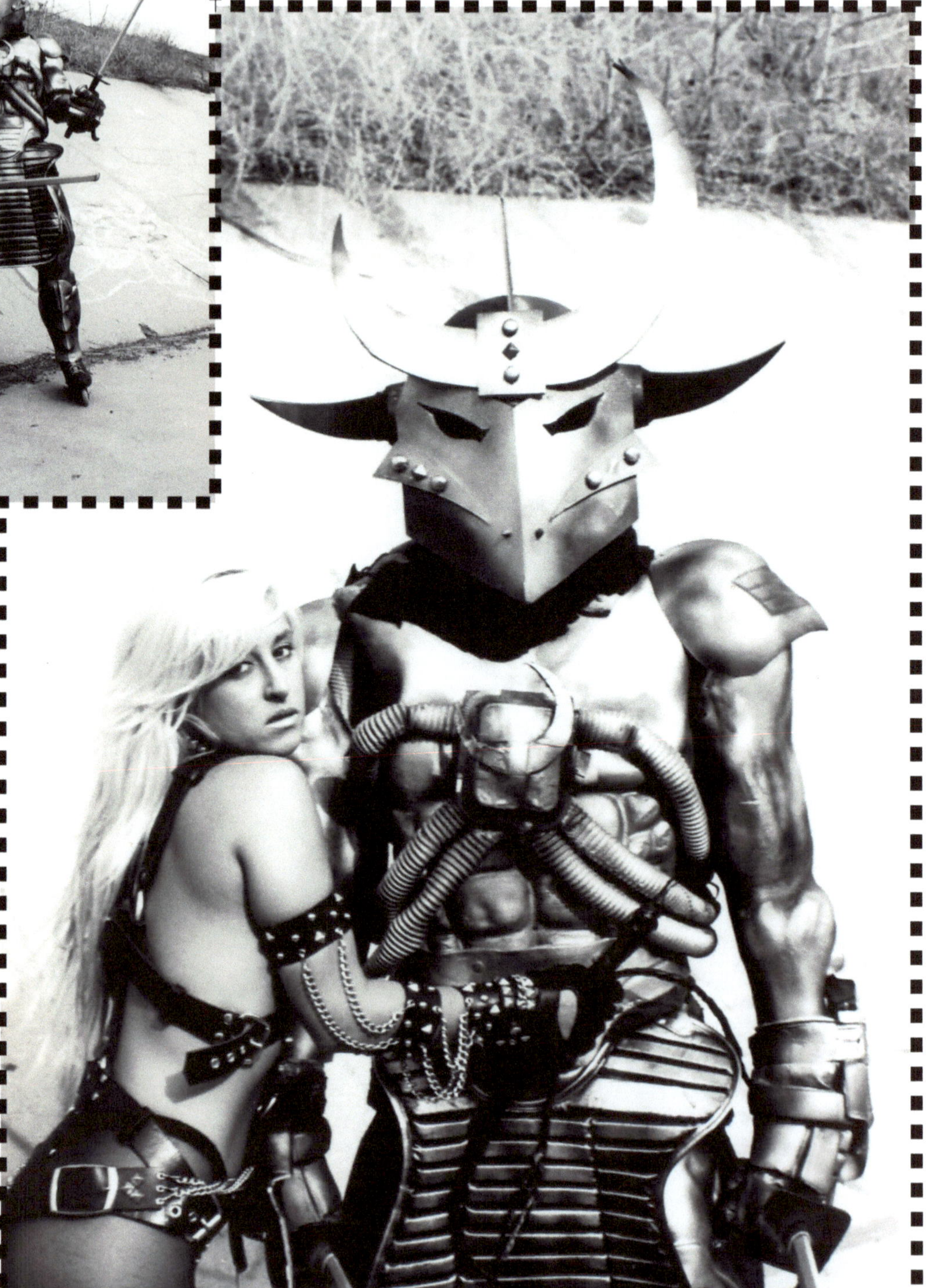

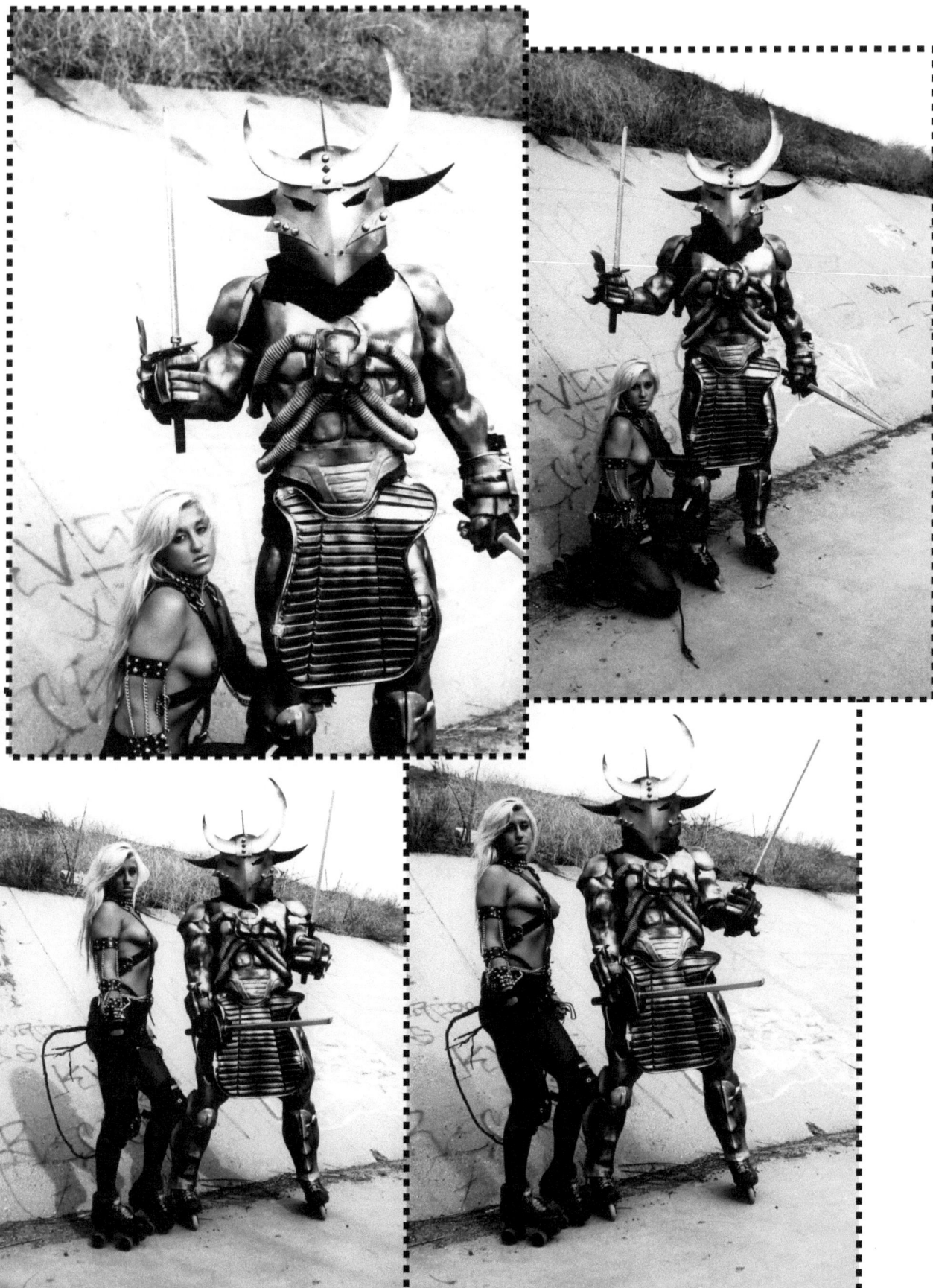

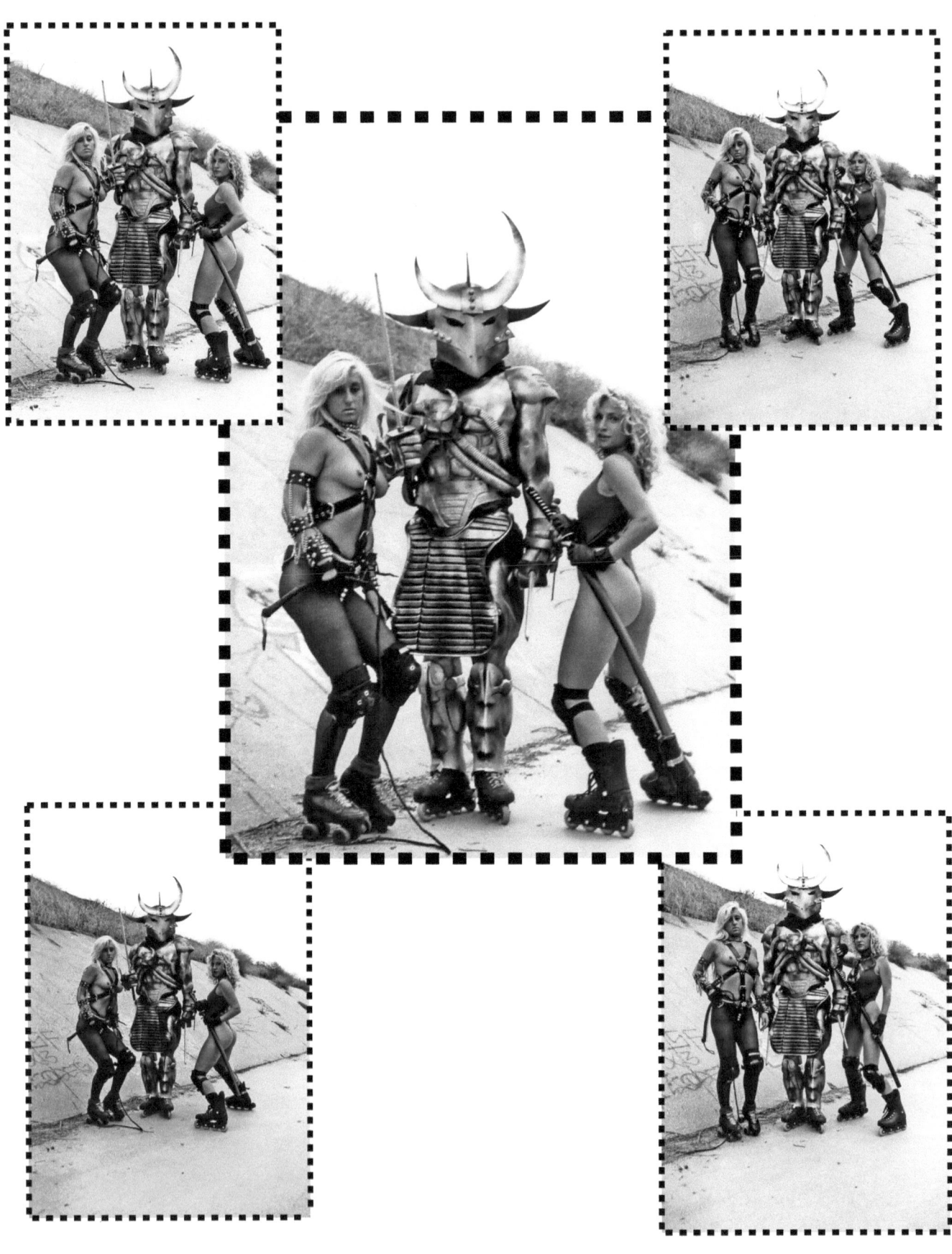

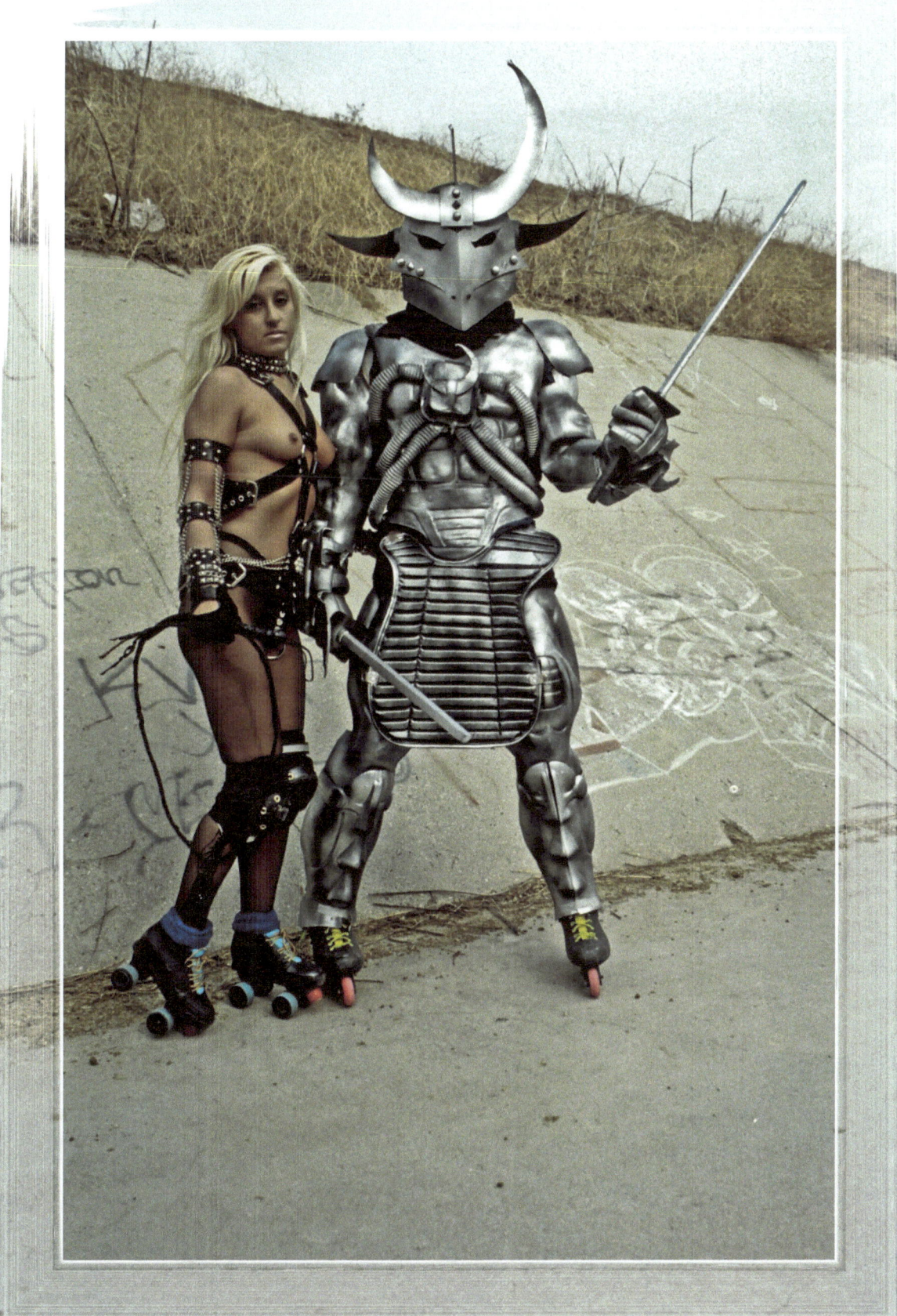

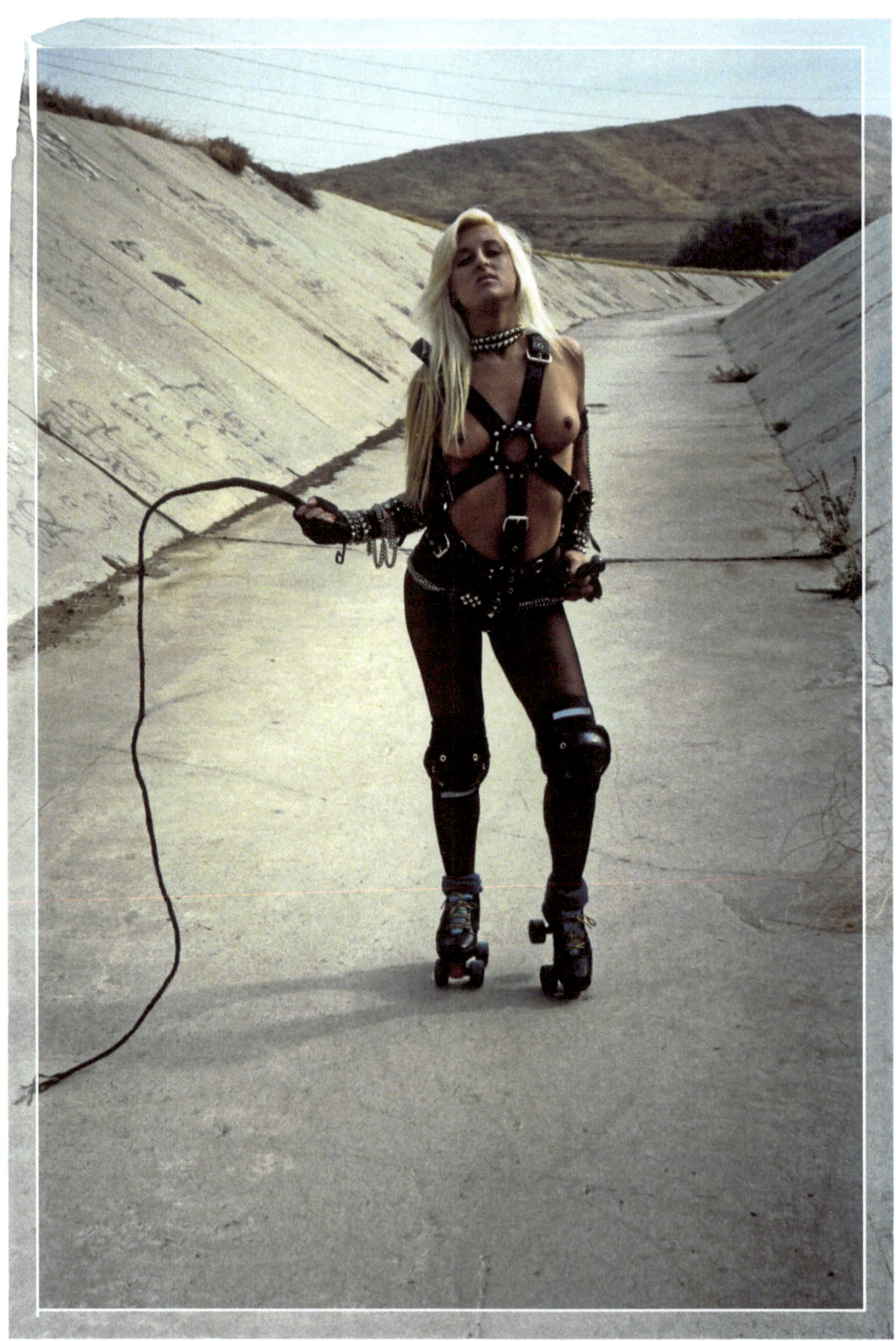

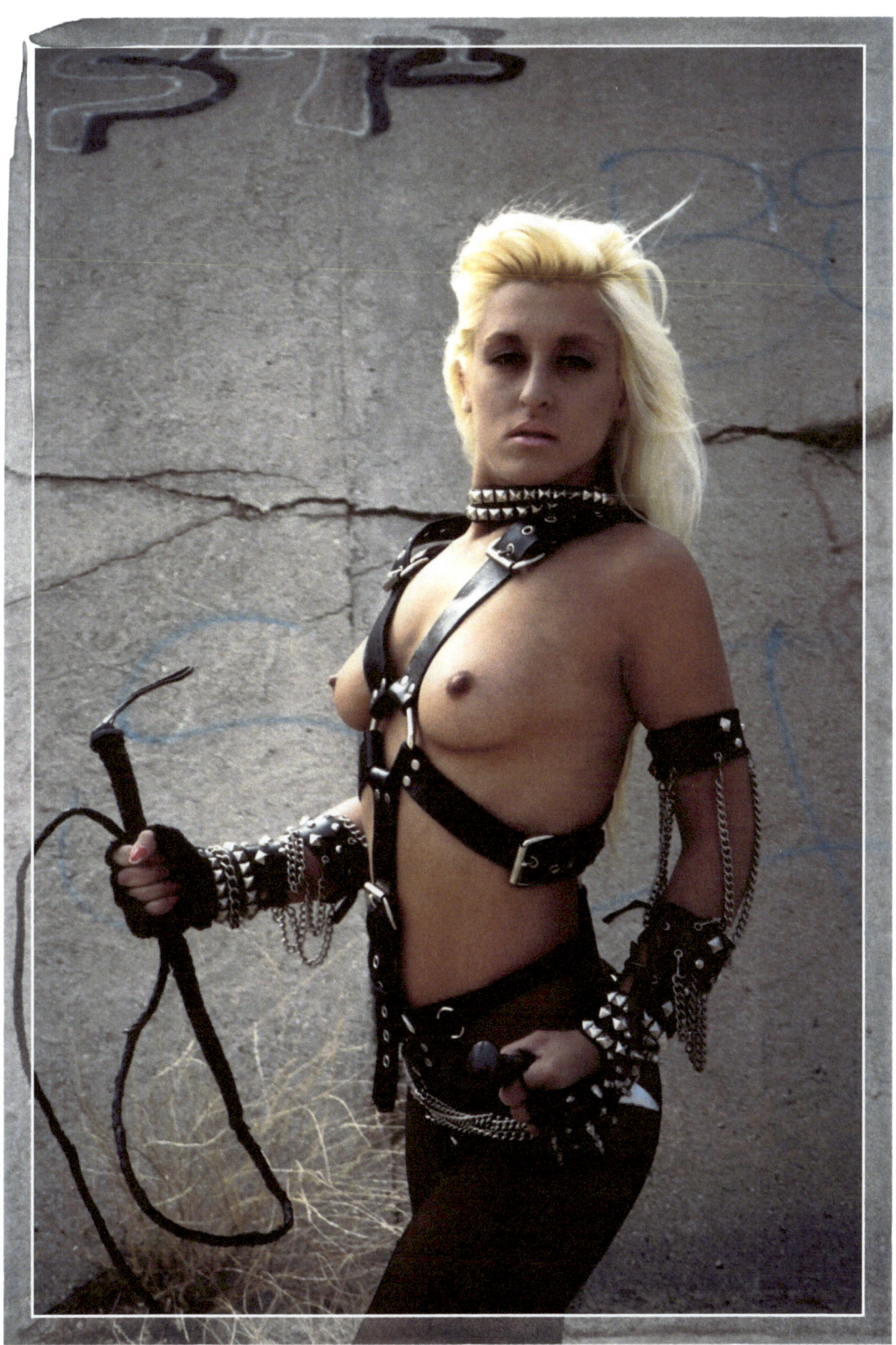

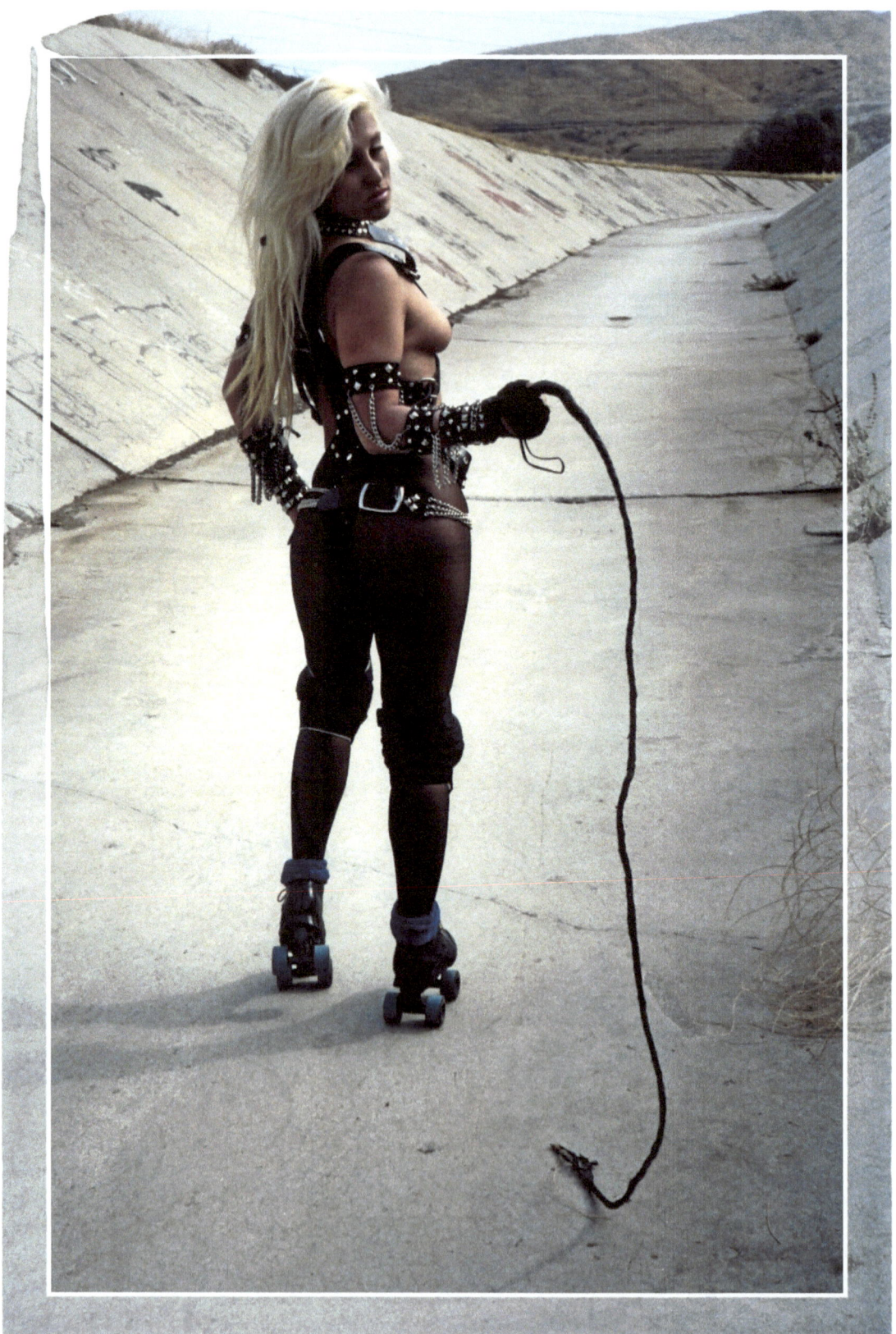

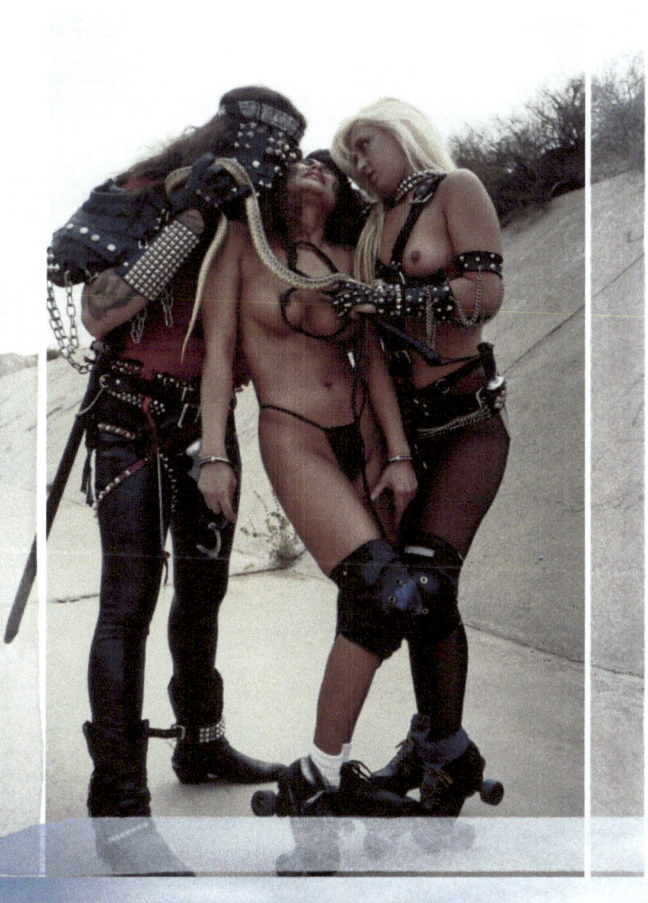

WITH MARK WILLIAMS AS HEAVY METAL

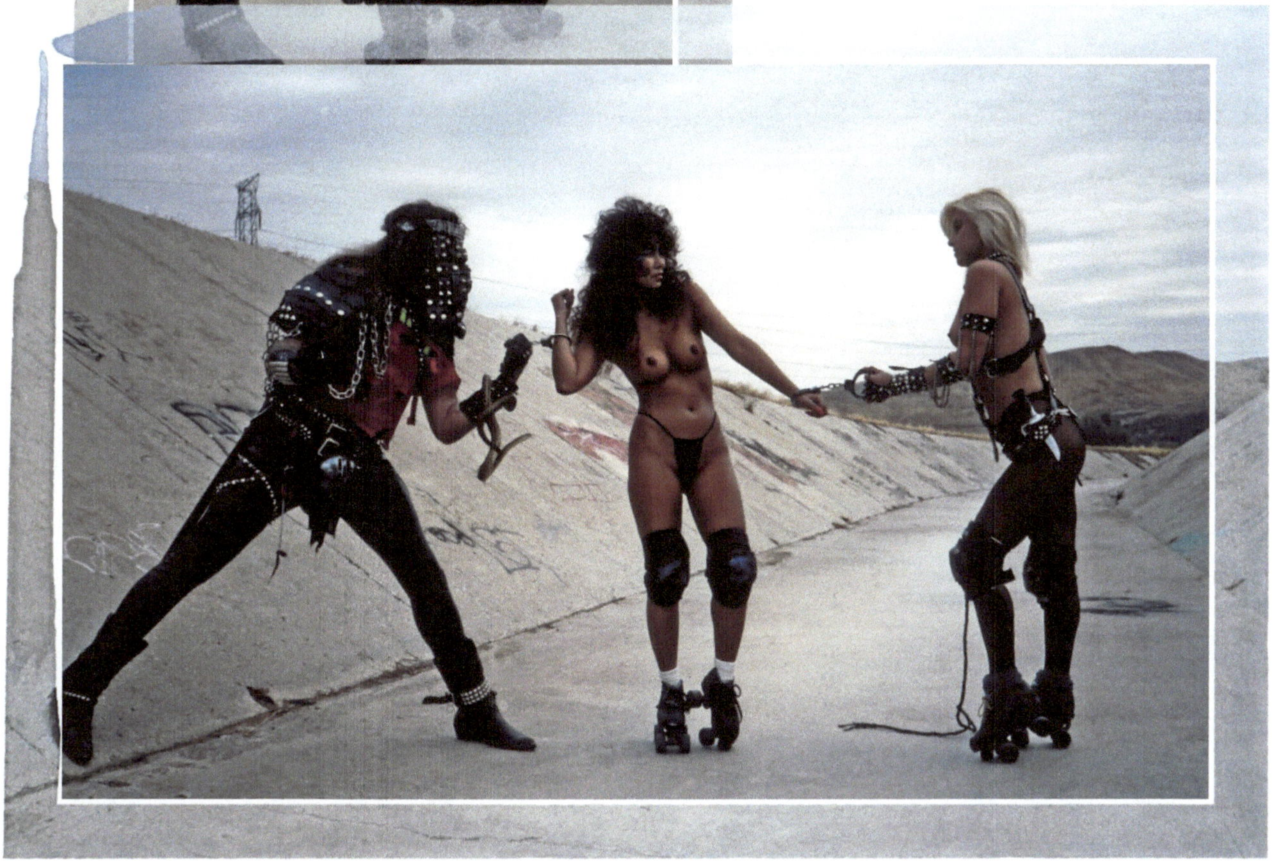

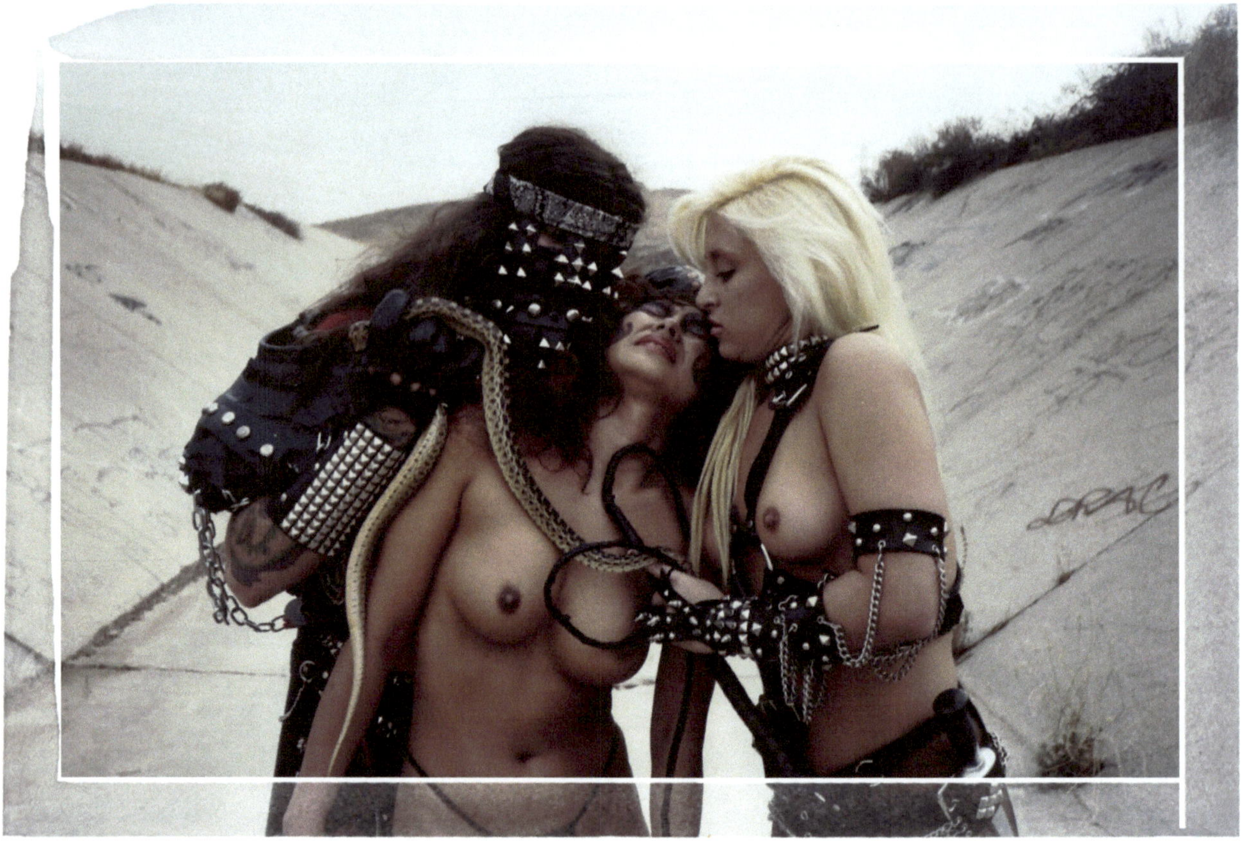

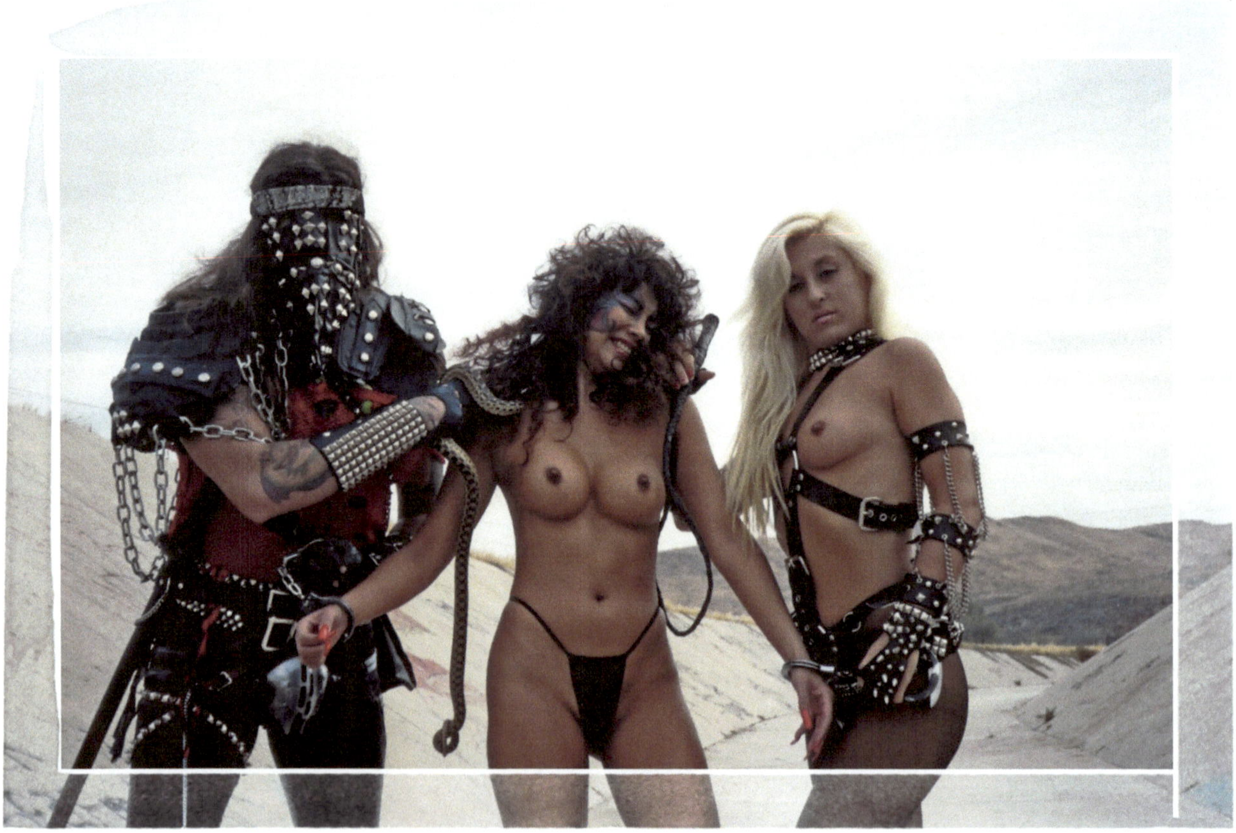

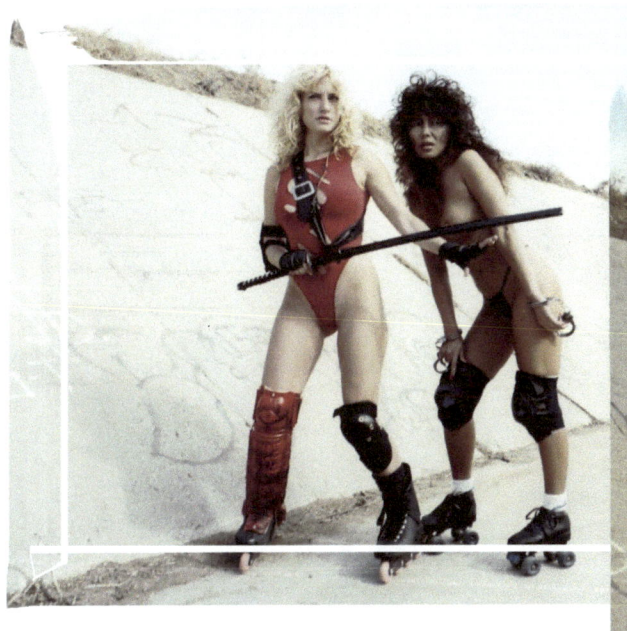

AND JADE EAST

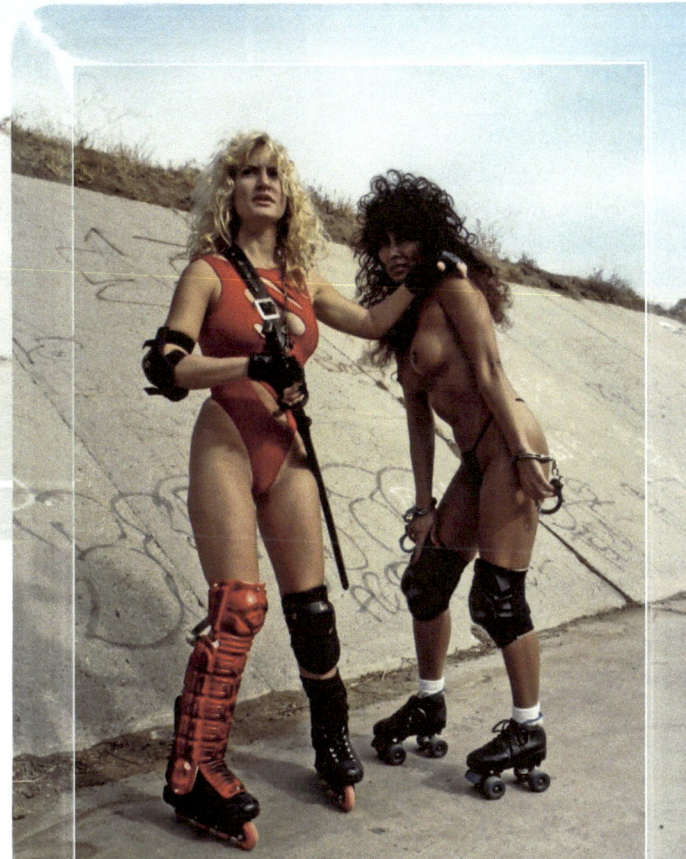

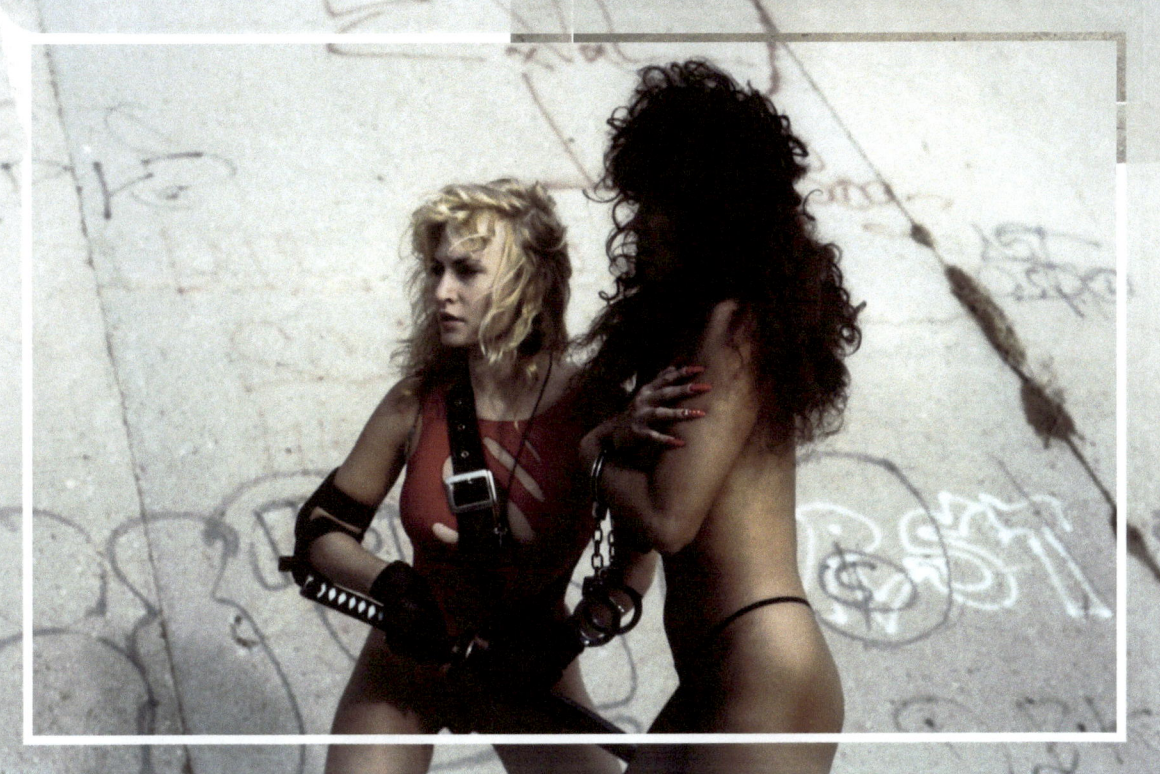

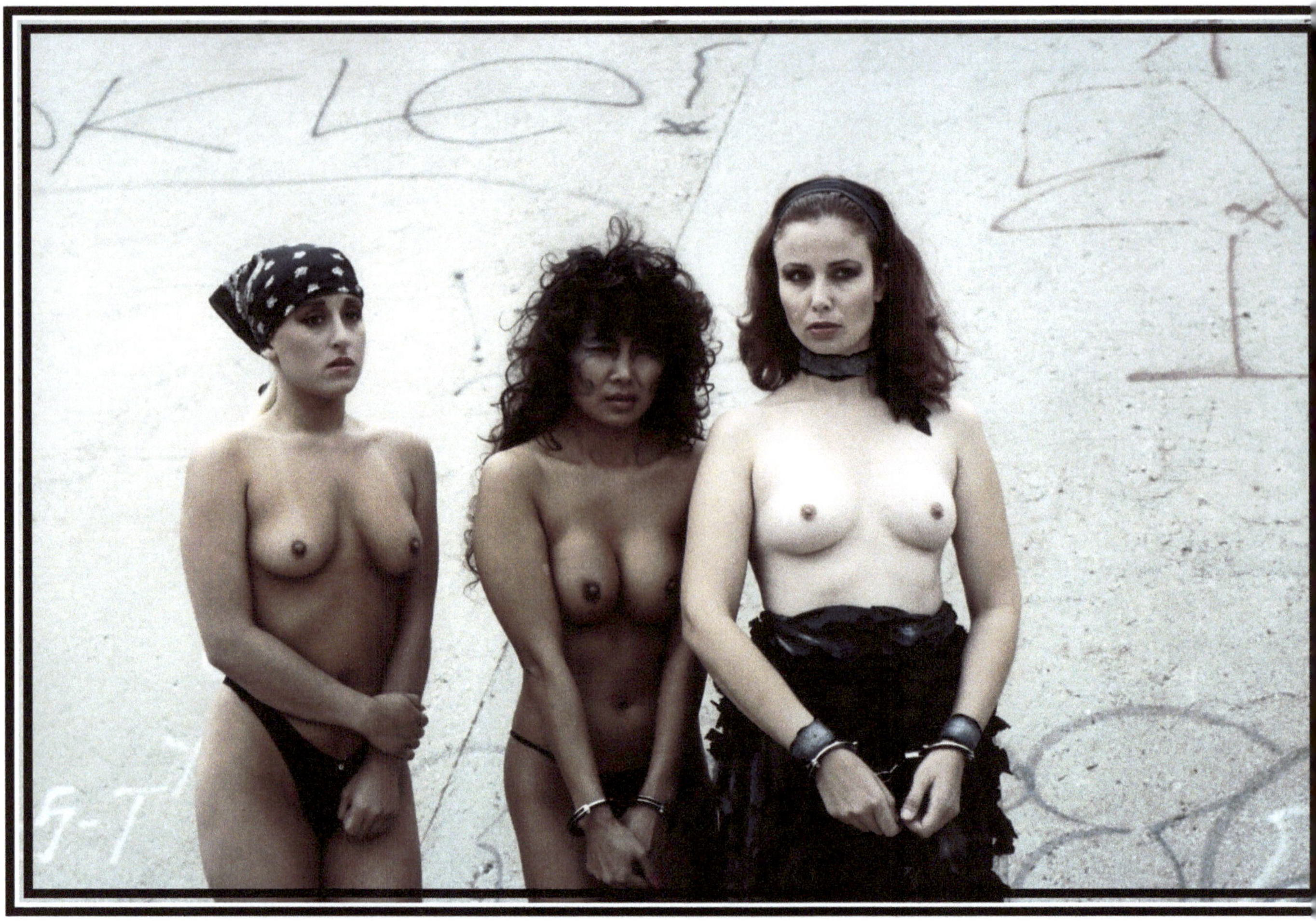

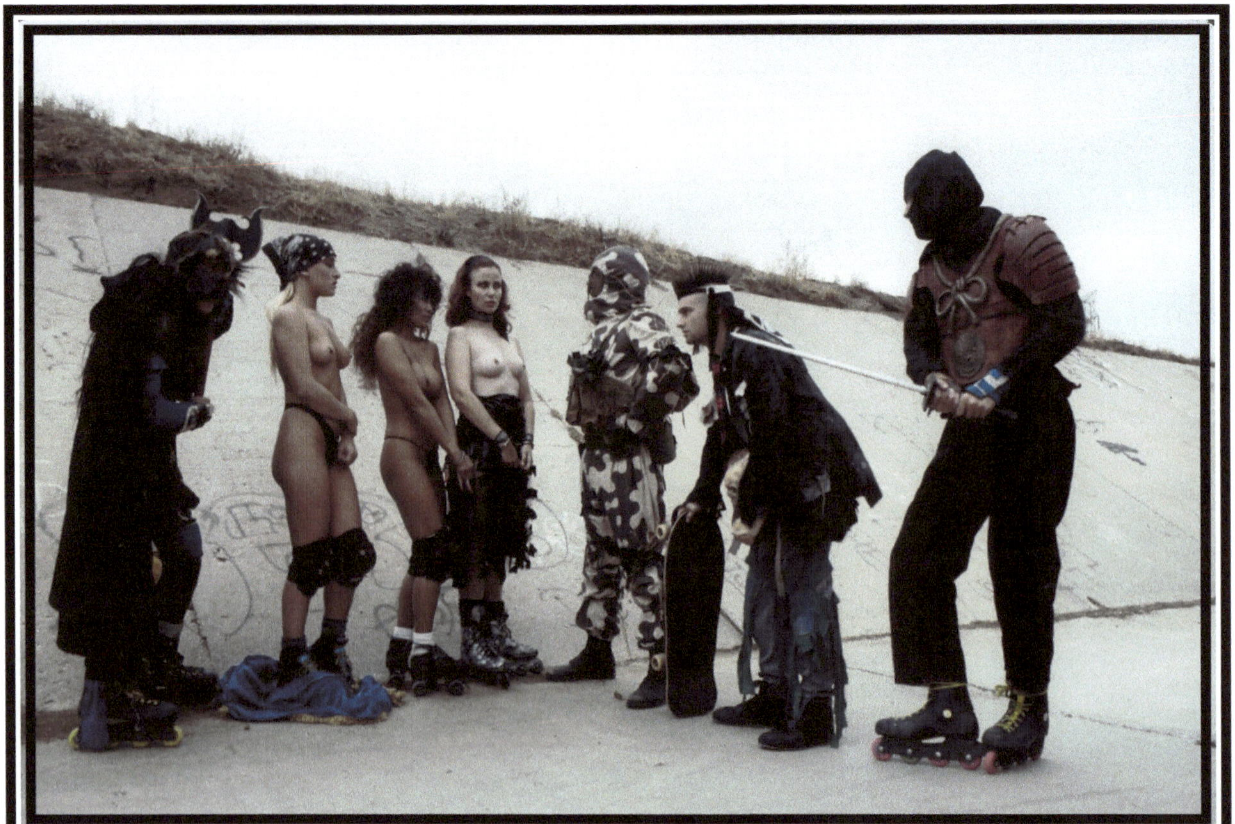

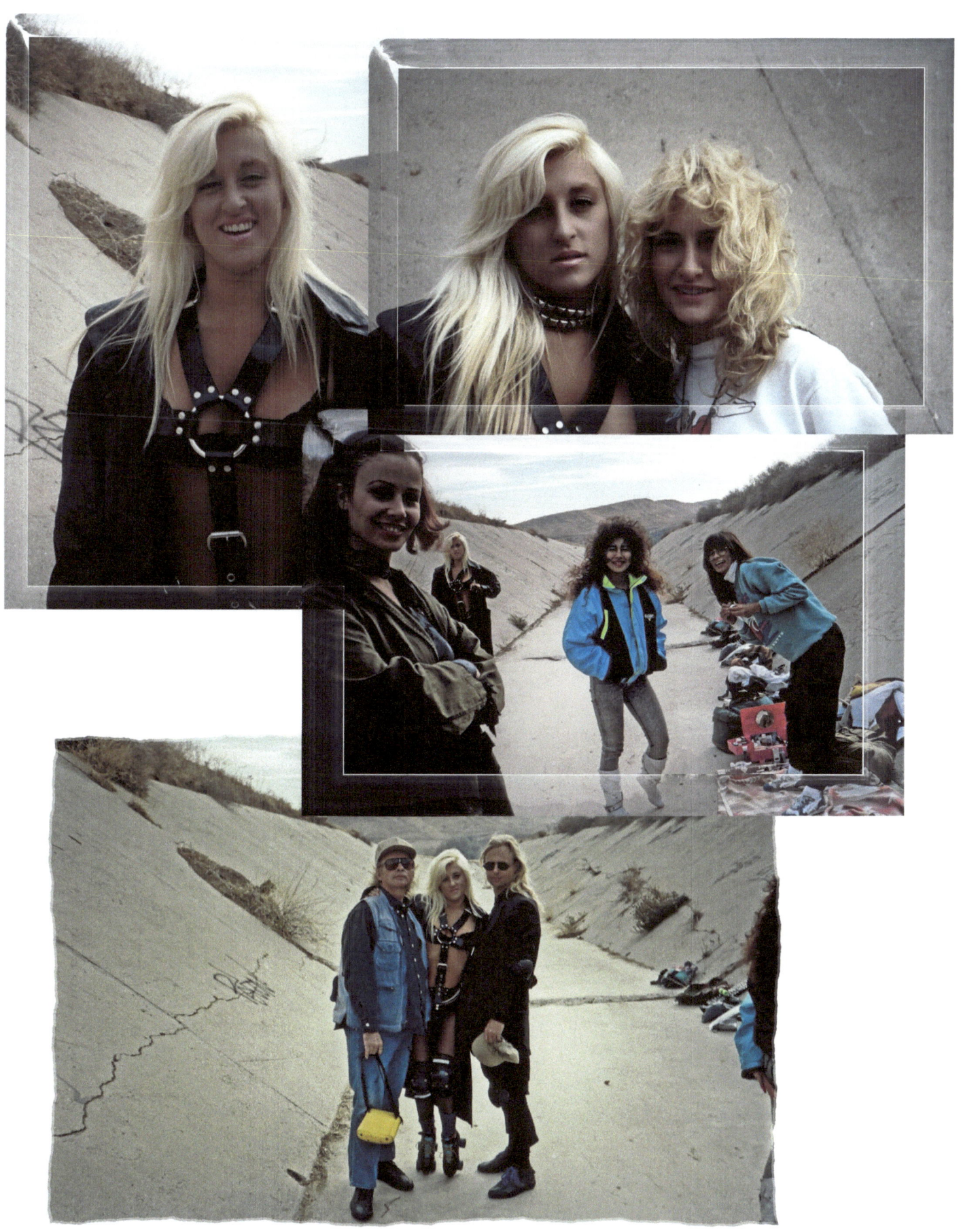

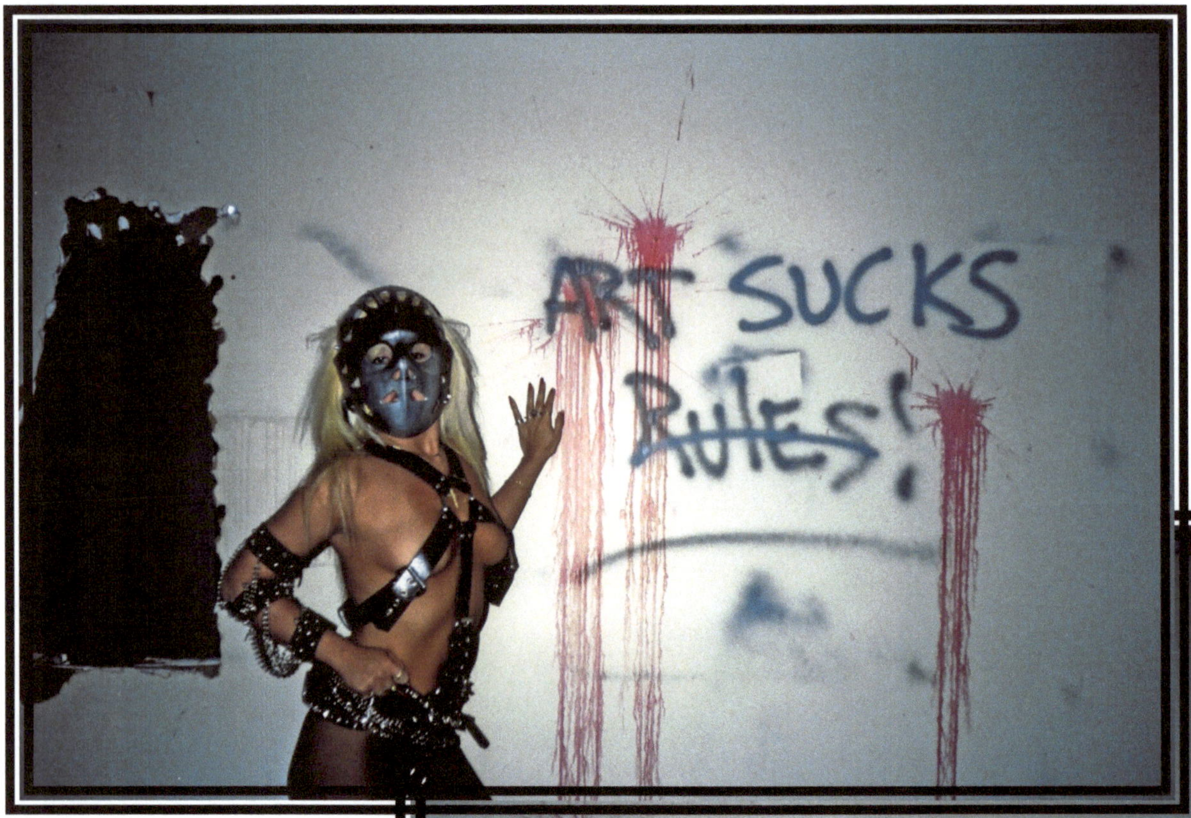

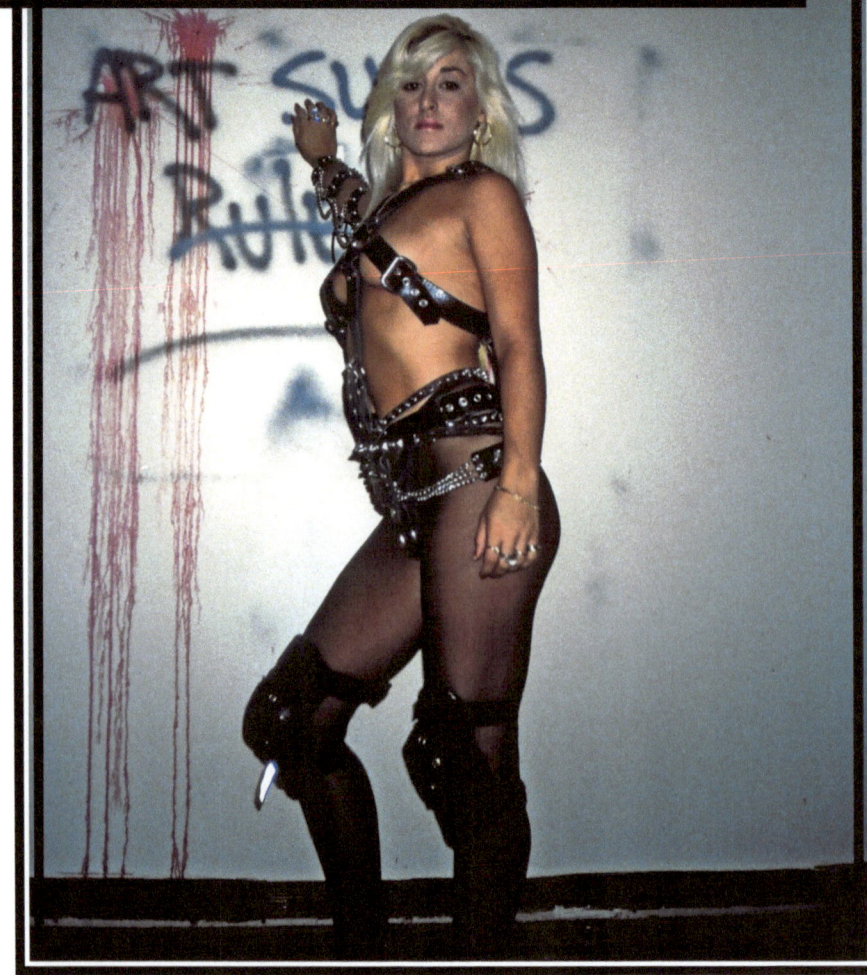

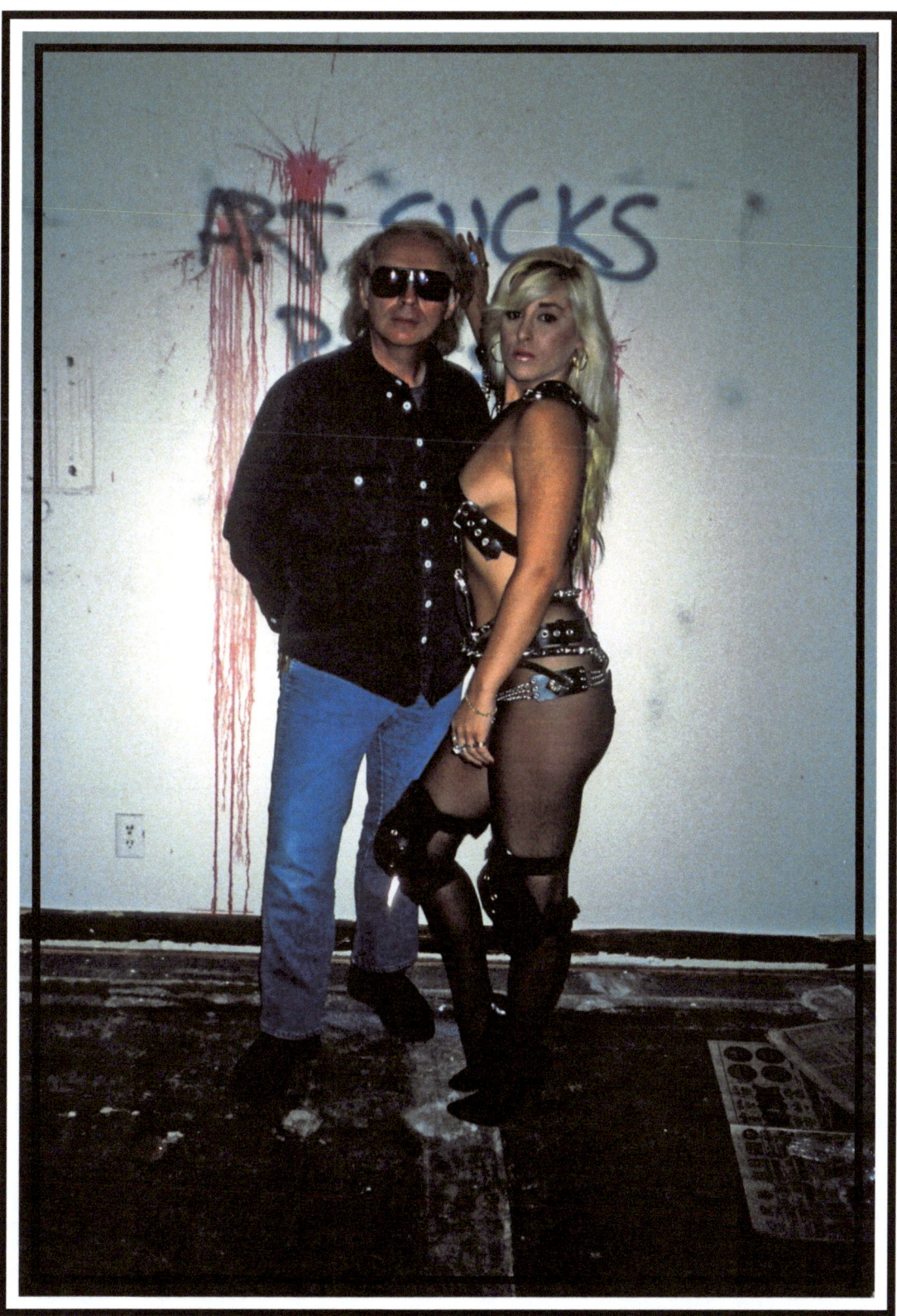

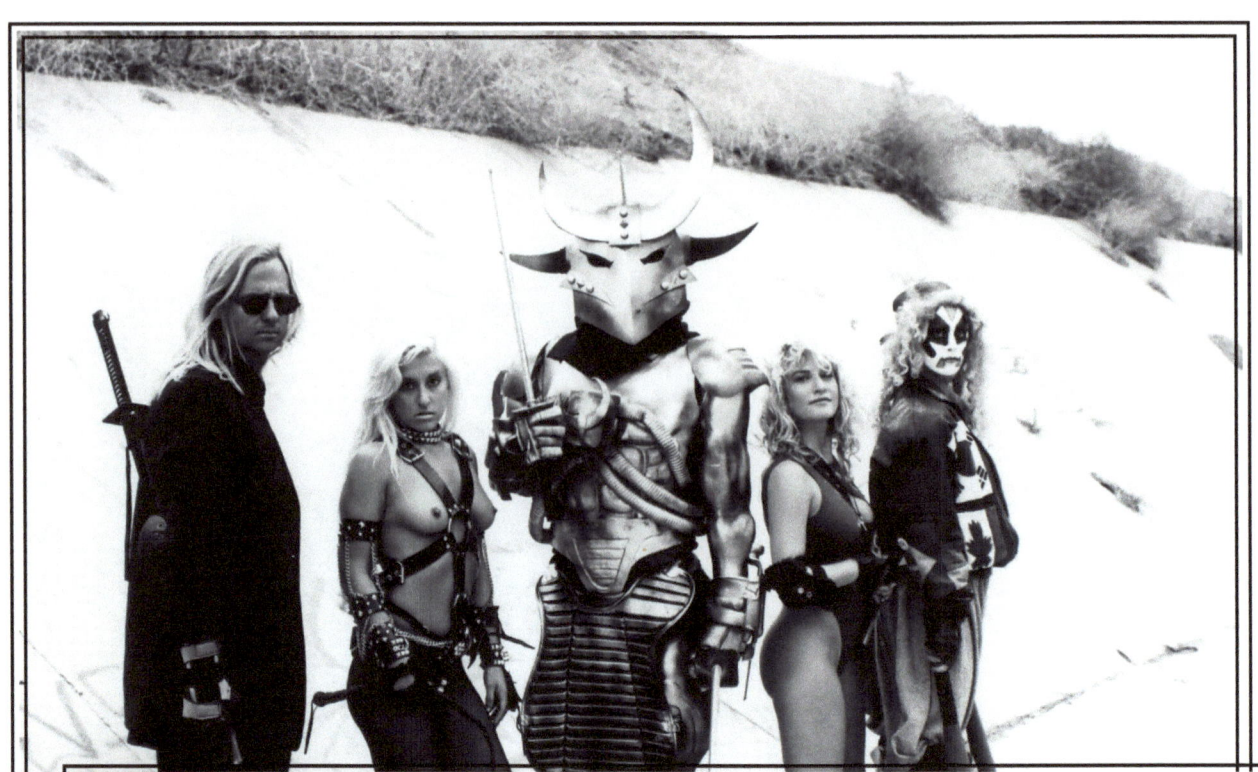

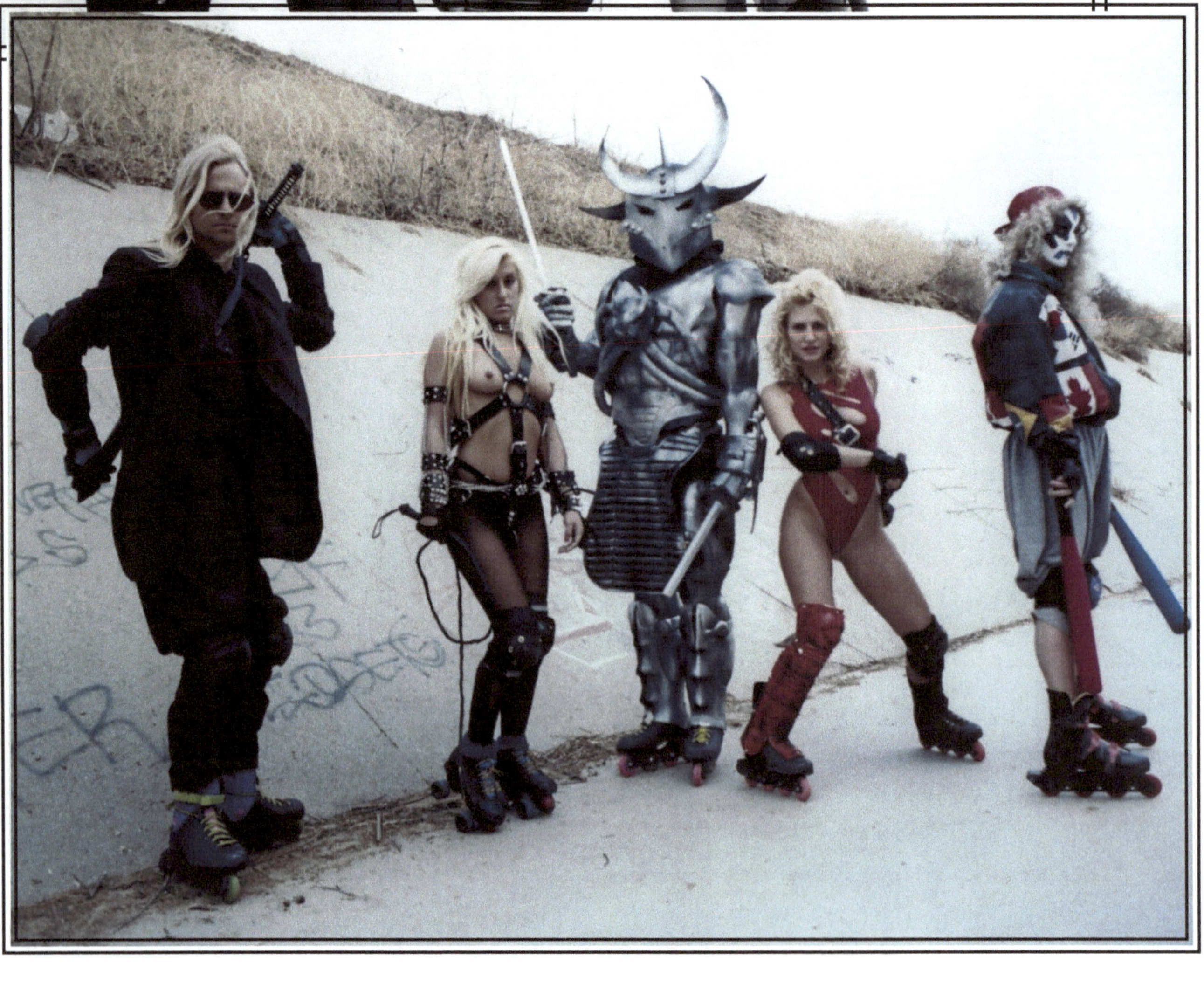

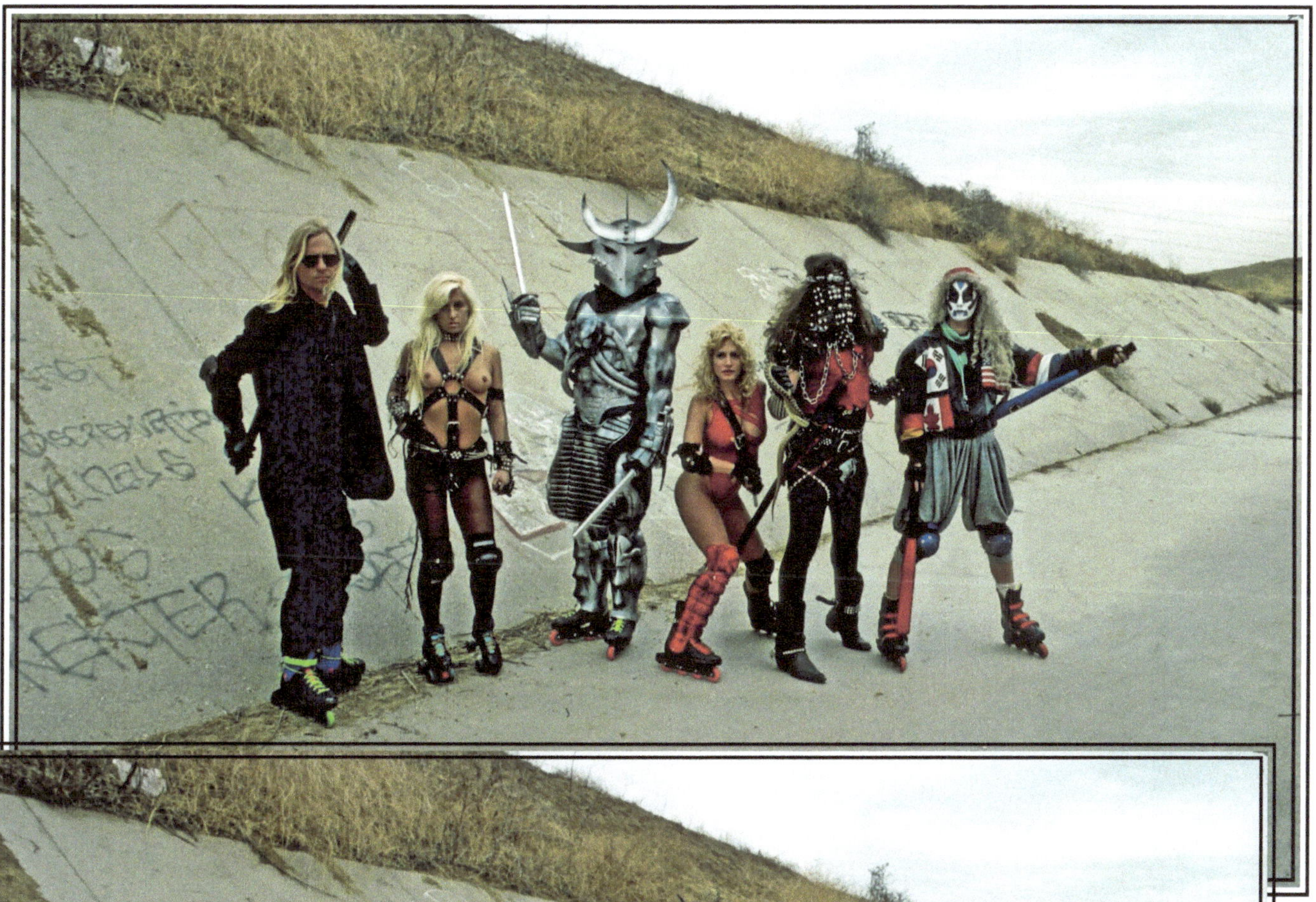

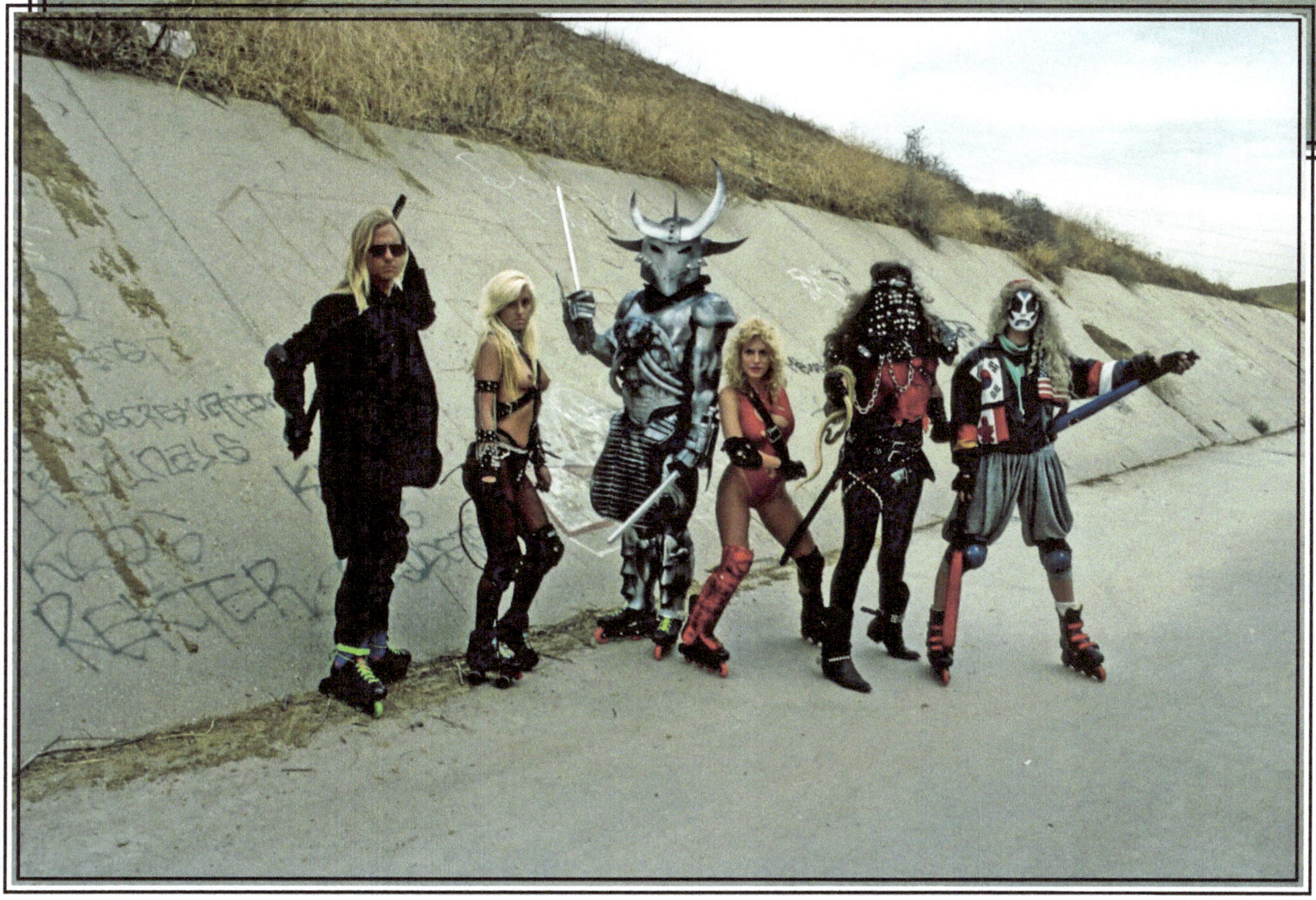

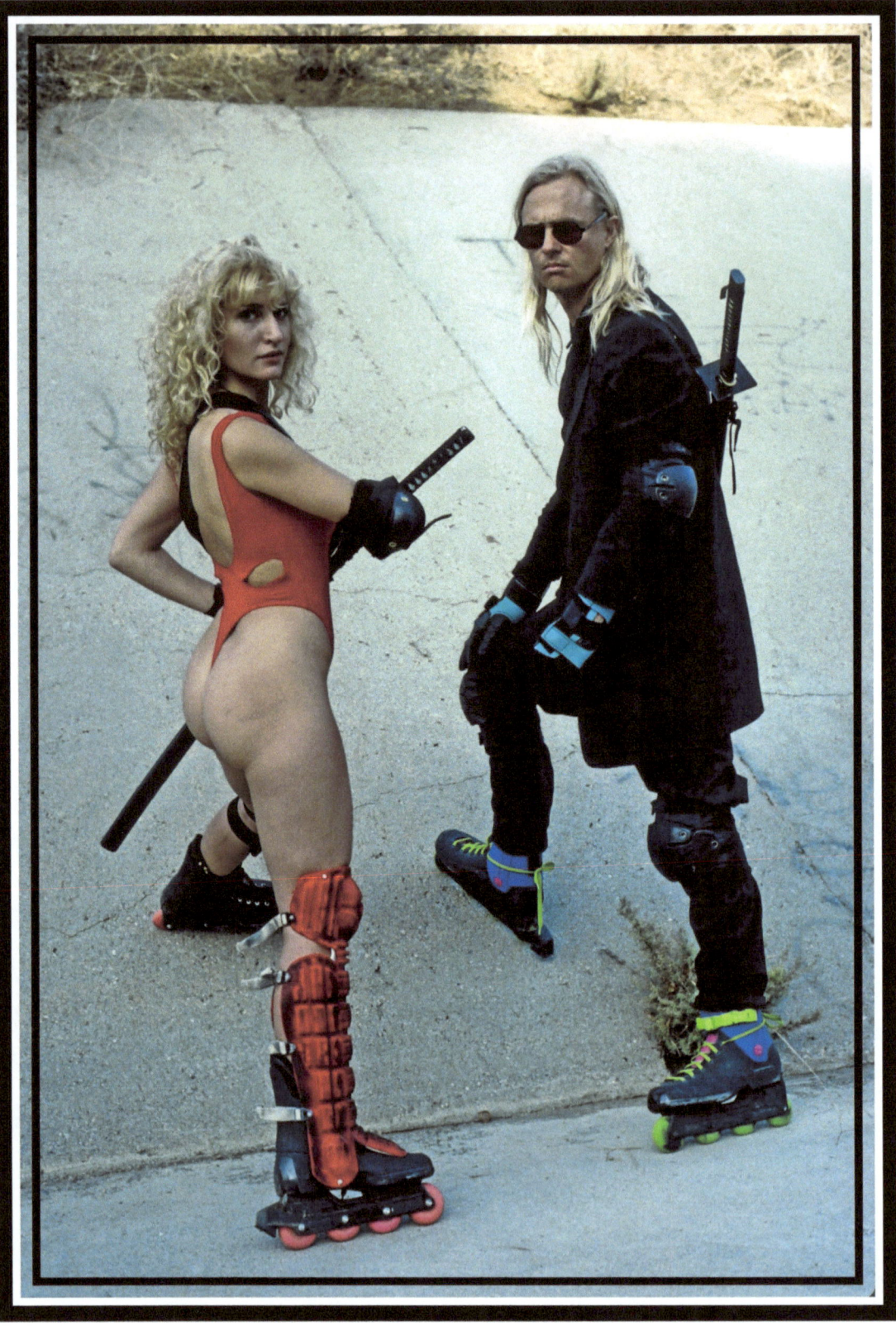

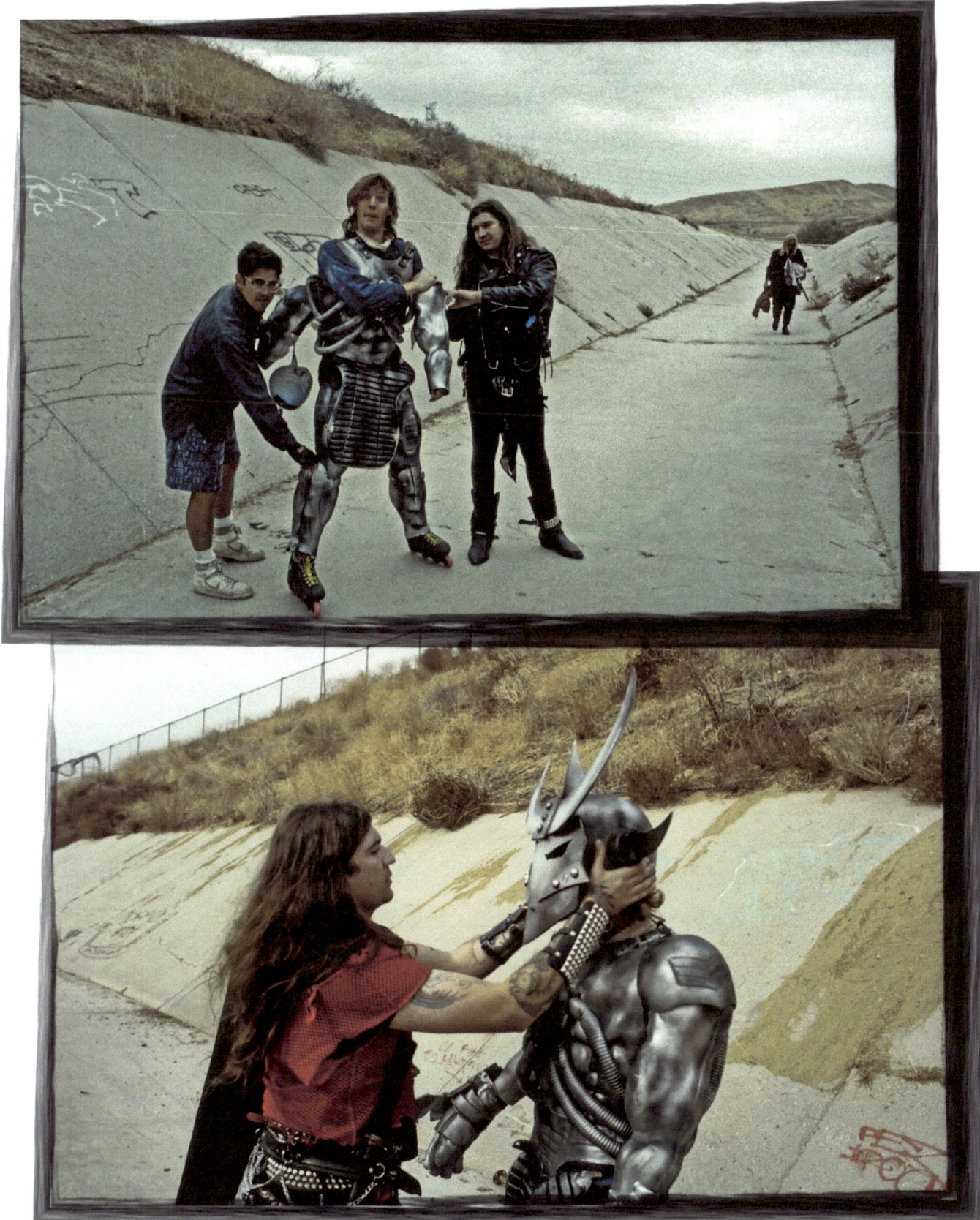

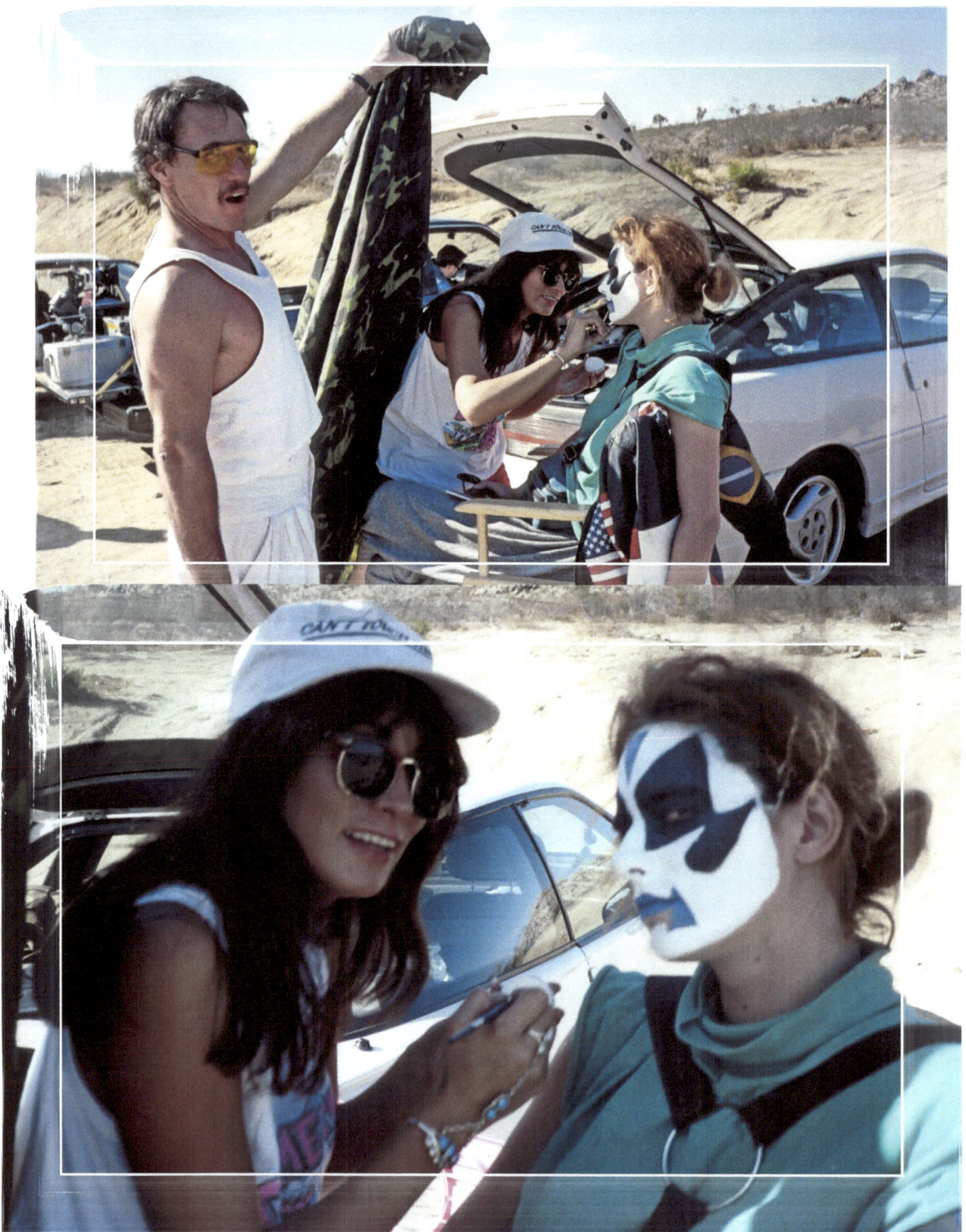

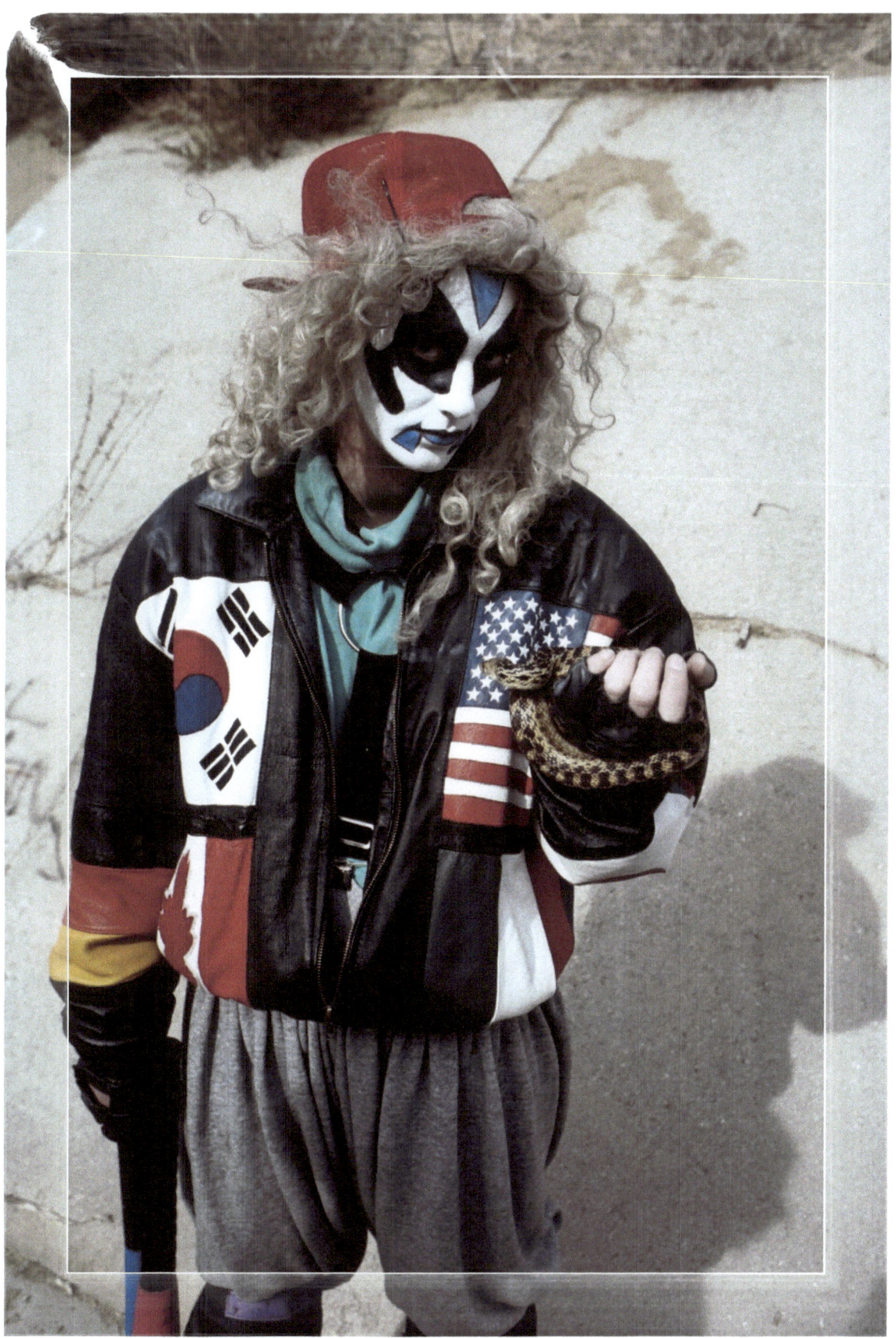

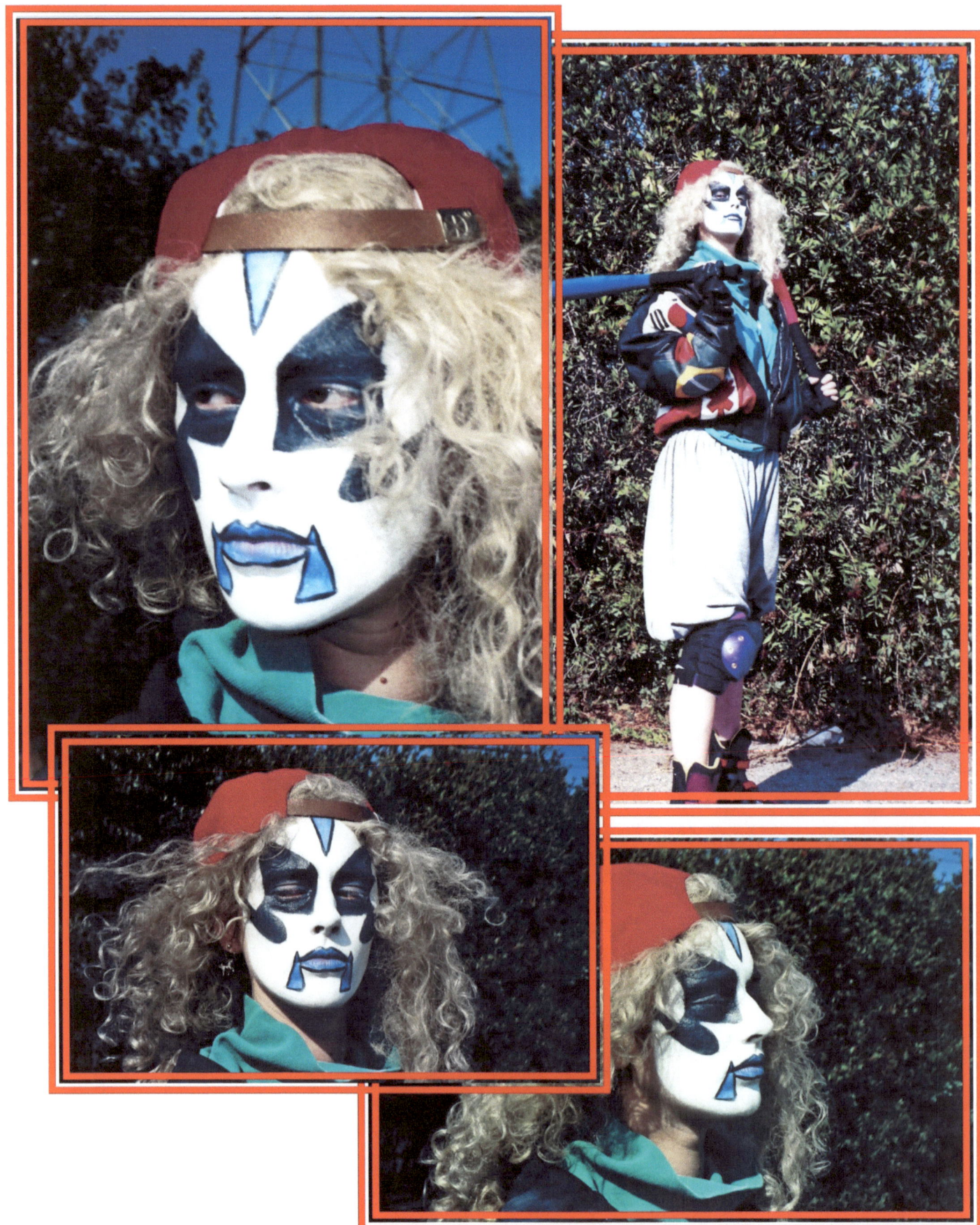

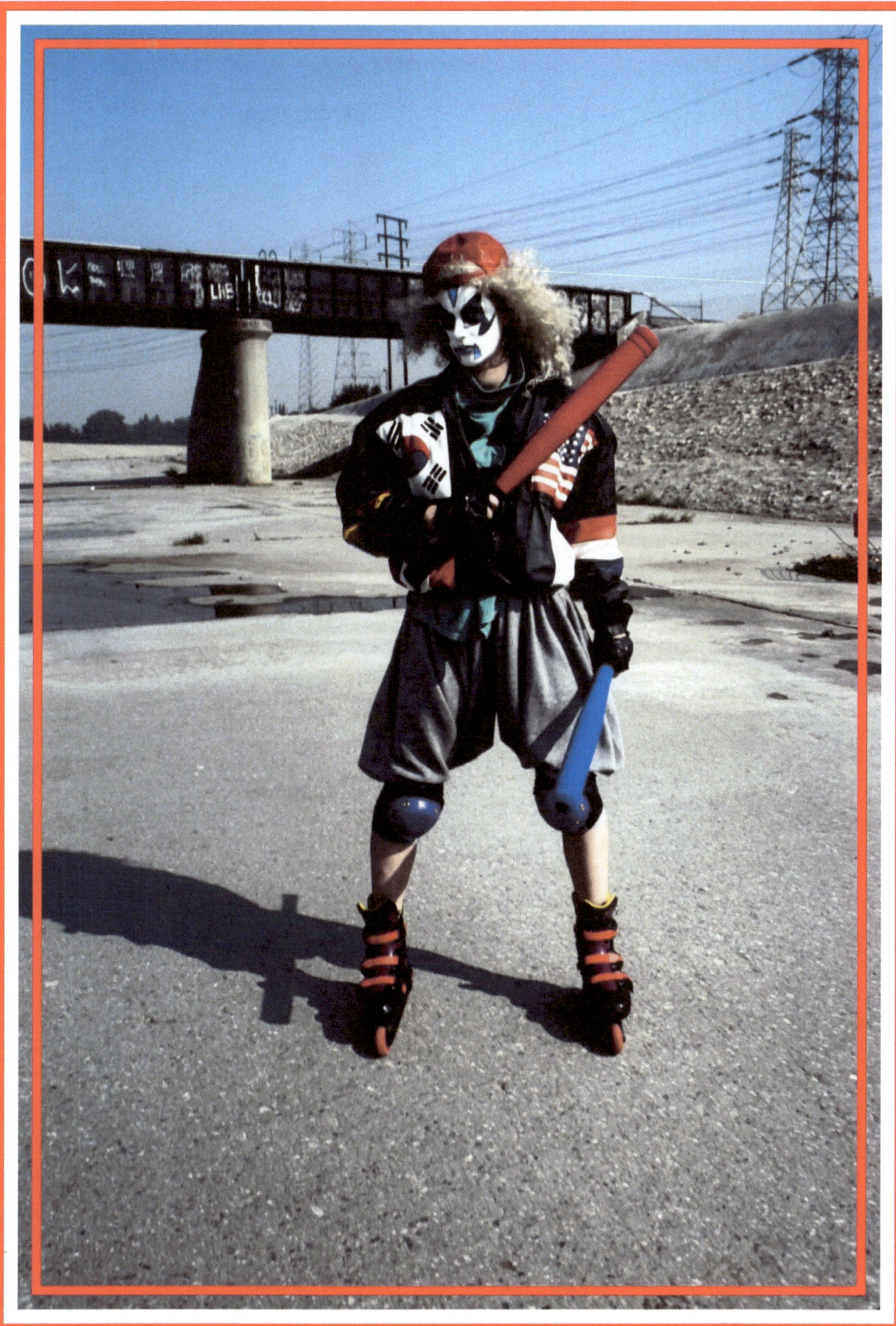

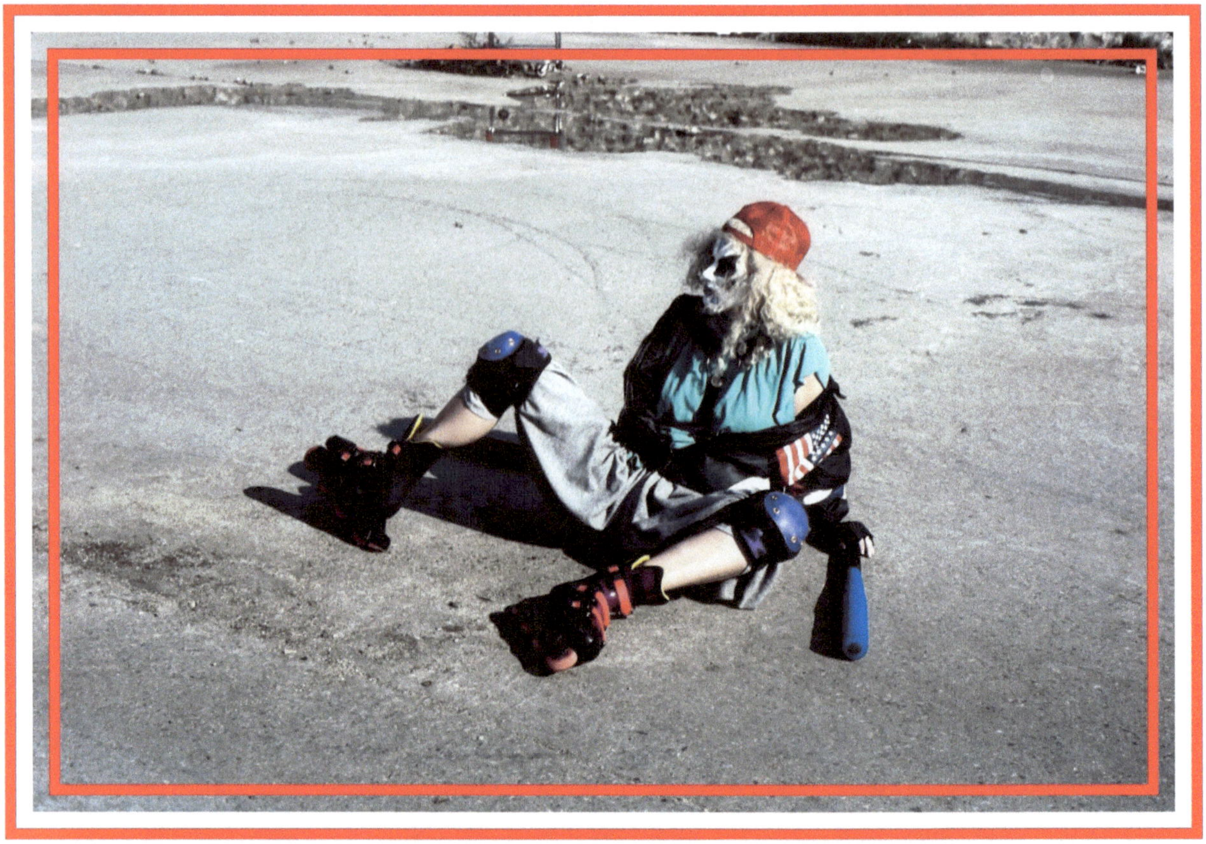

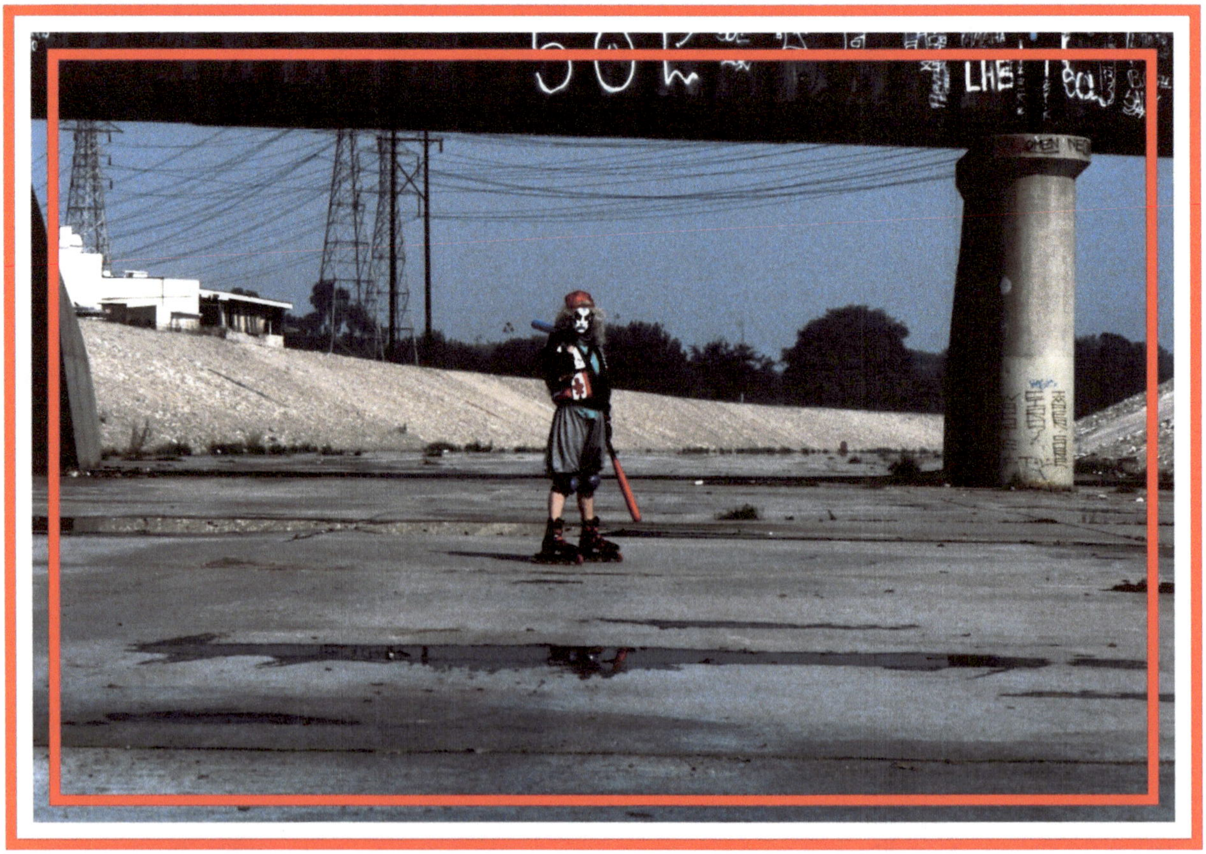

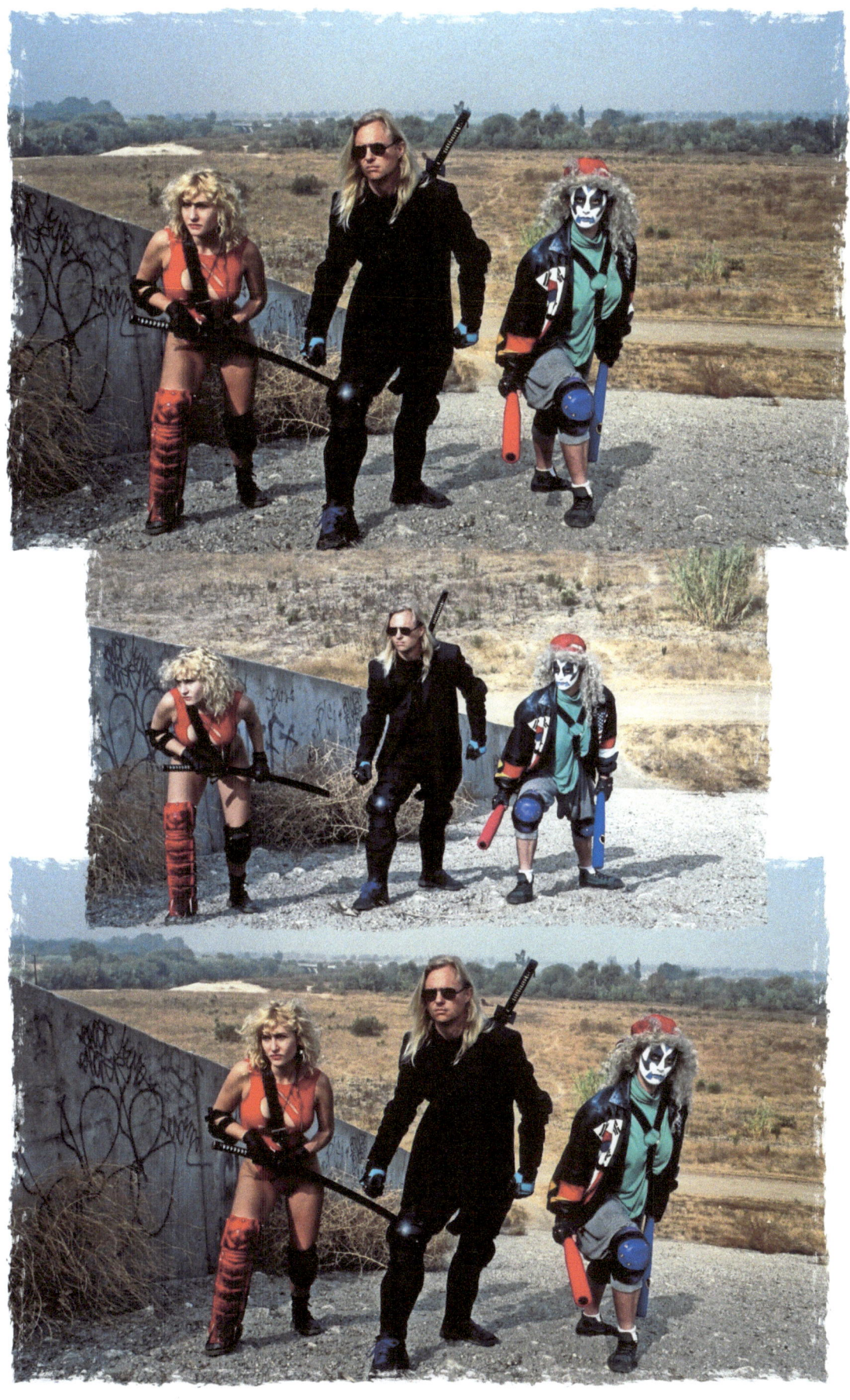

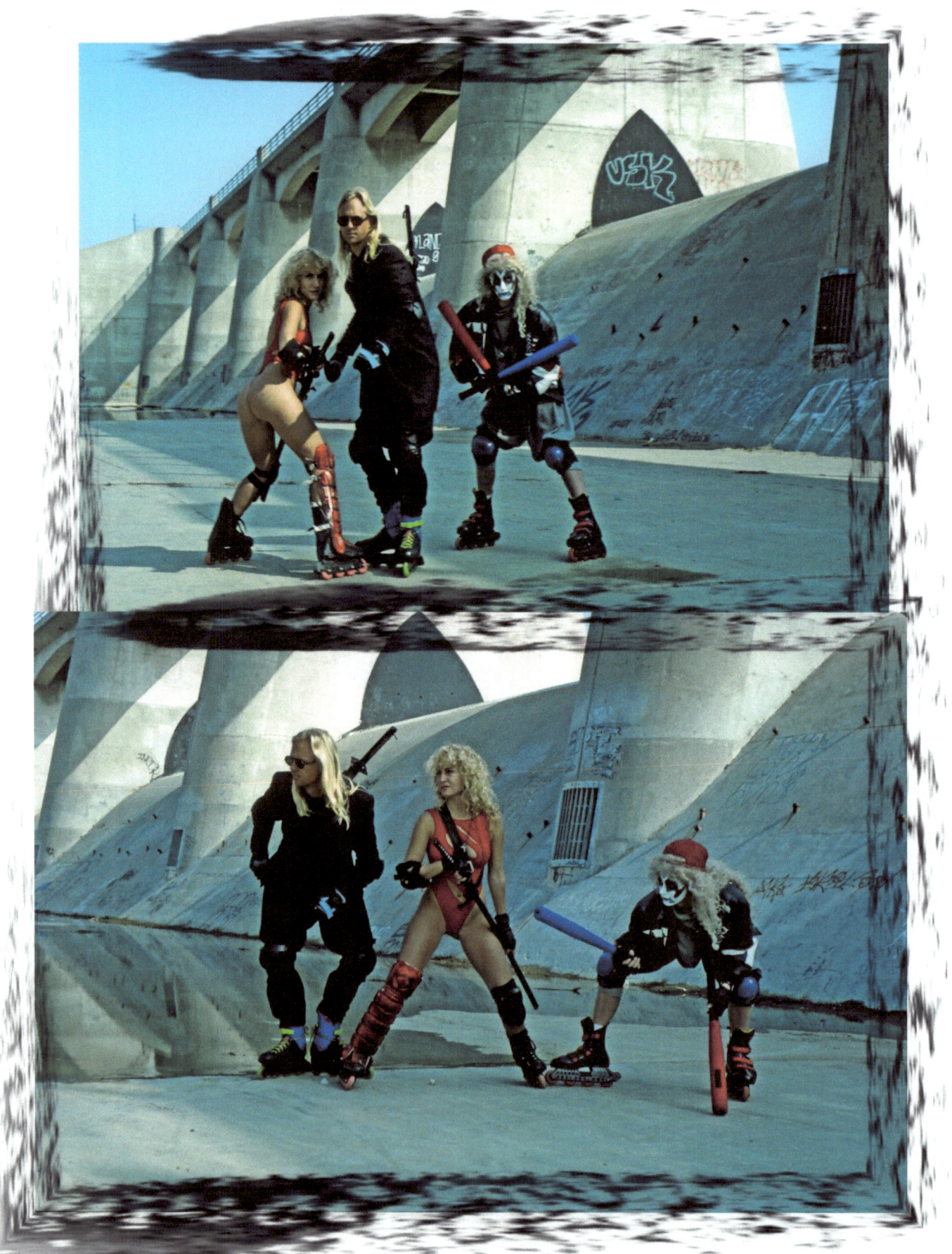

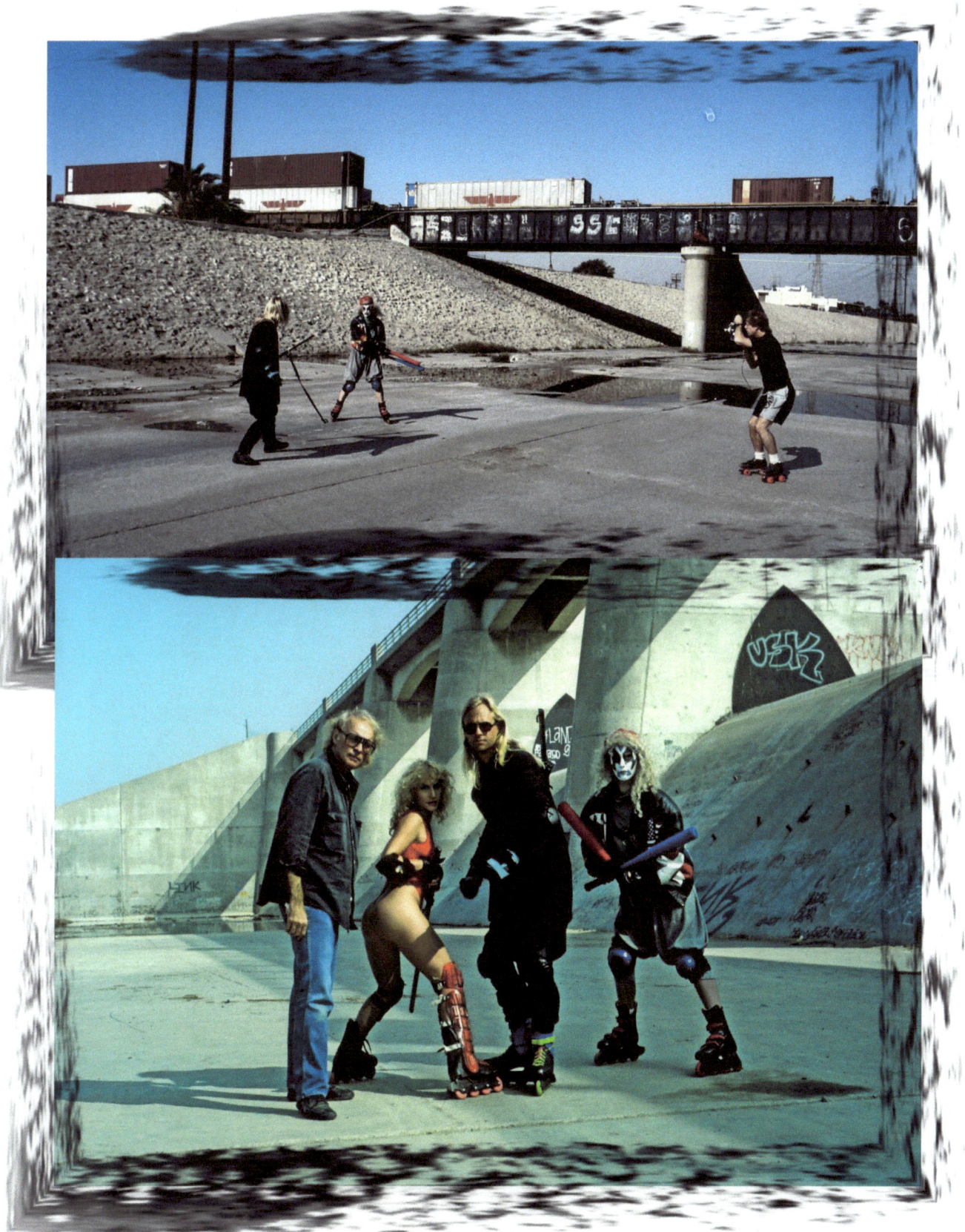

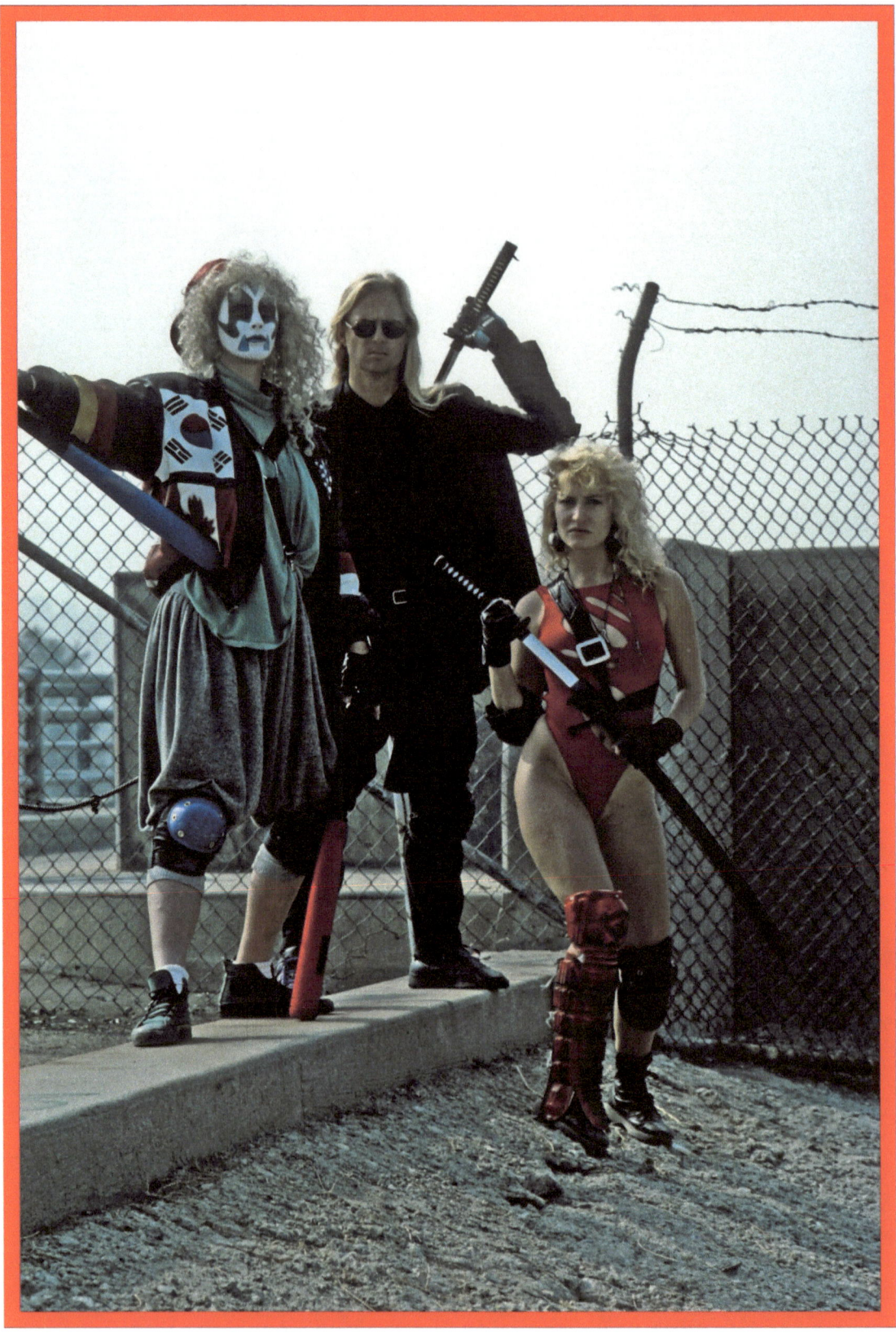

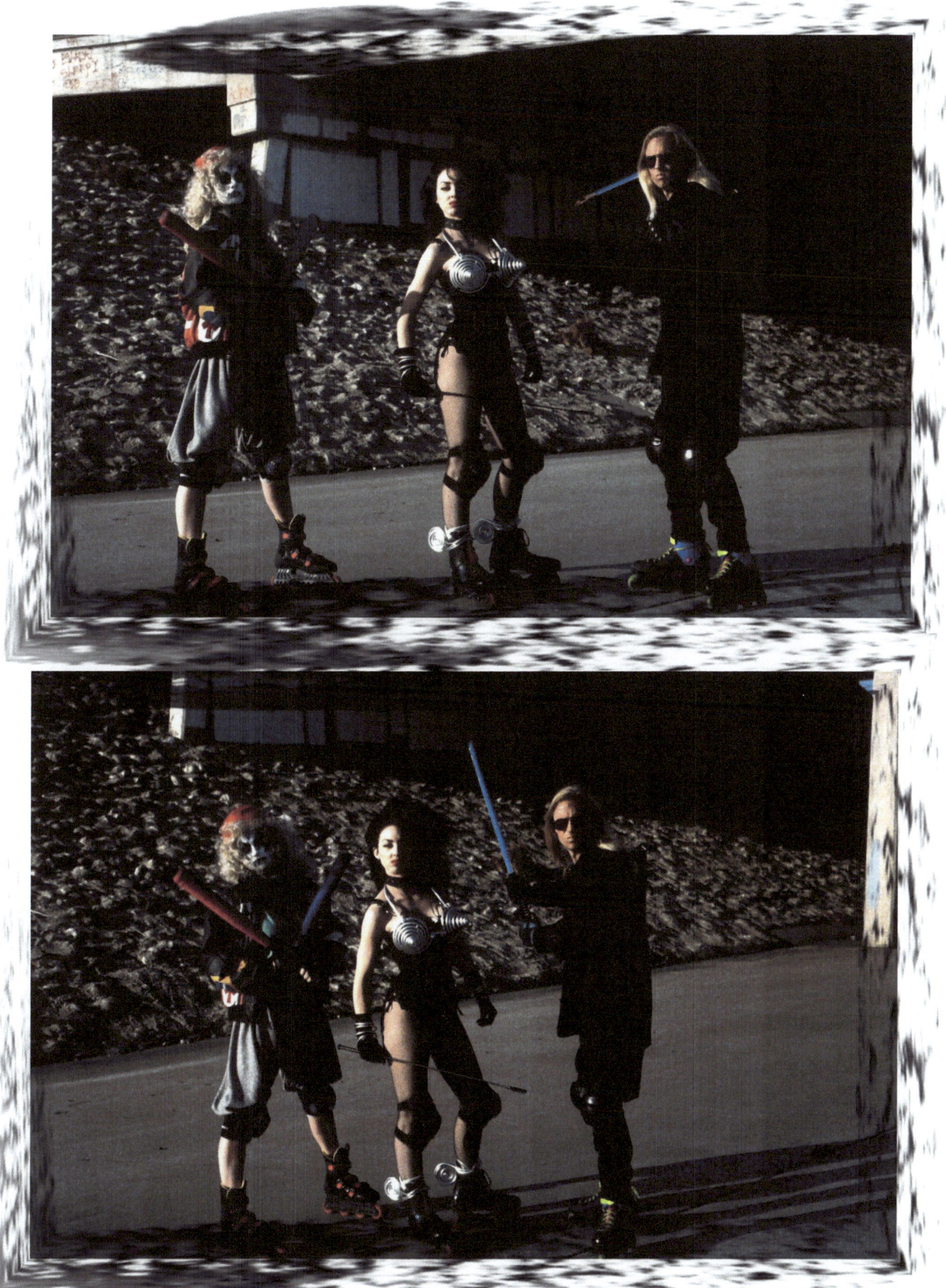

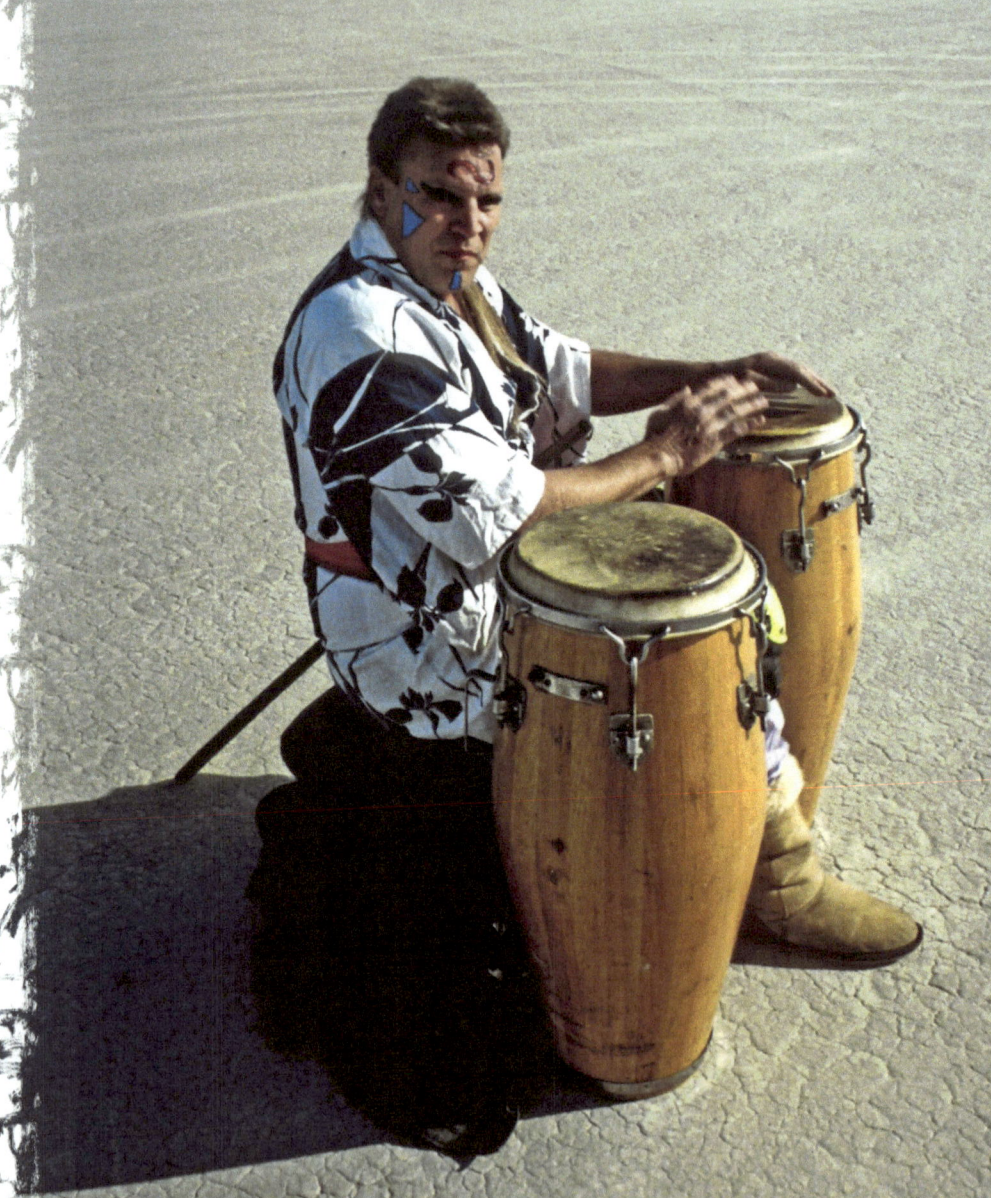

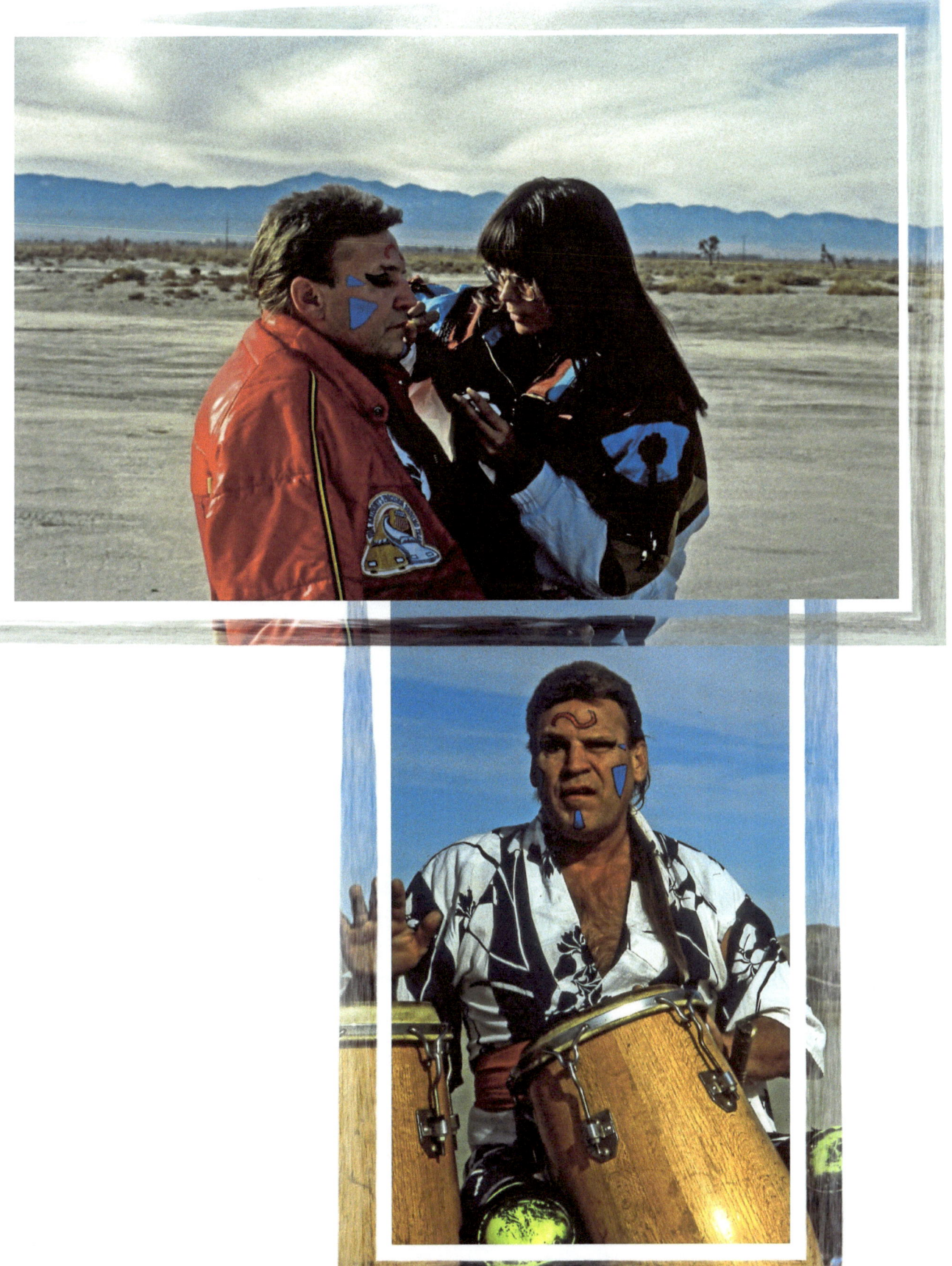

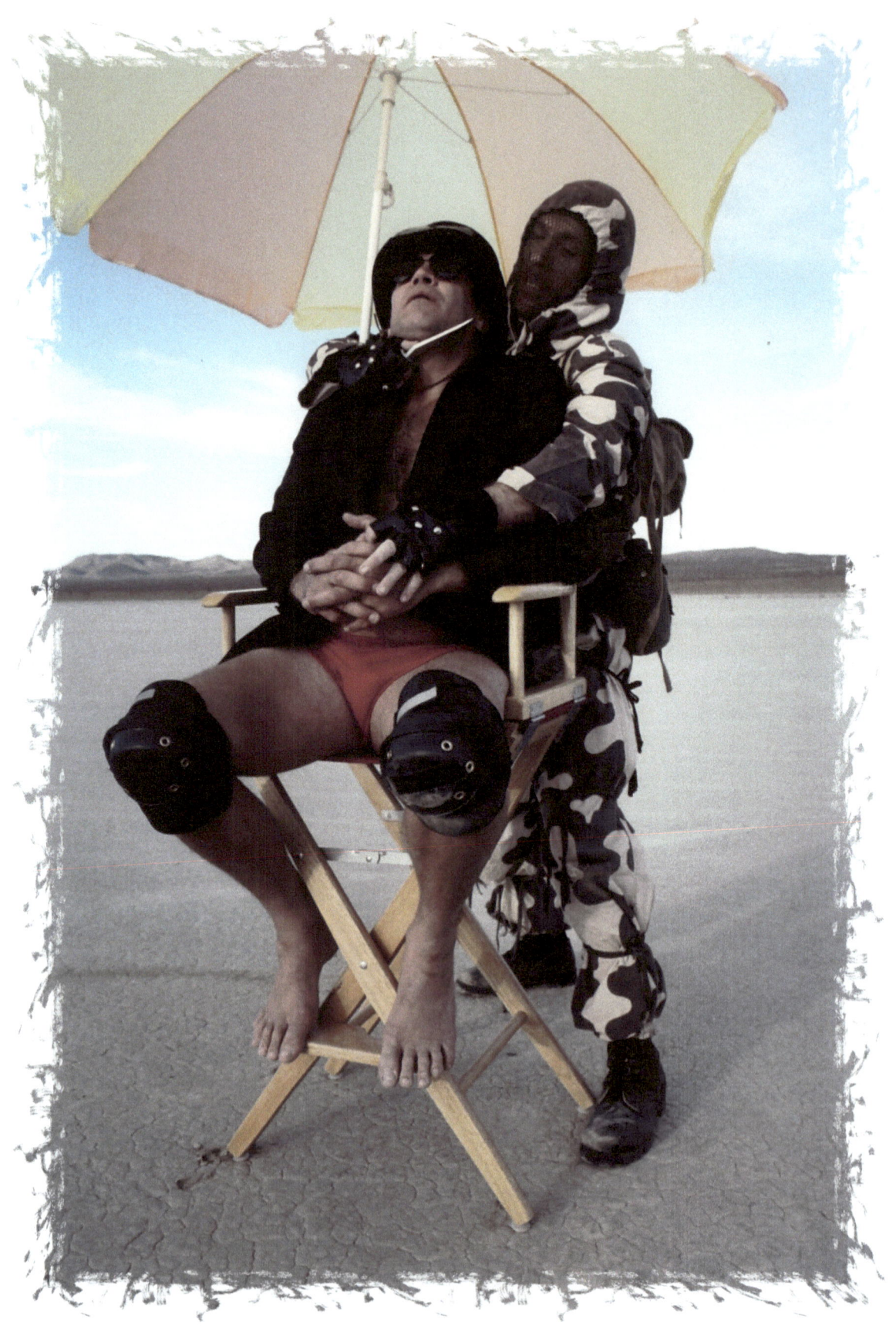

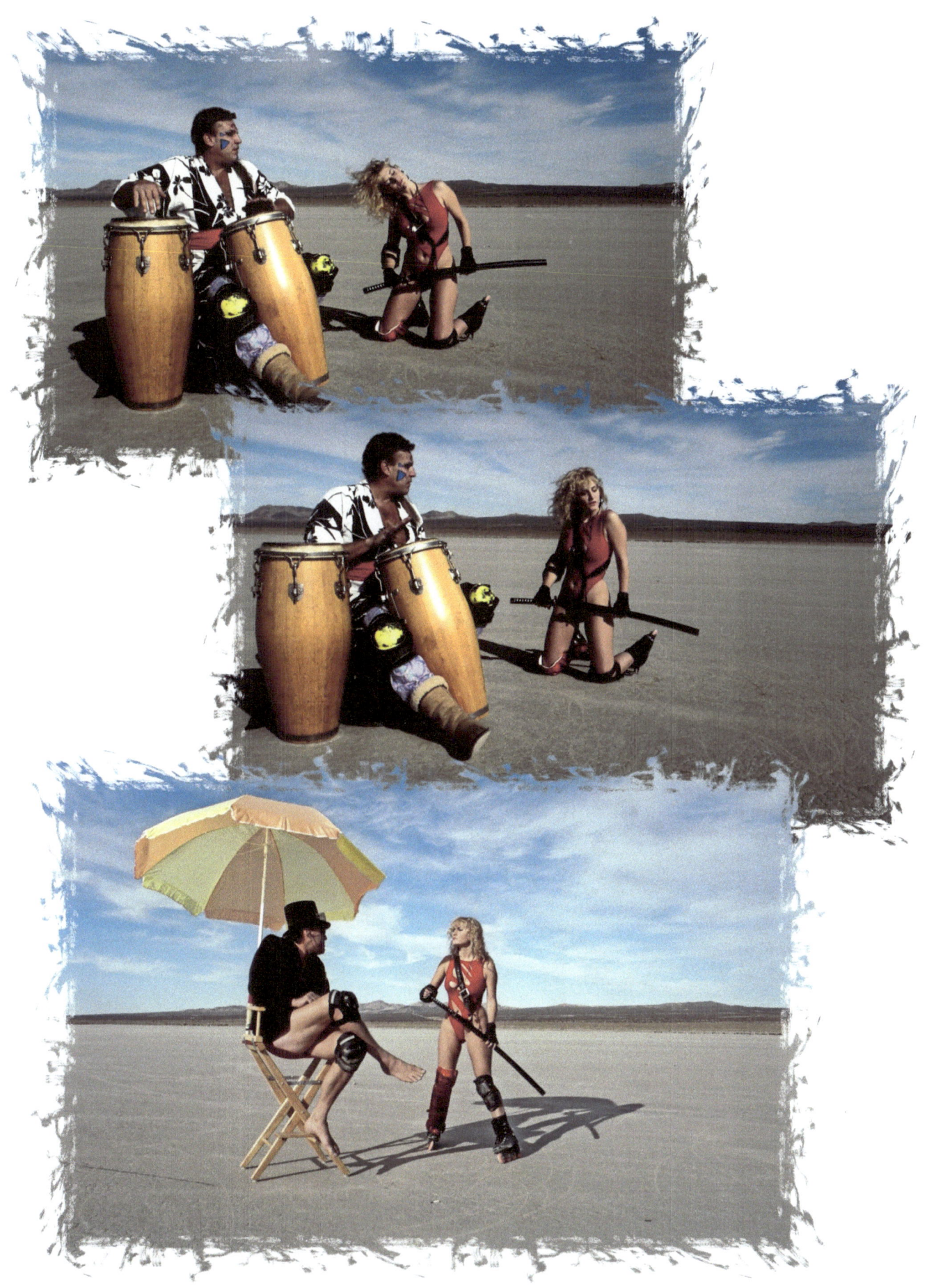

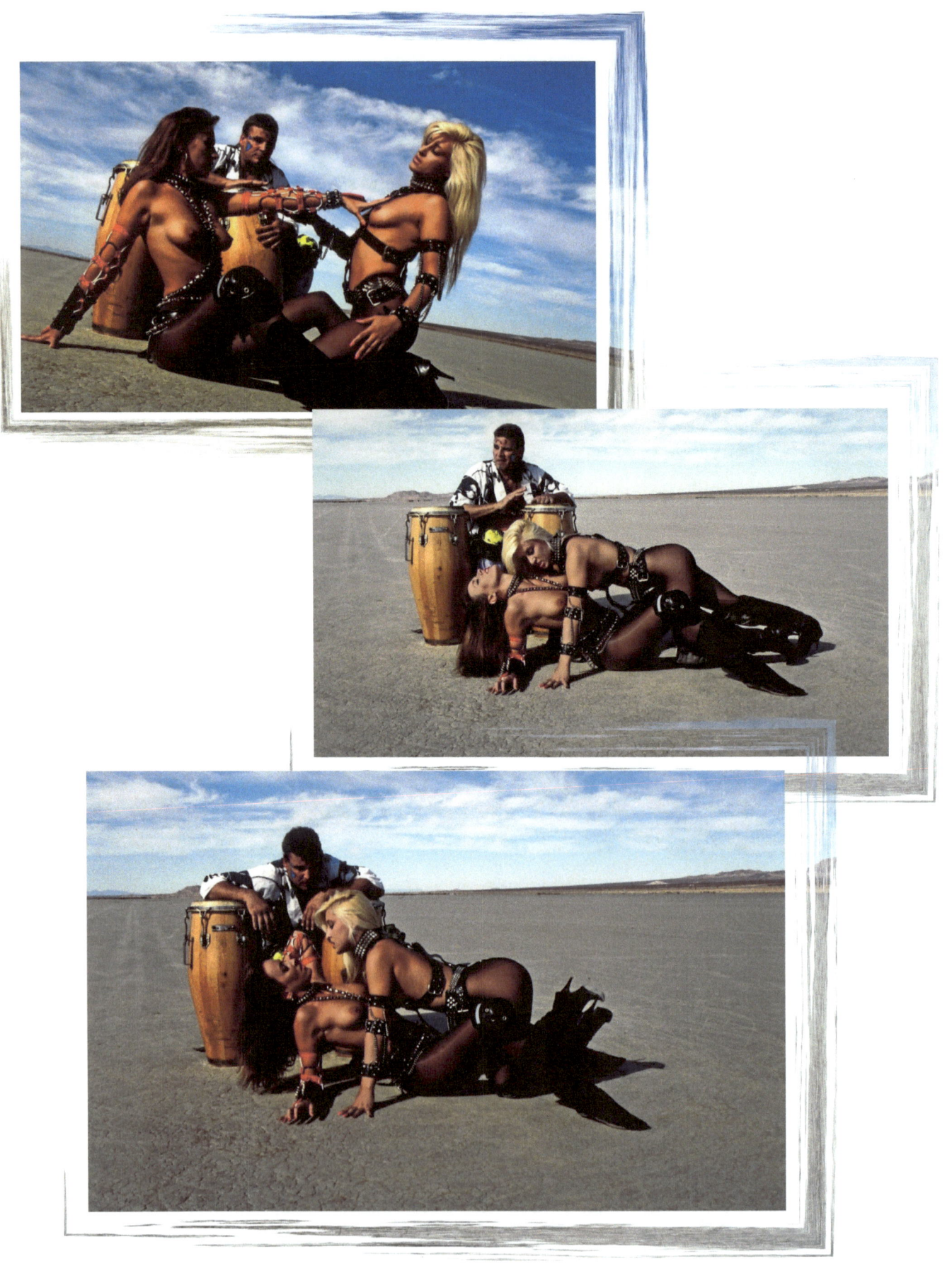

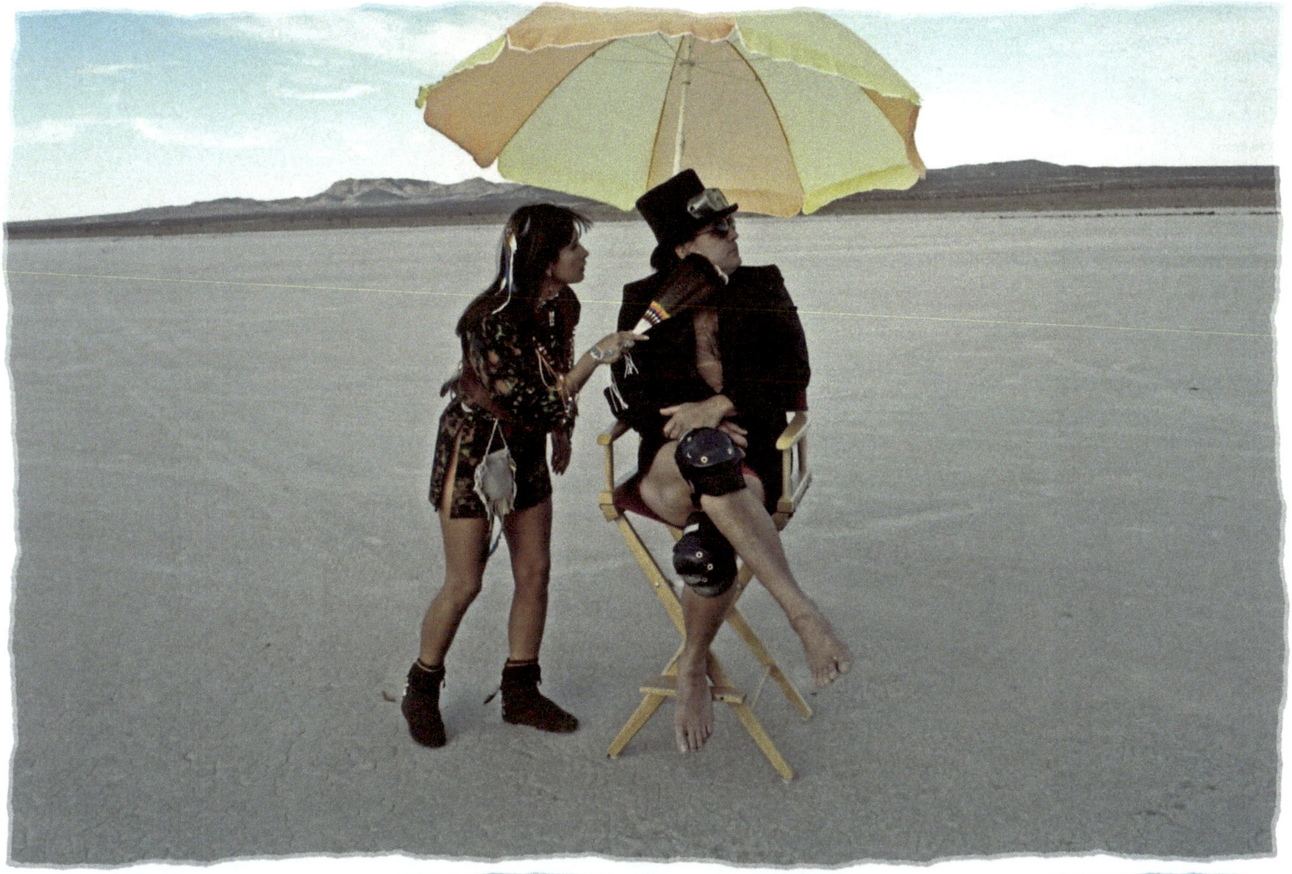

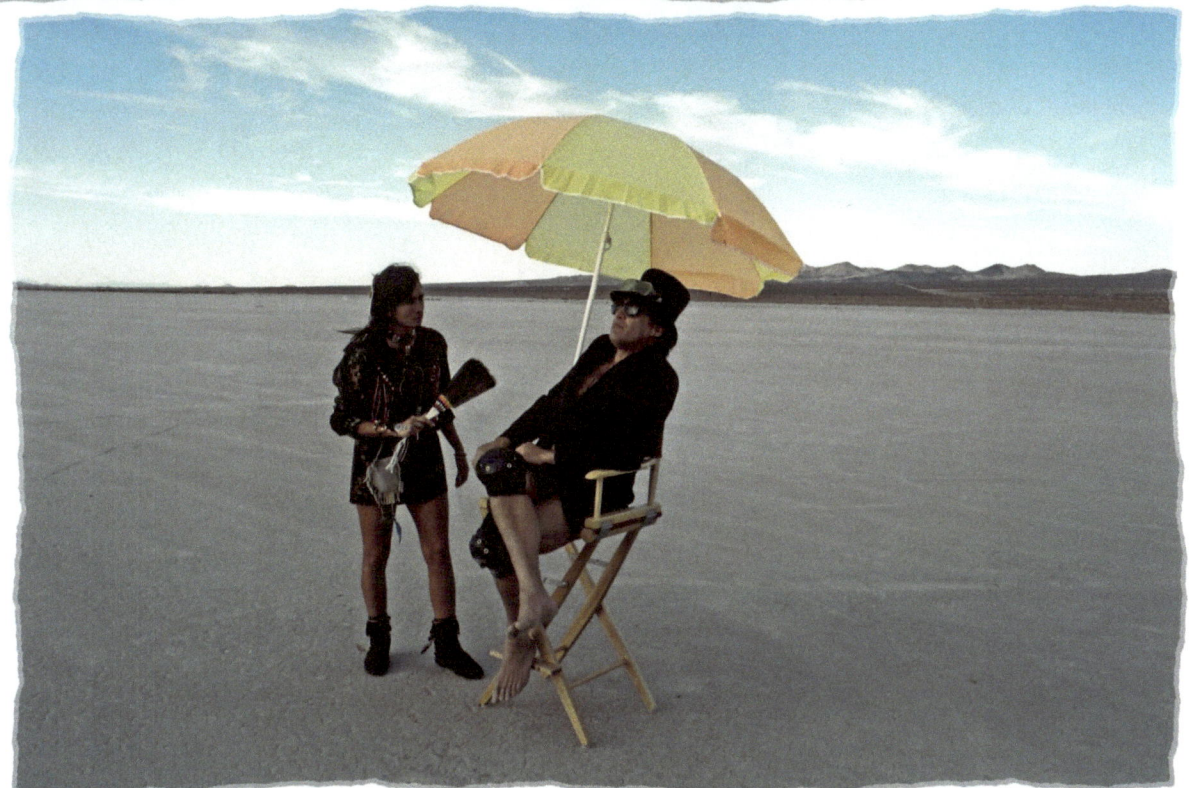

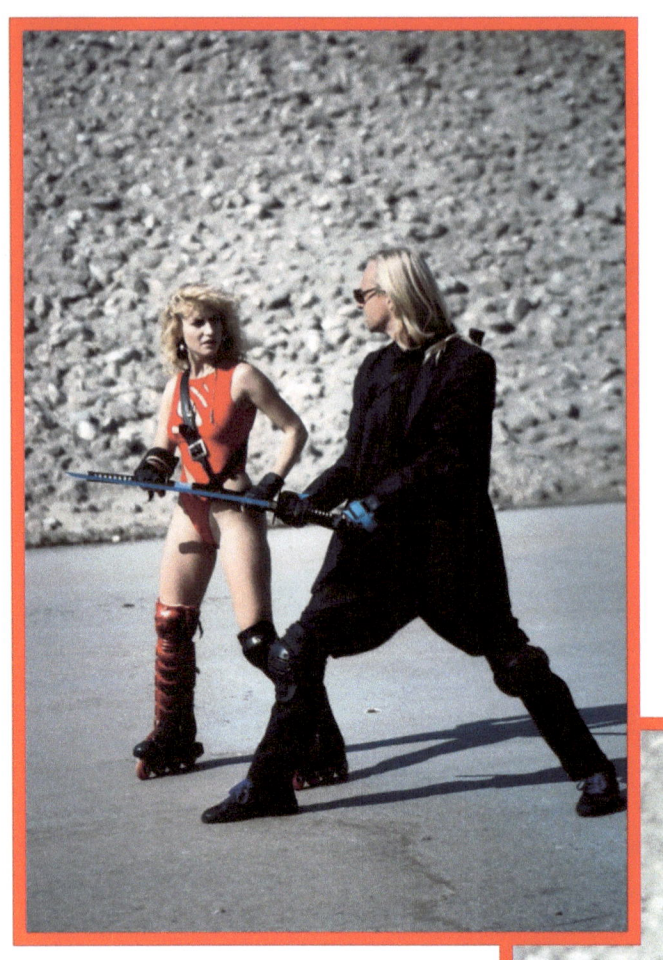
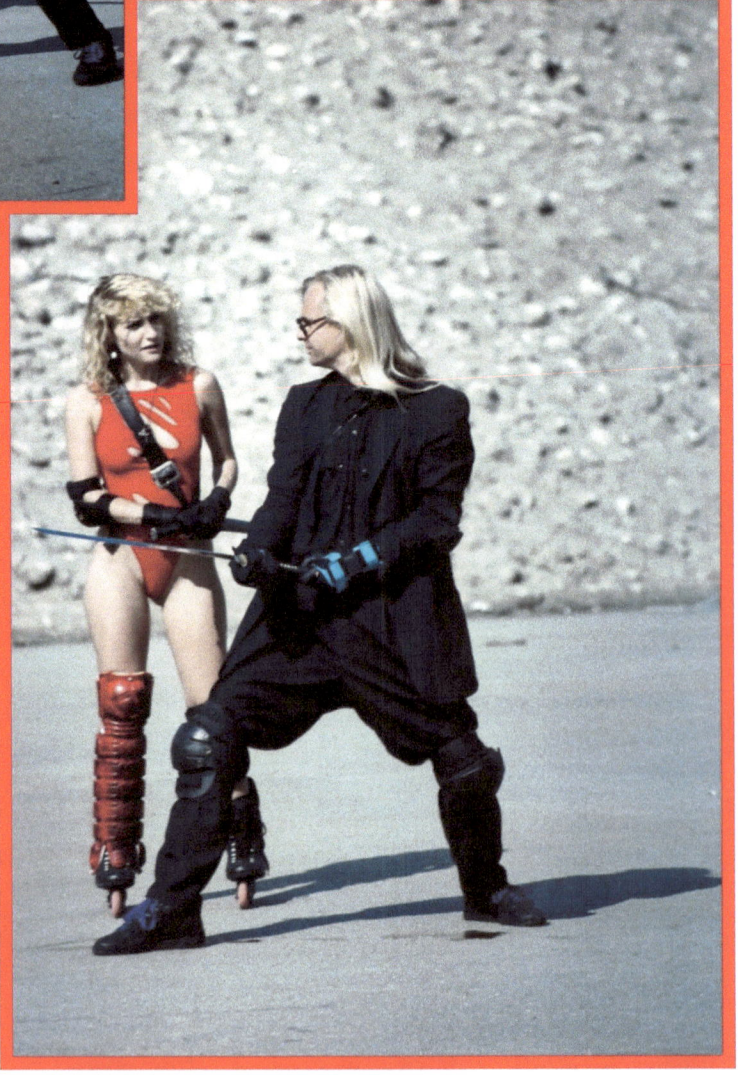

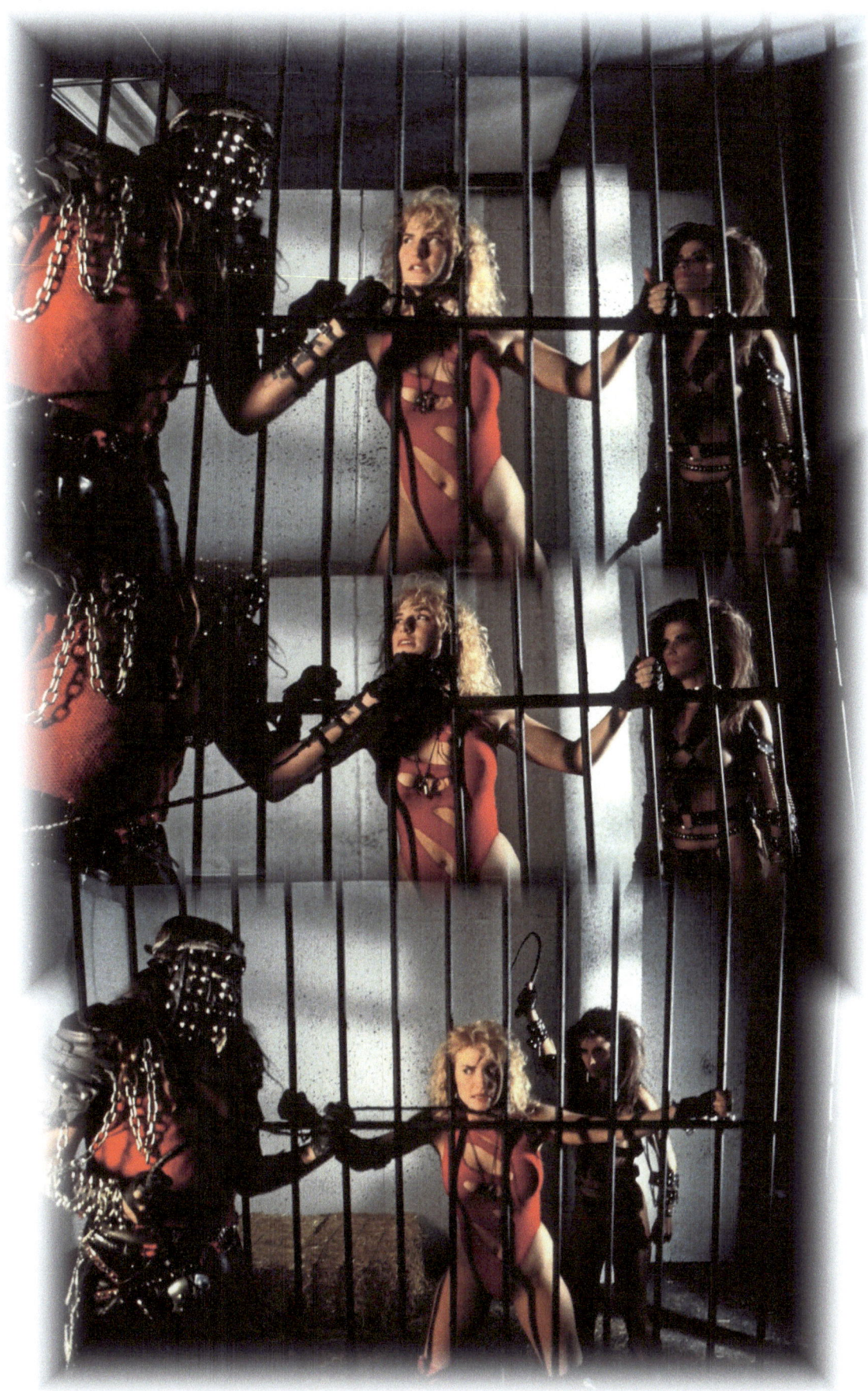

KAREN BLACK

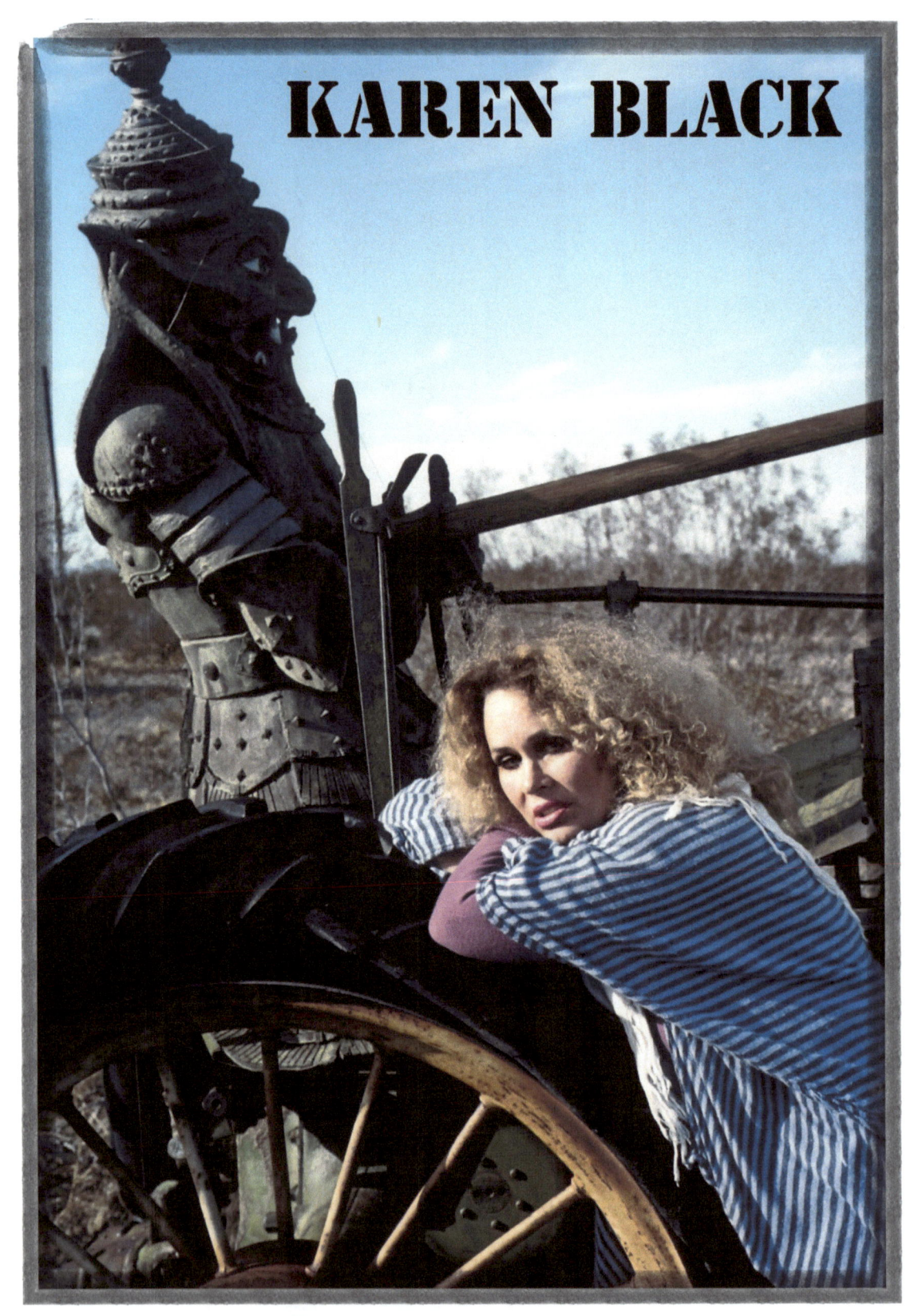

AS TAROT

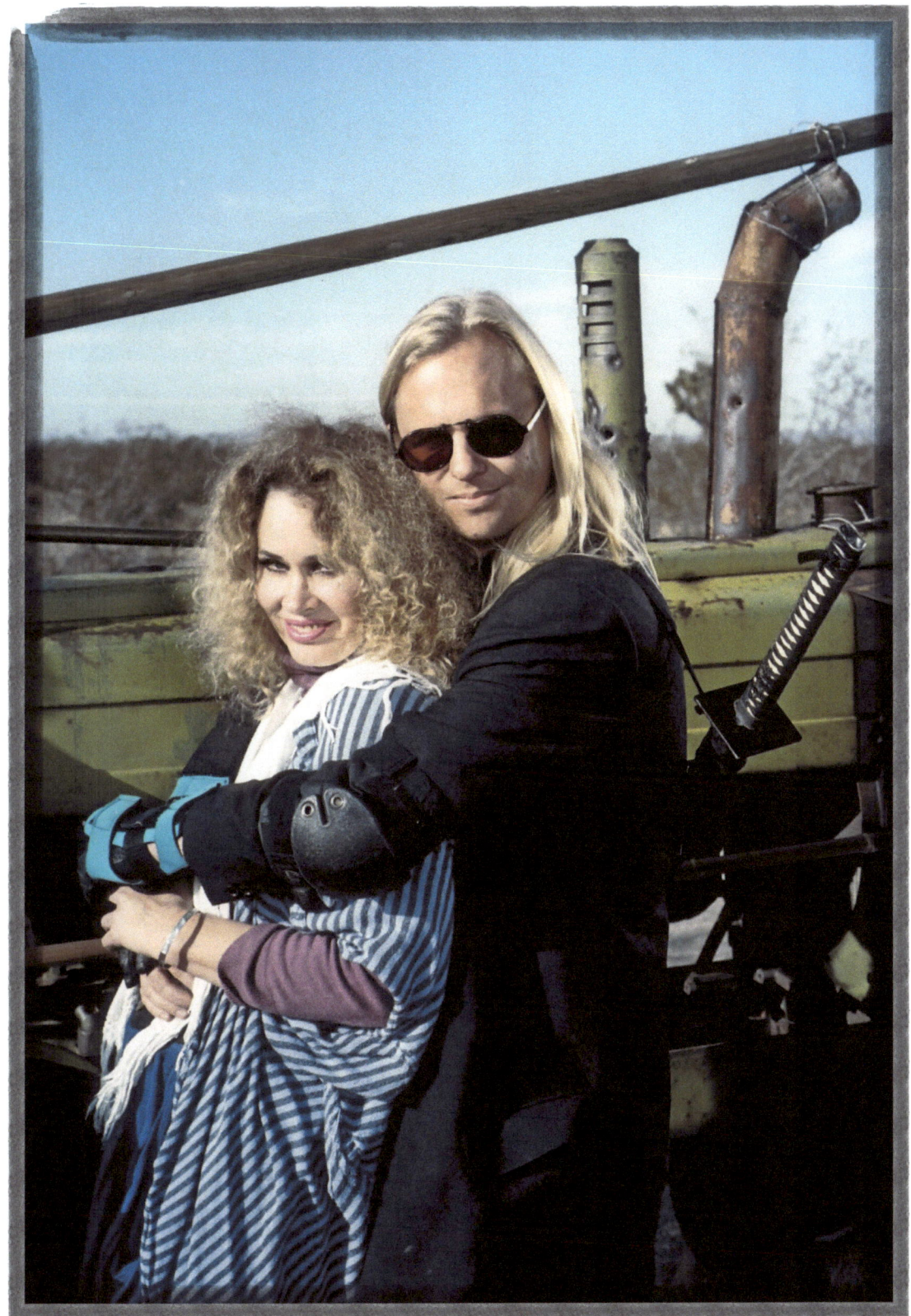

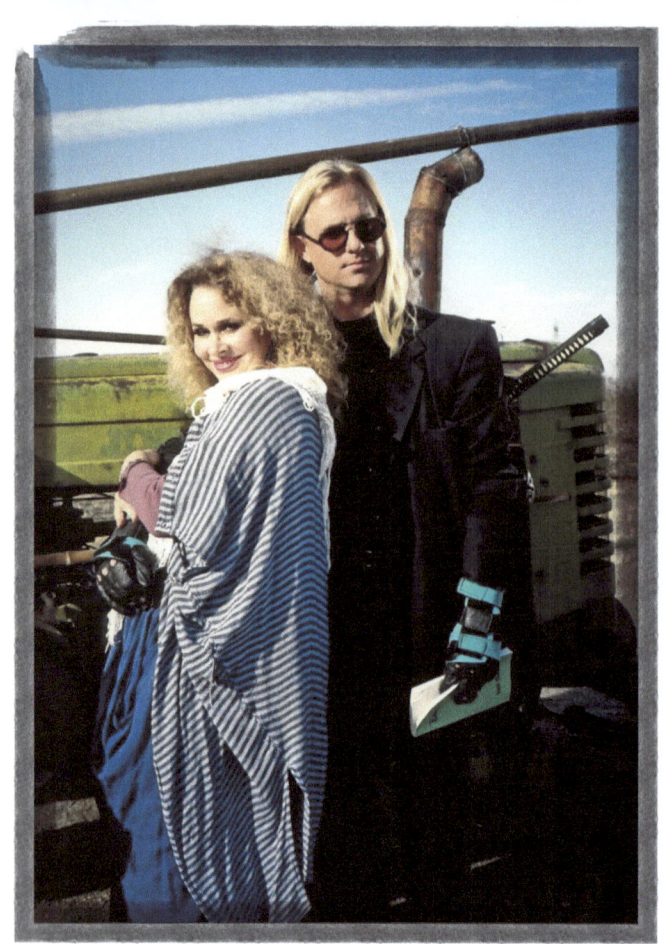
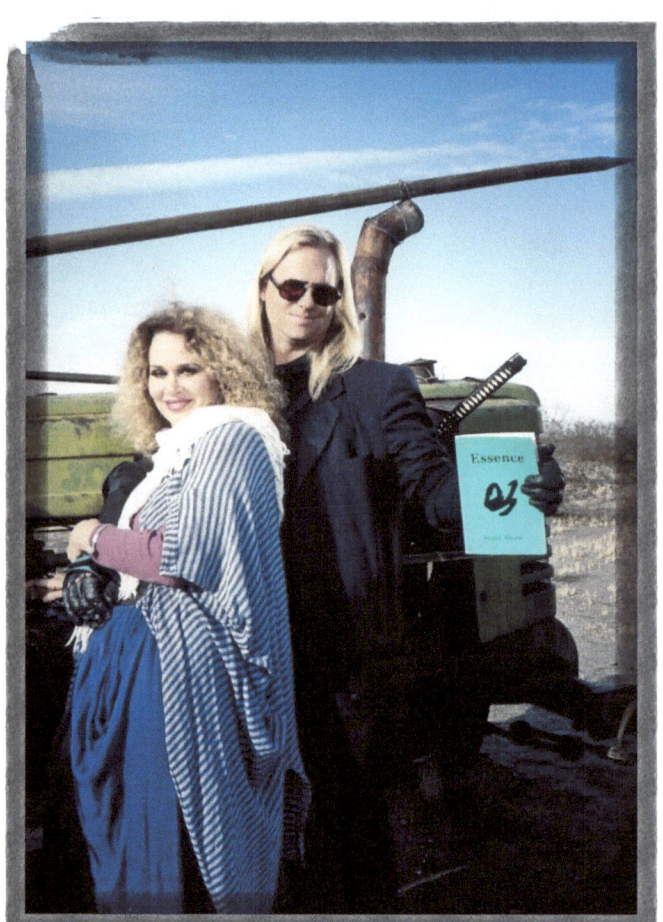

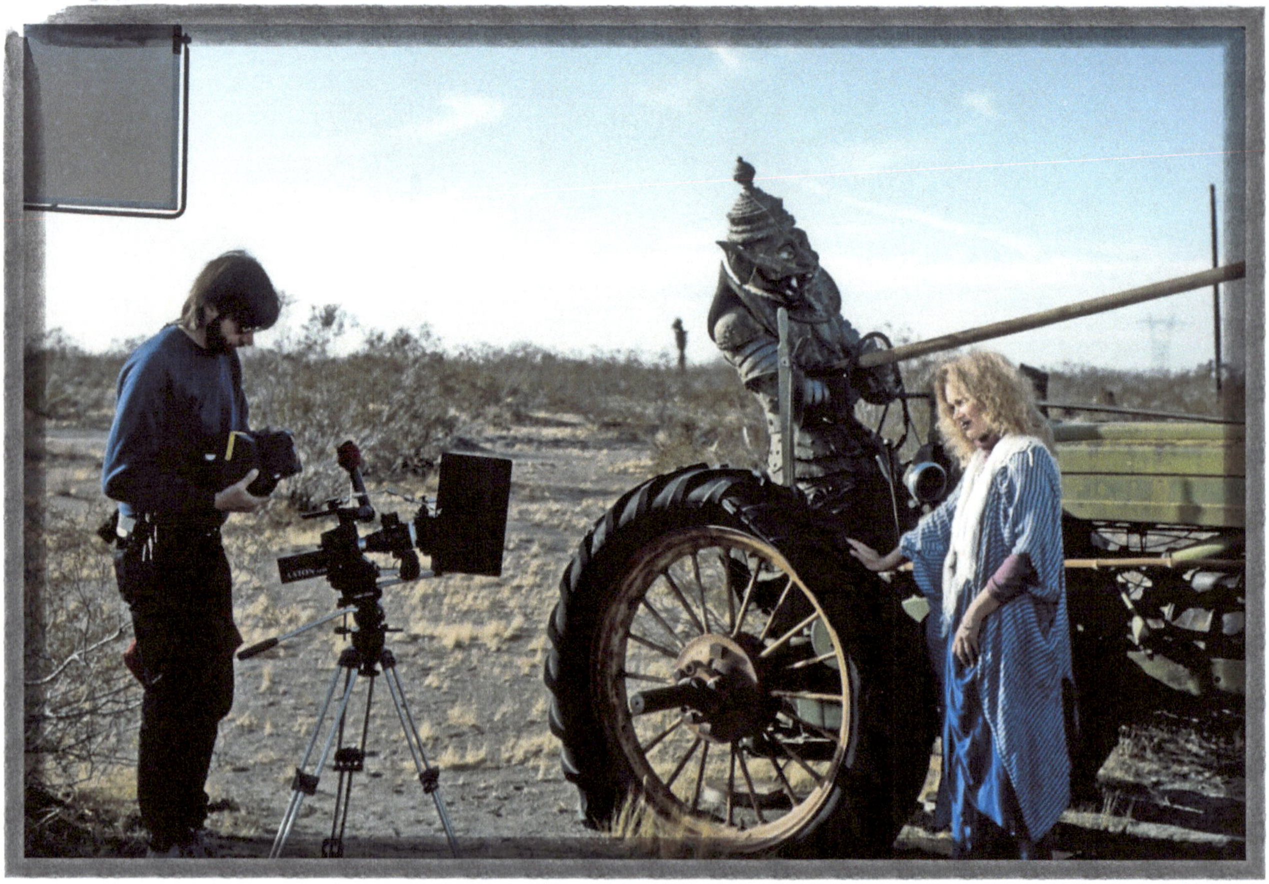

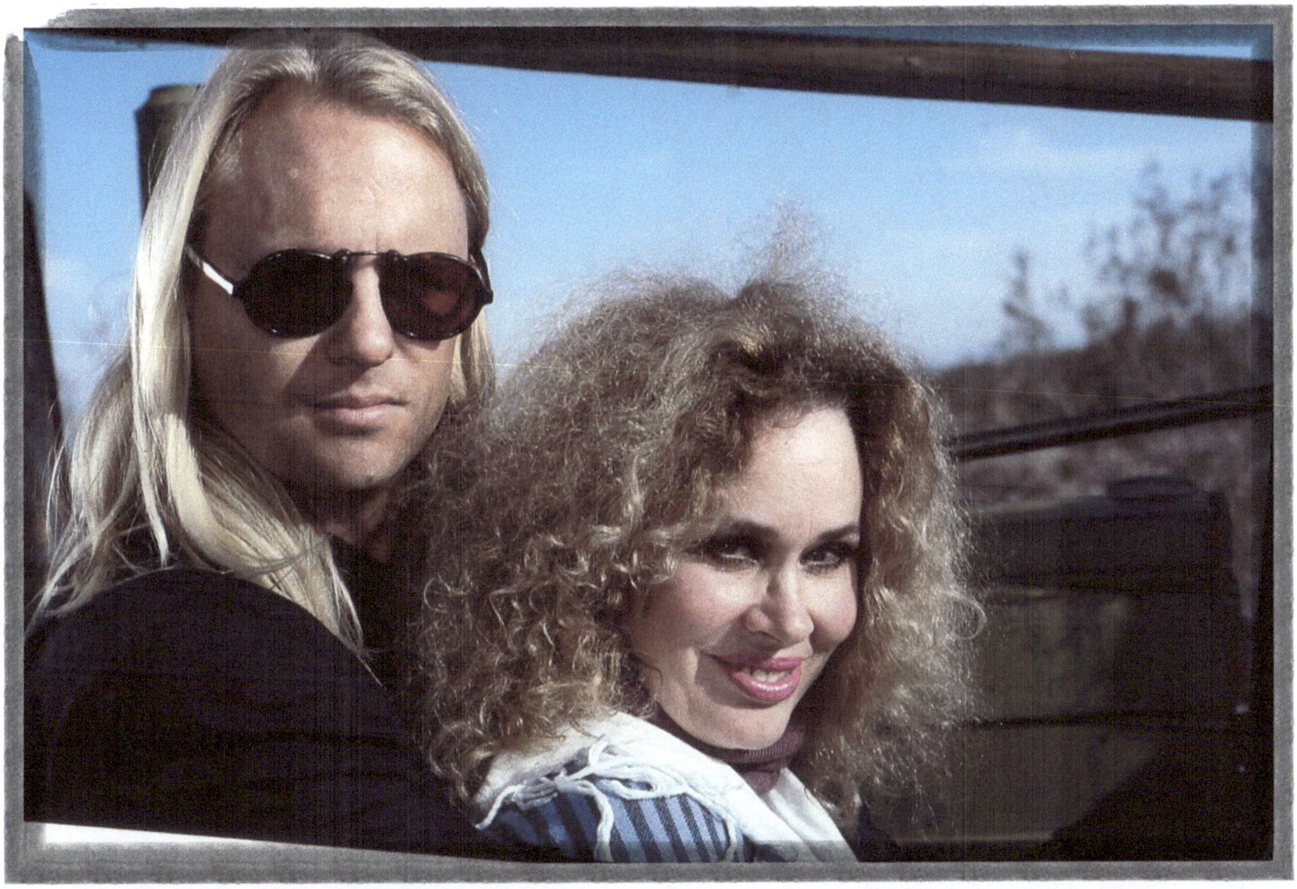

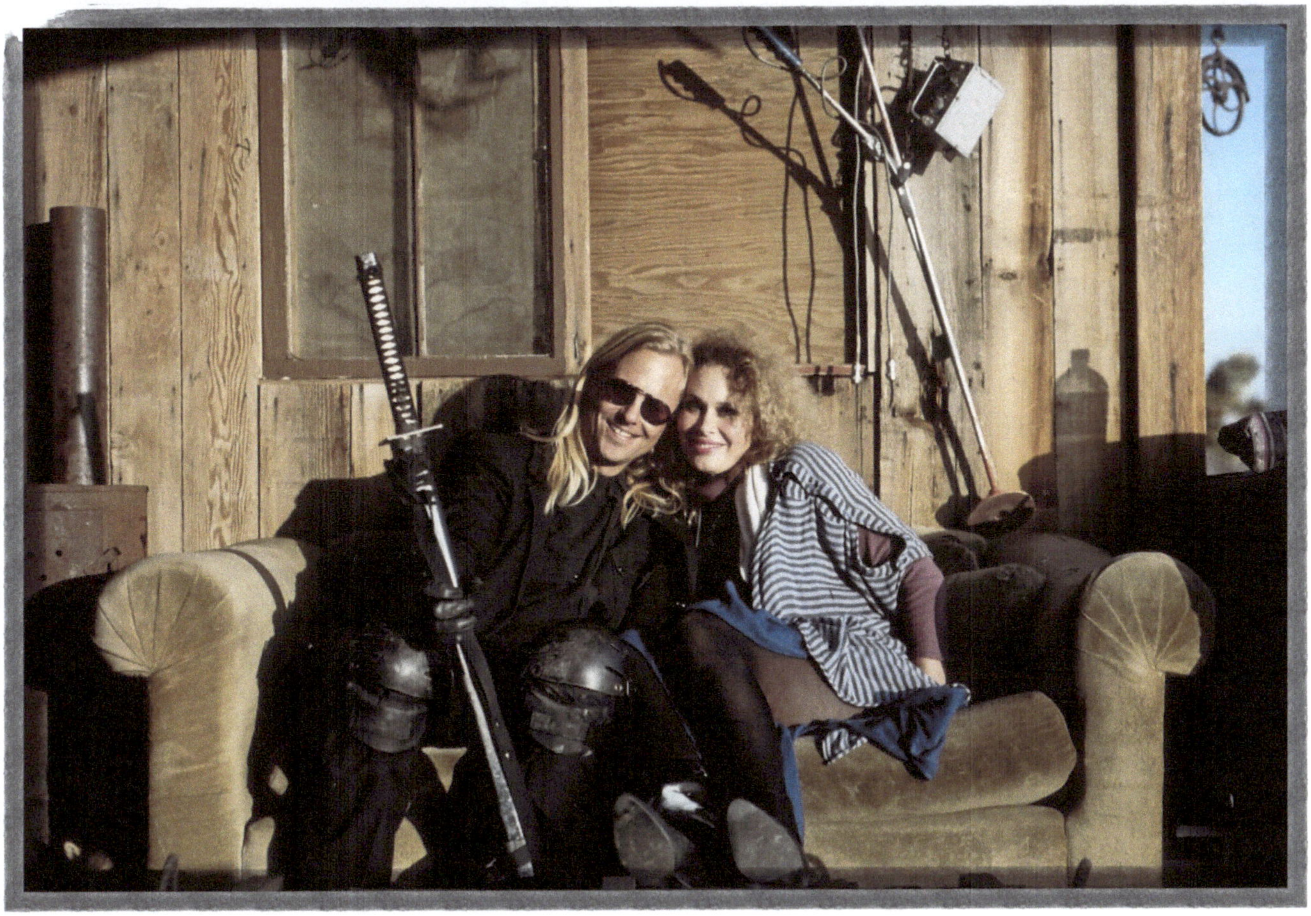

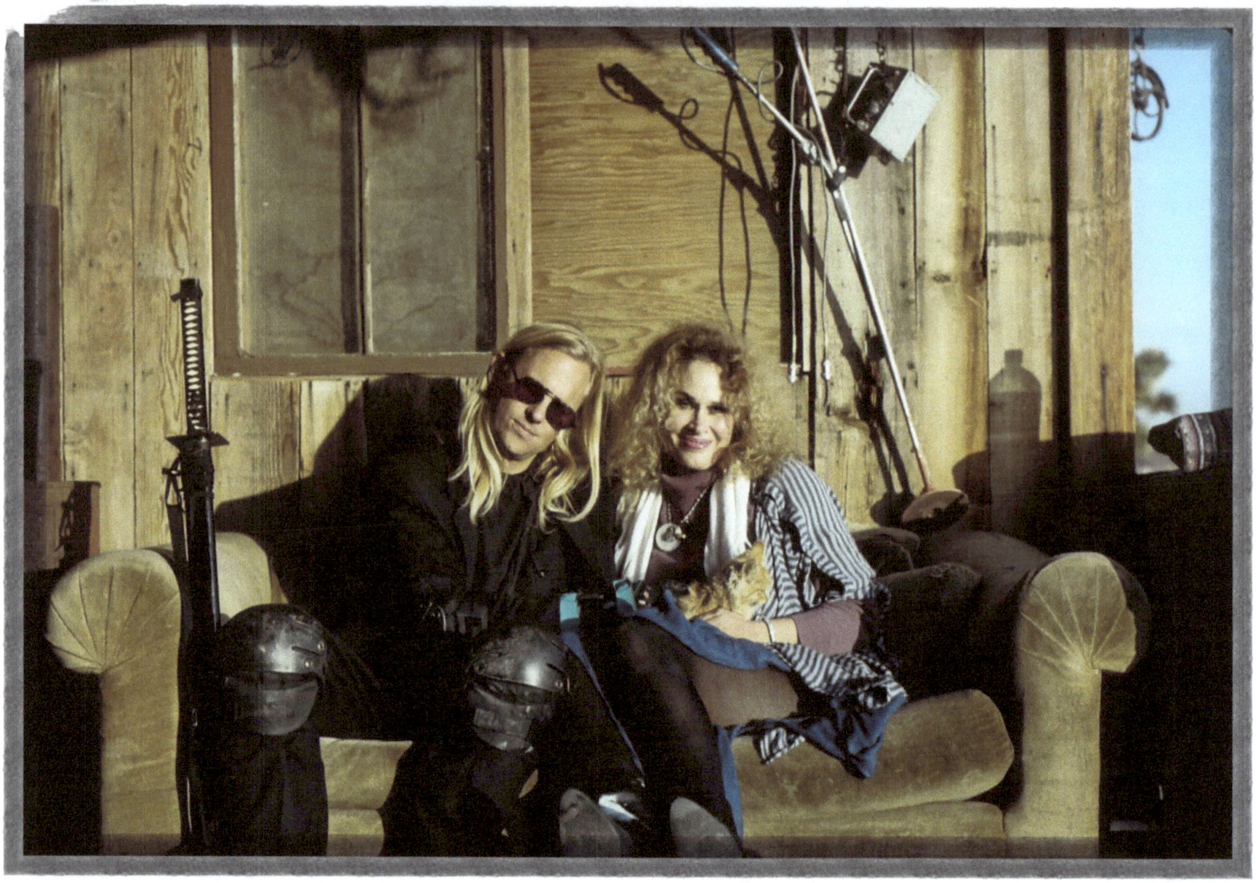

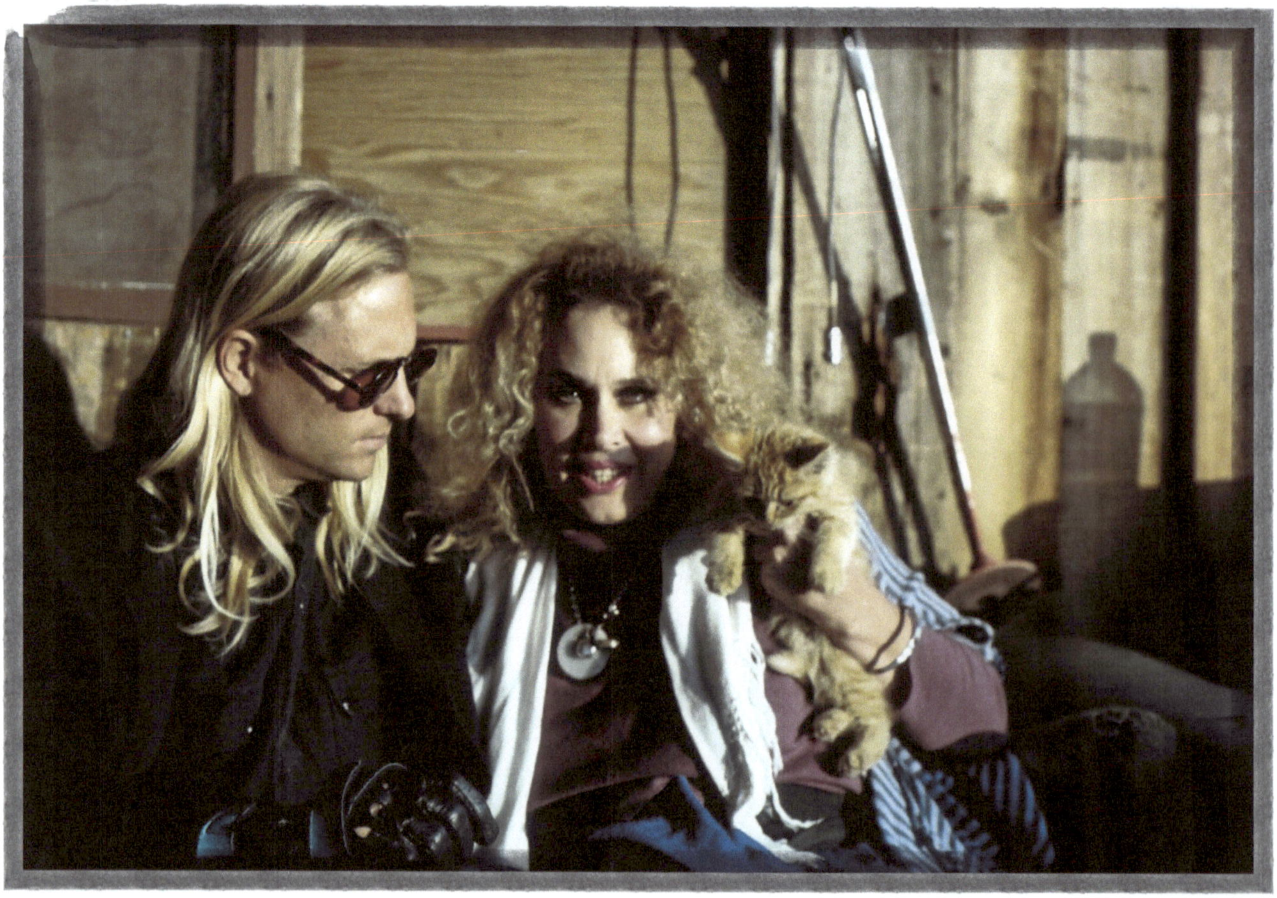

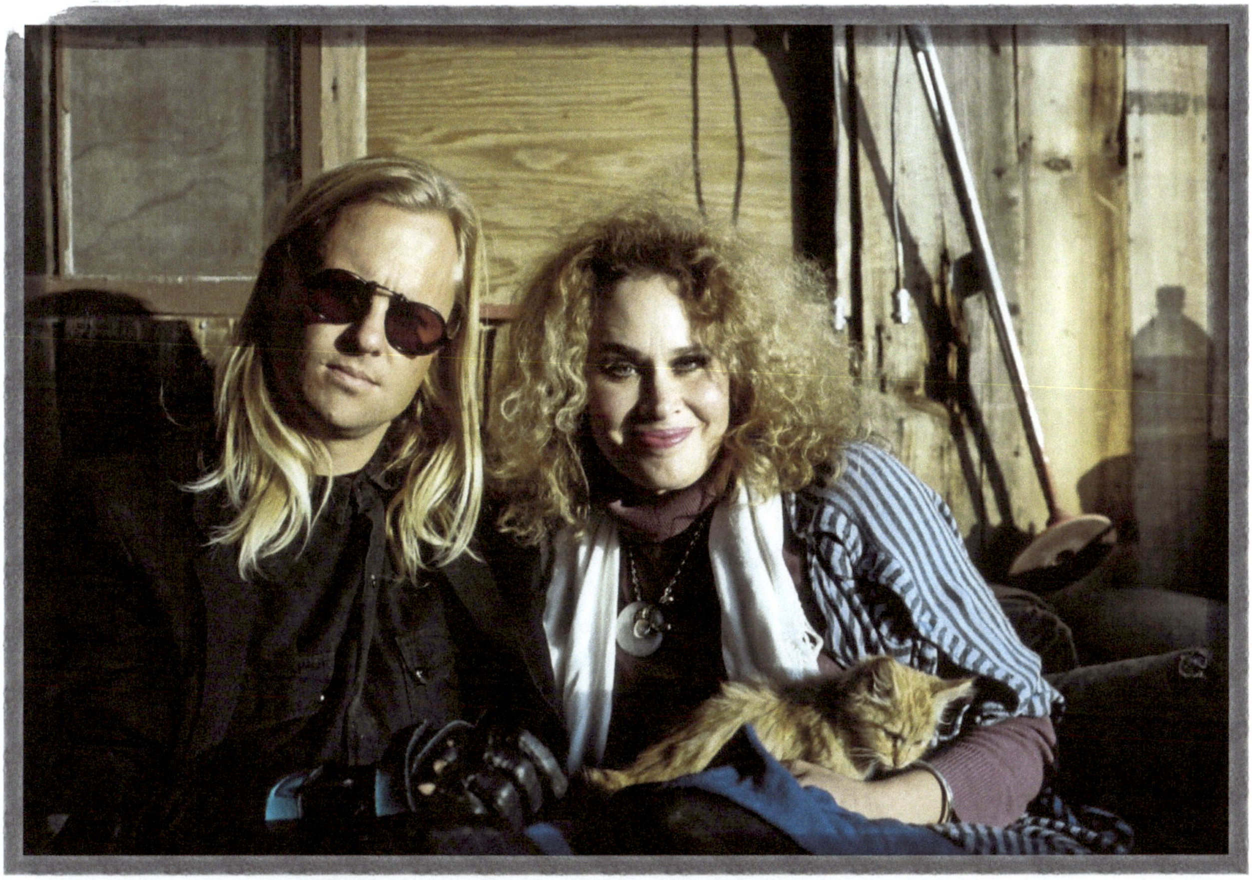

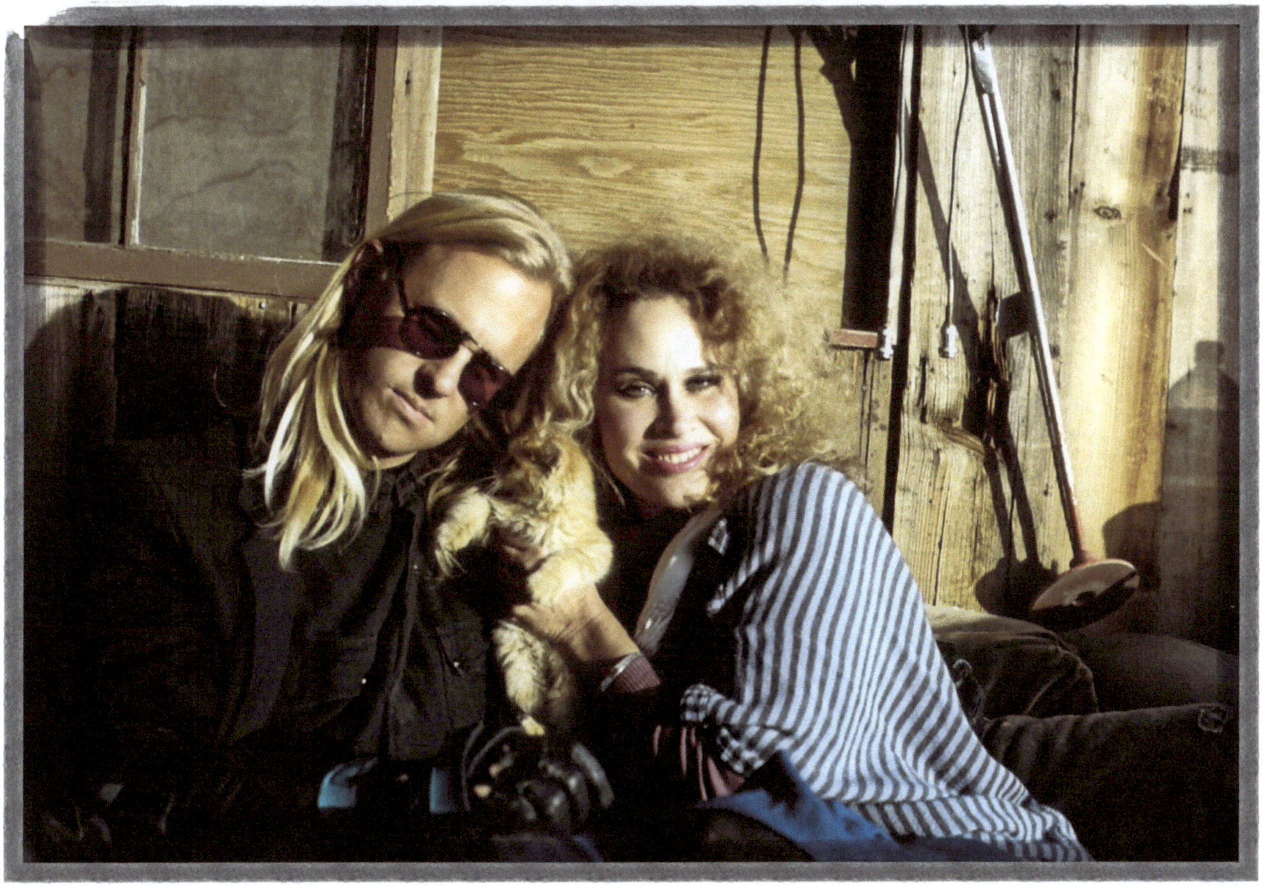

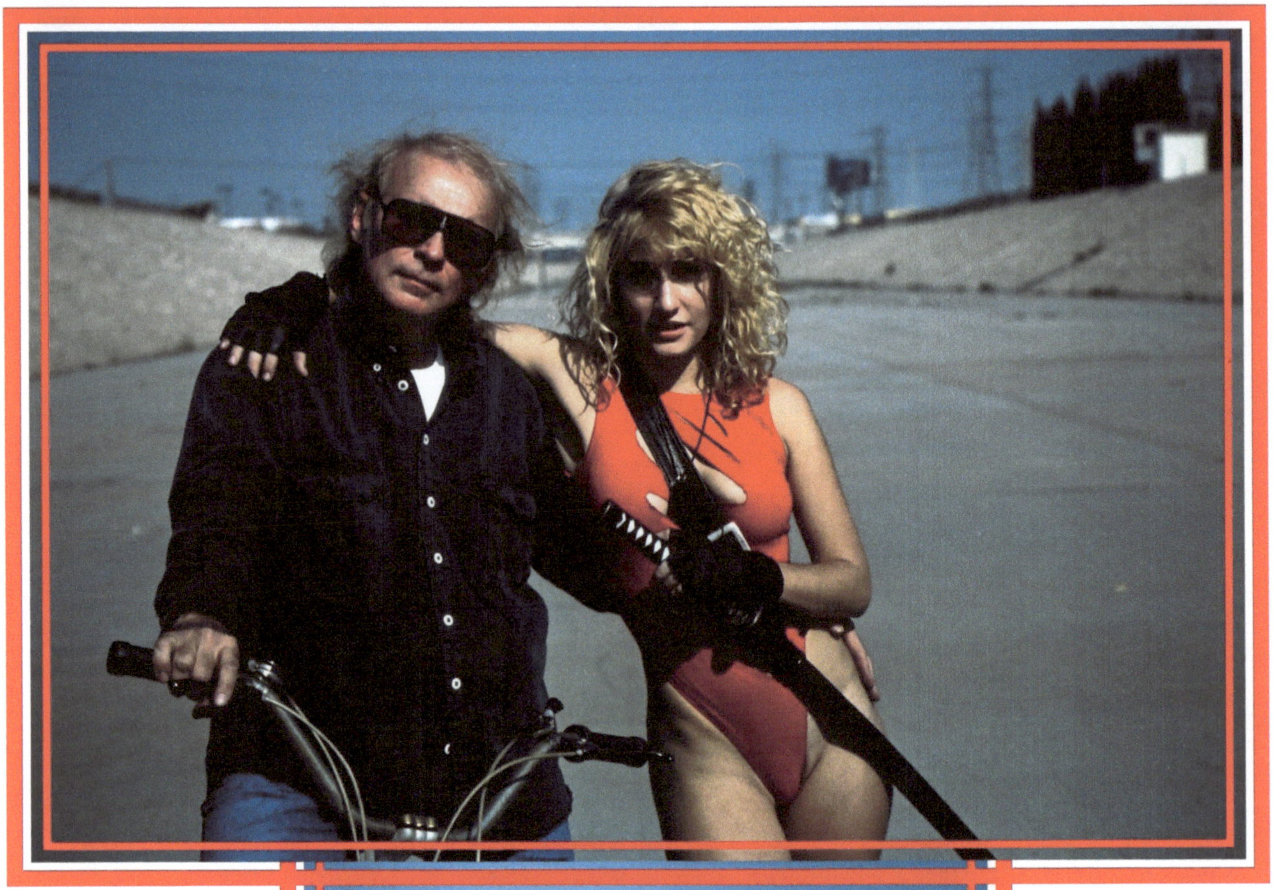

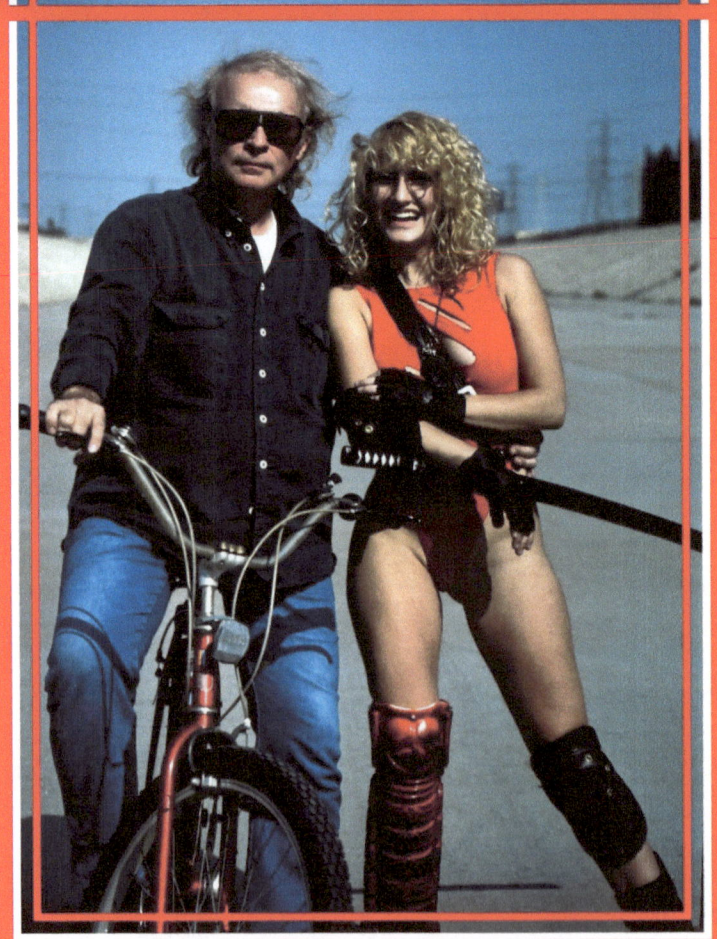

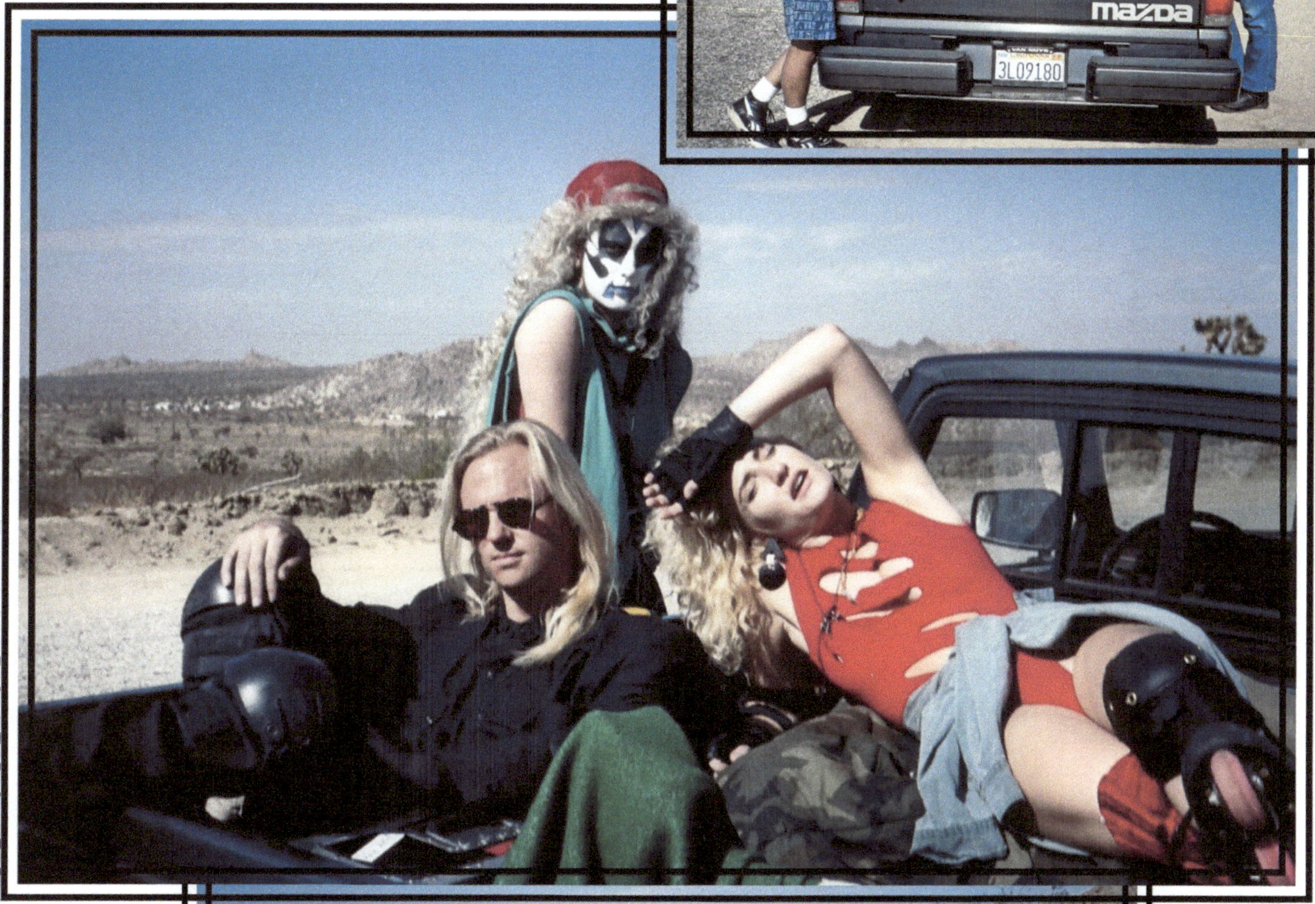

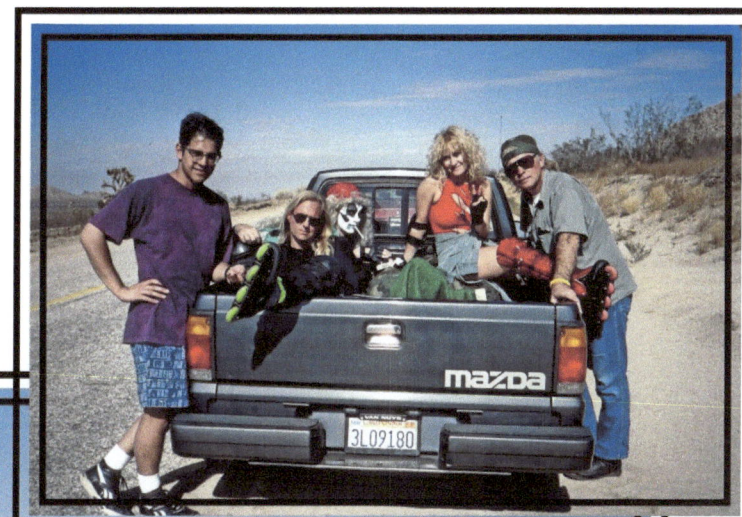
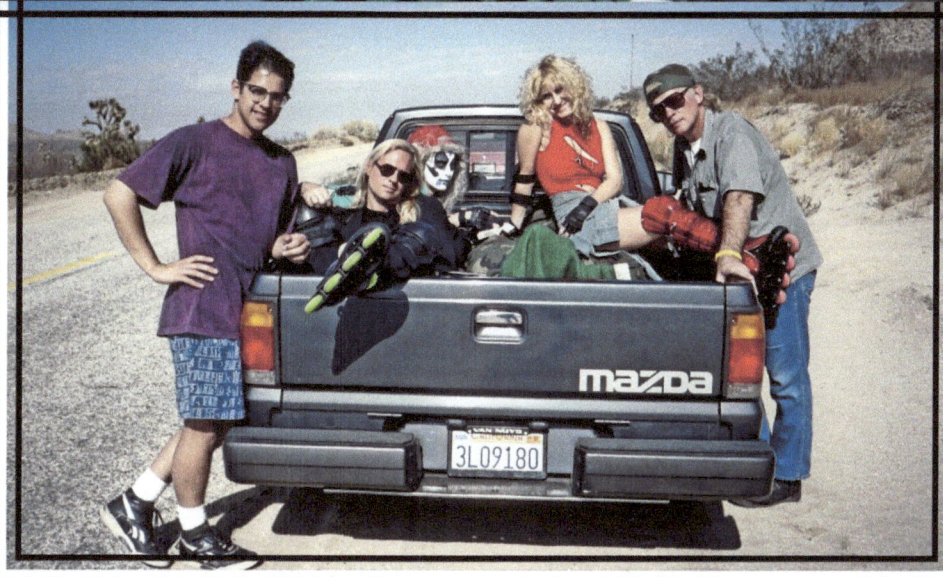

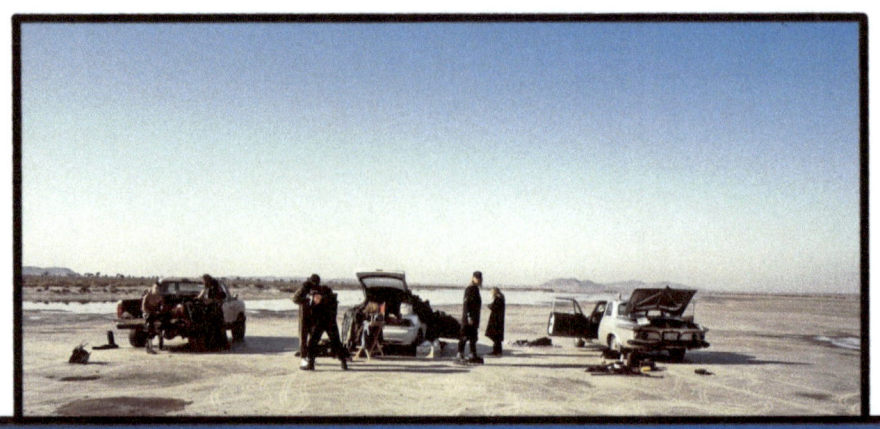

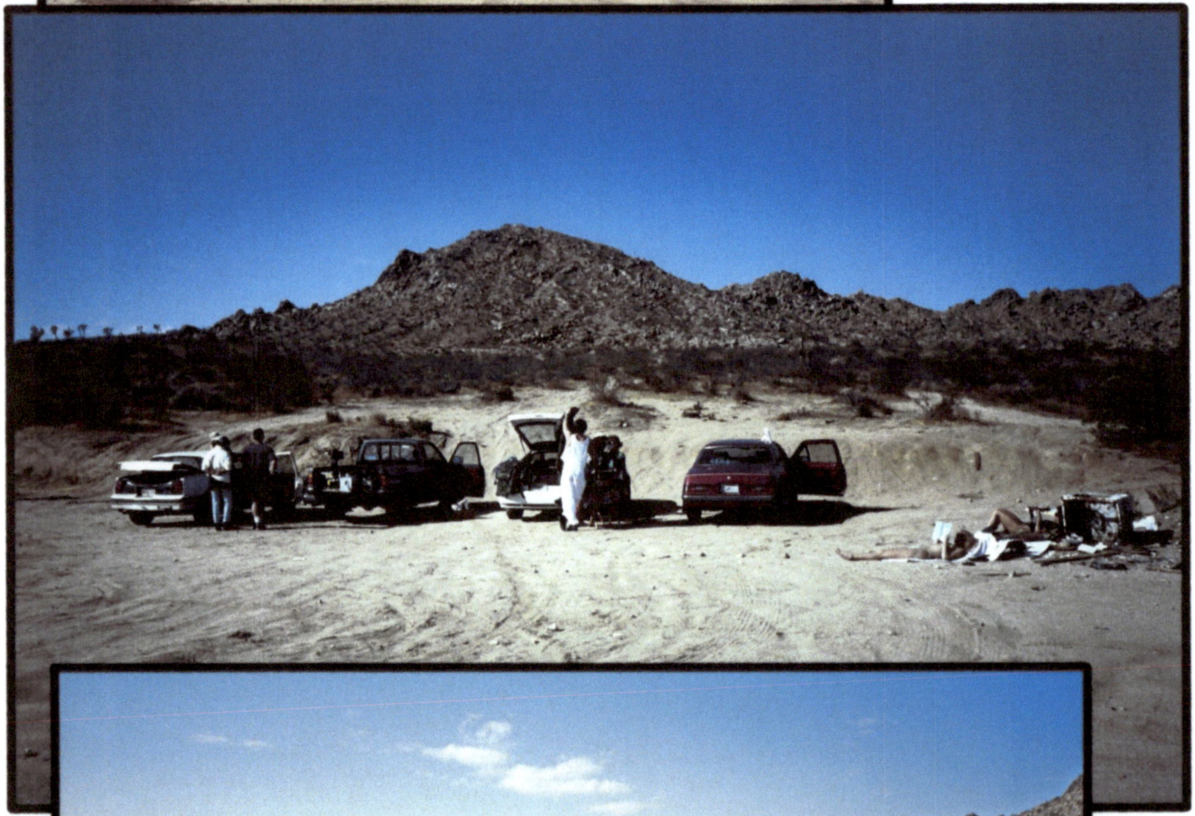

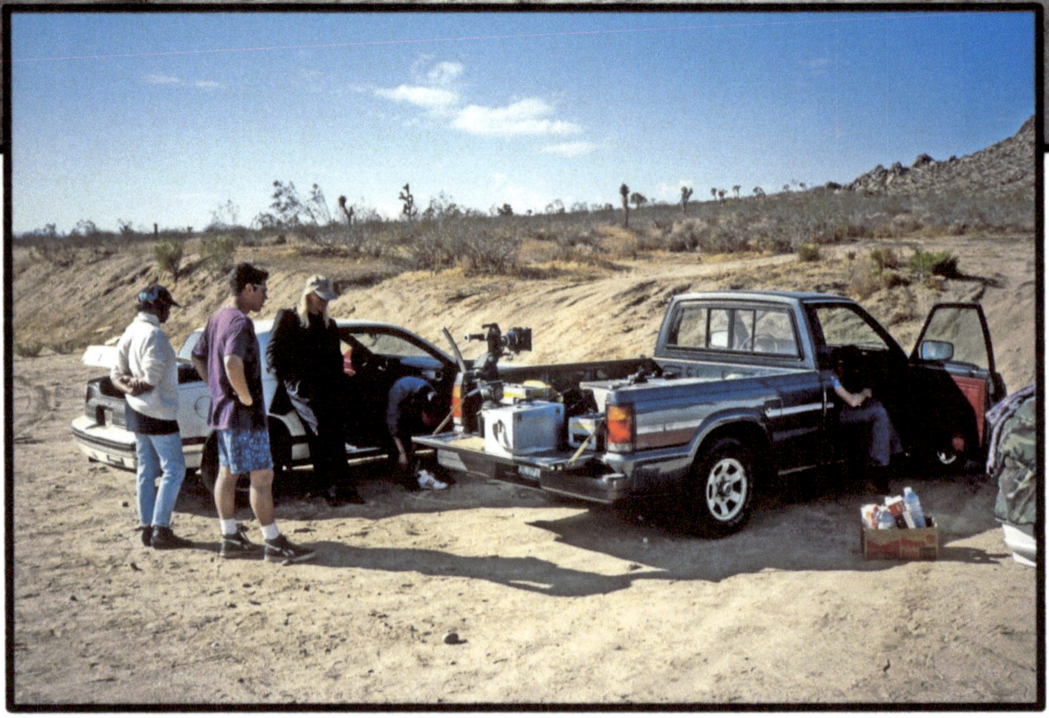

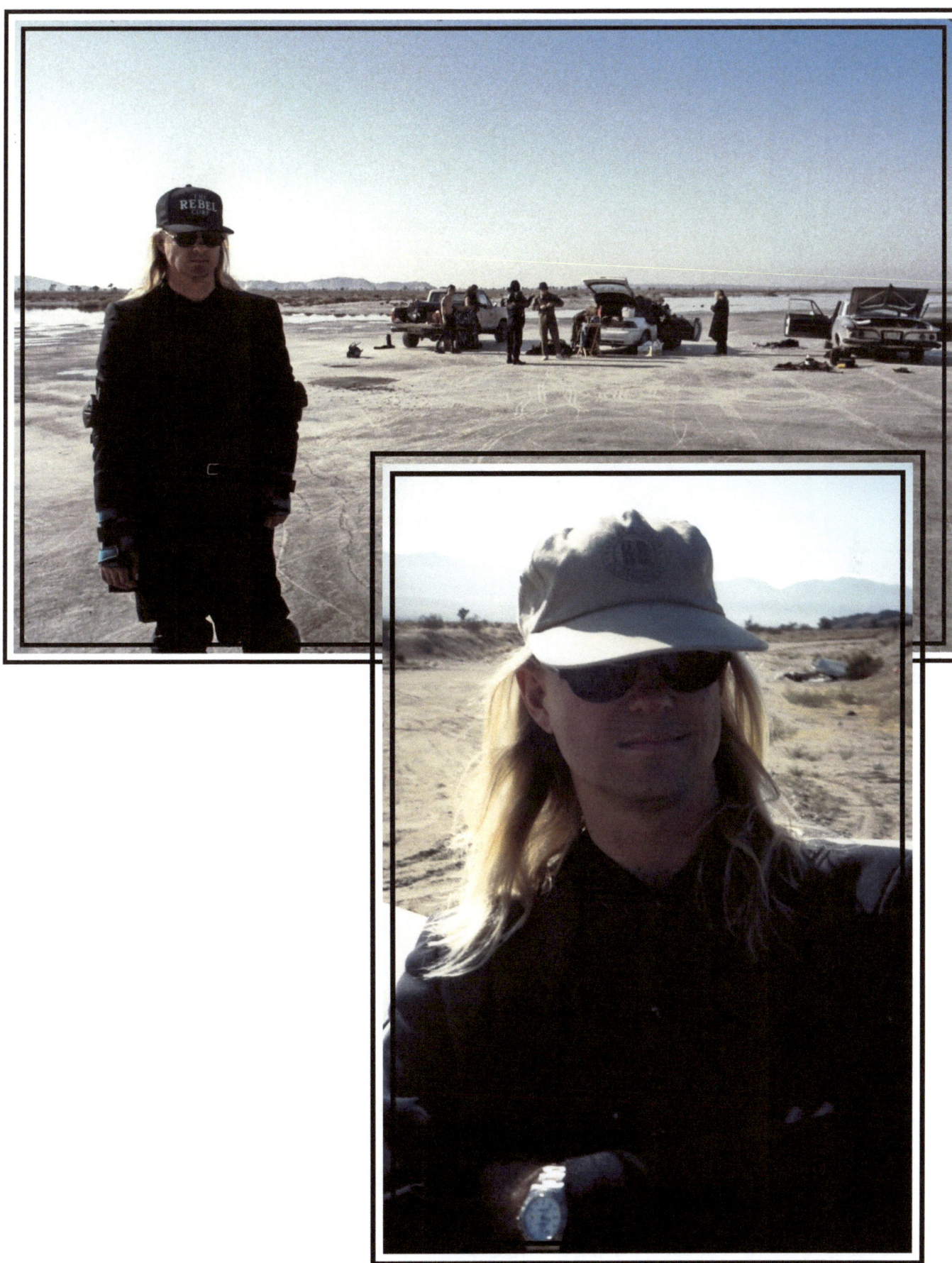

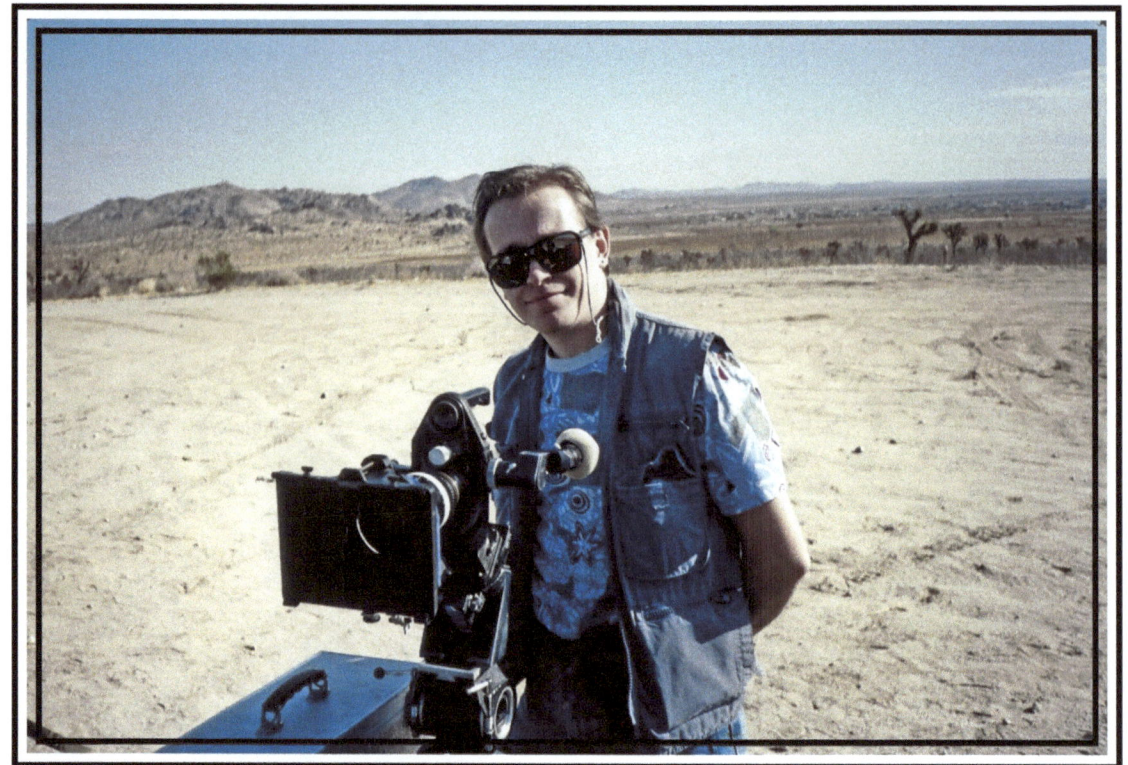

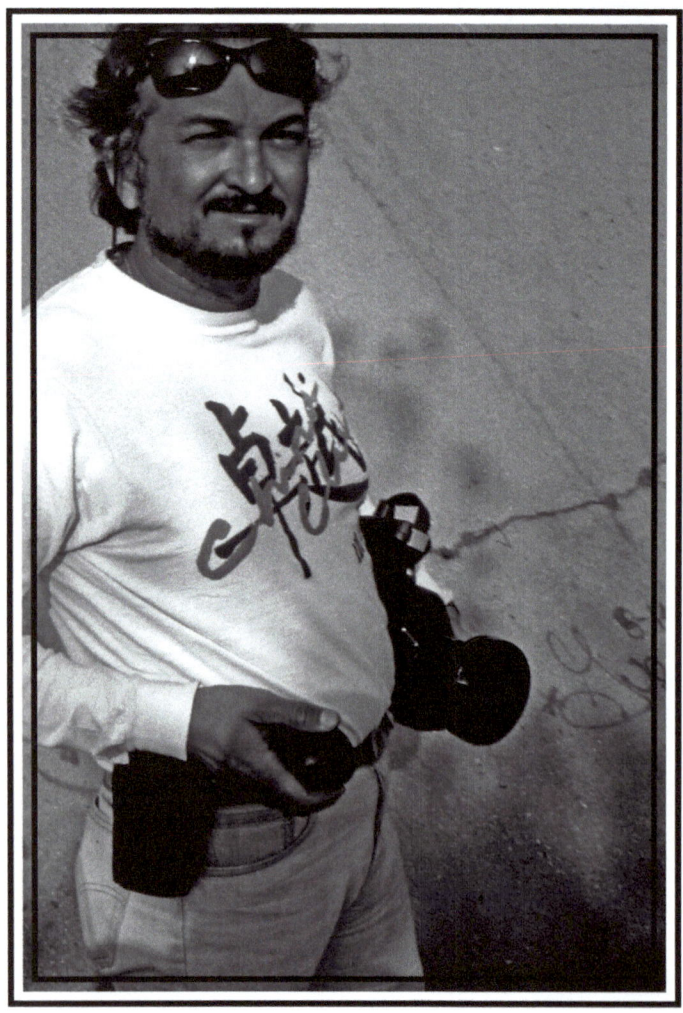

SERGIO CORO
ASSISTANT CAMERA

Future Director of Photography
for
Samurai Vampire Bikers from Hell.

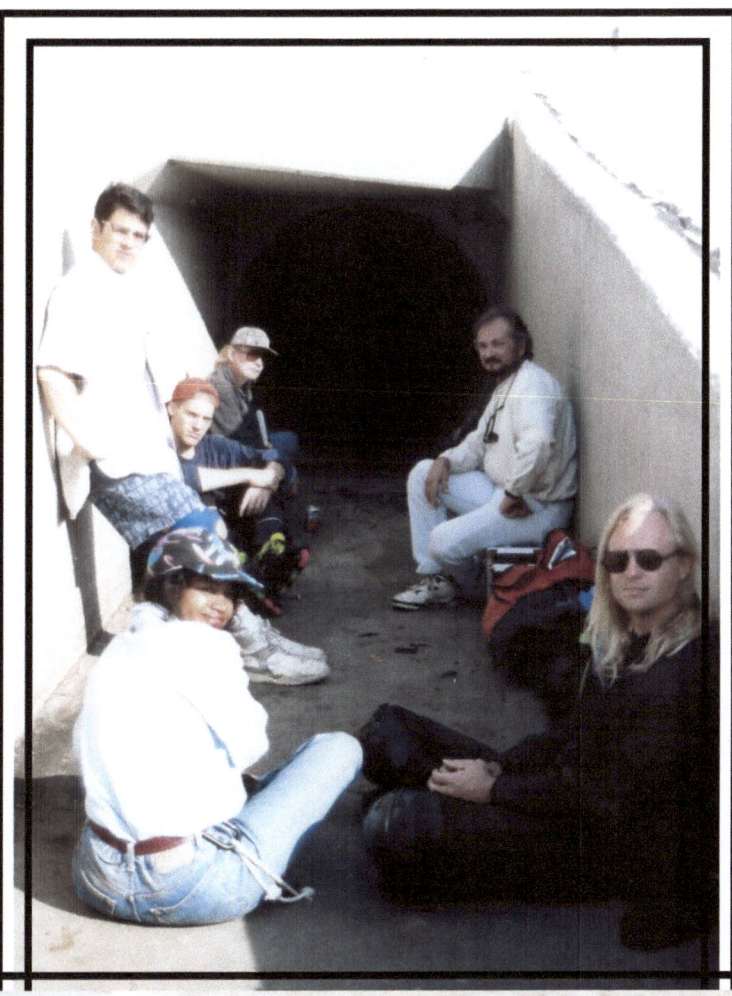
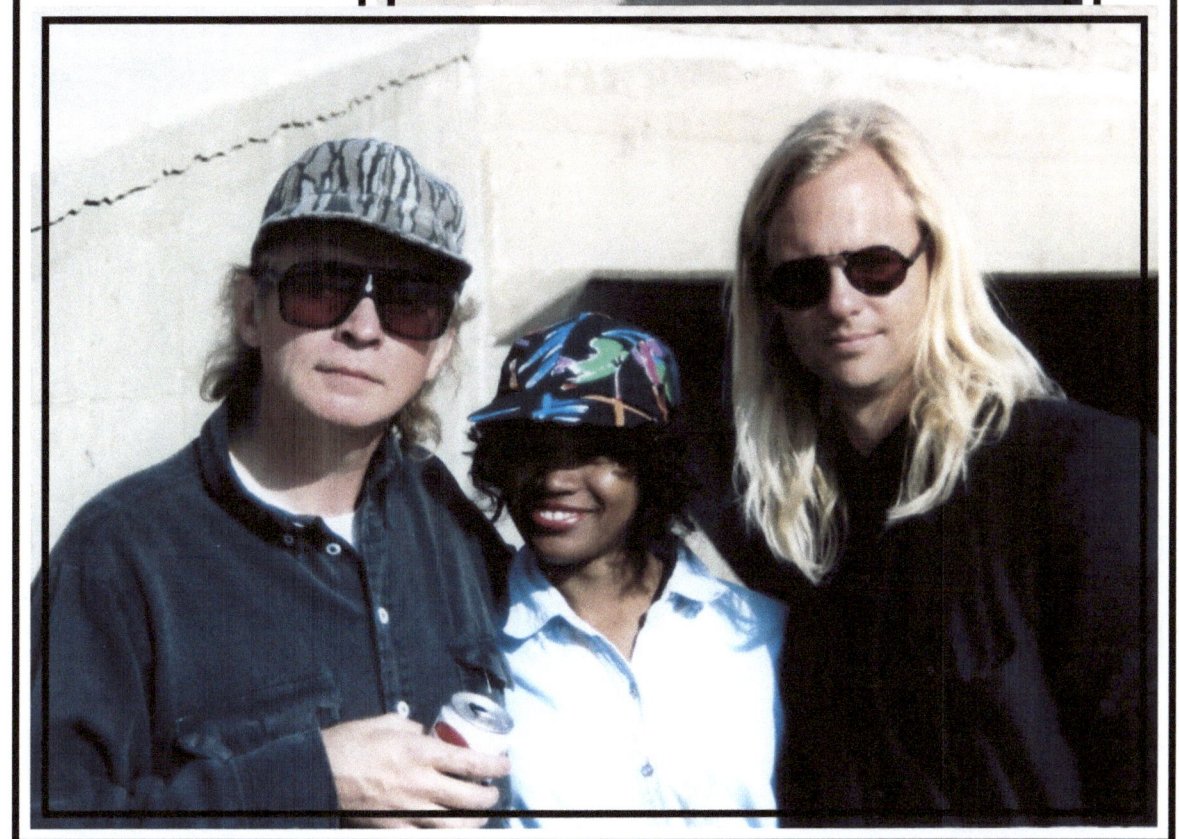

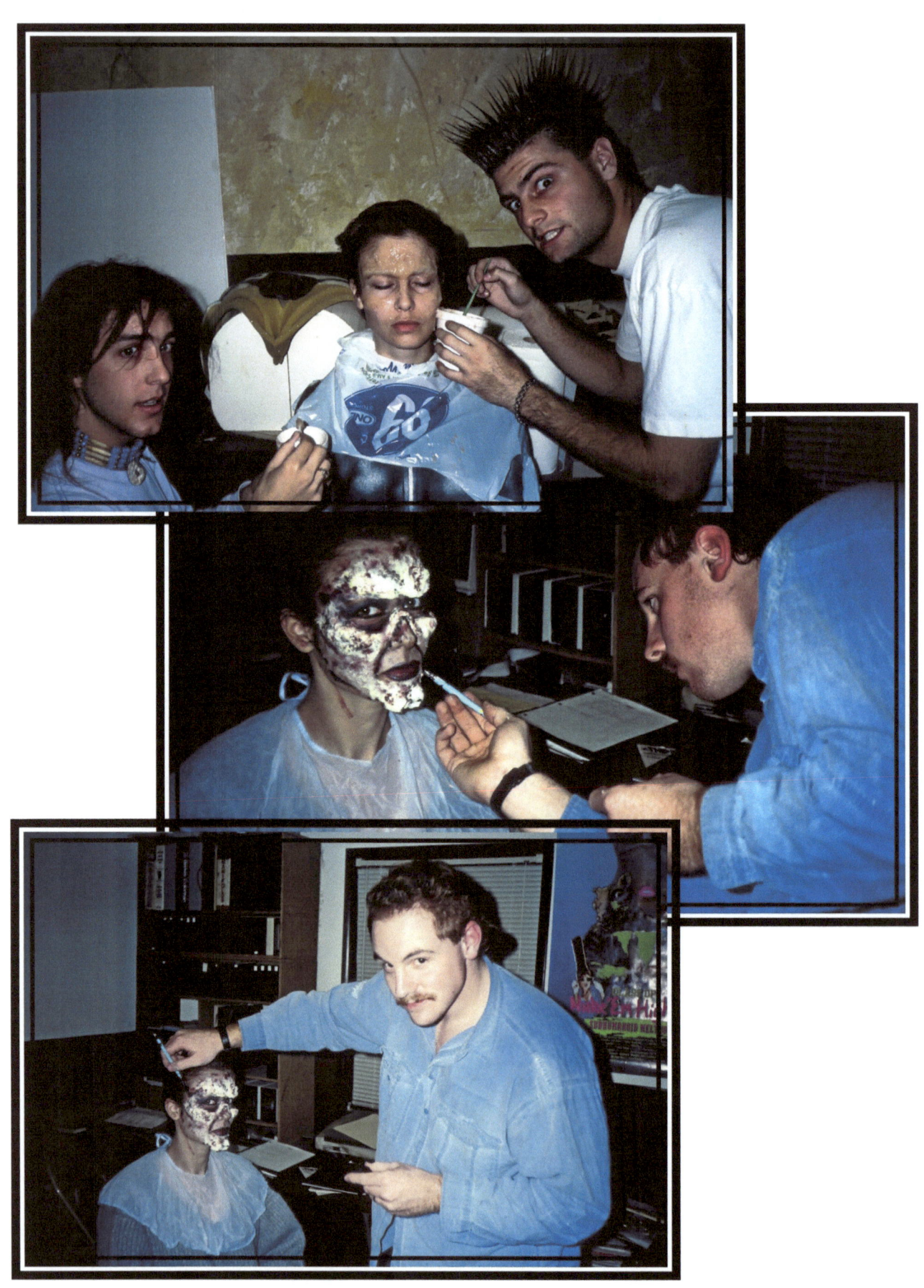

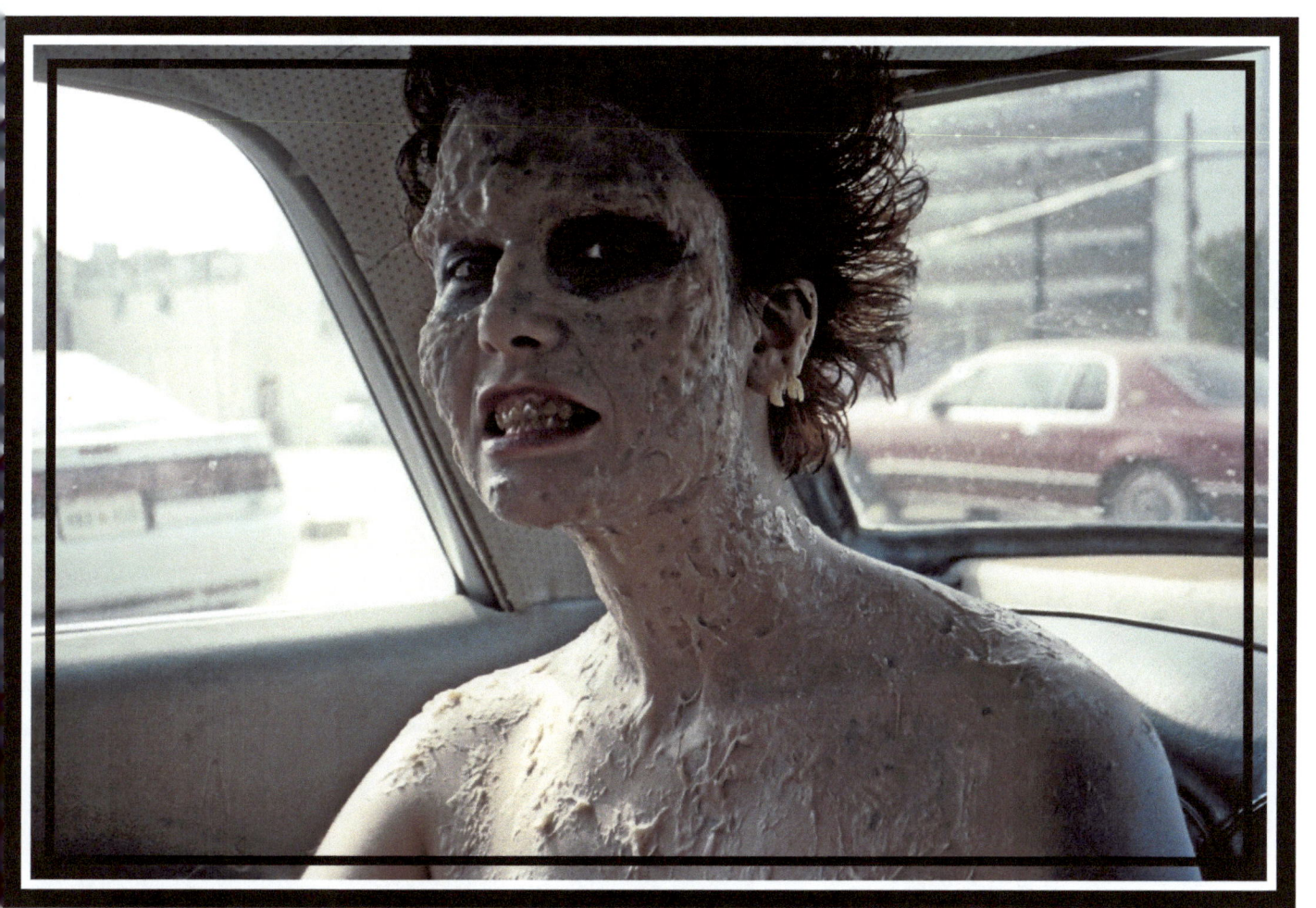

ZONA JAGUAR AS ONIBABA

"Devil Demon Doll Disciple from Hell."

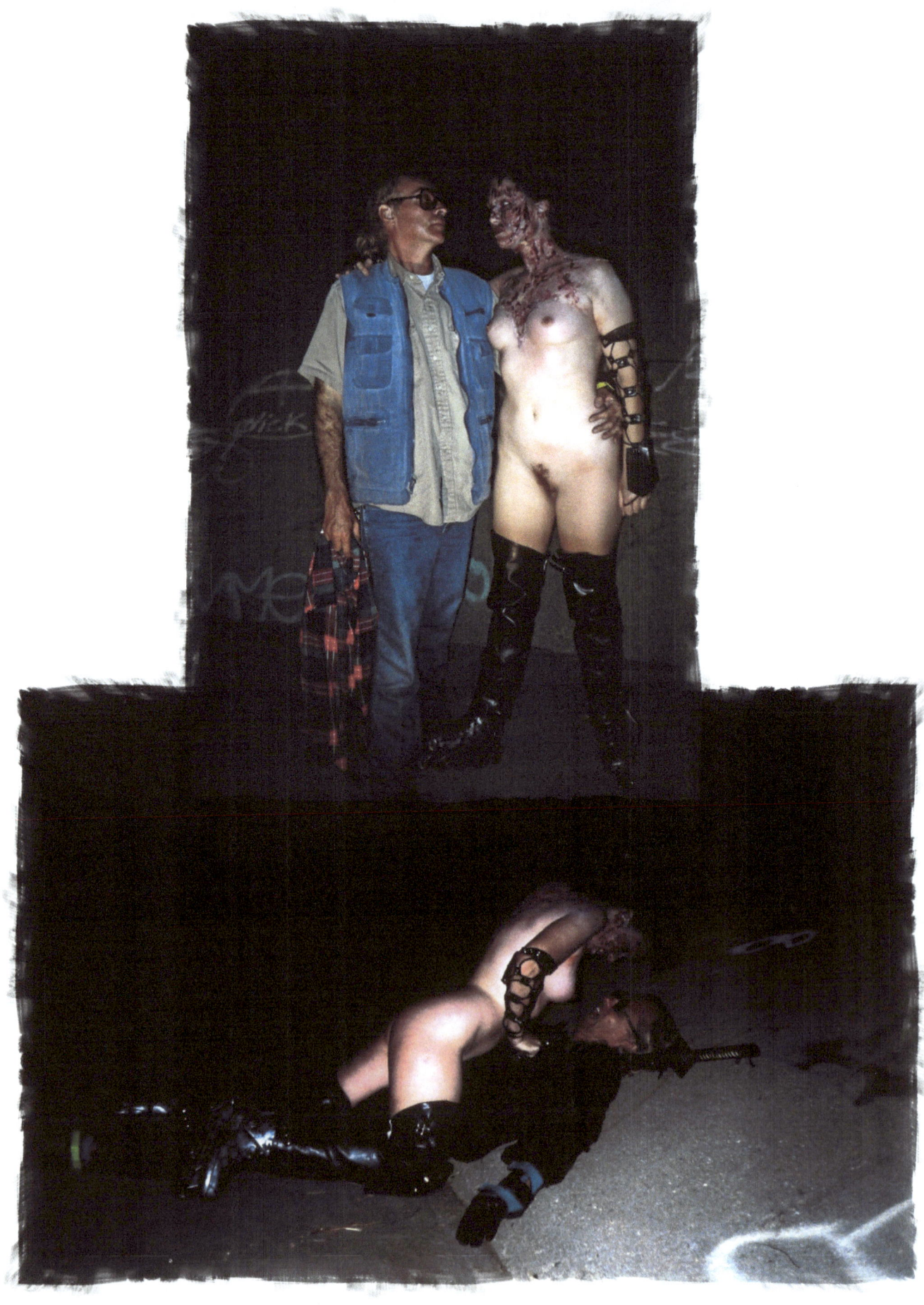

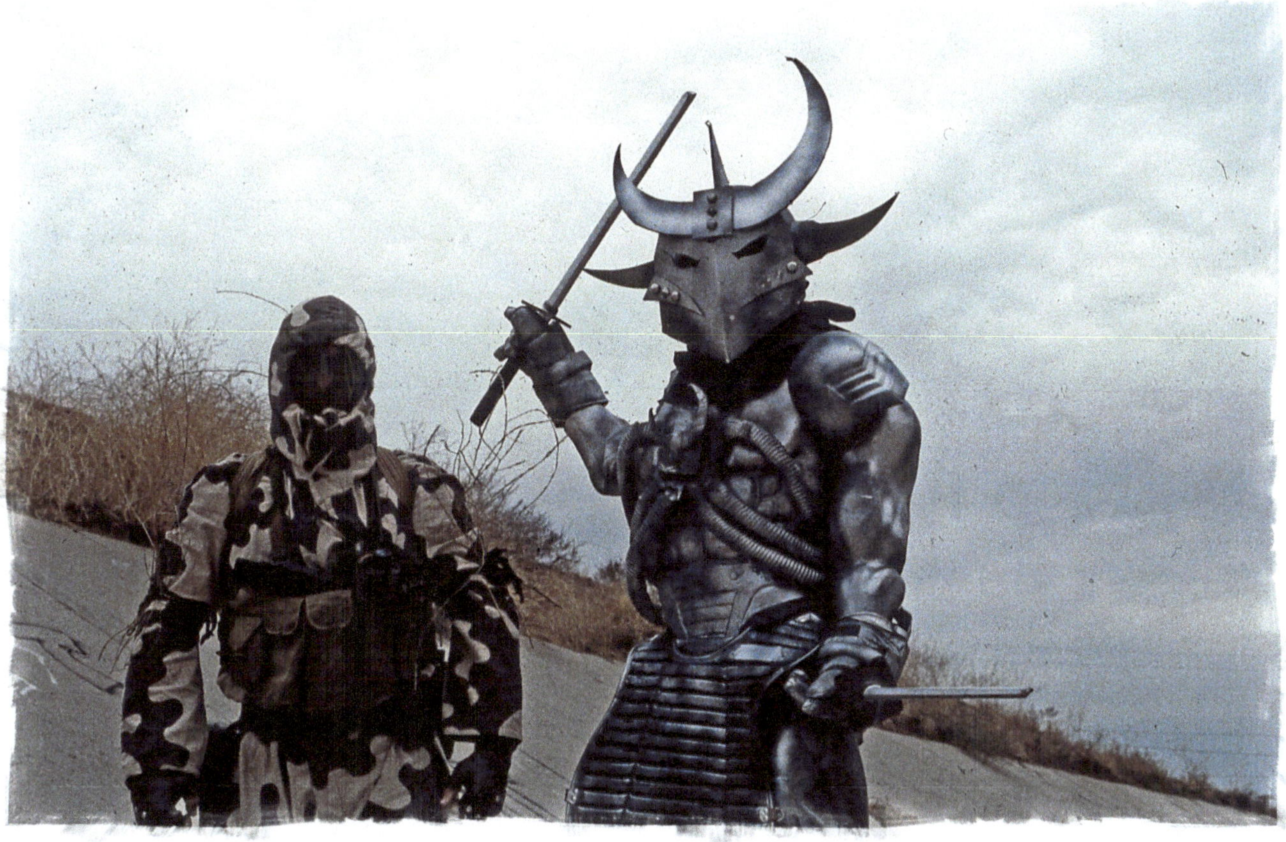

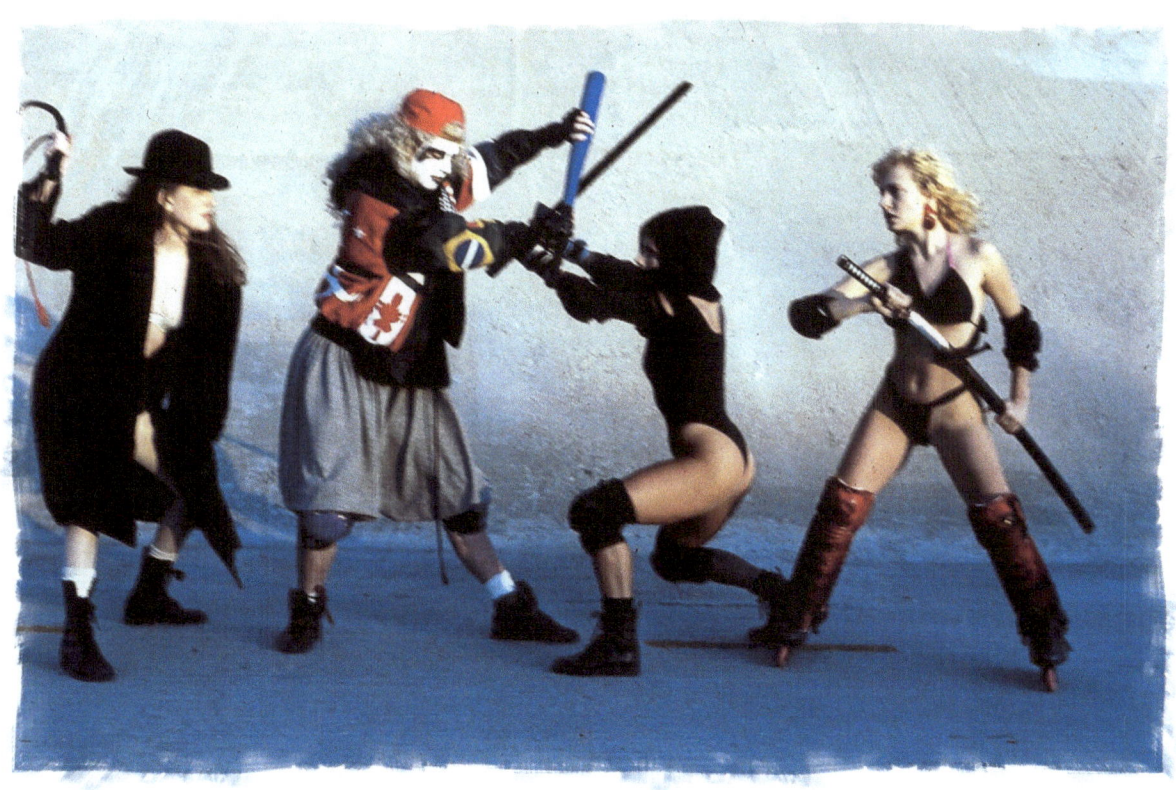

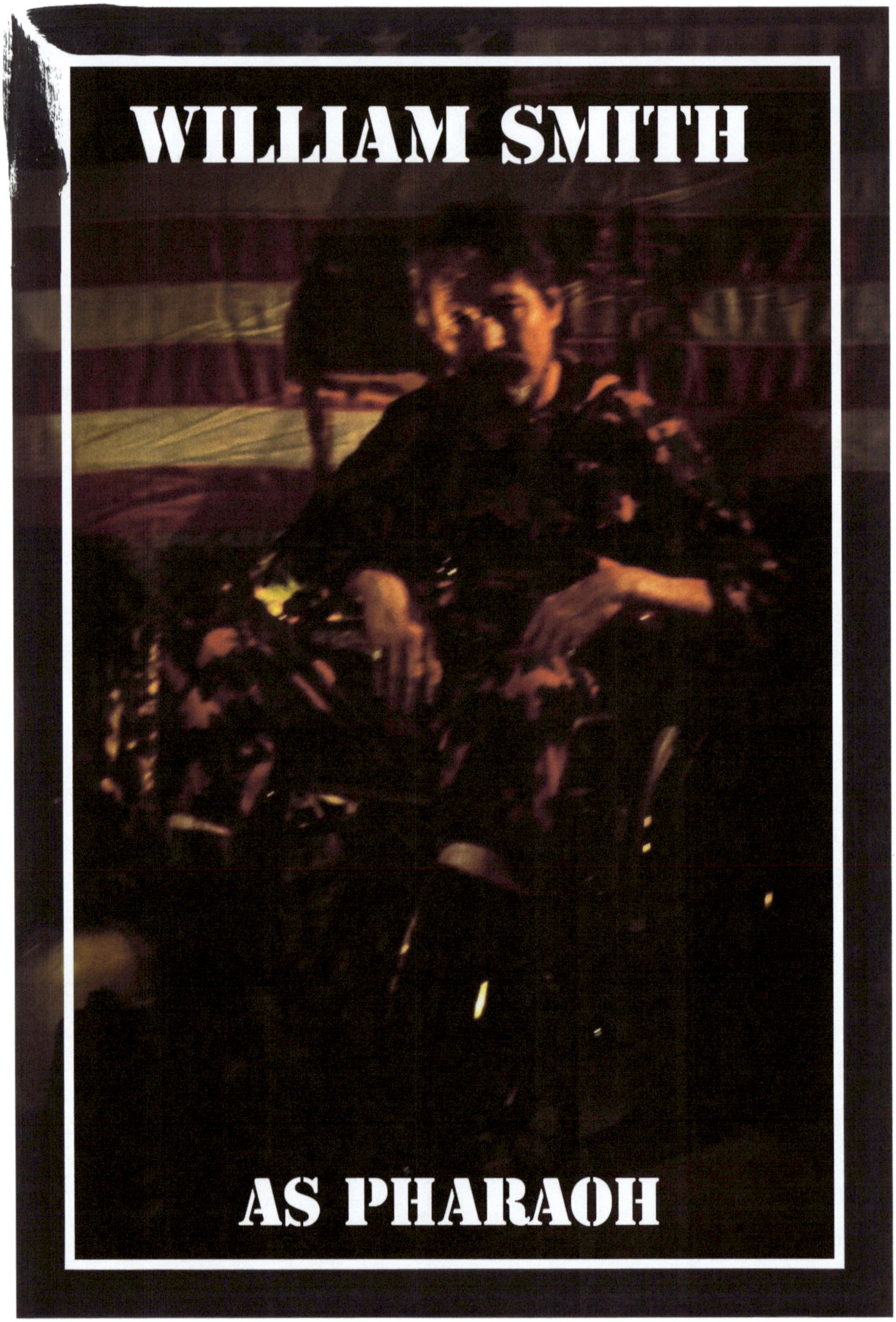

WILLIAM SMITH

AS PHARAOH

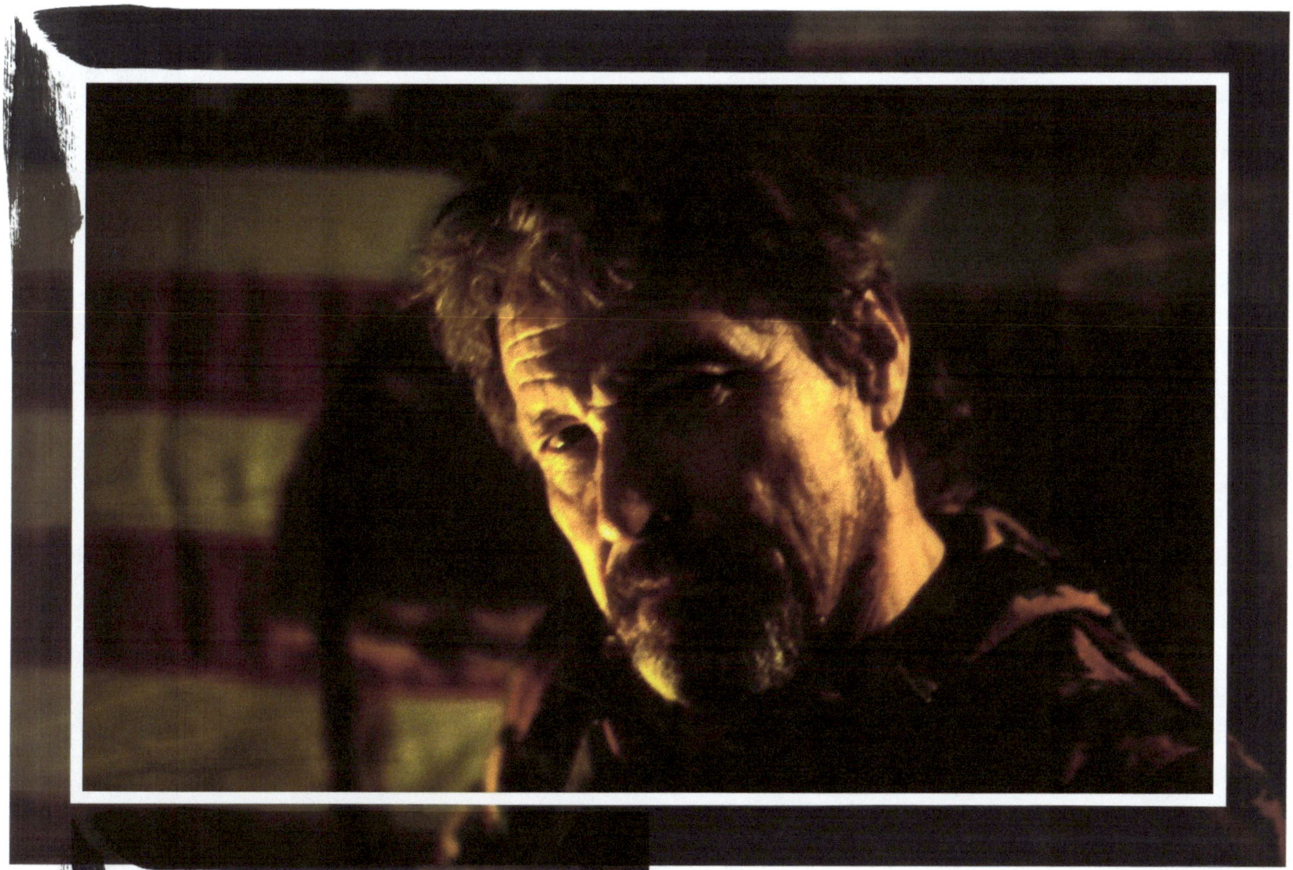

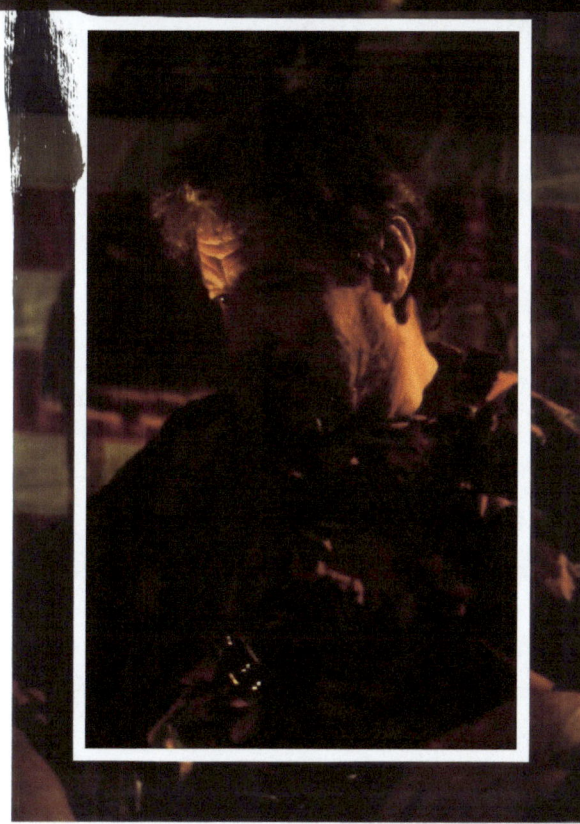

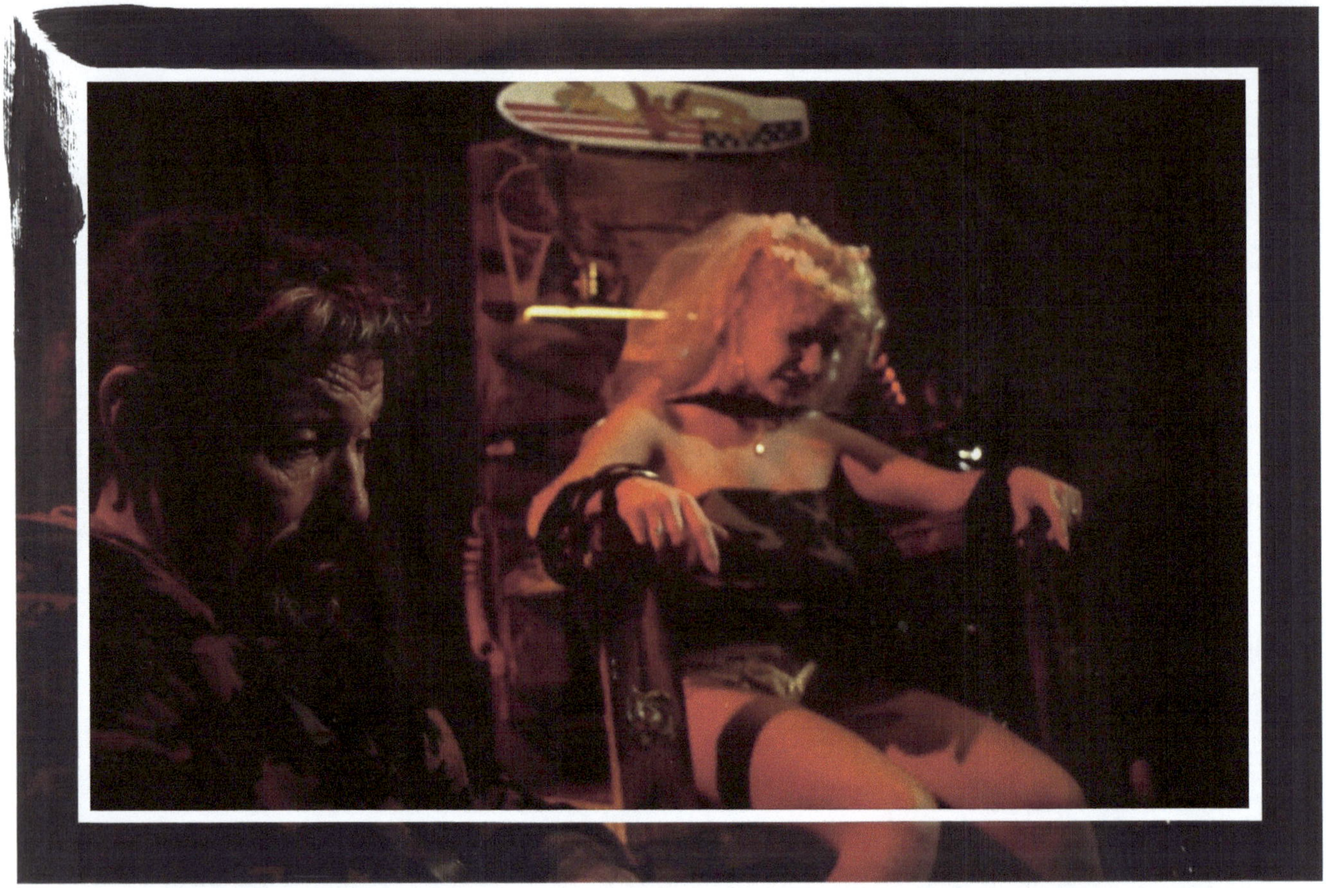

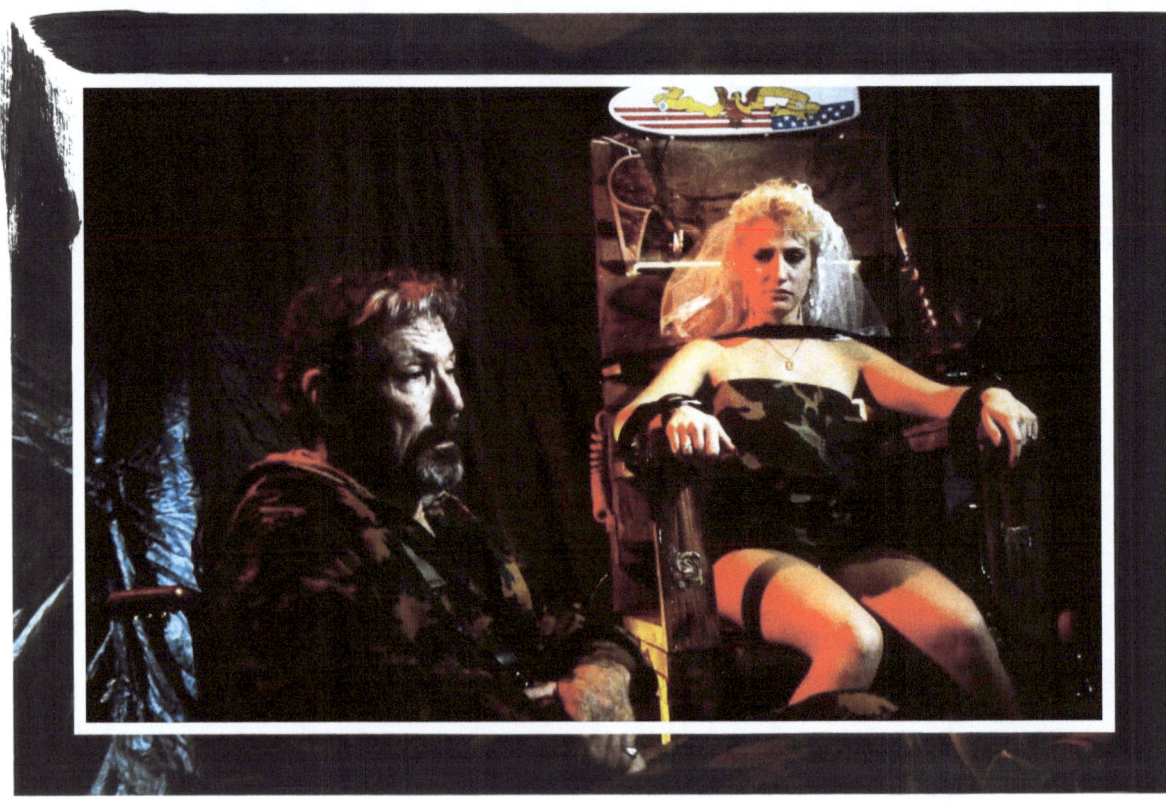

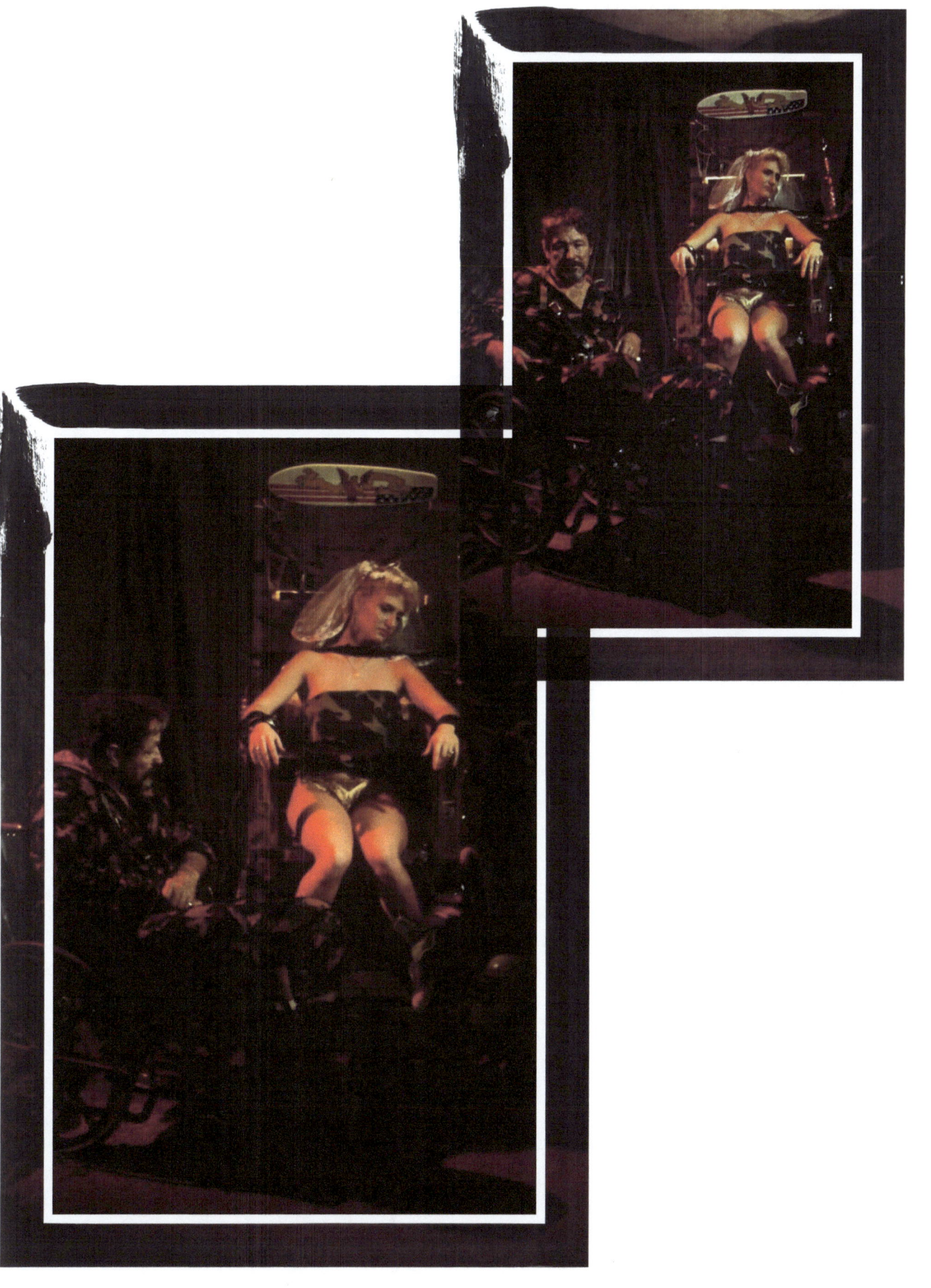

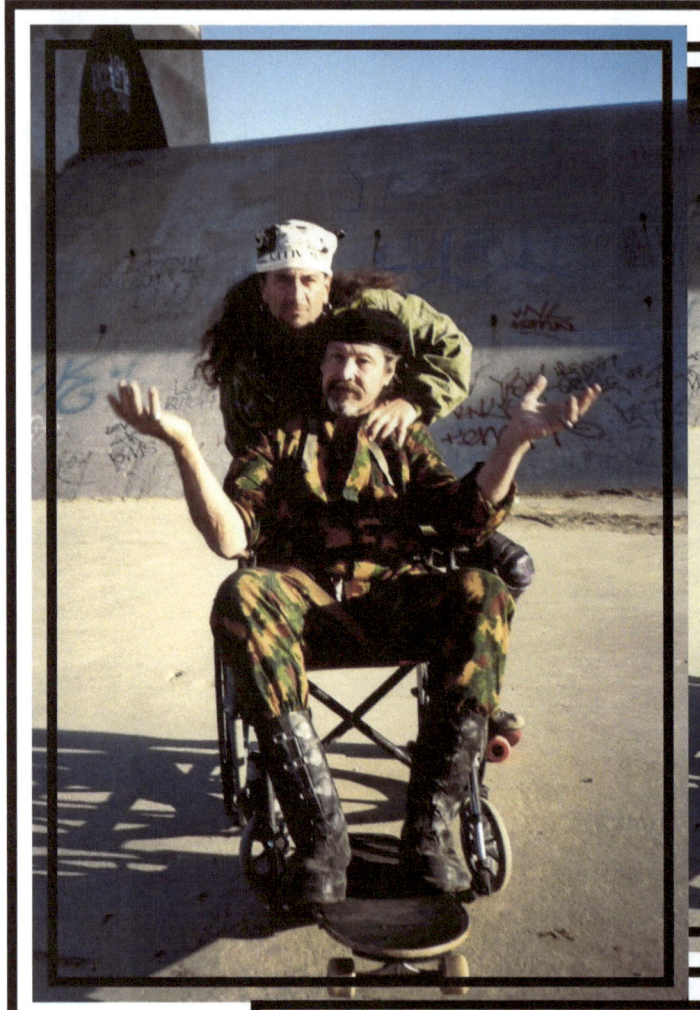
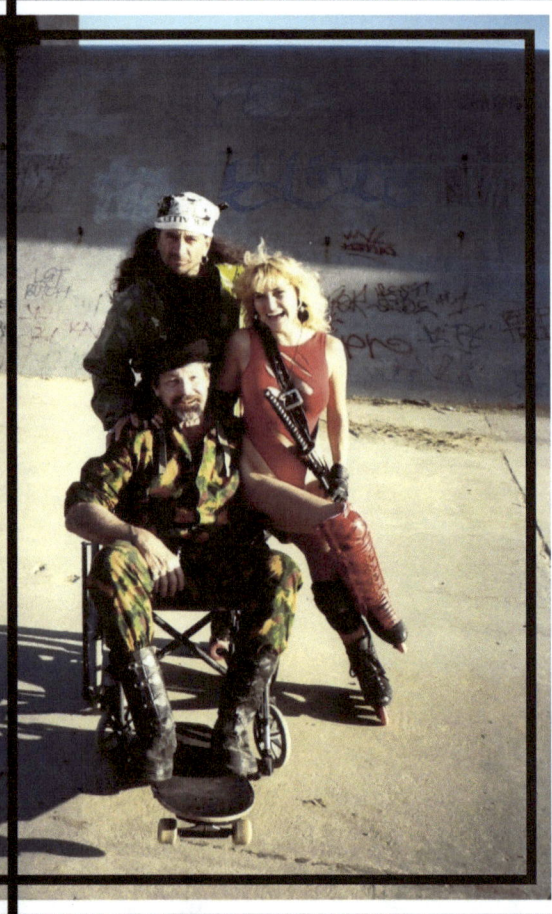
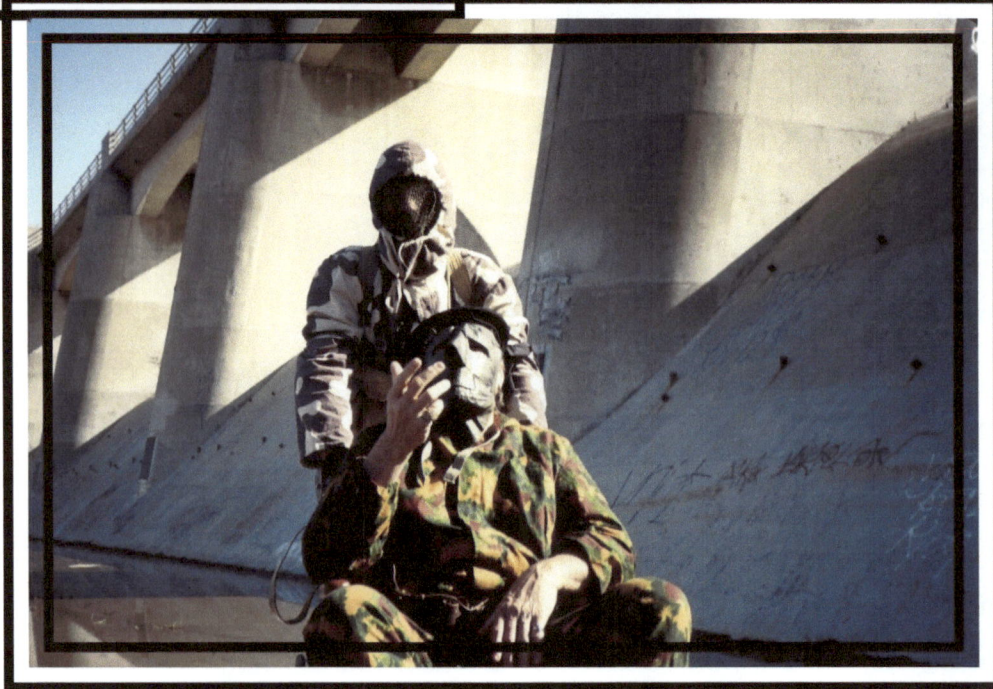

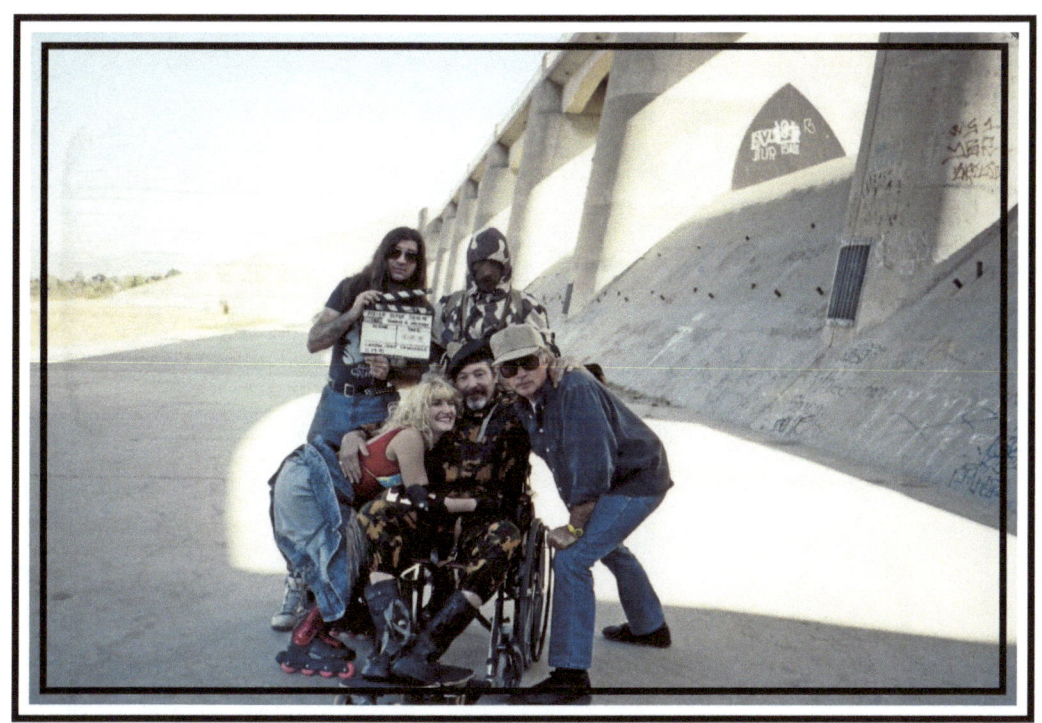

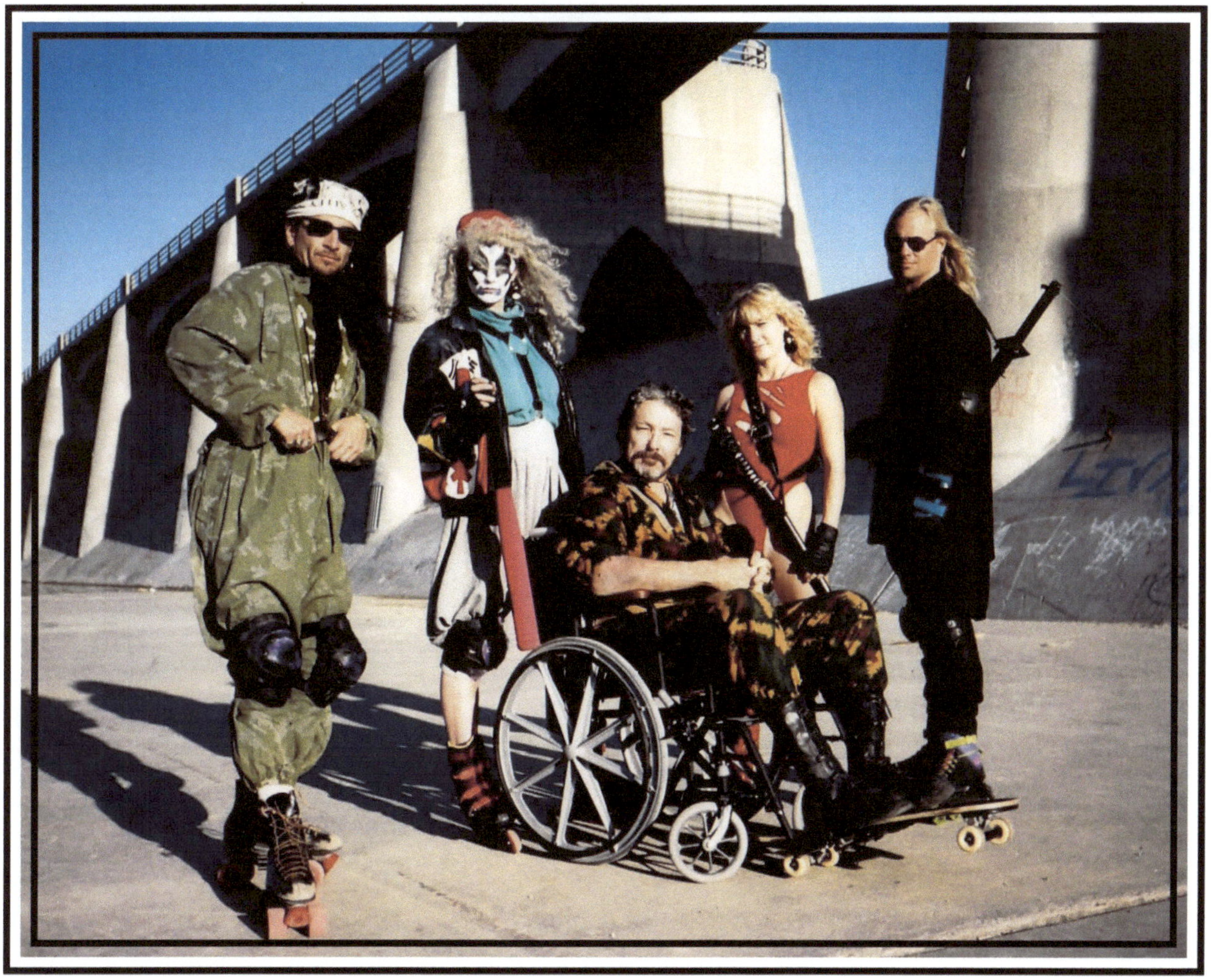

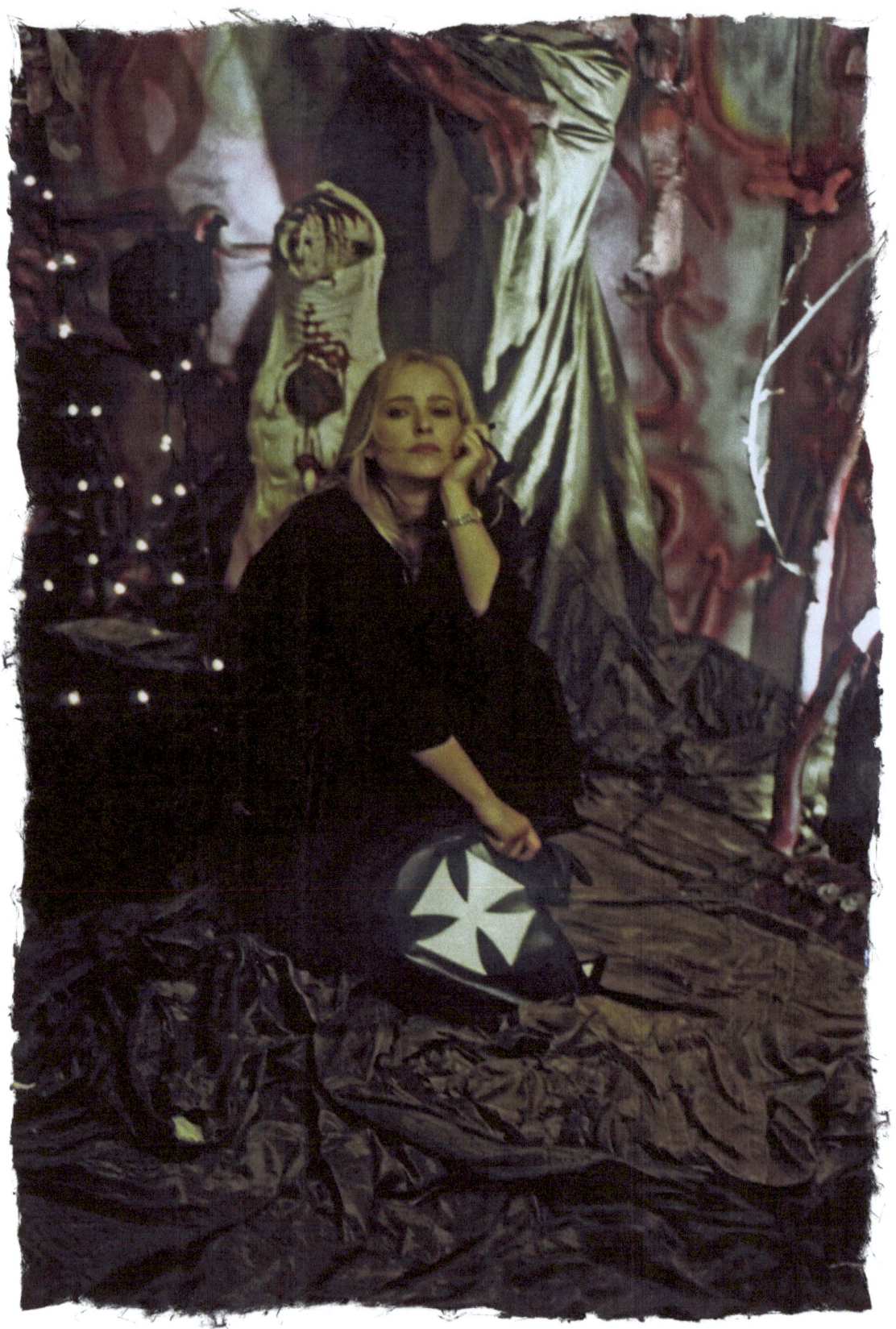

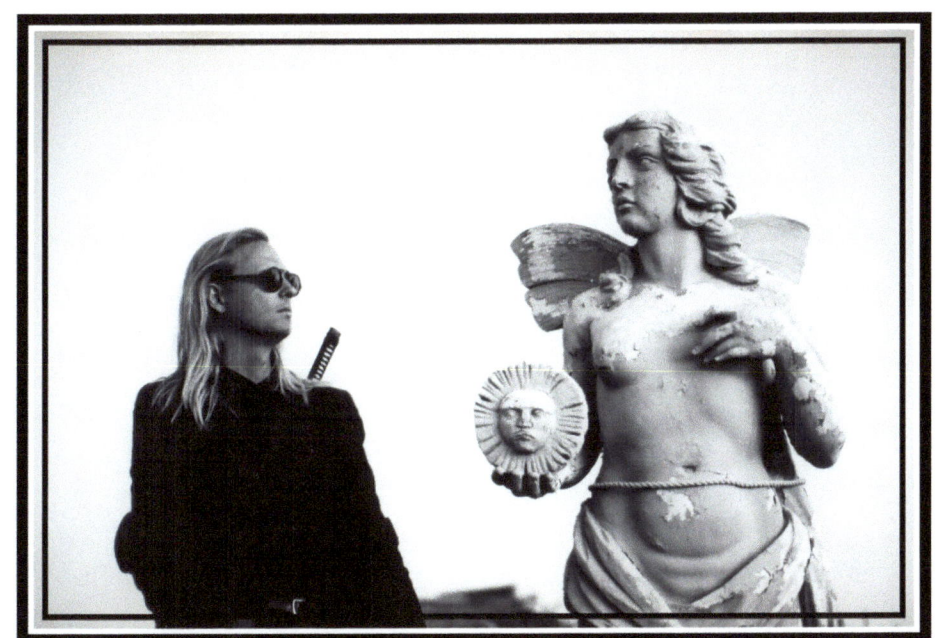

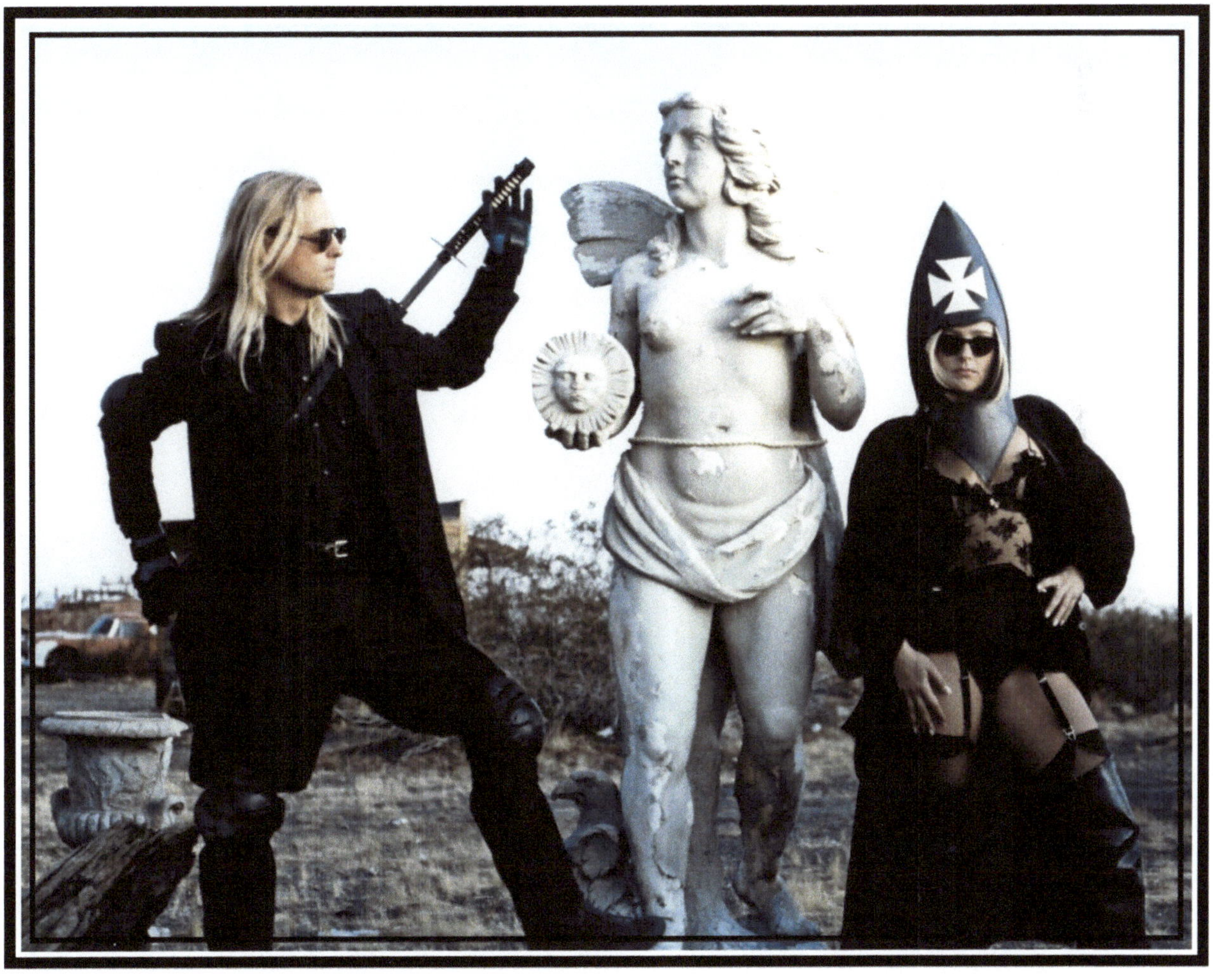

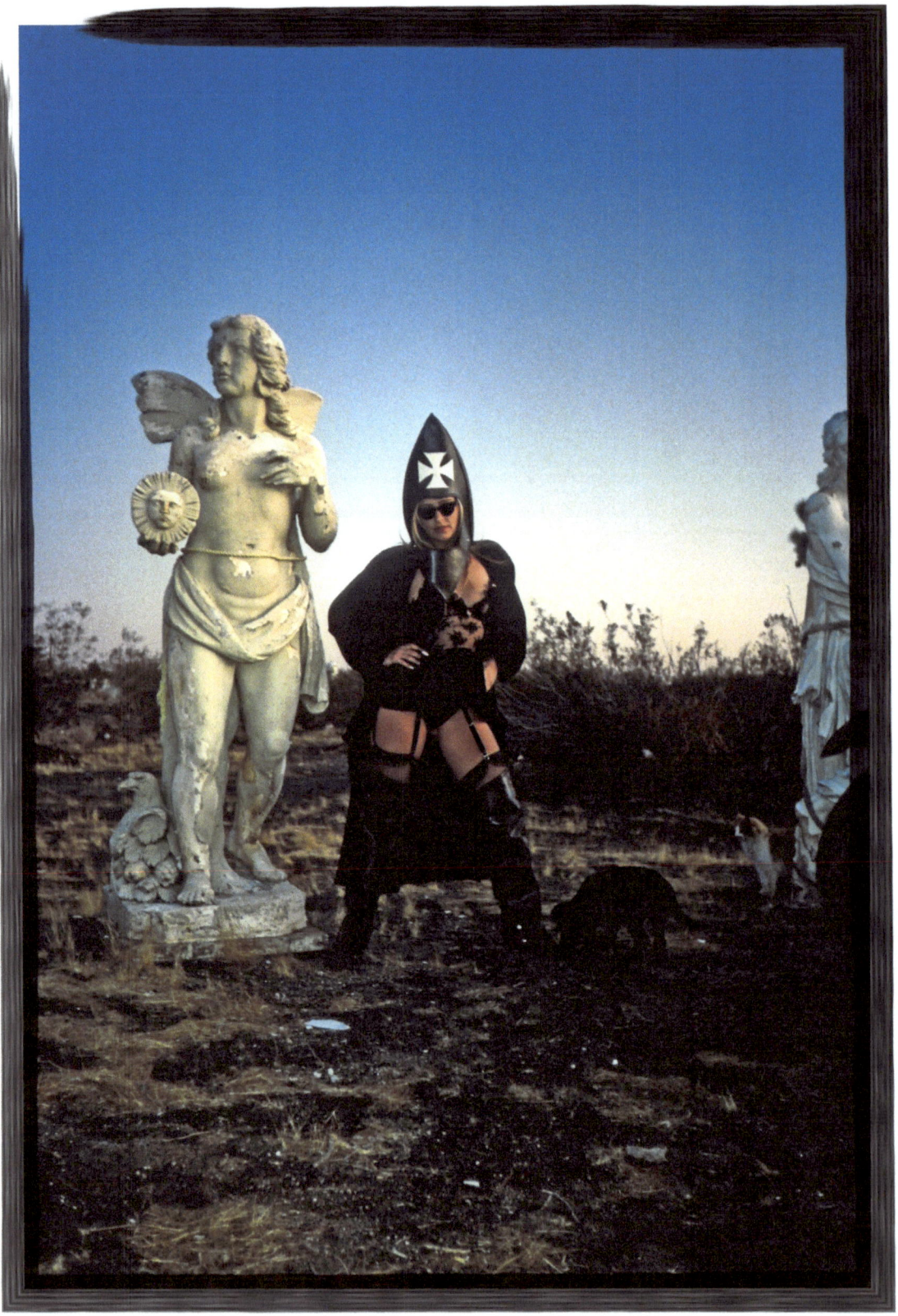

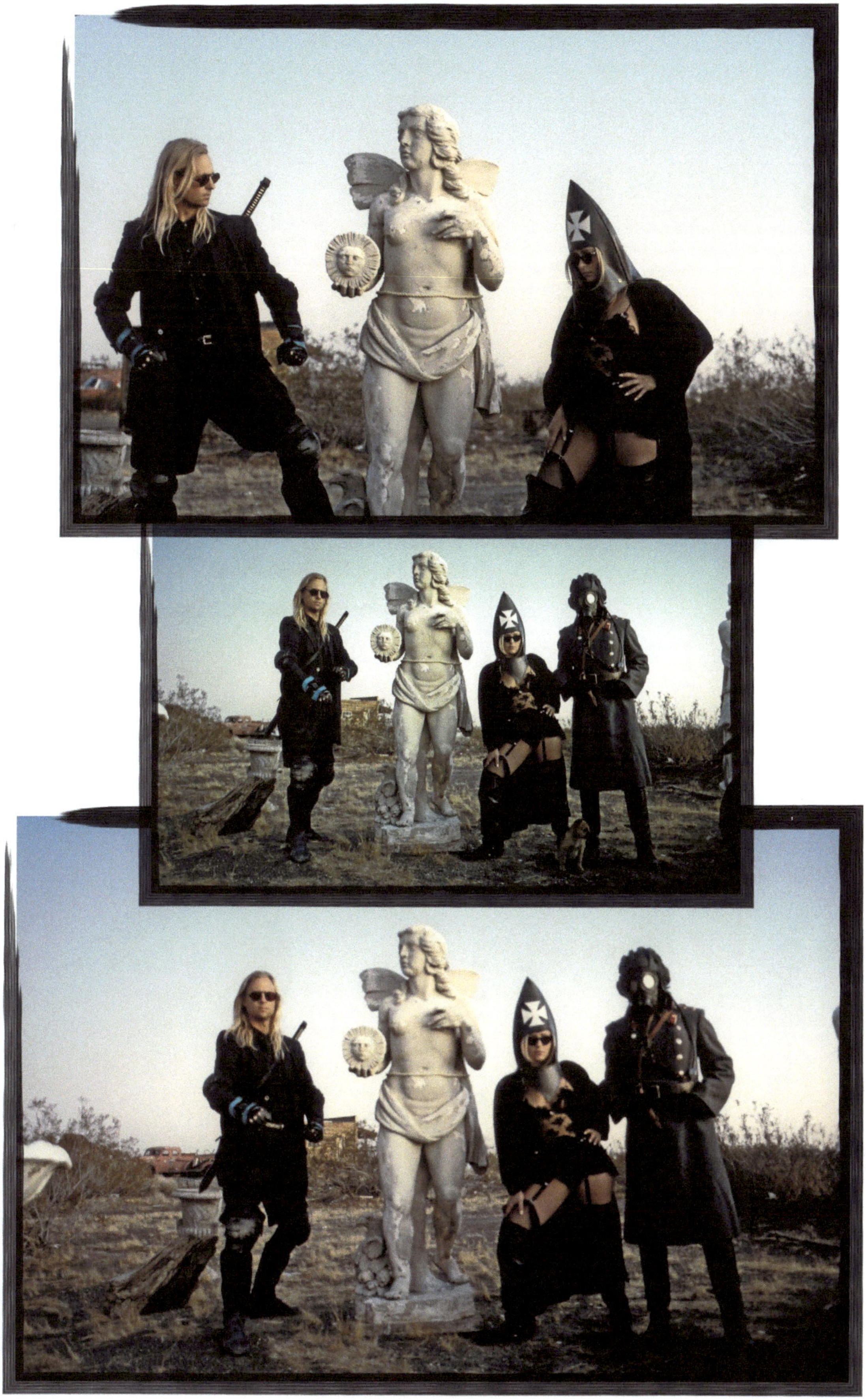

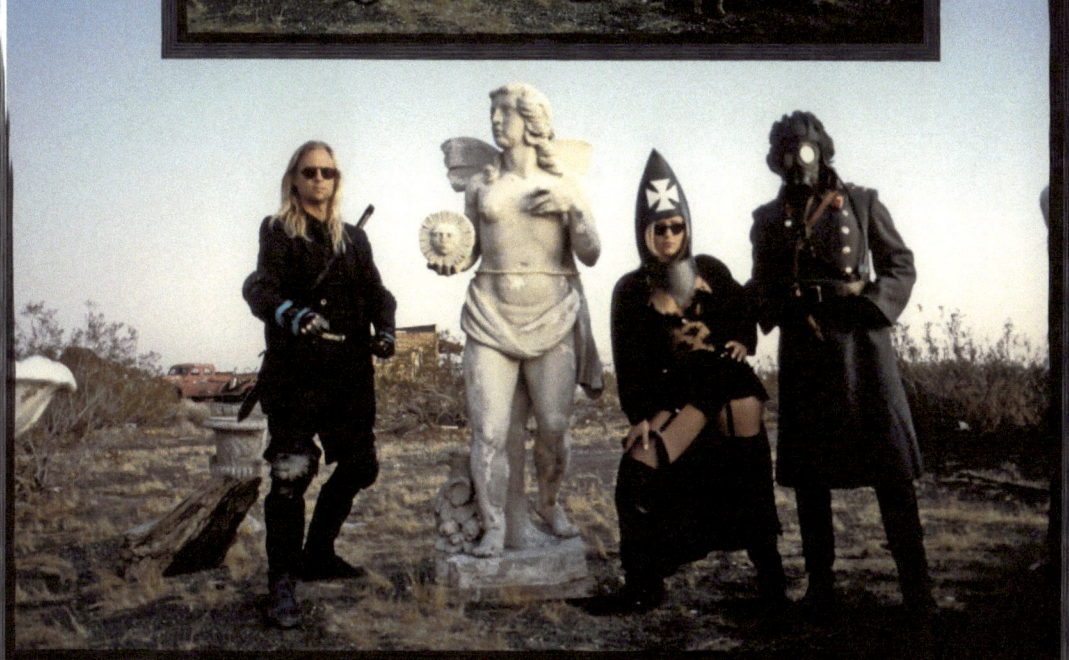

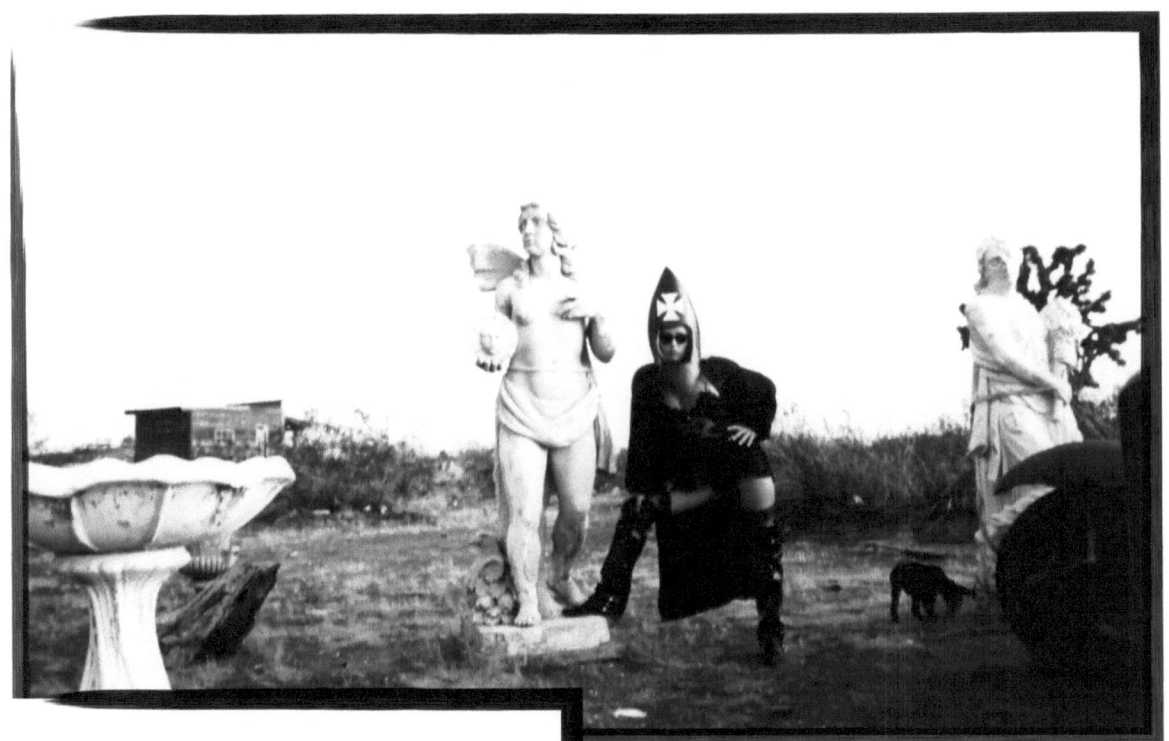
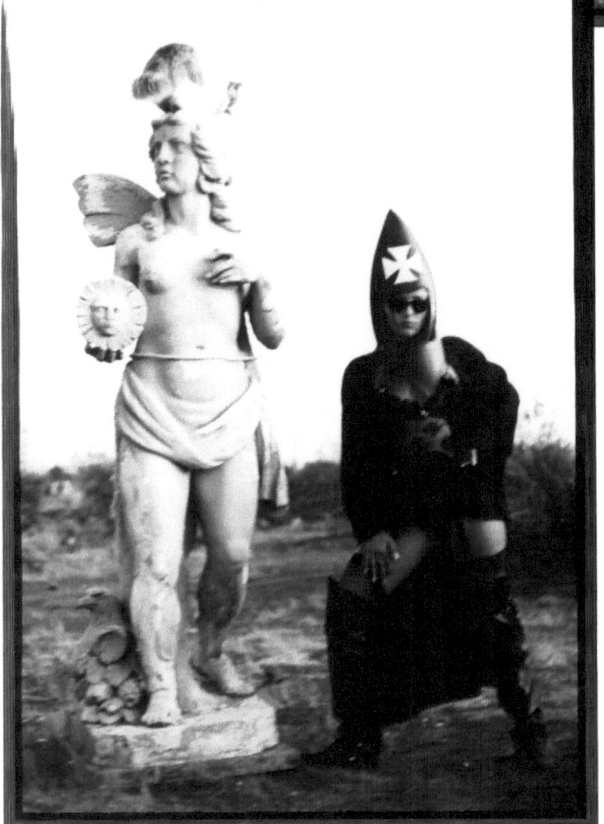
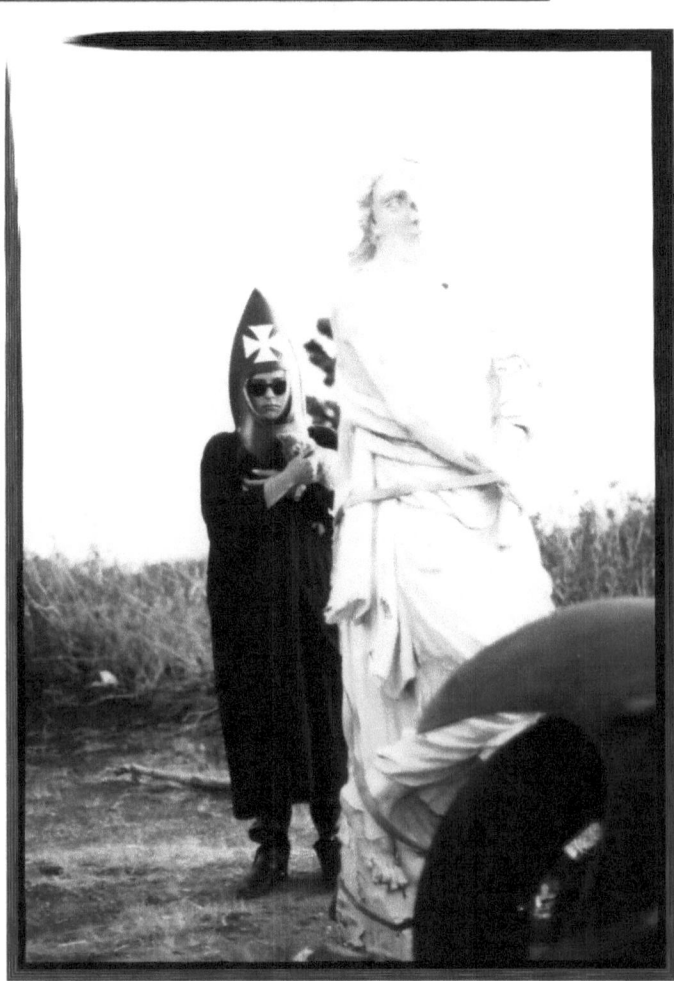

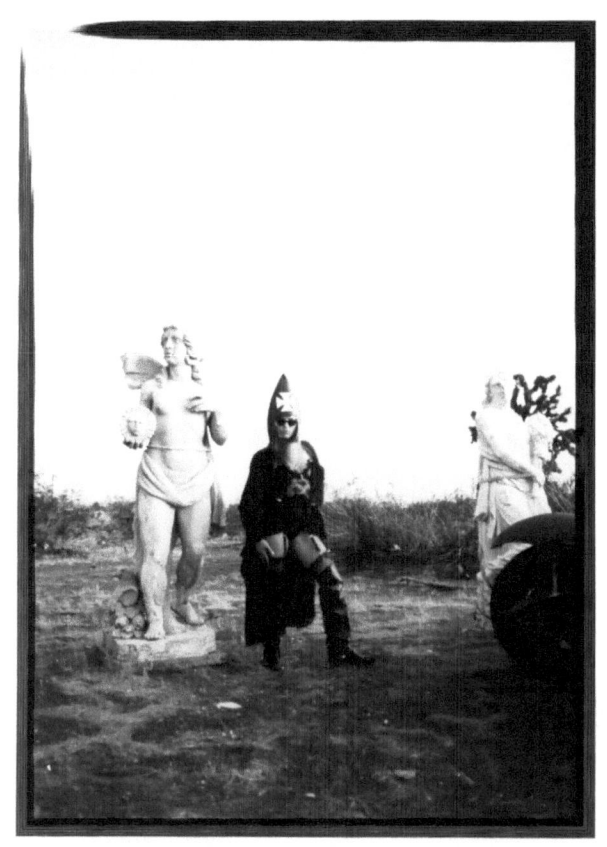
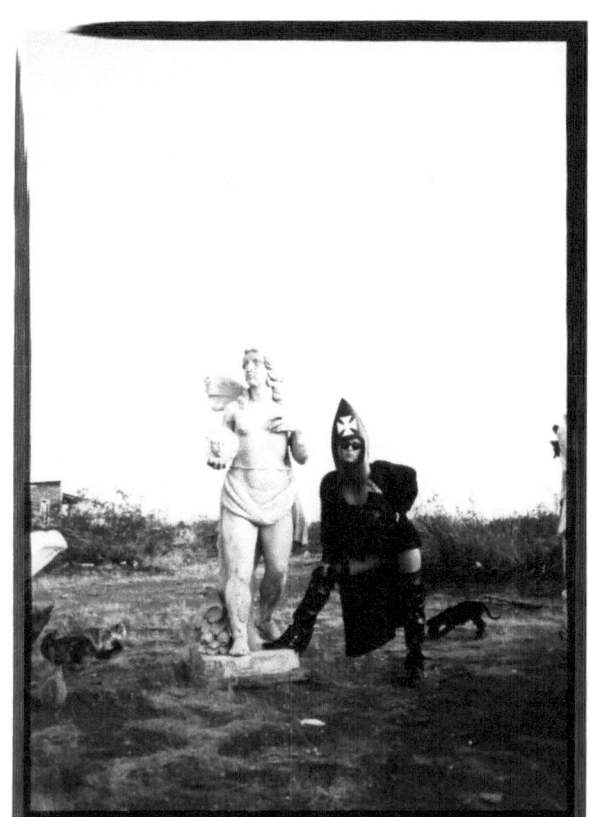
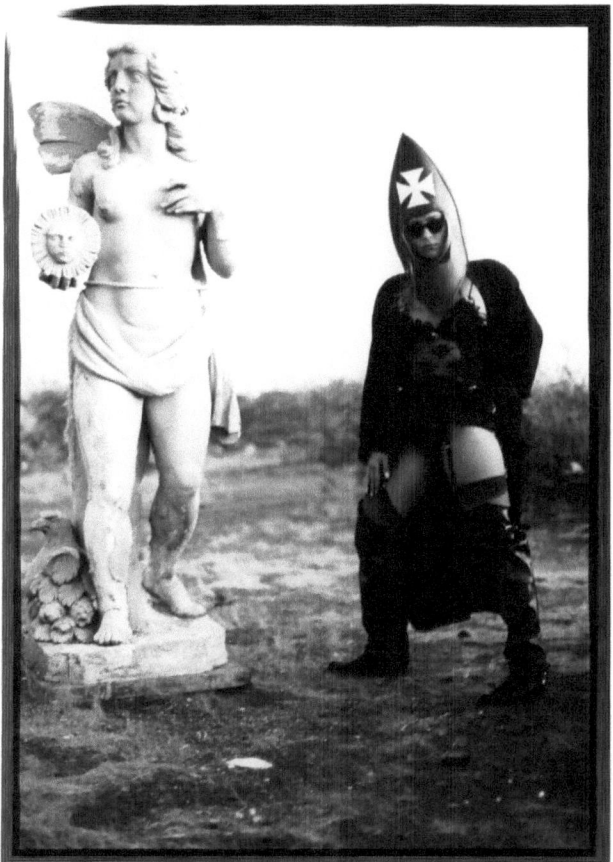
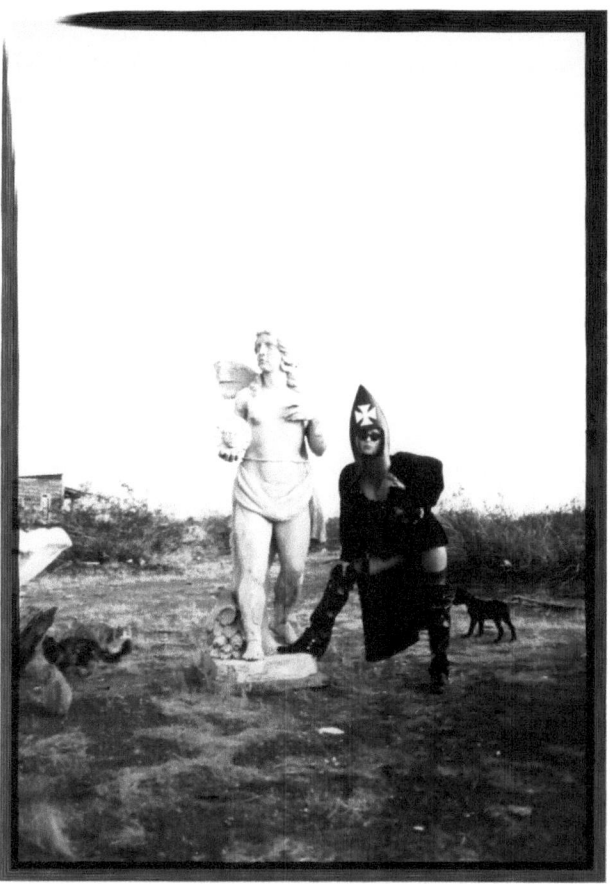

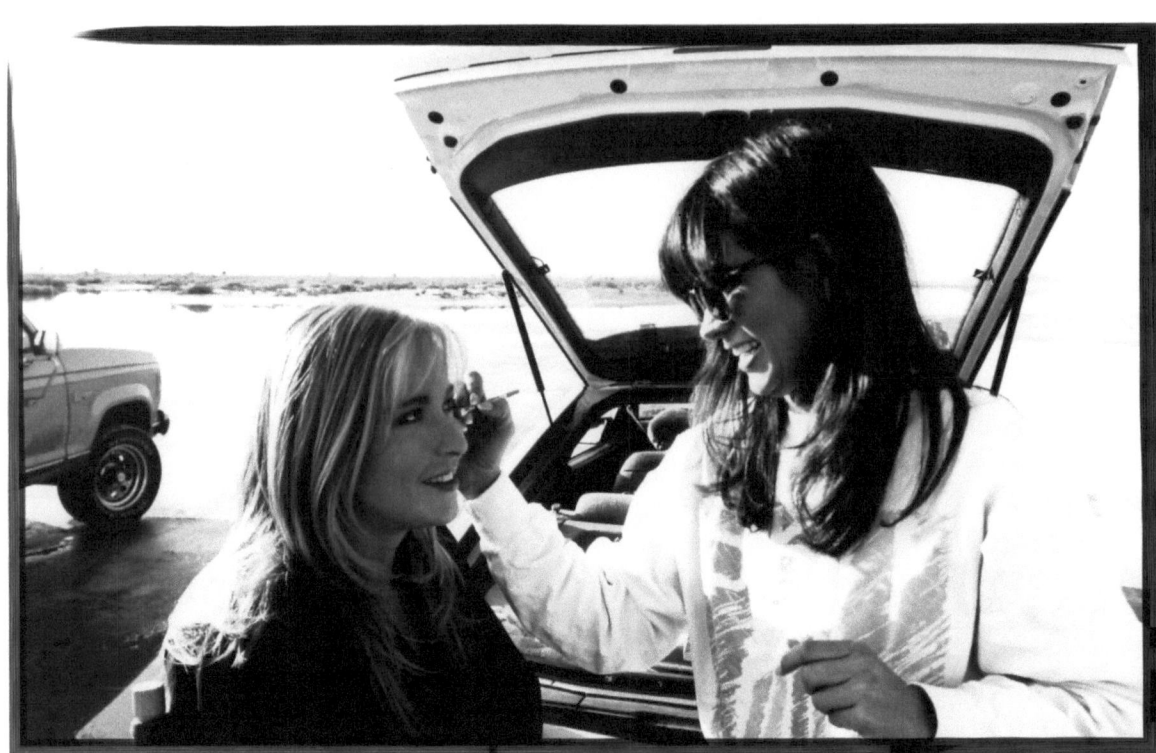
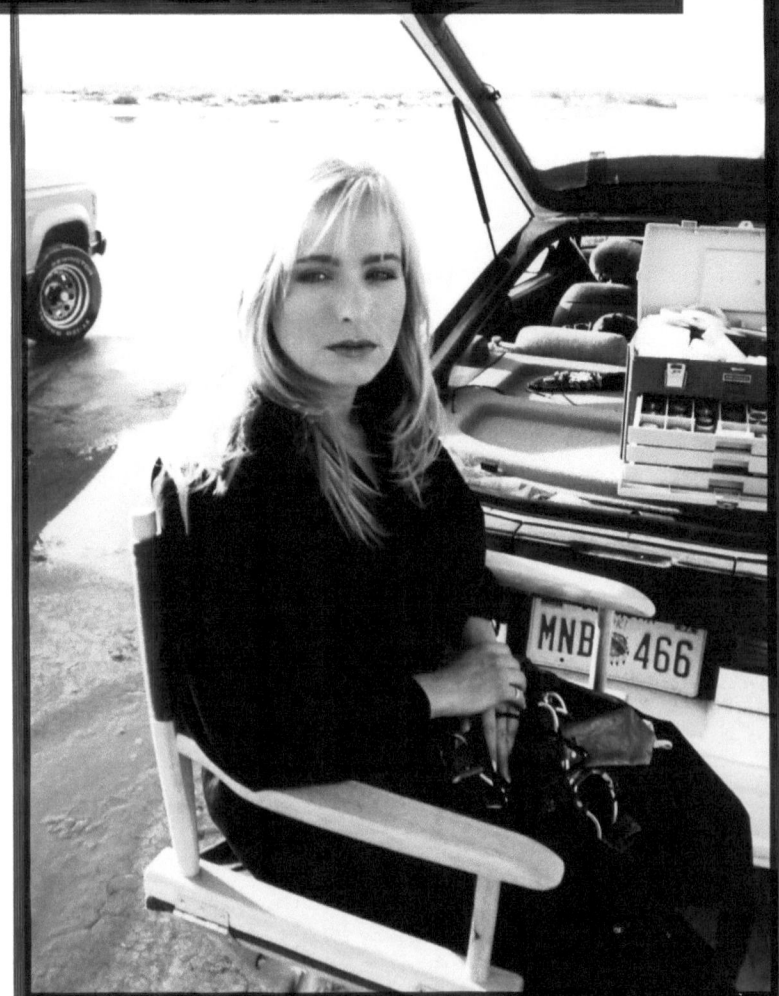

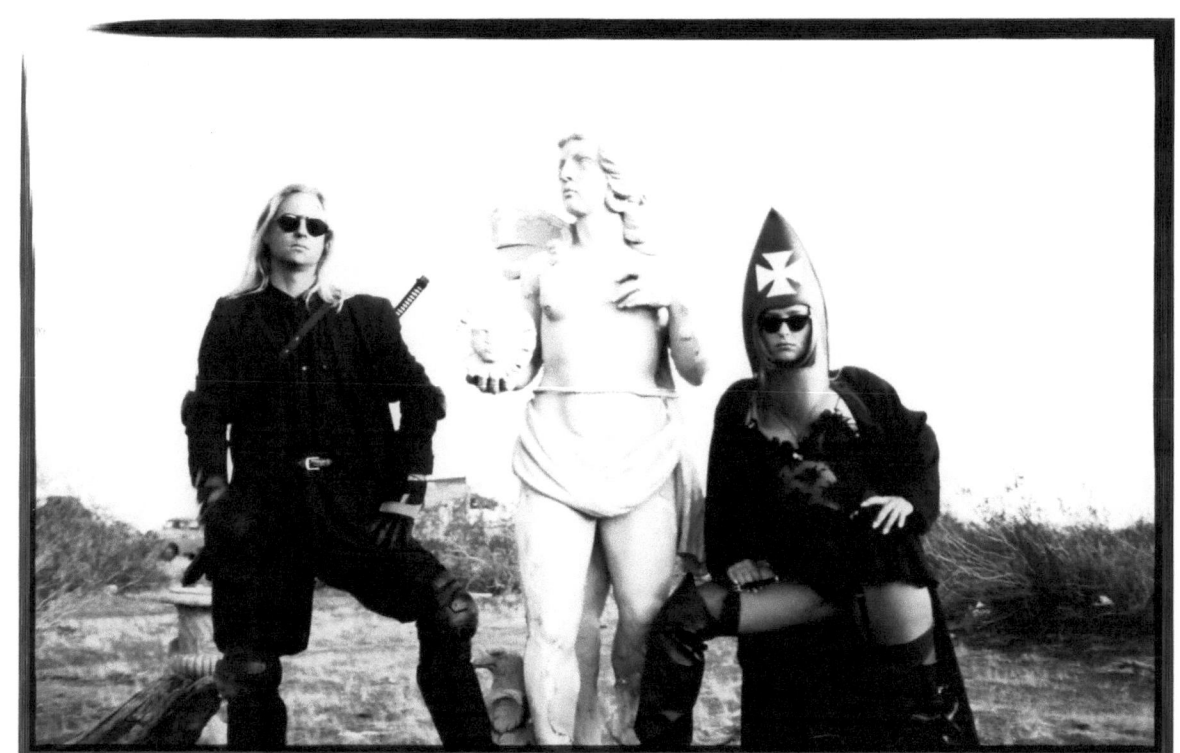
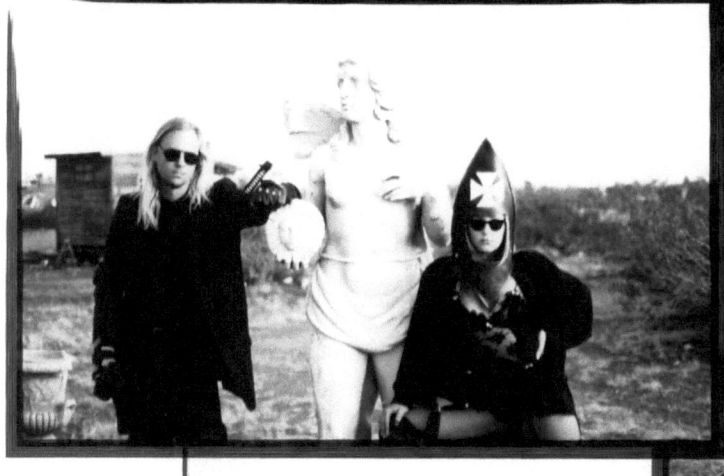
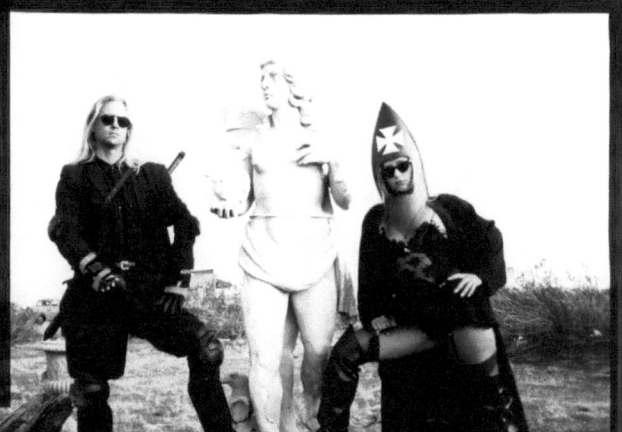
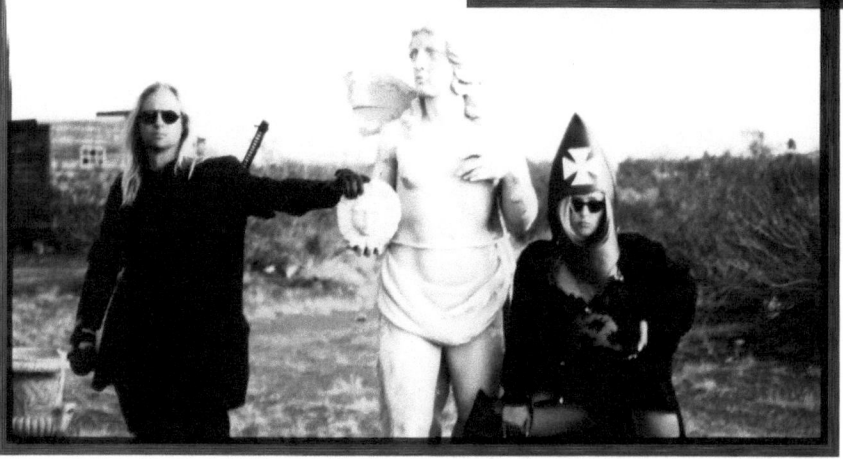

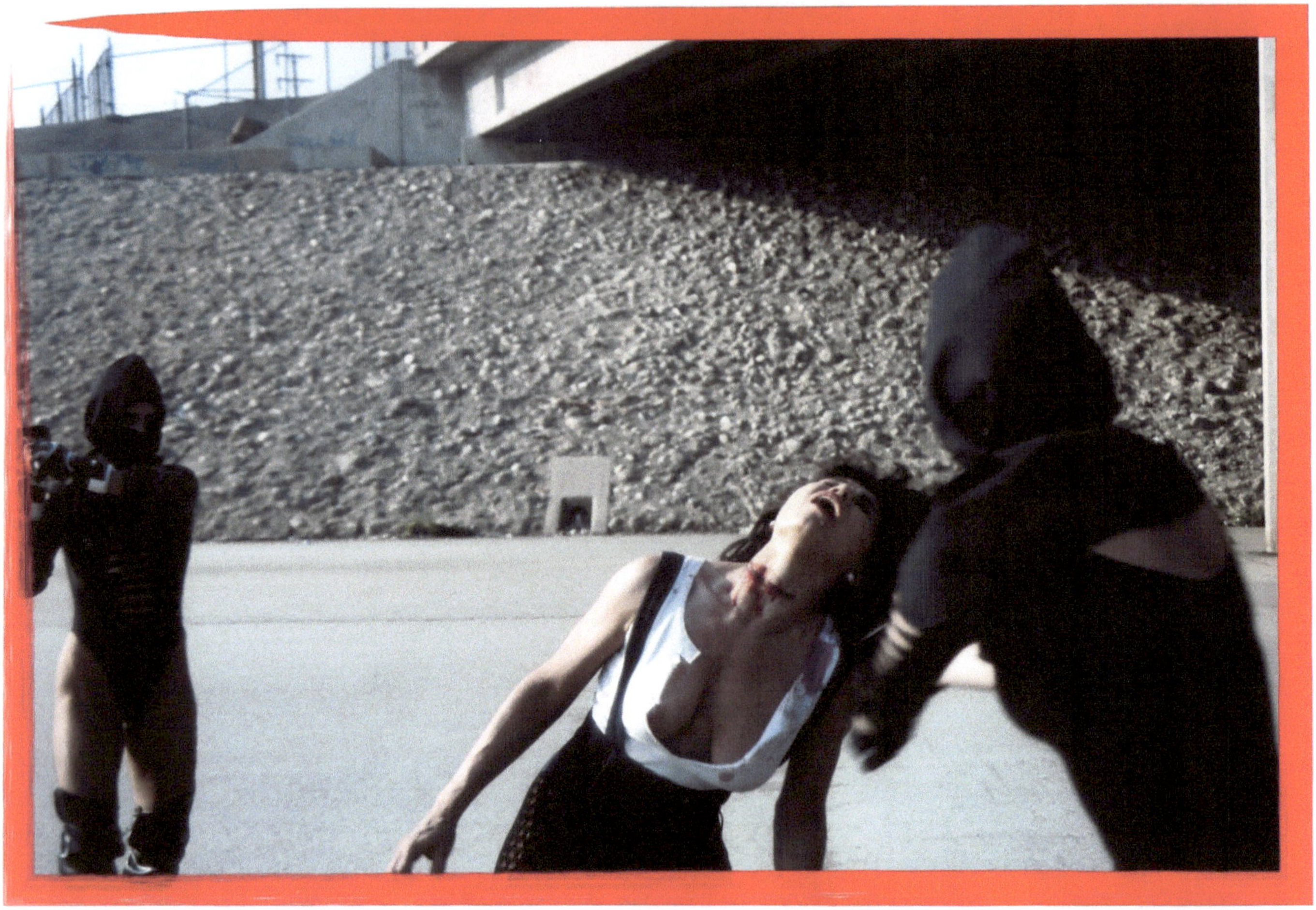

ROLLER BLADE FIRE DRILL

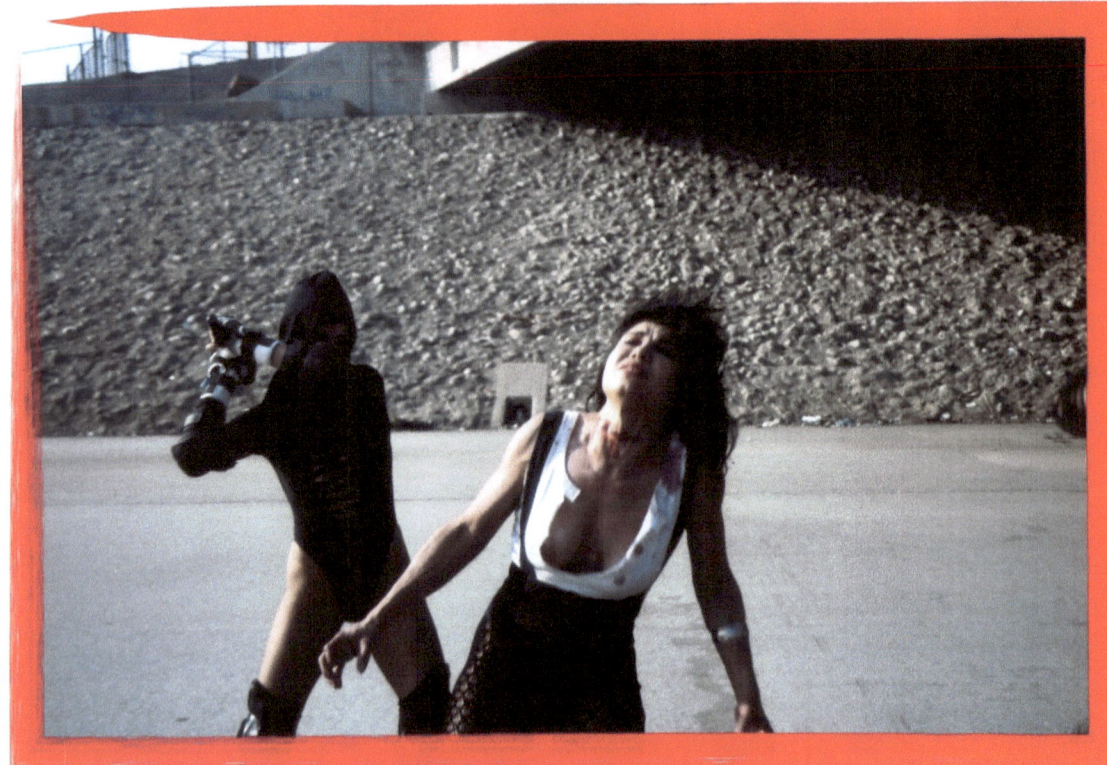

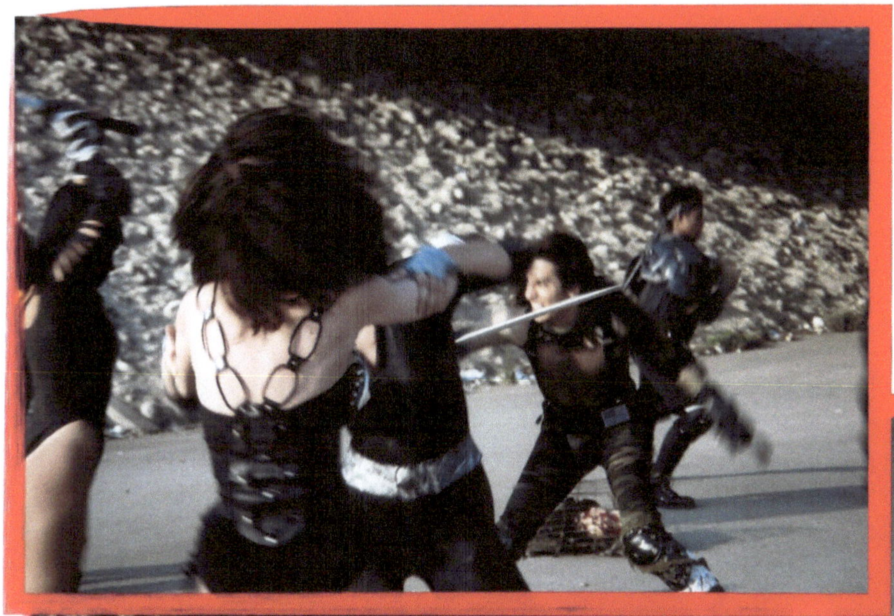

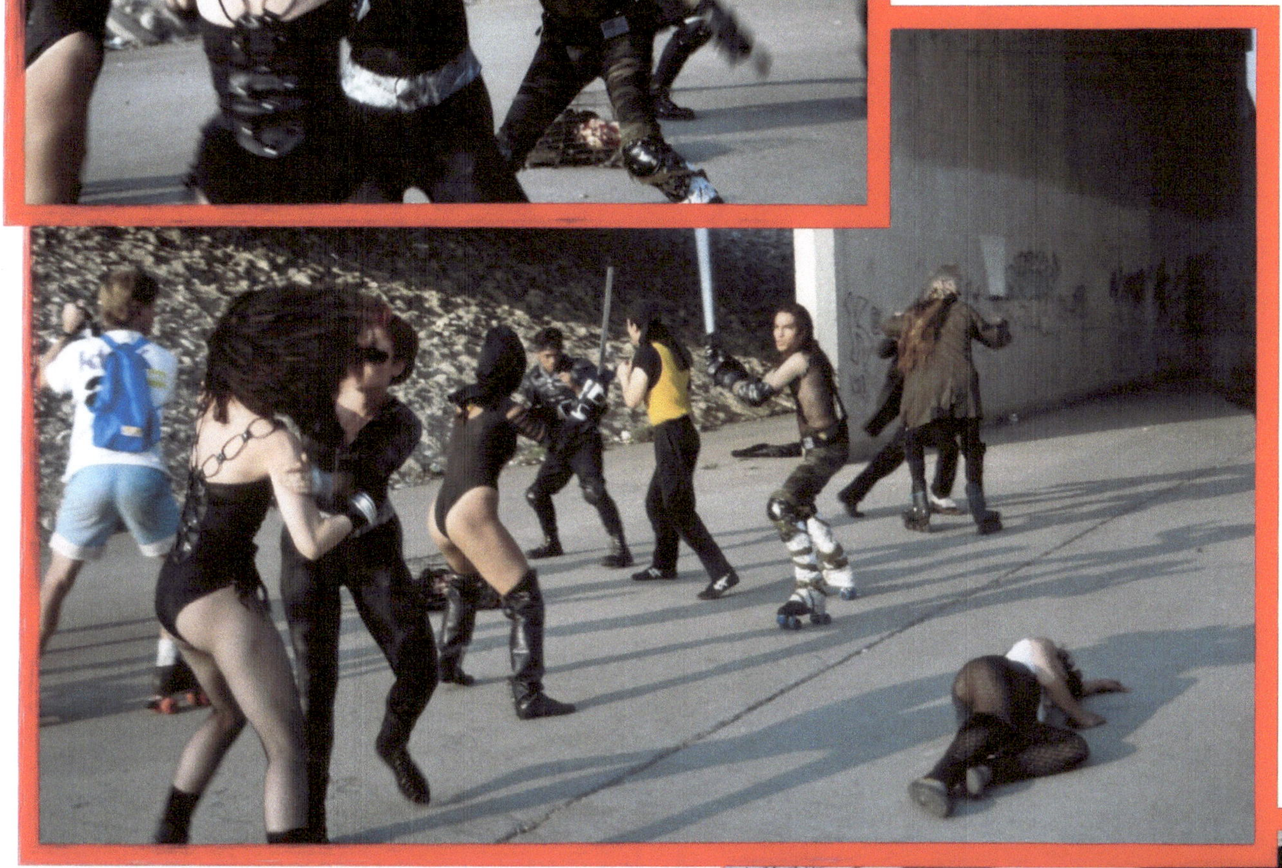

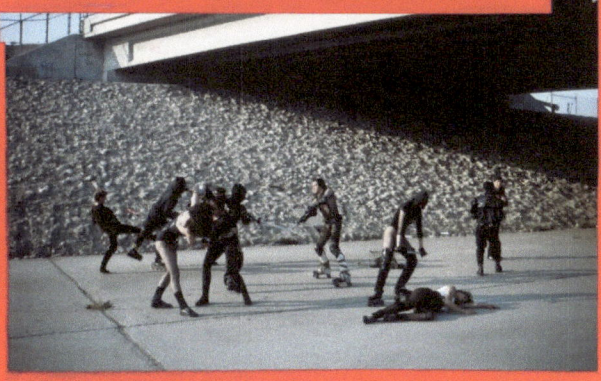
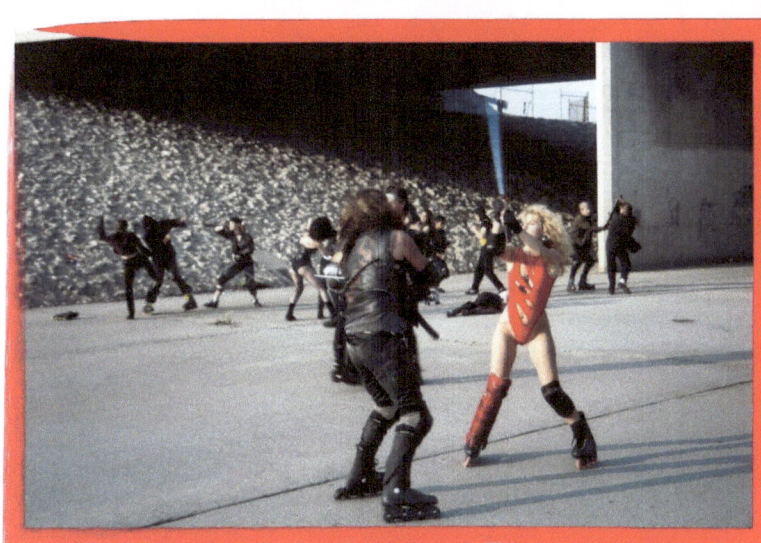

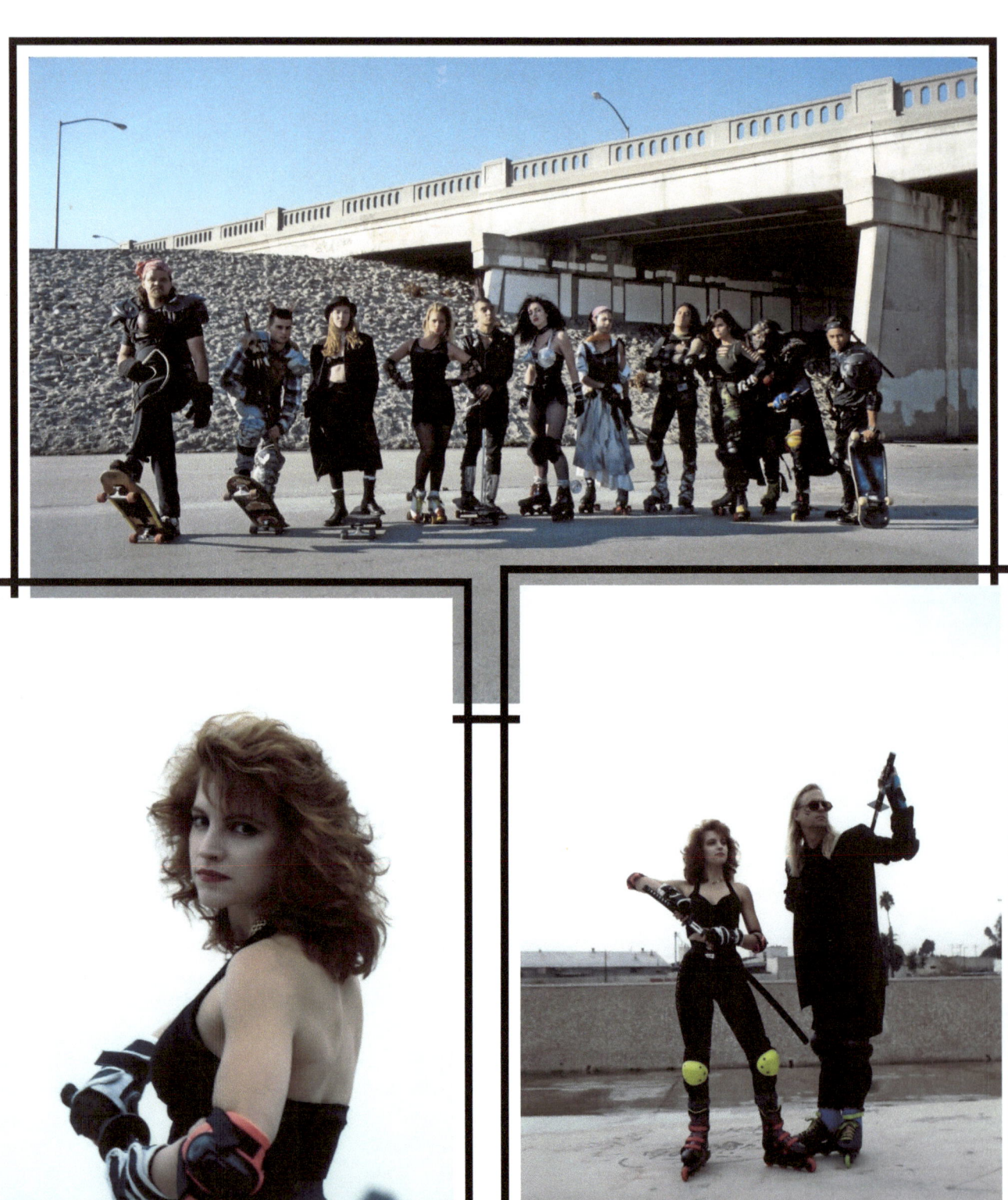

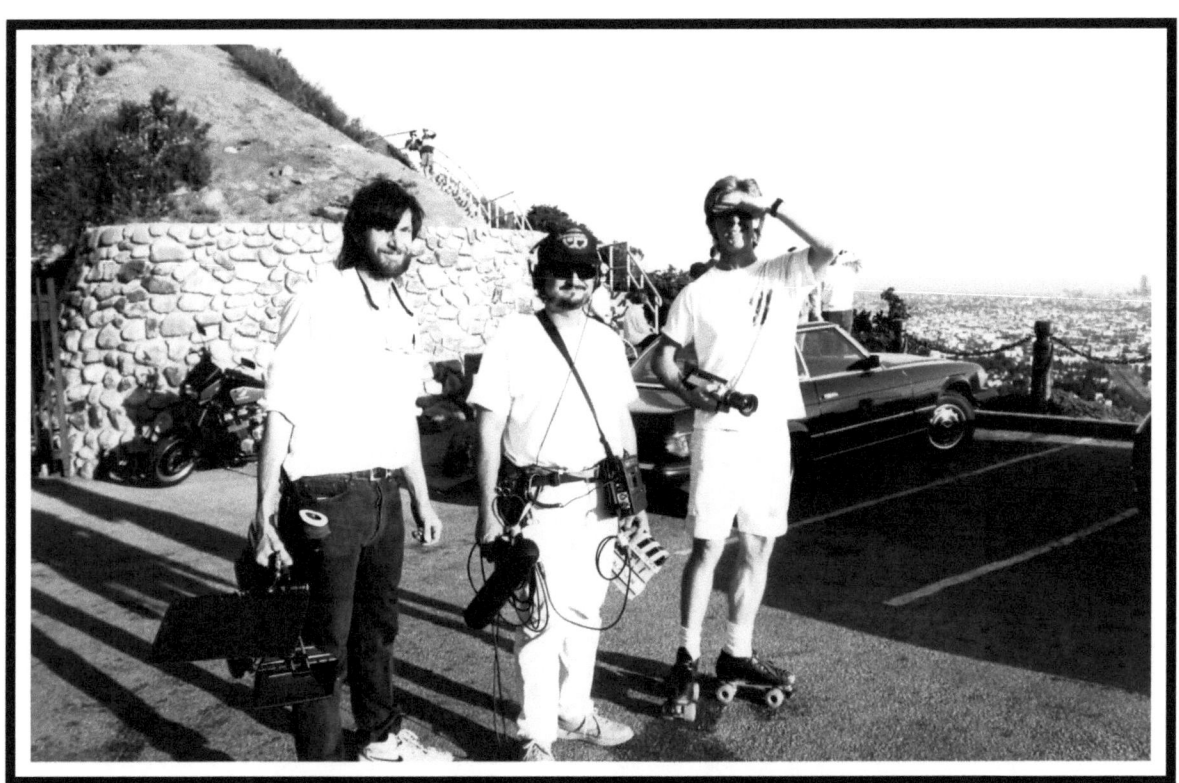
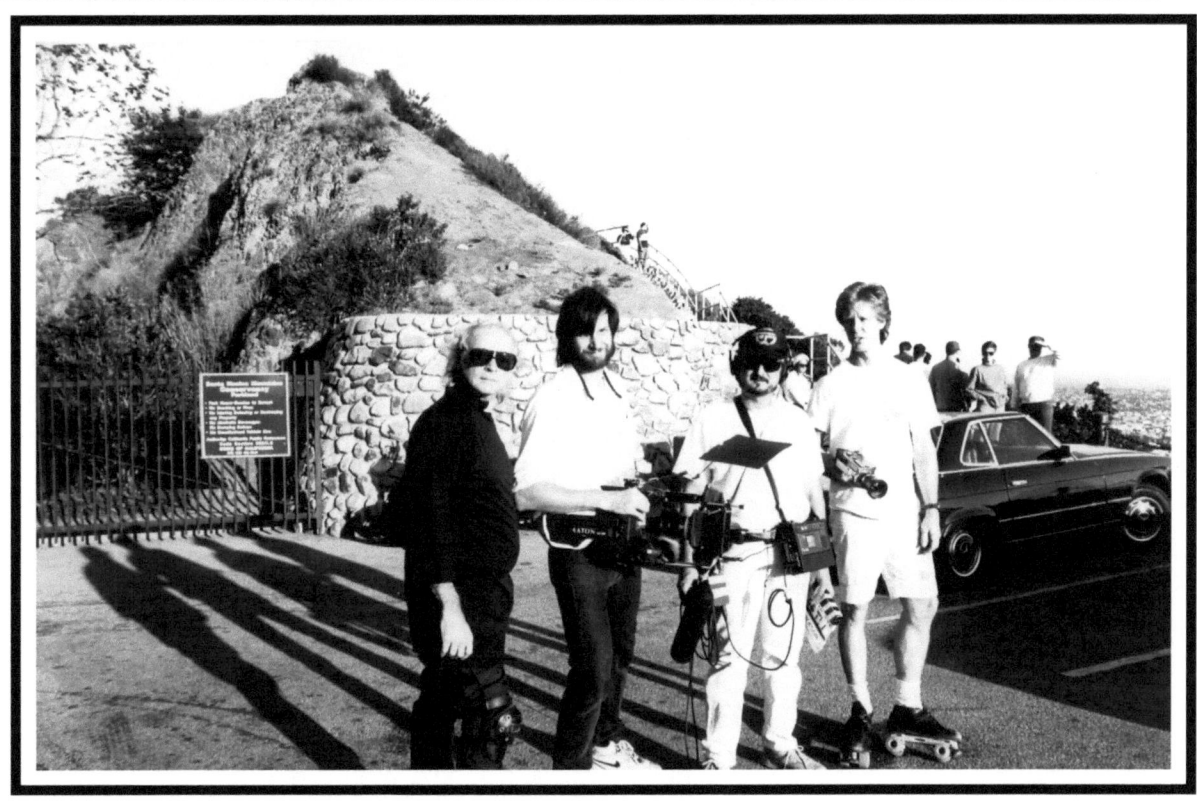

FRANK STALLONE

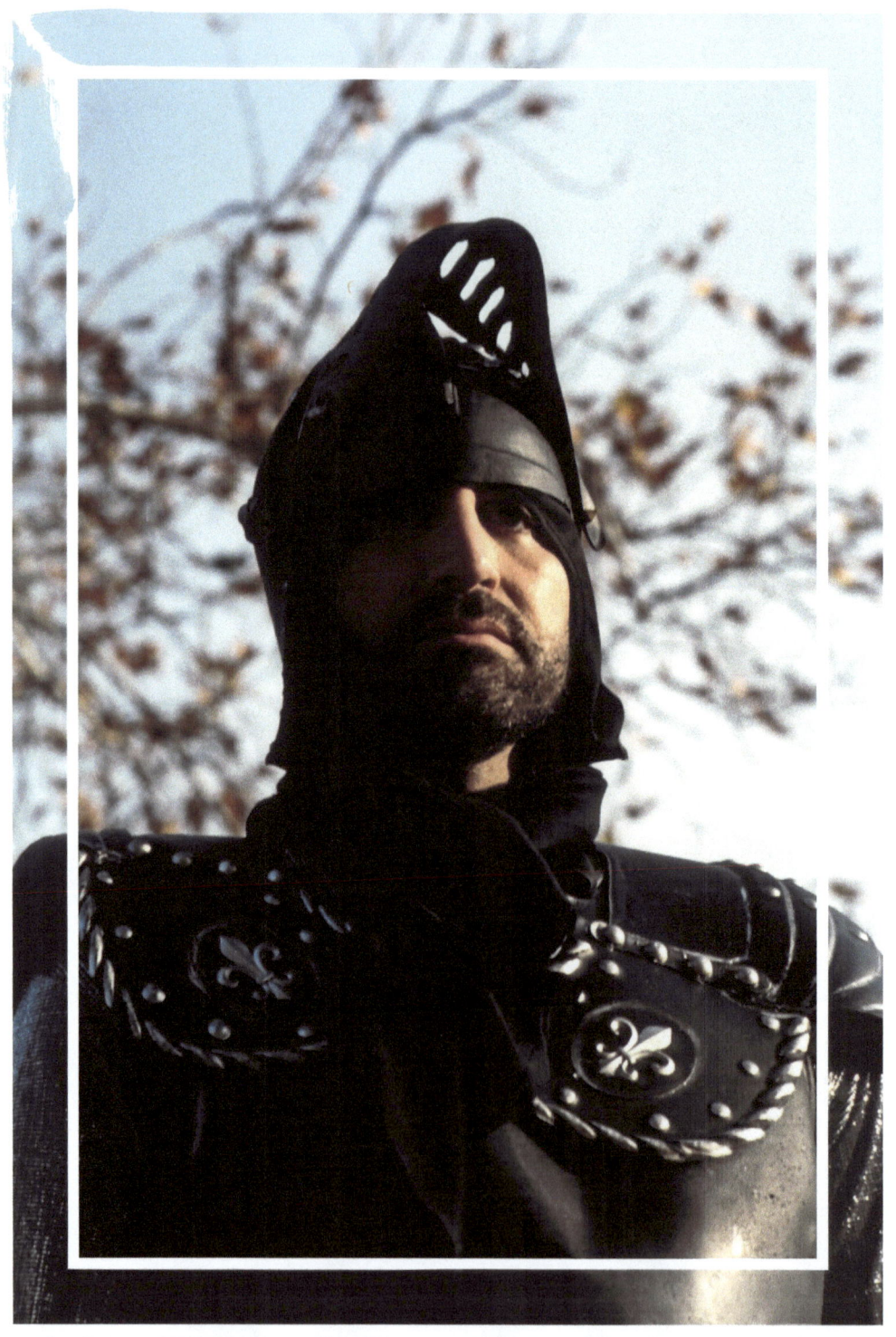

AS THE BLACK KNIGHT

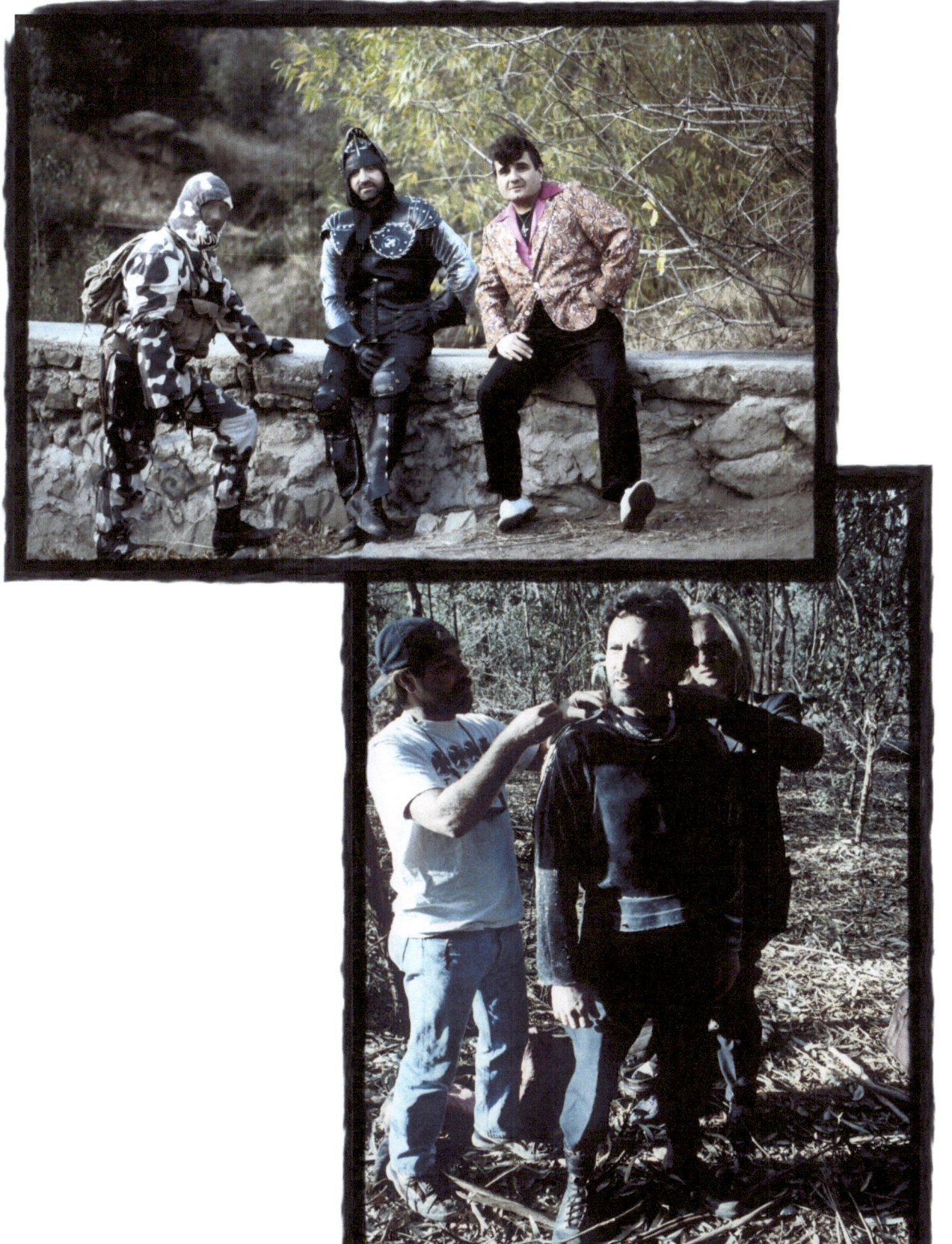

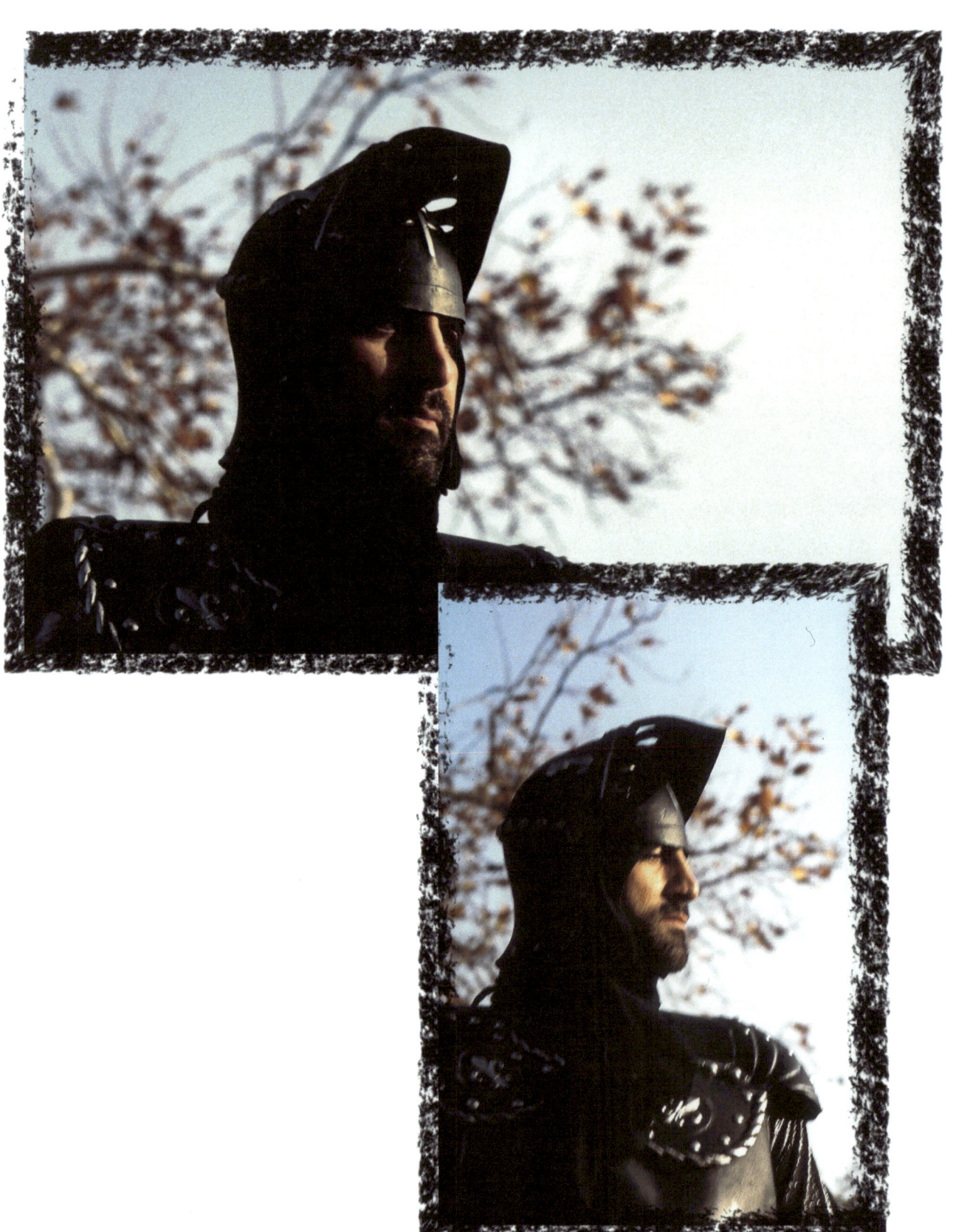

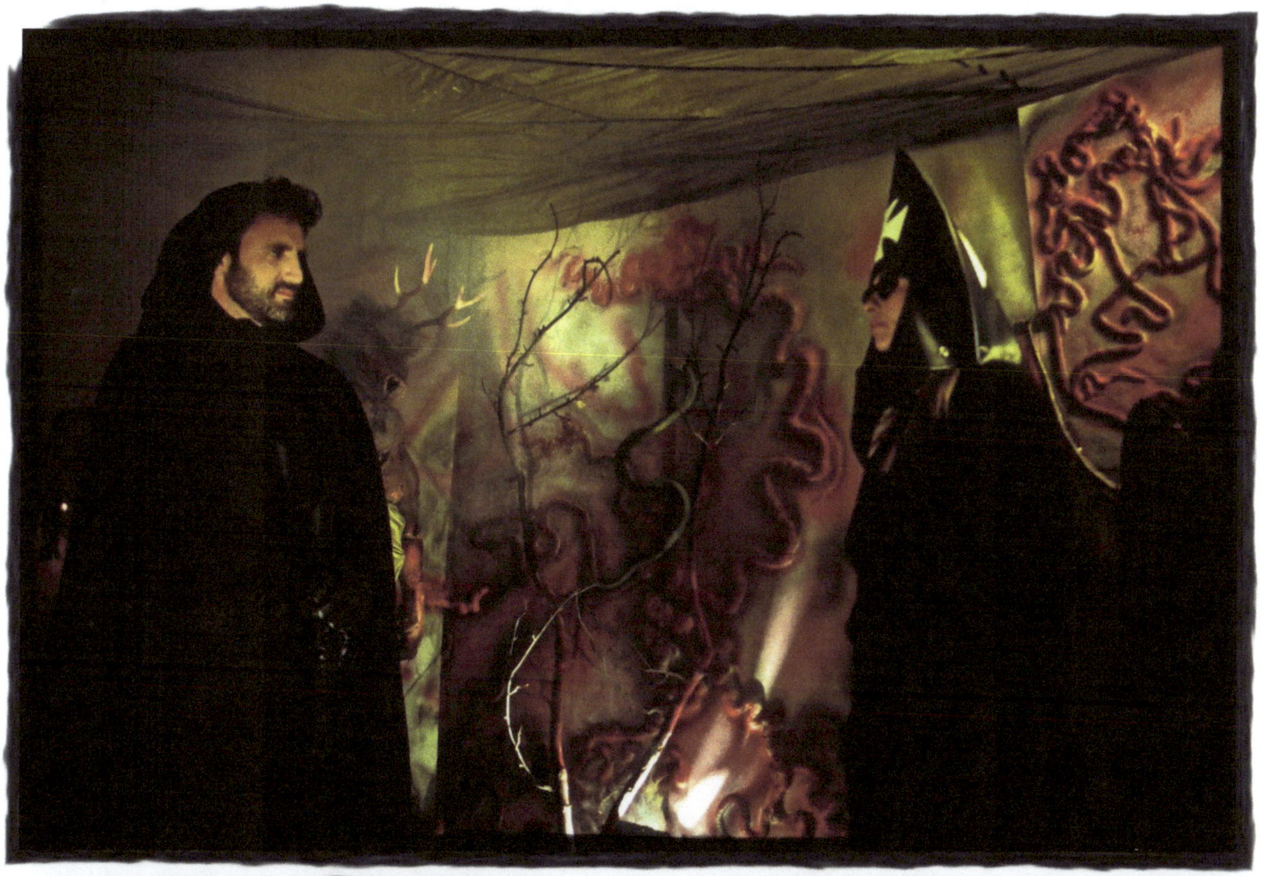

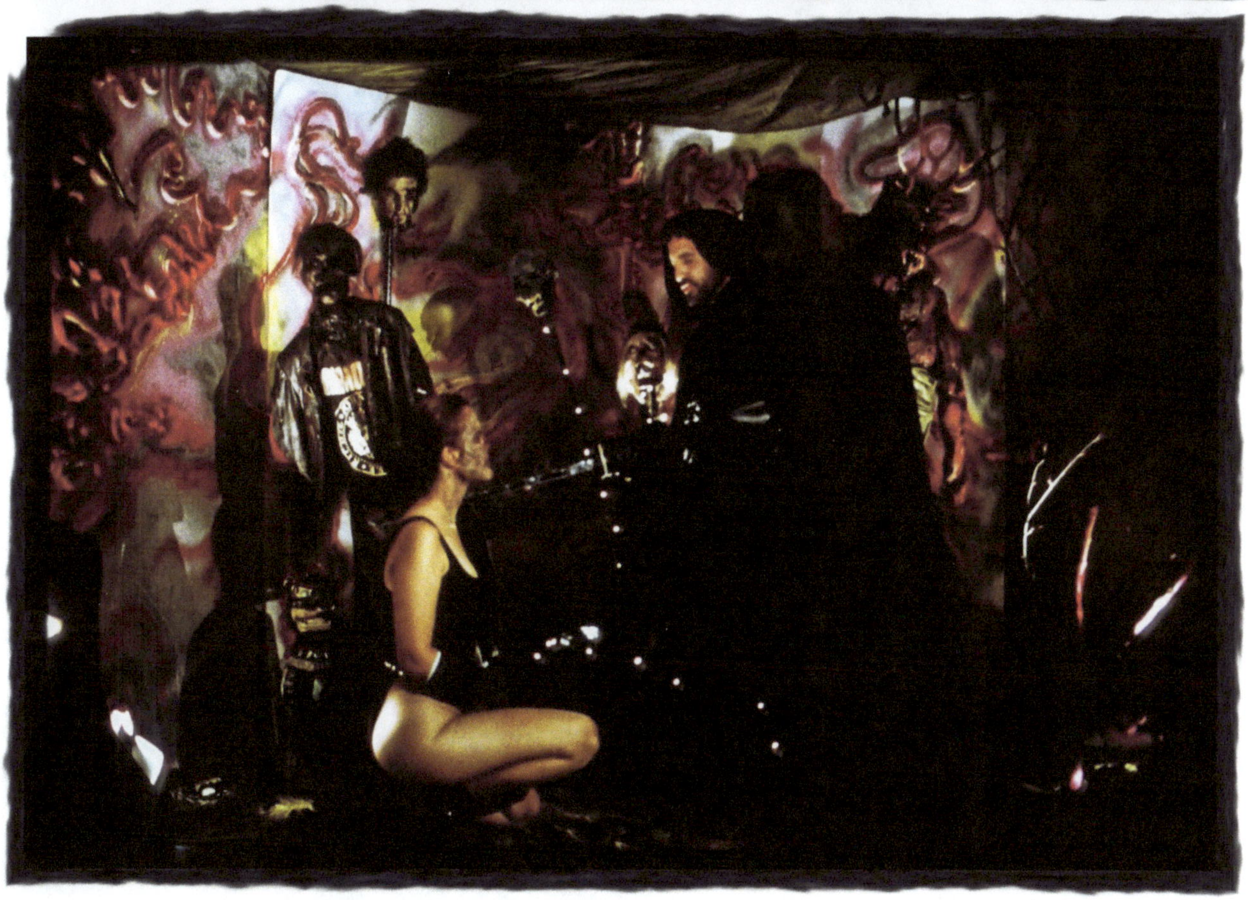

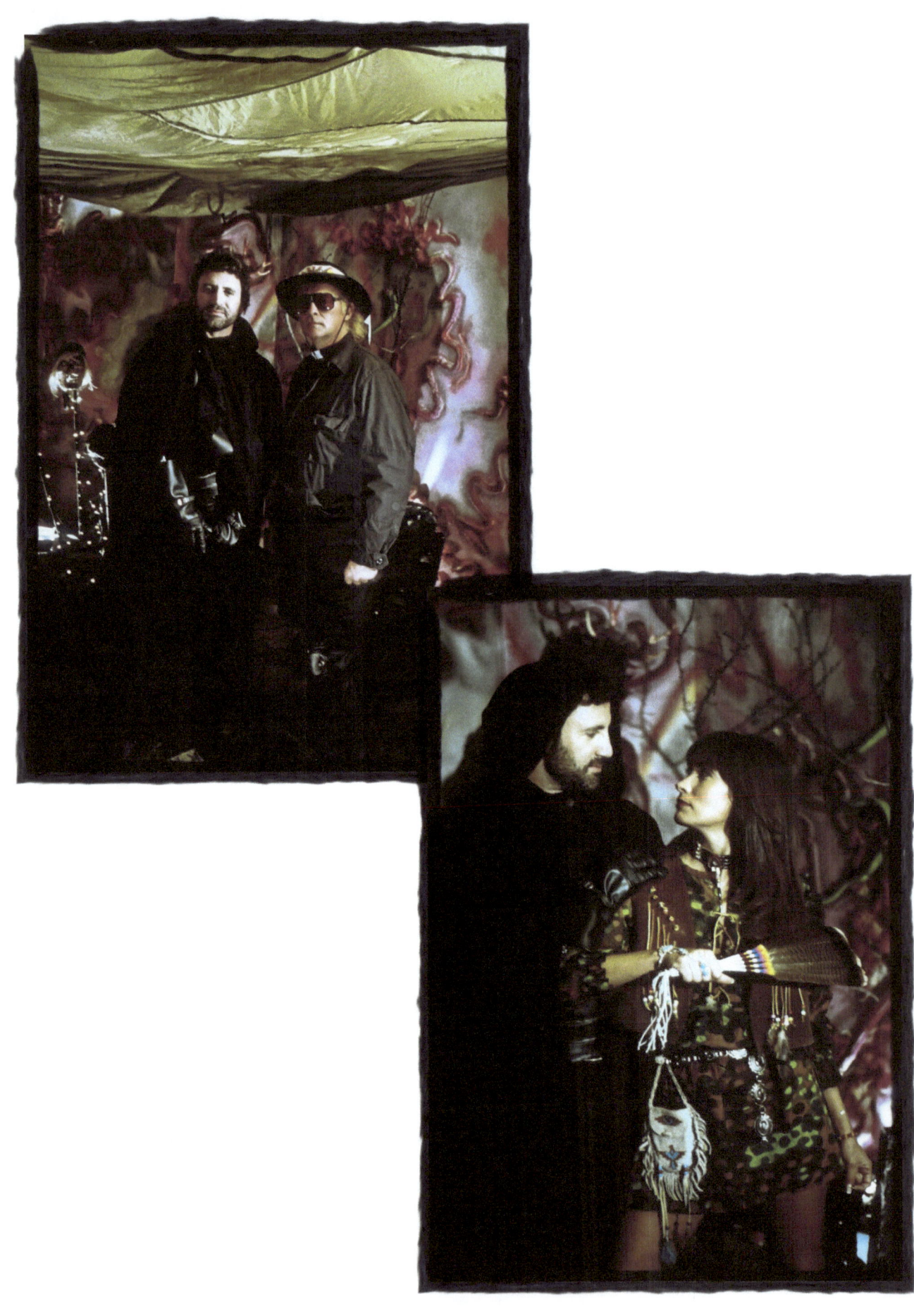

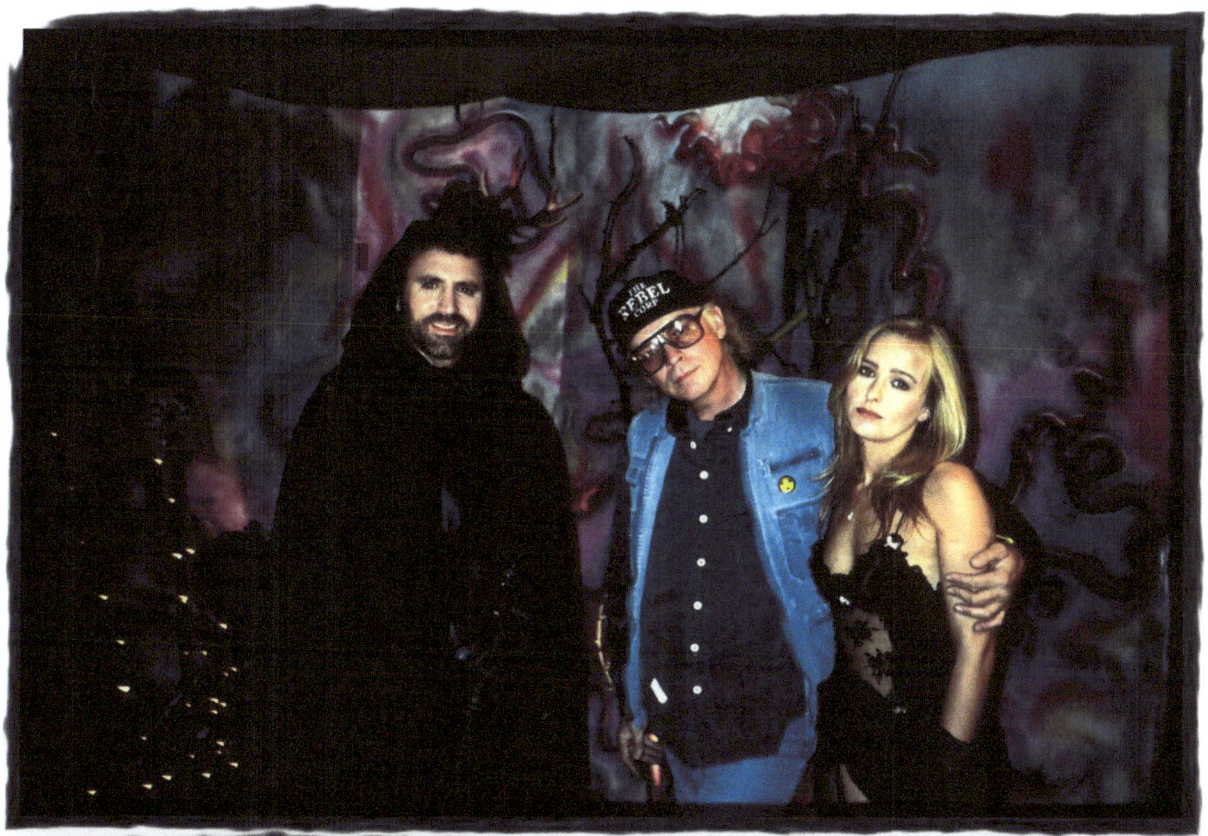

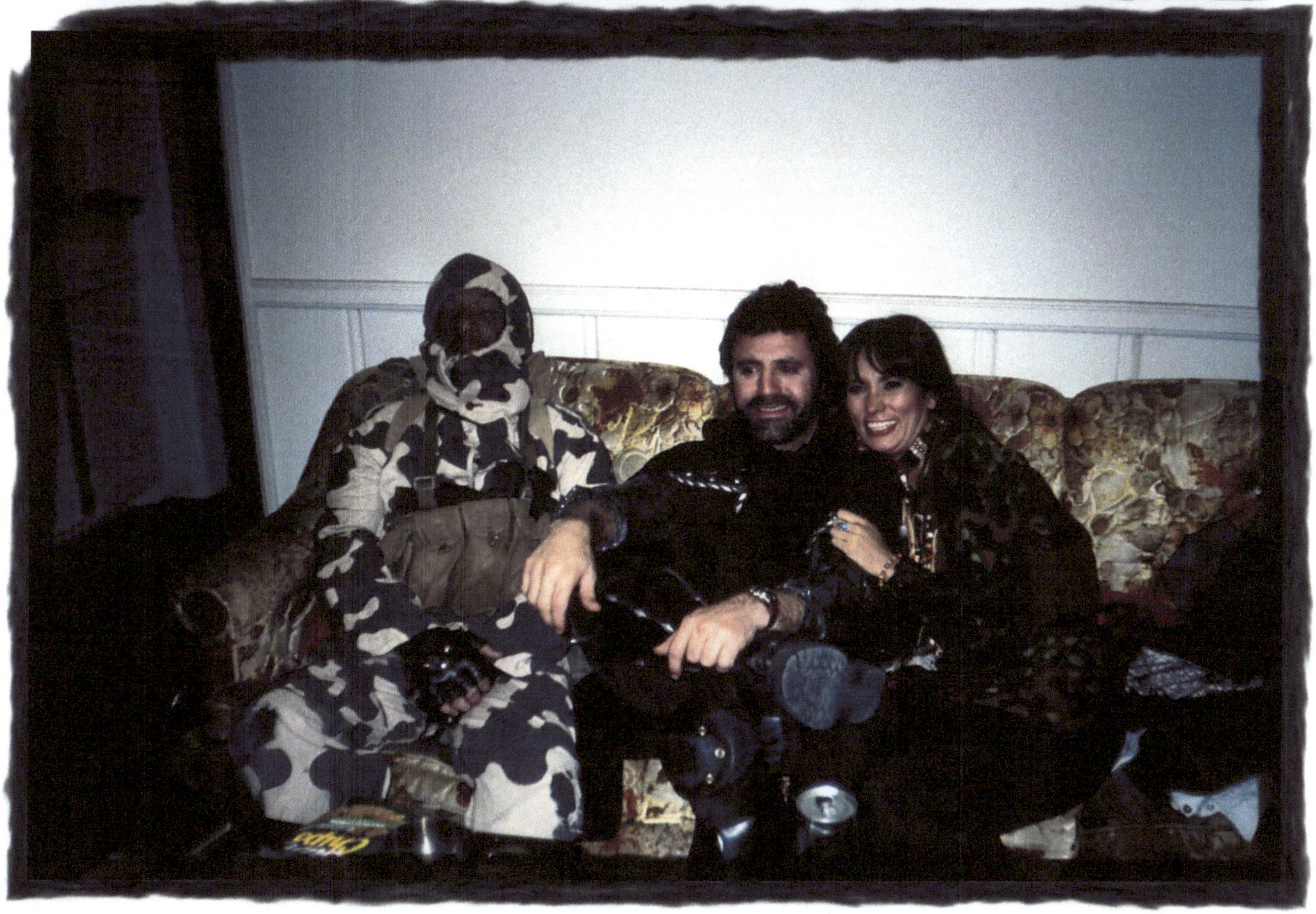

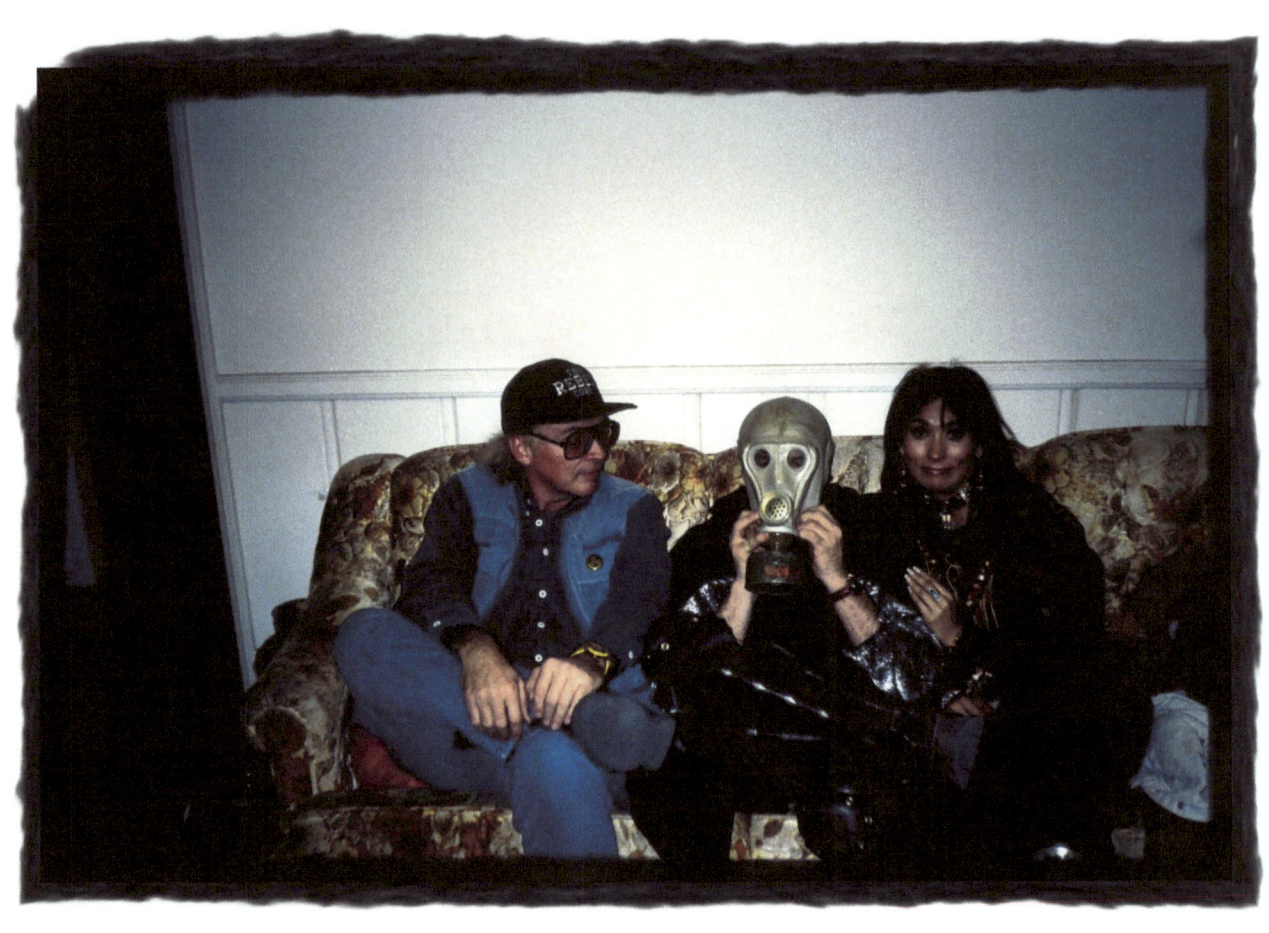

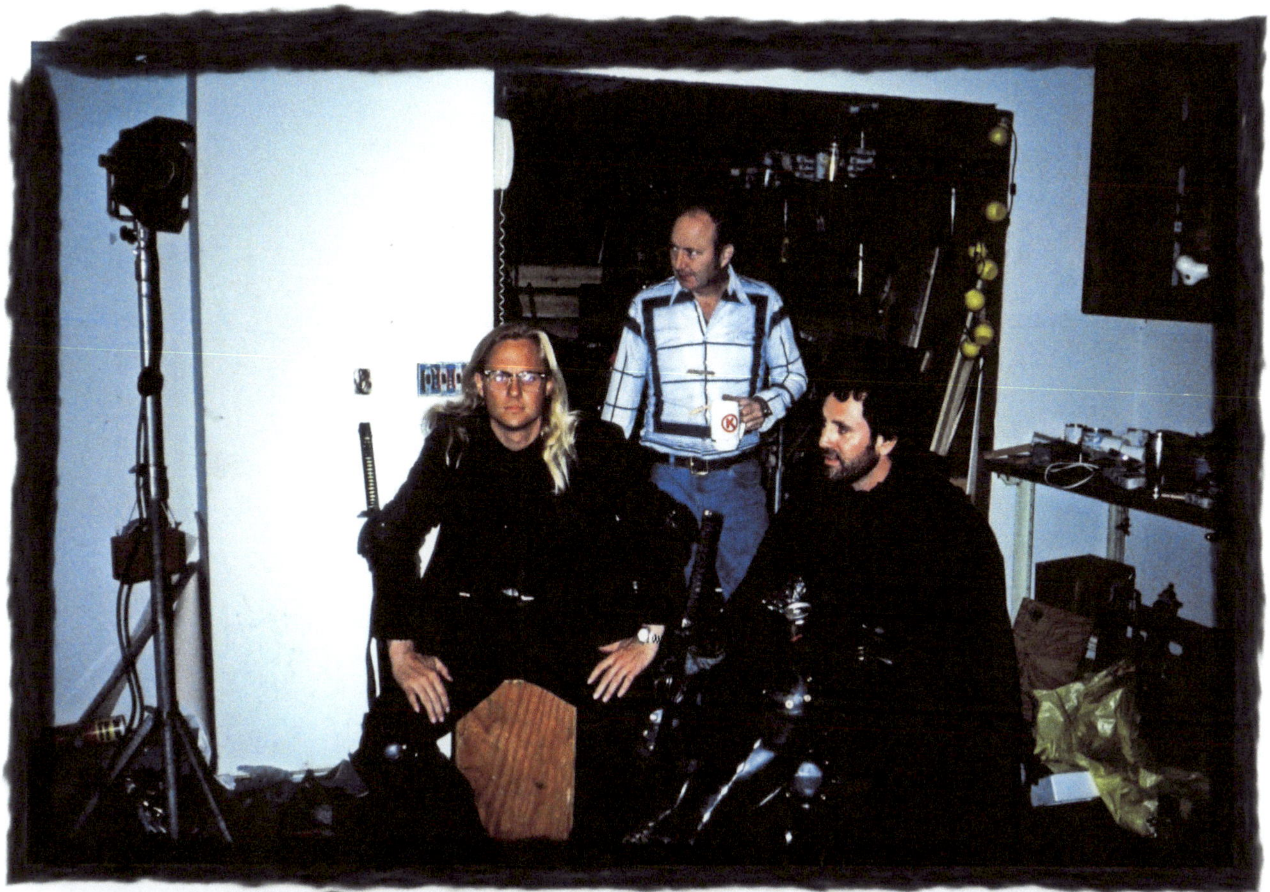

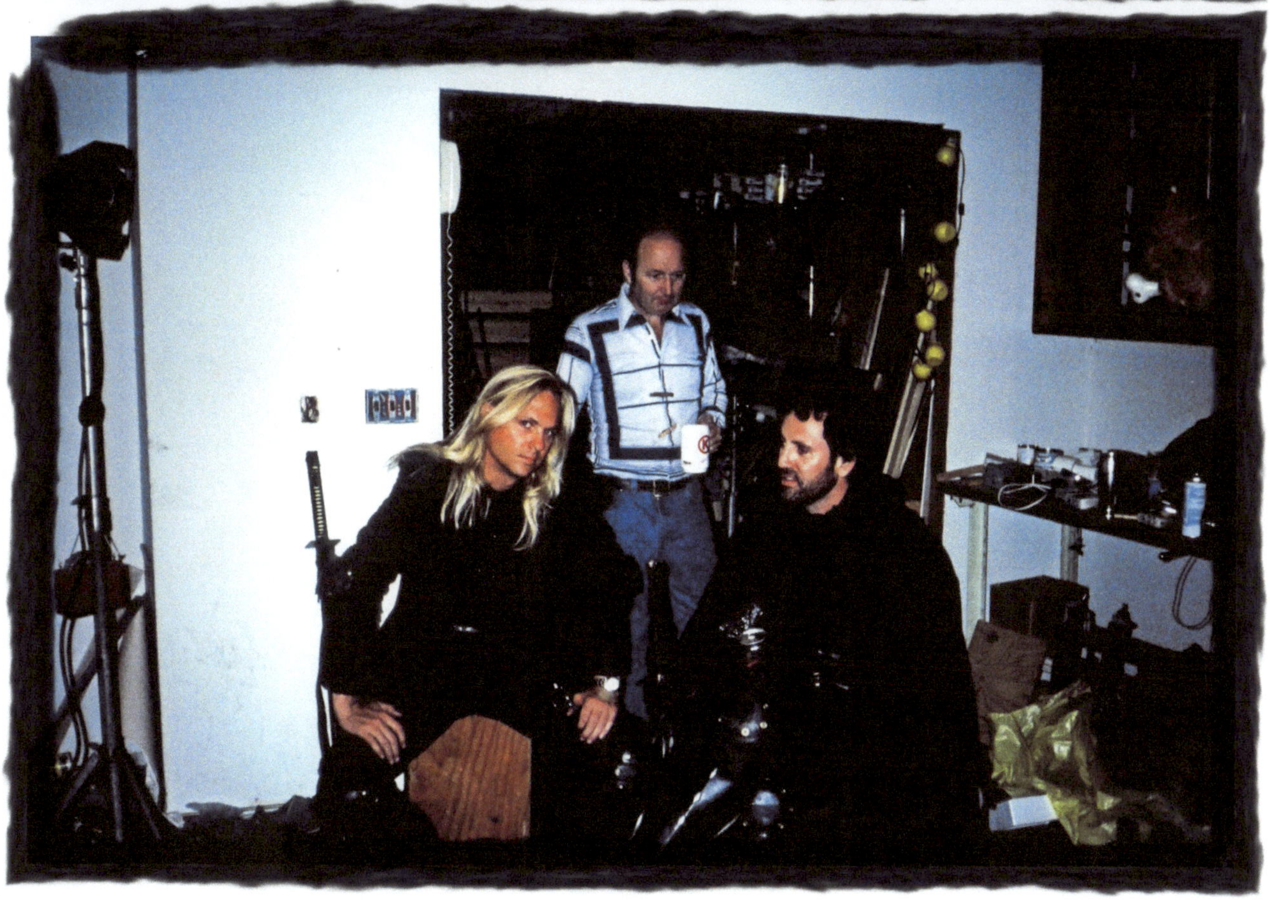

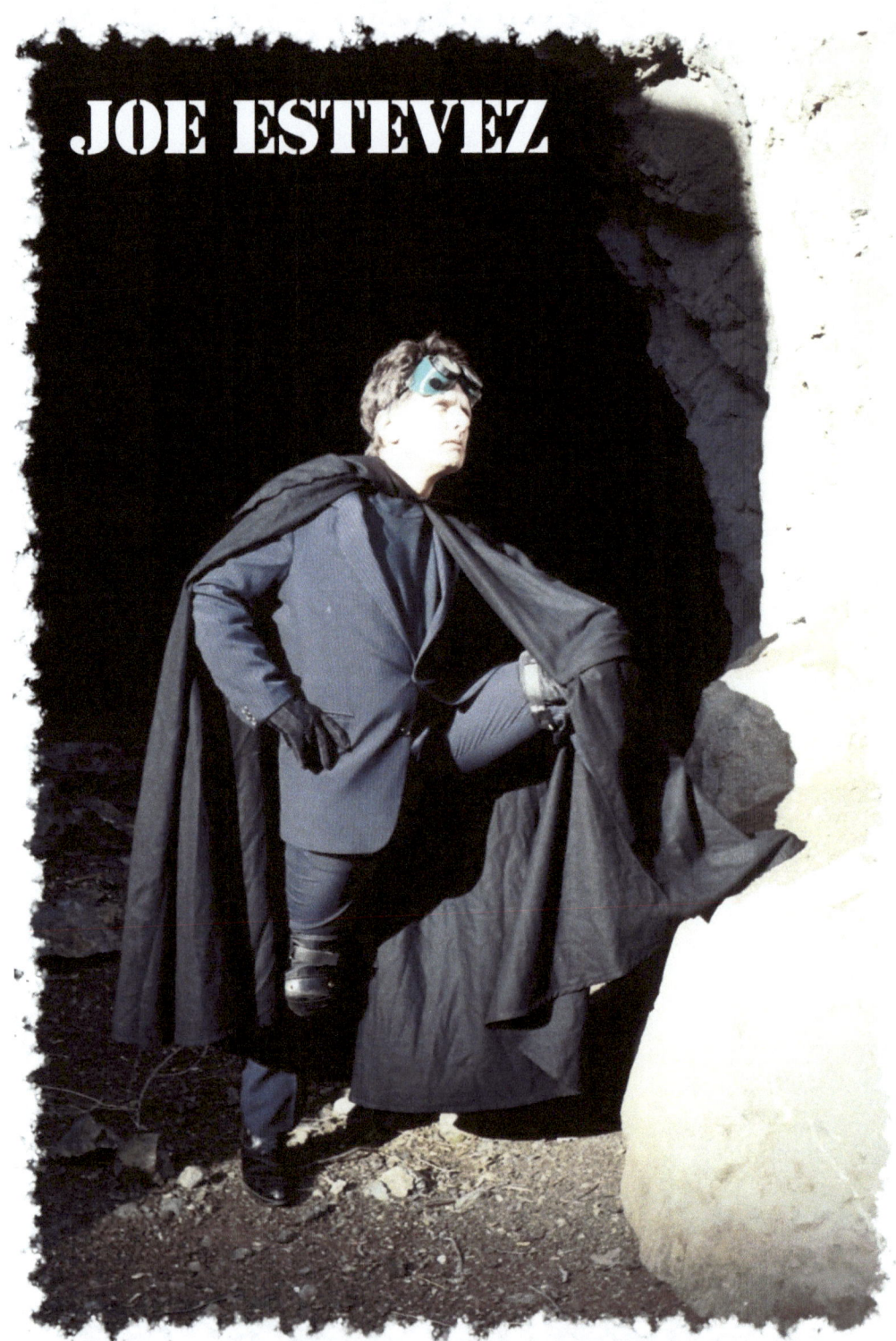

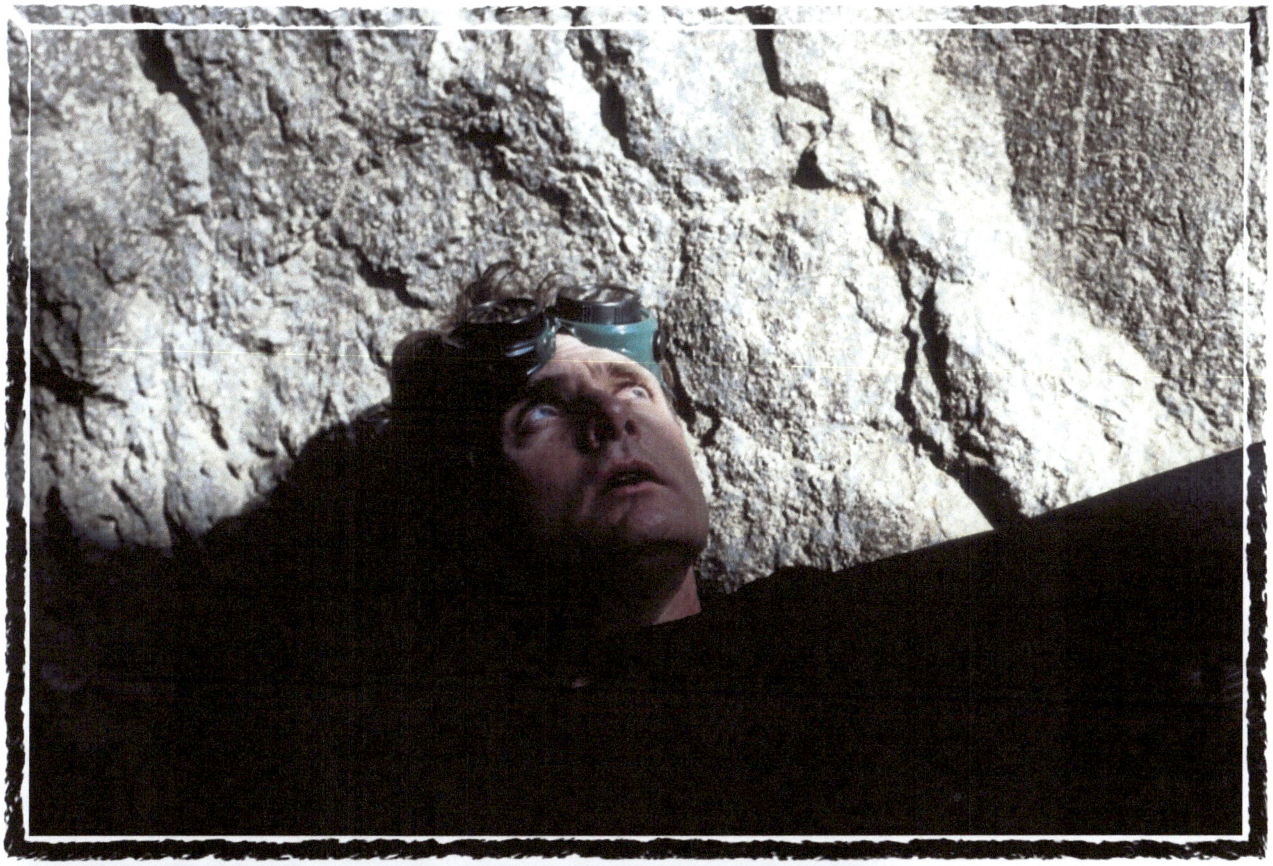

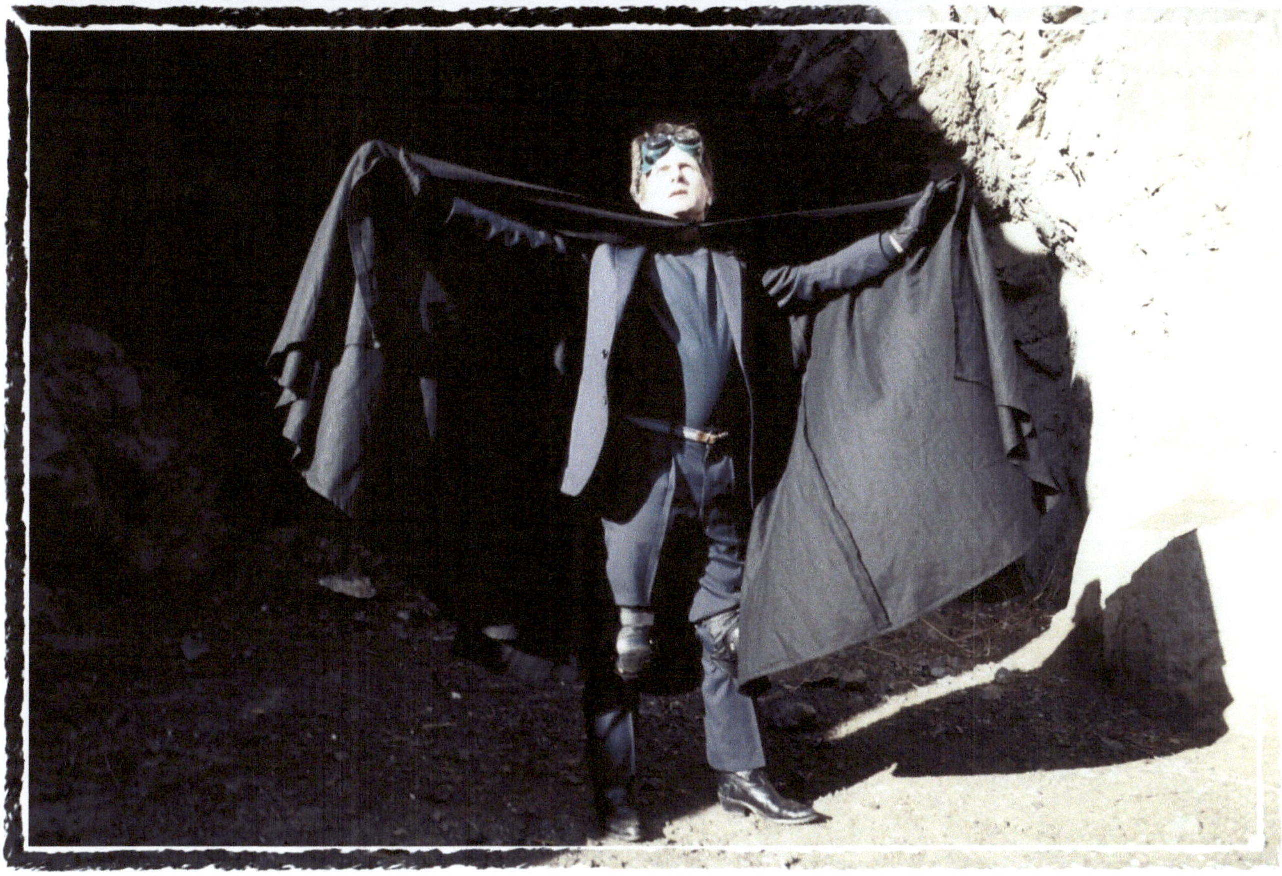

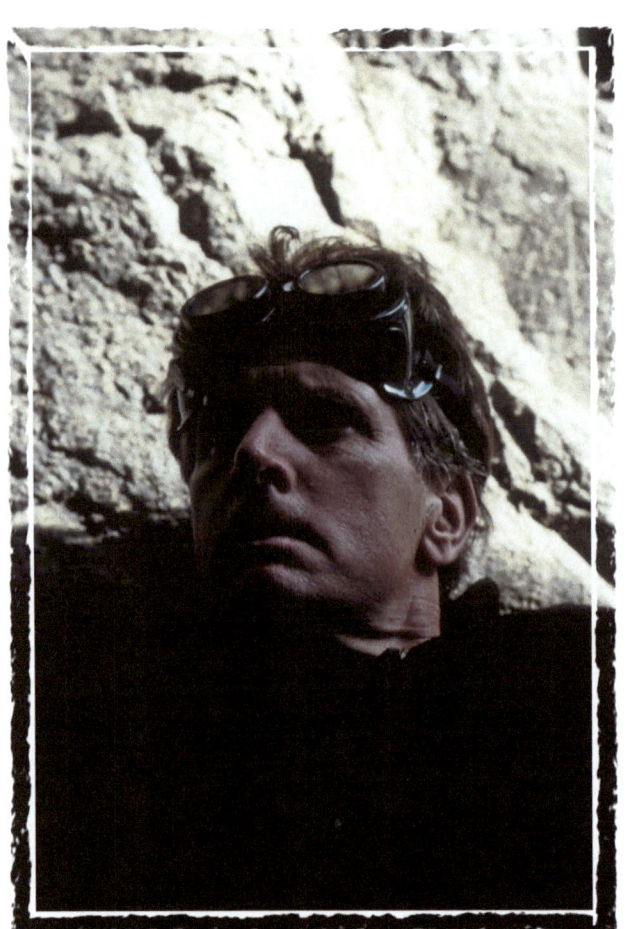
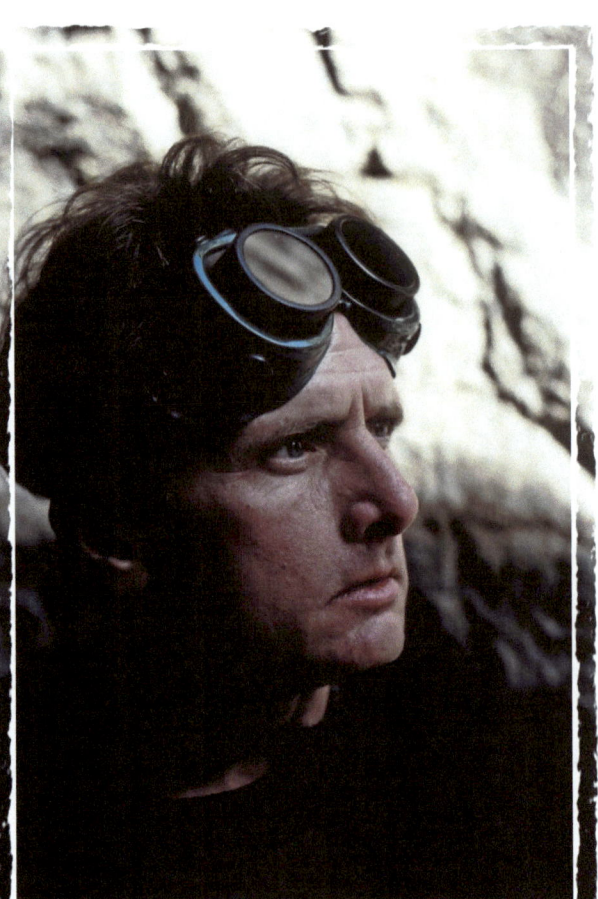

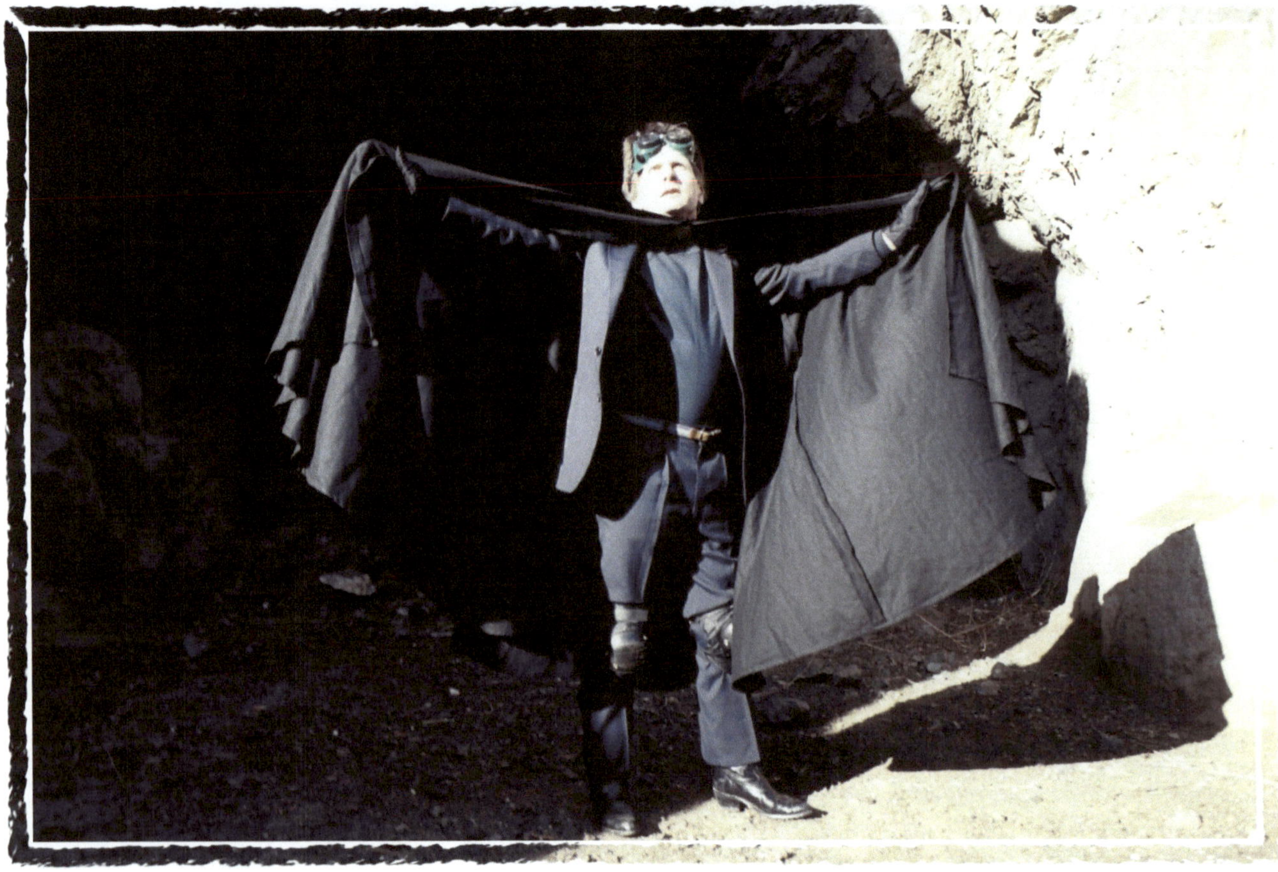

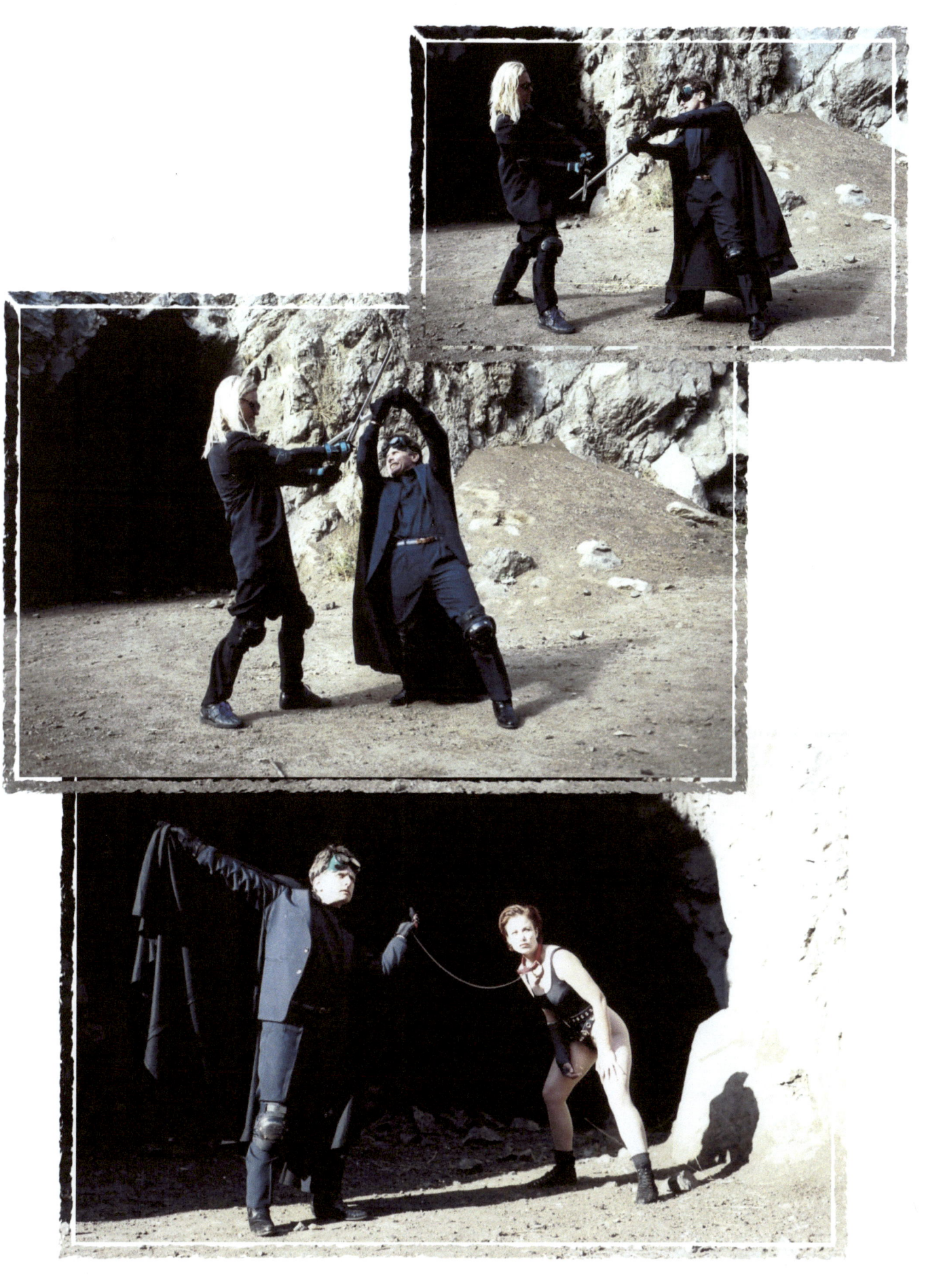

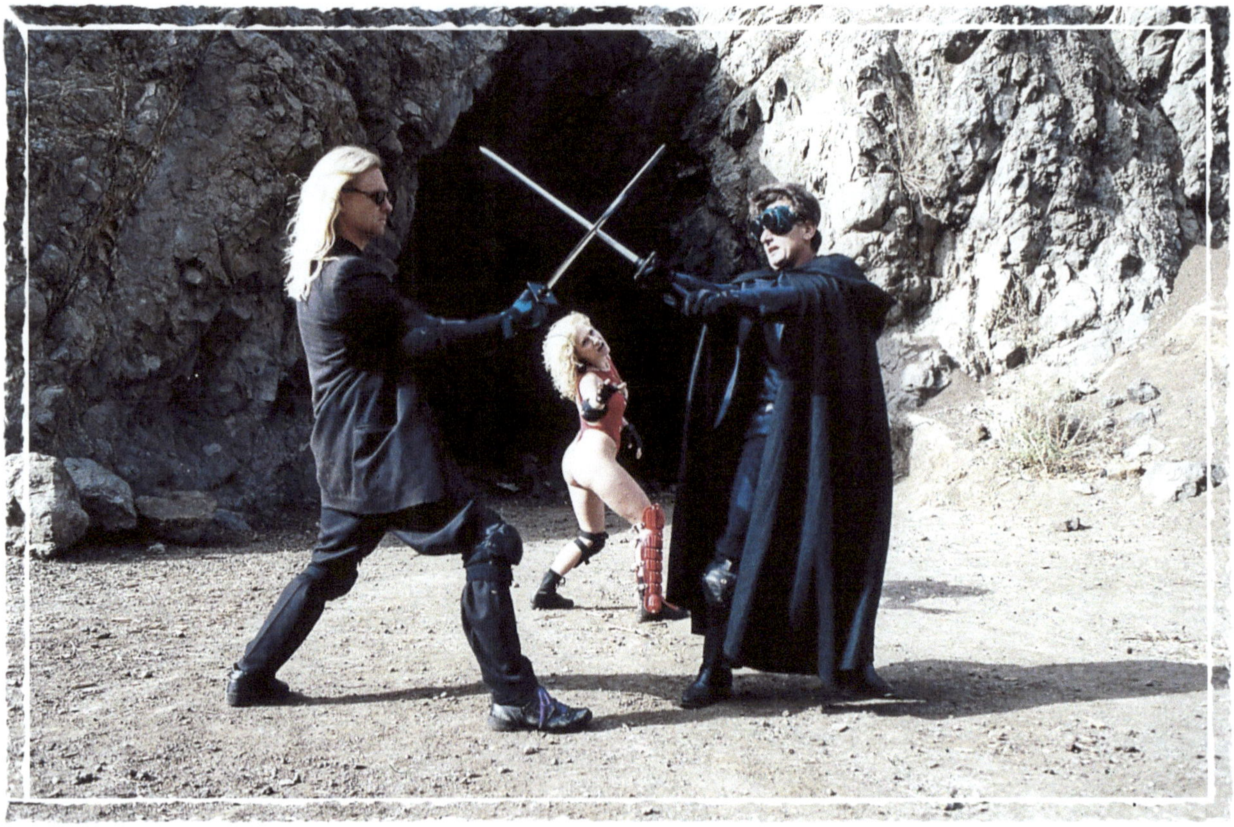

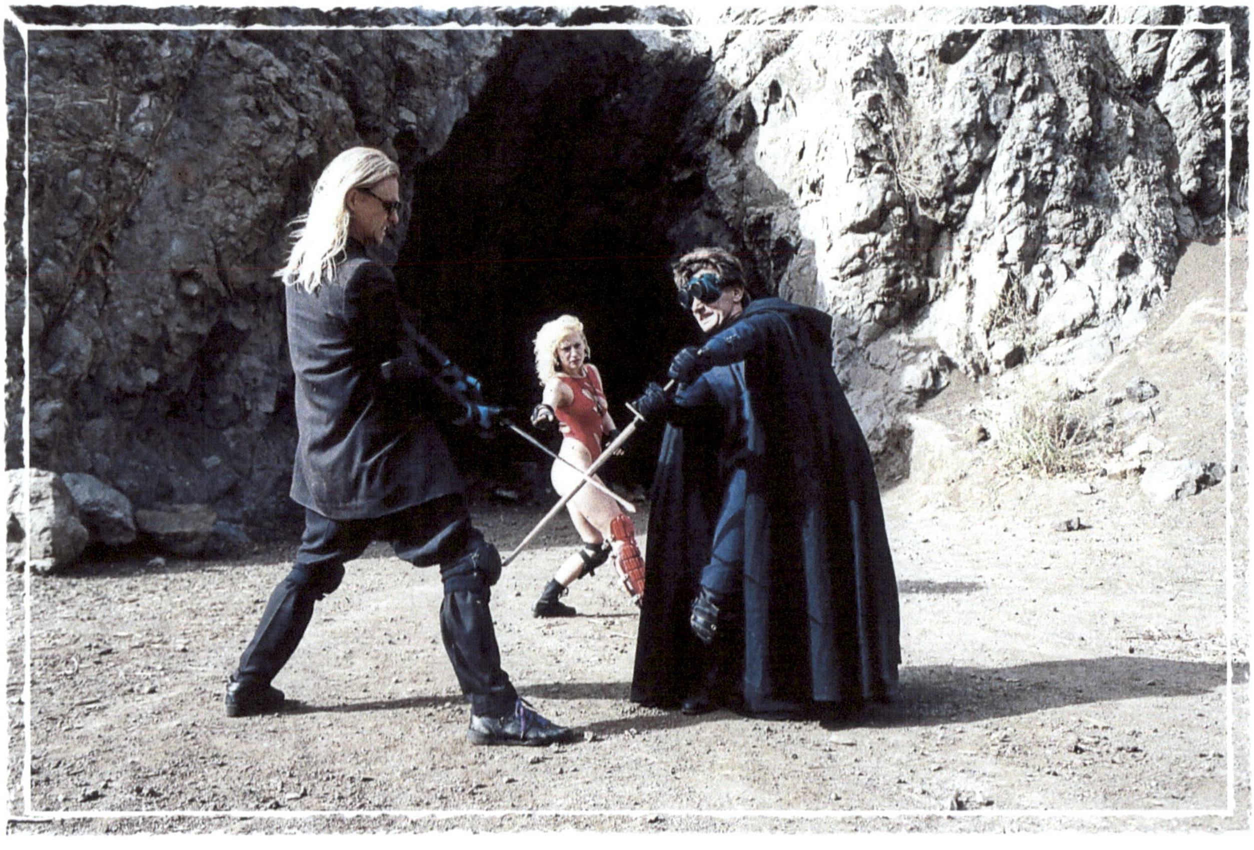

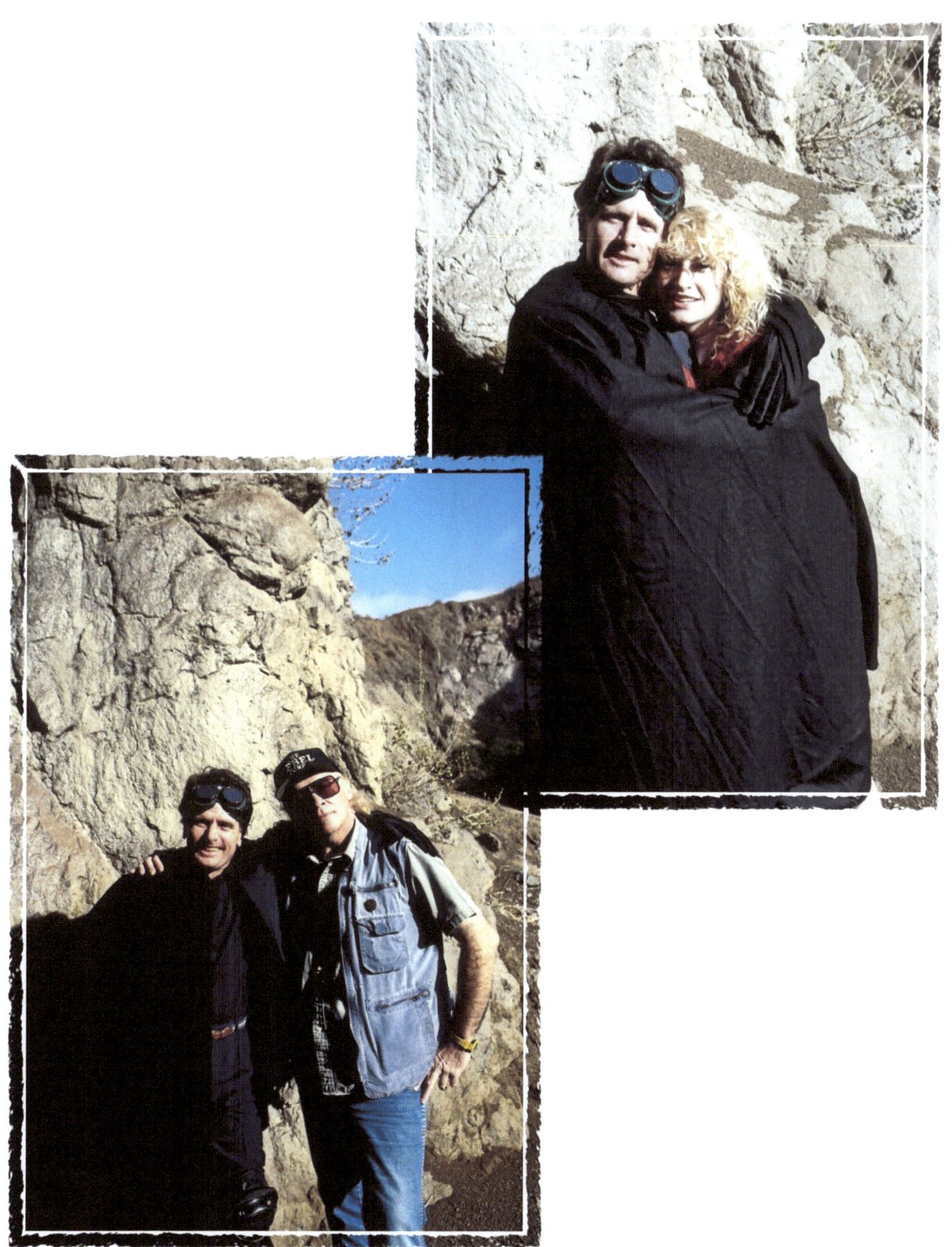

ROLLER BLADE SEVEN WEDDING

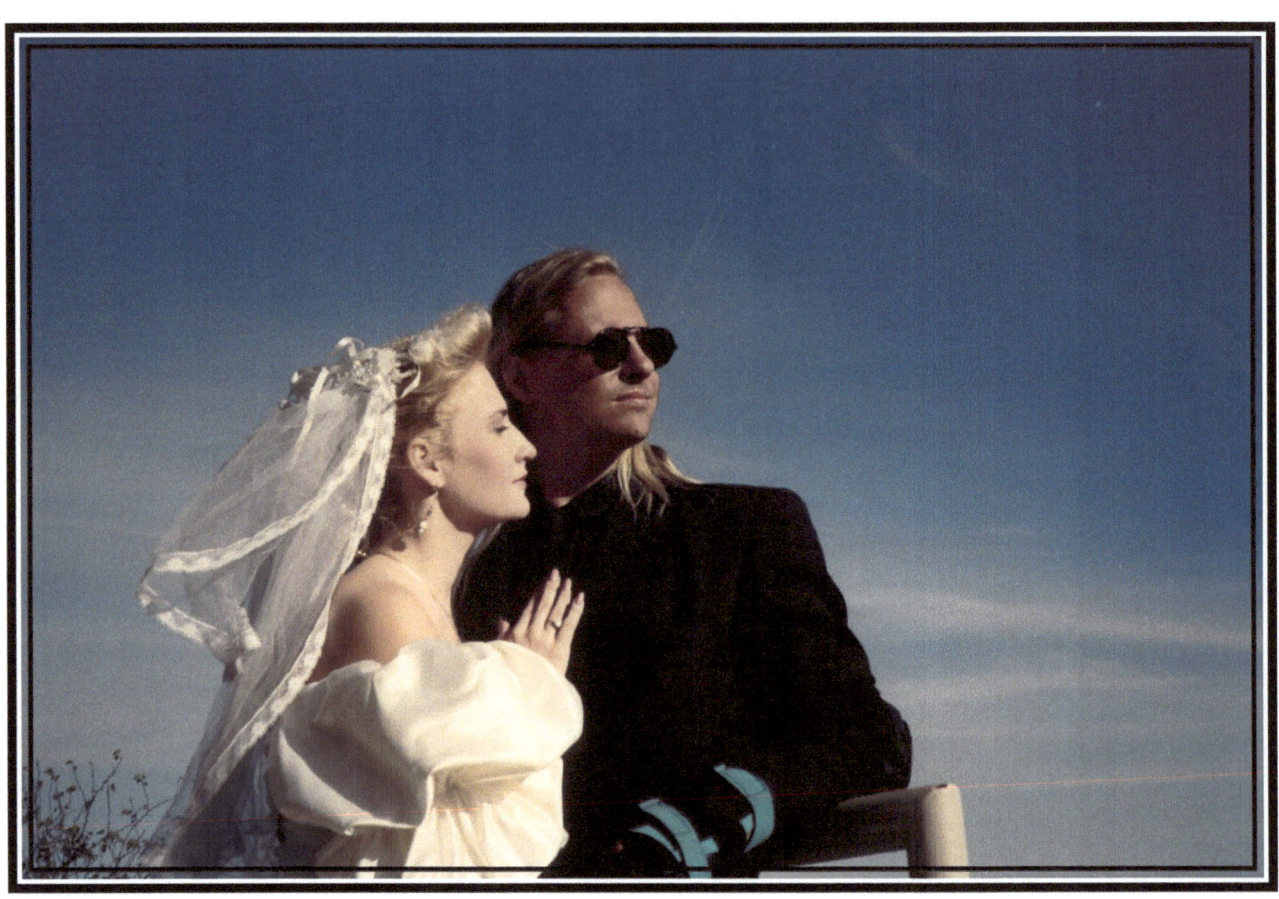

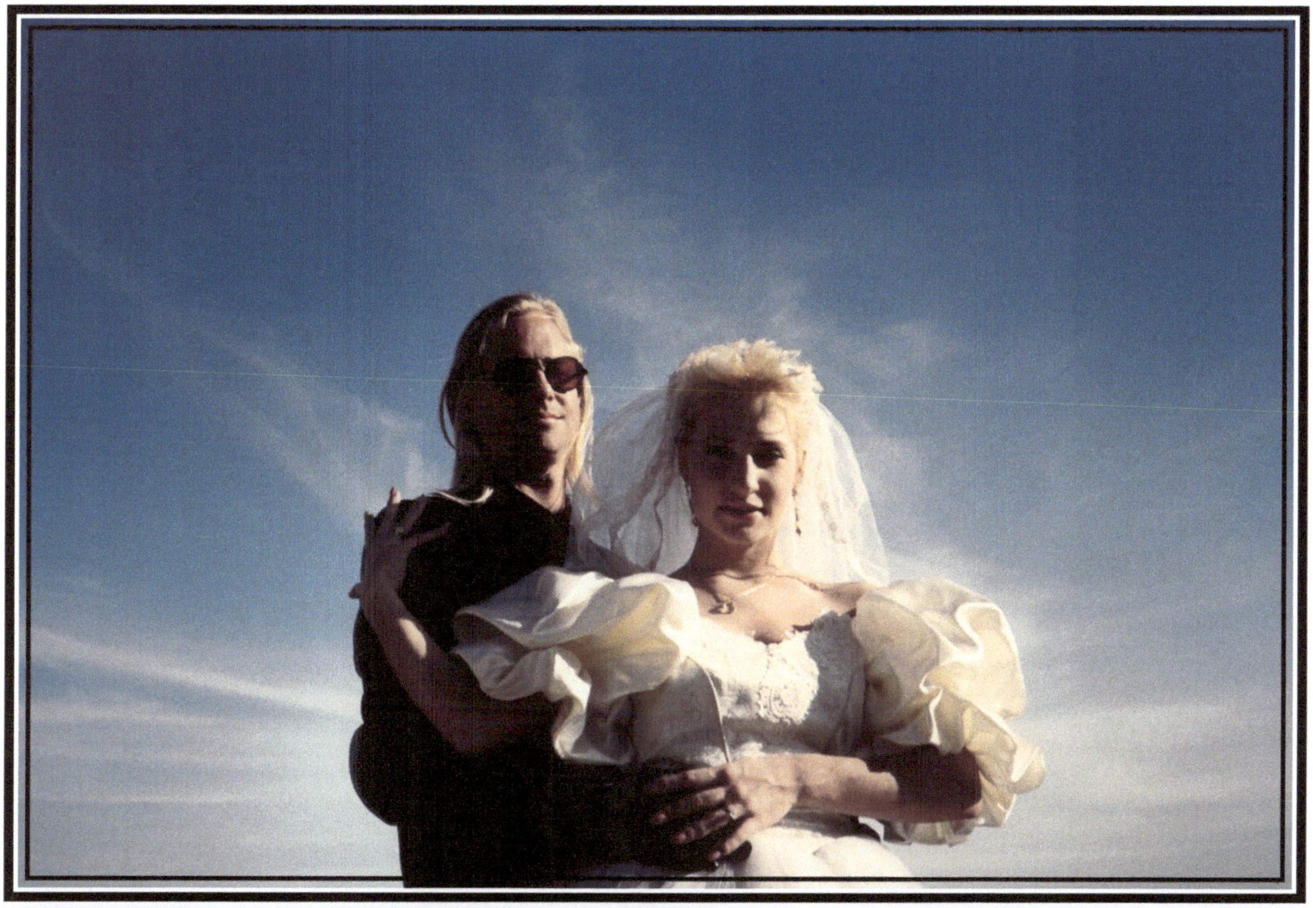

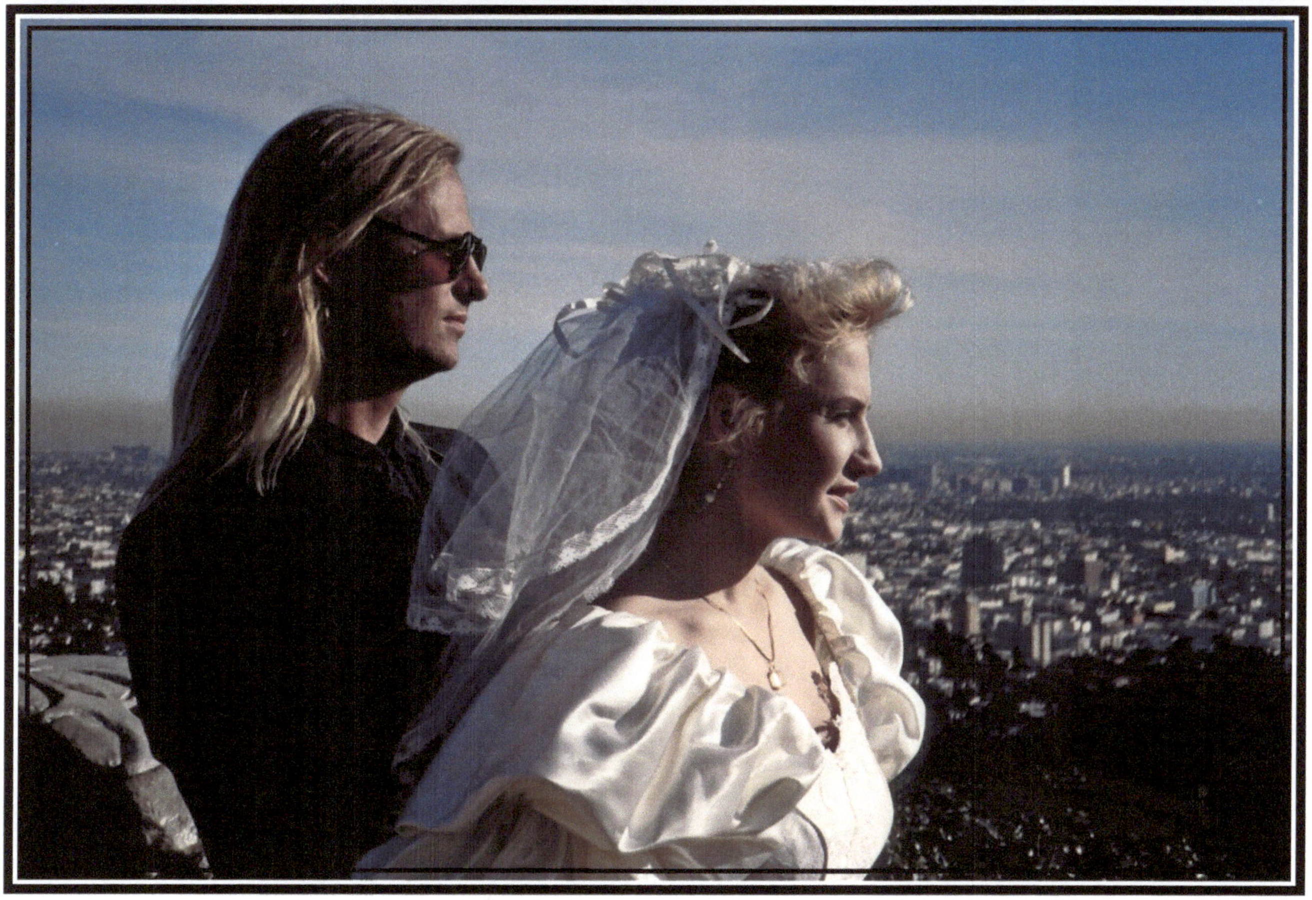

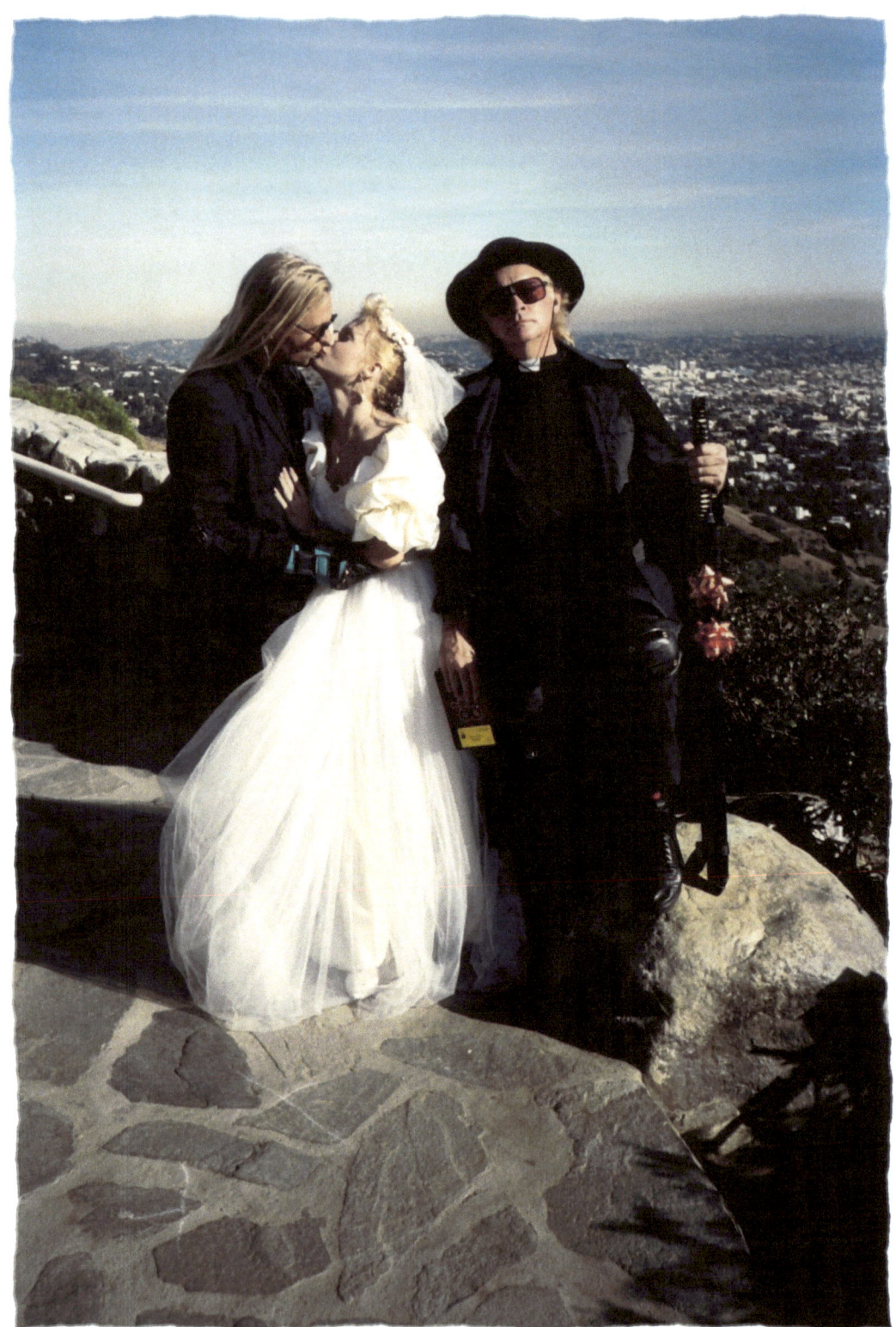

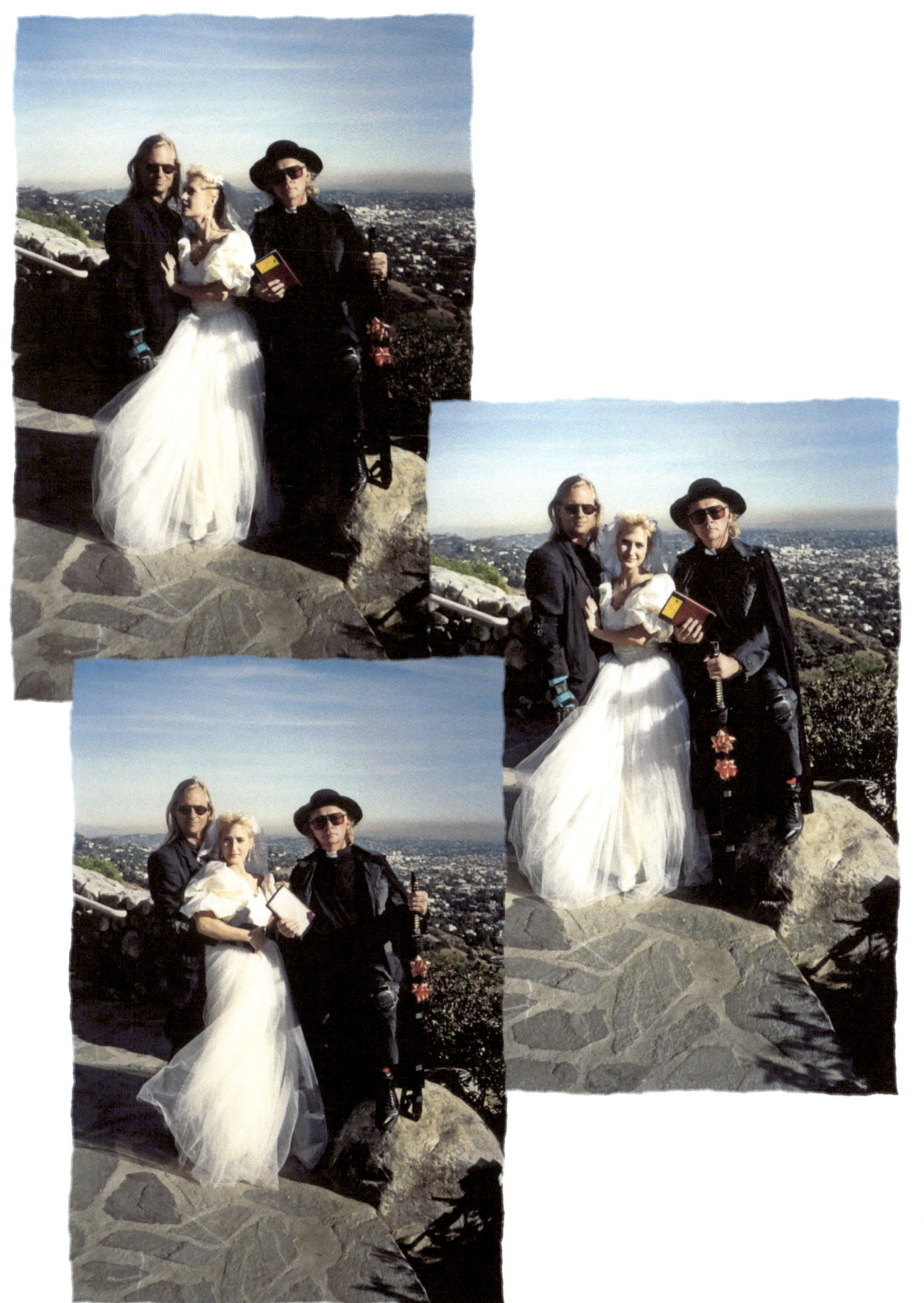

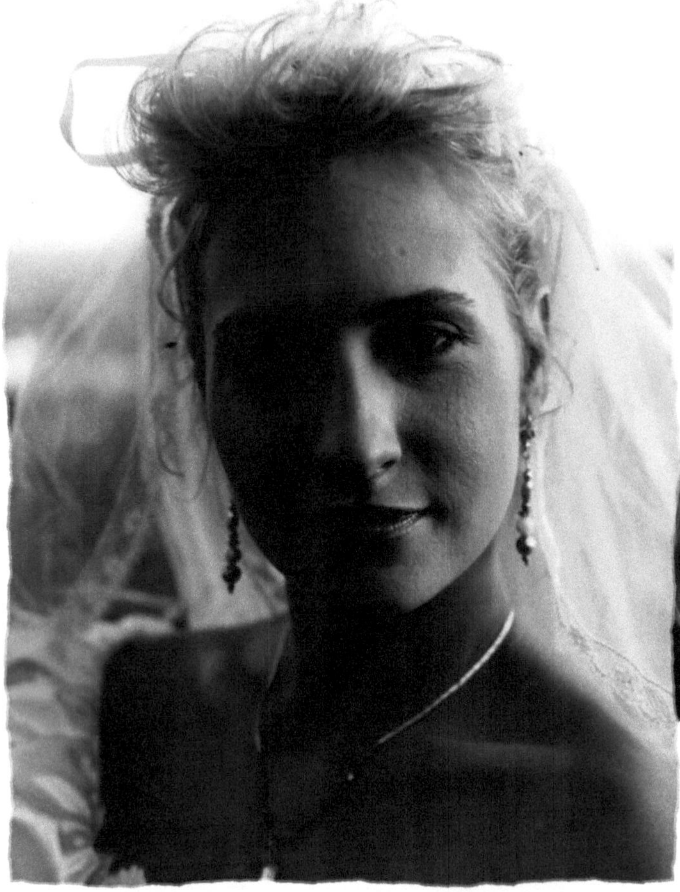

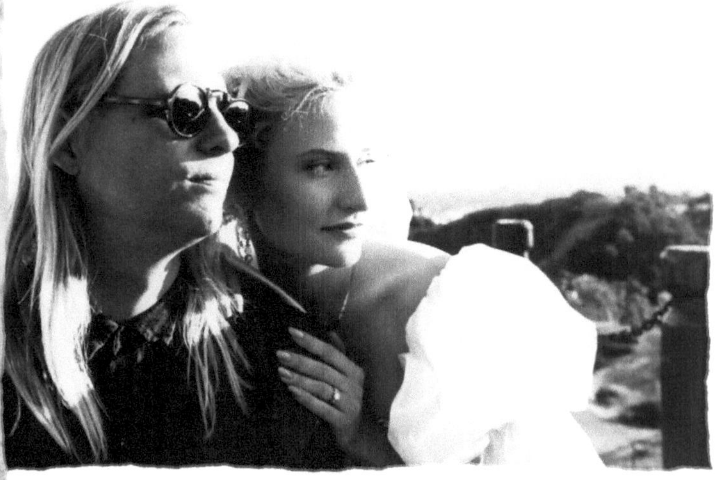

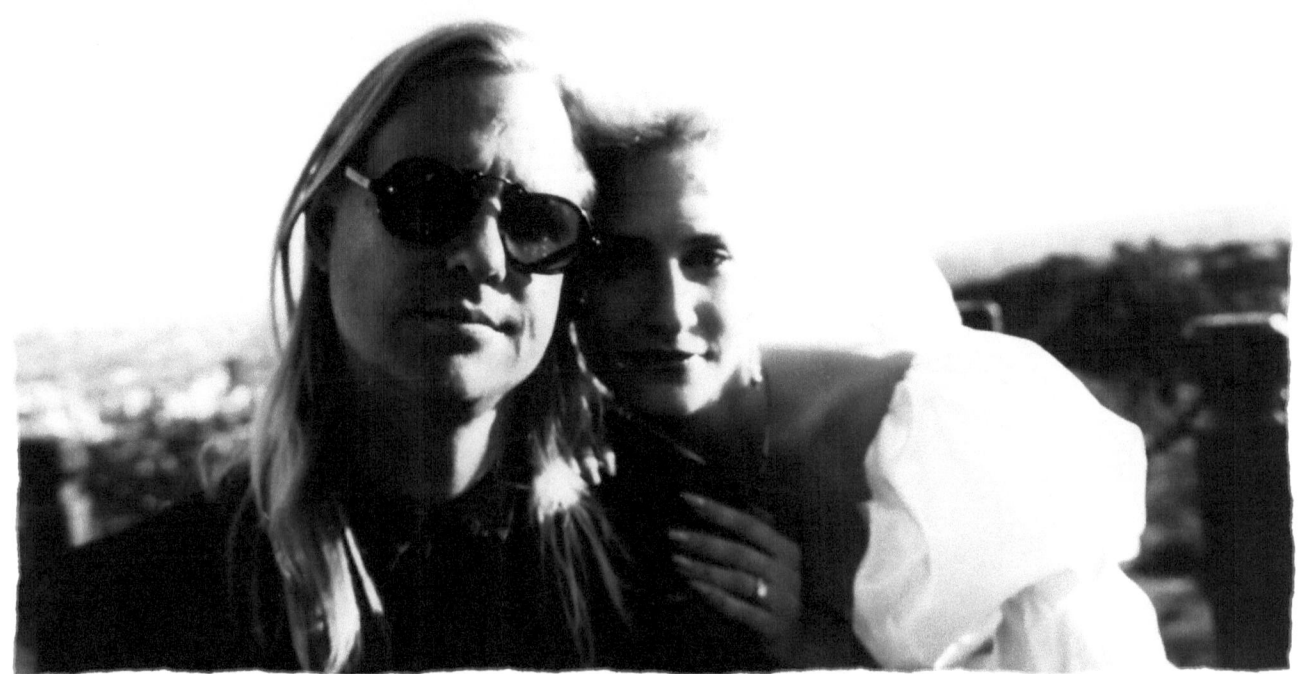

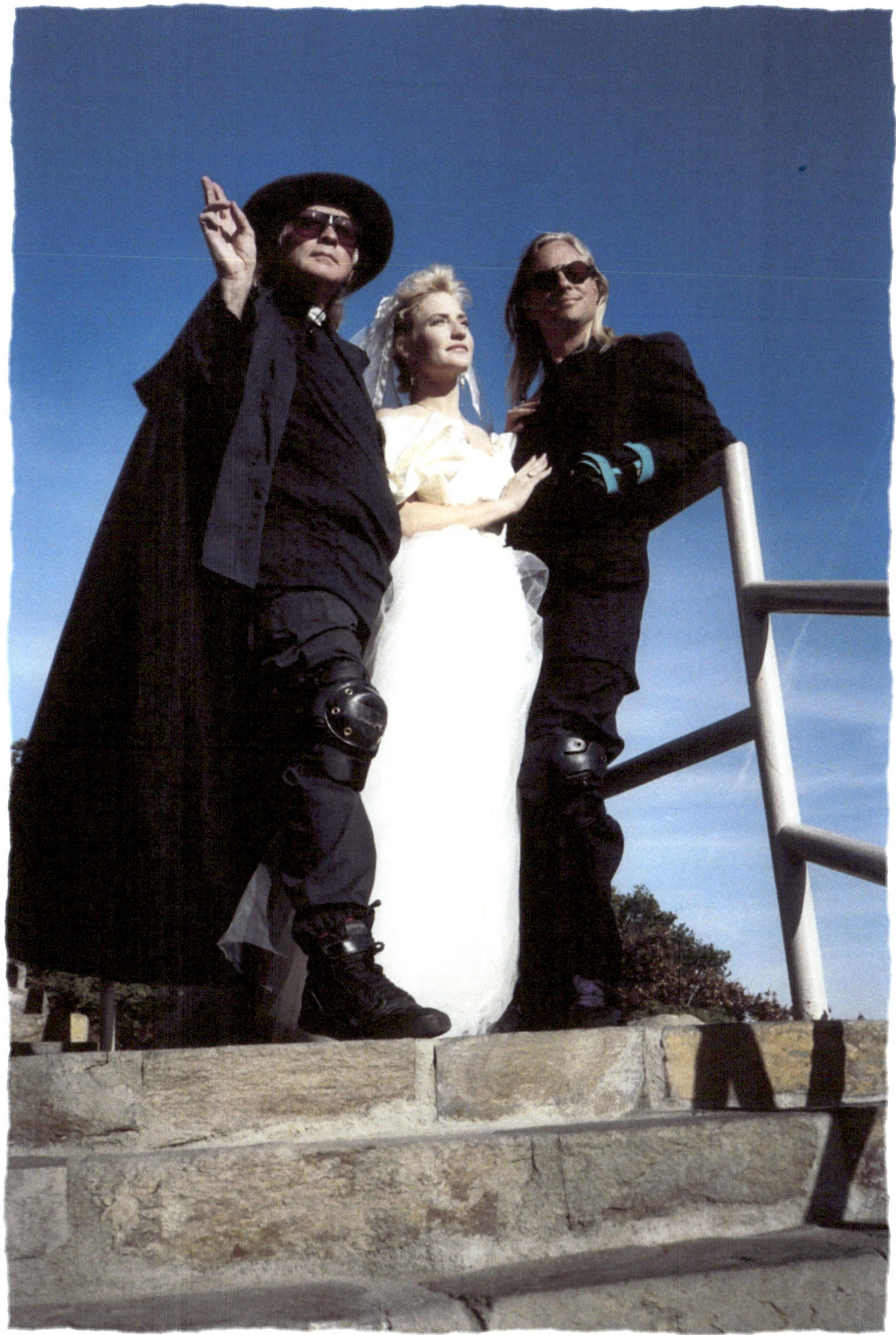

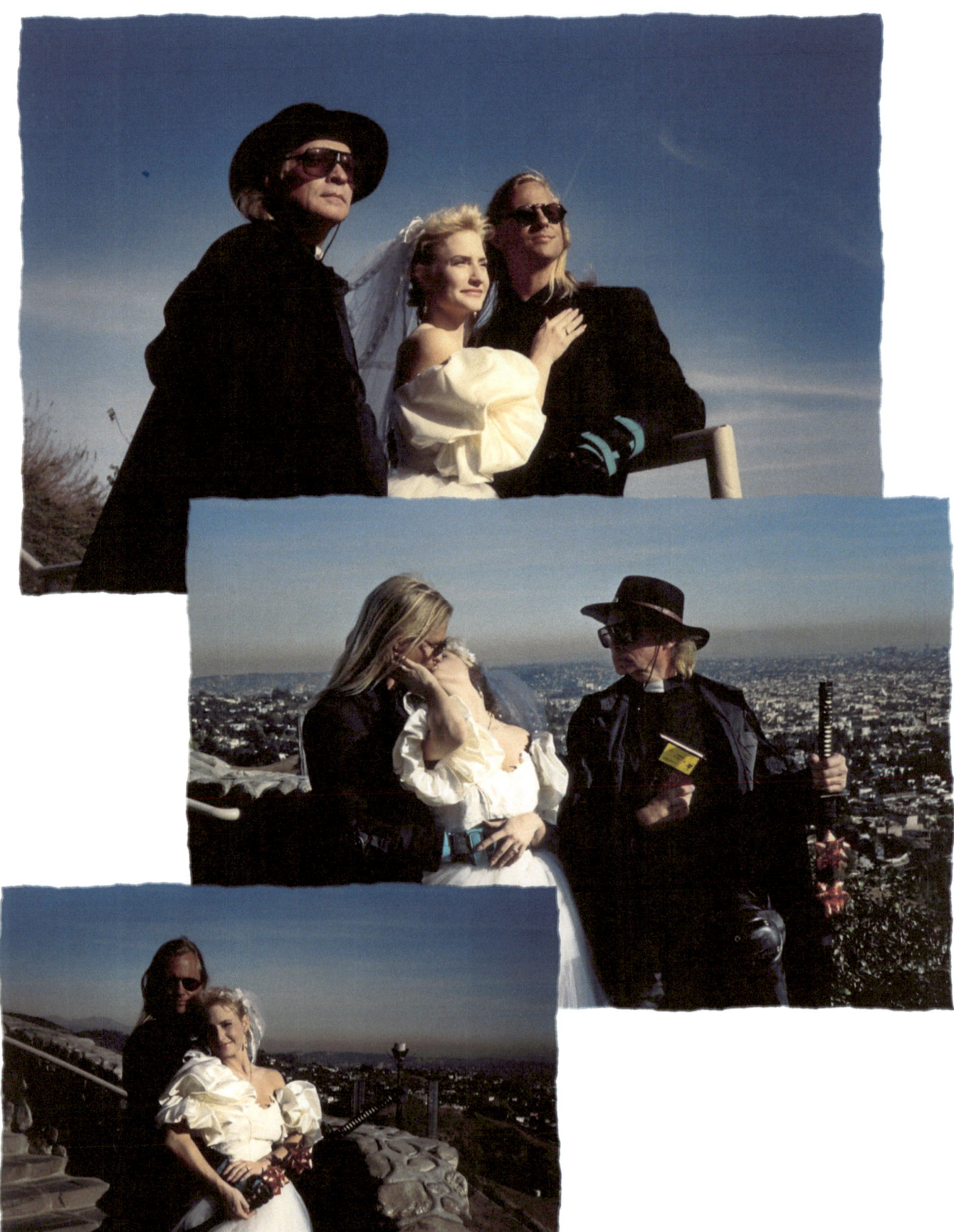

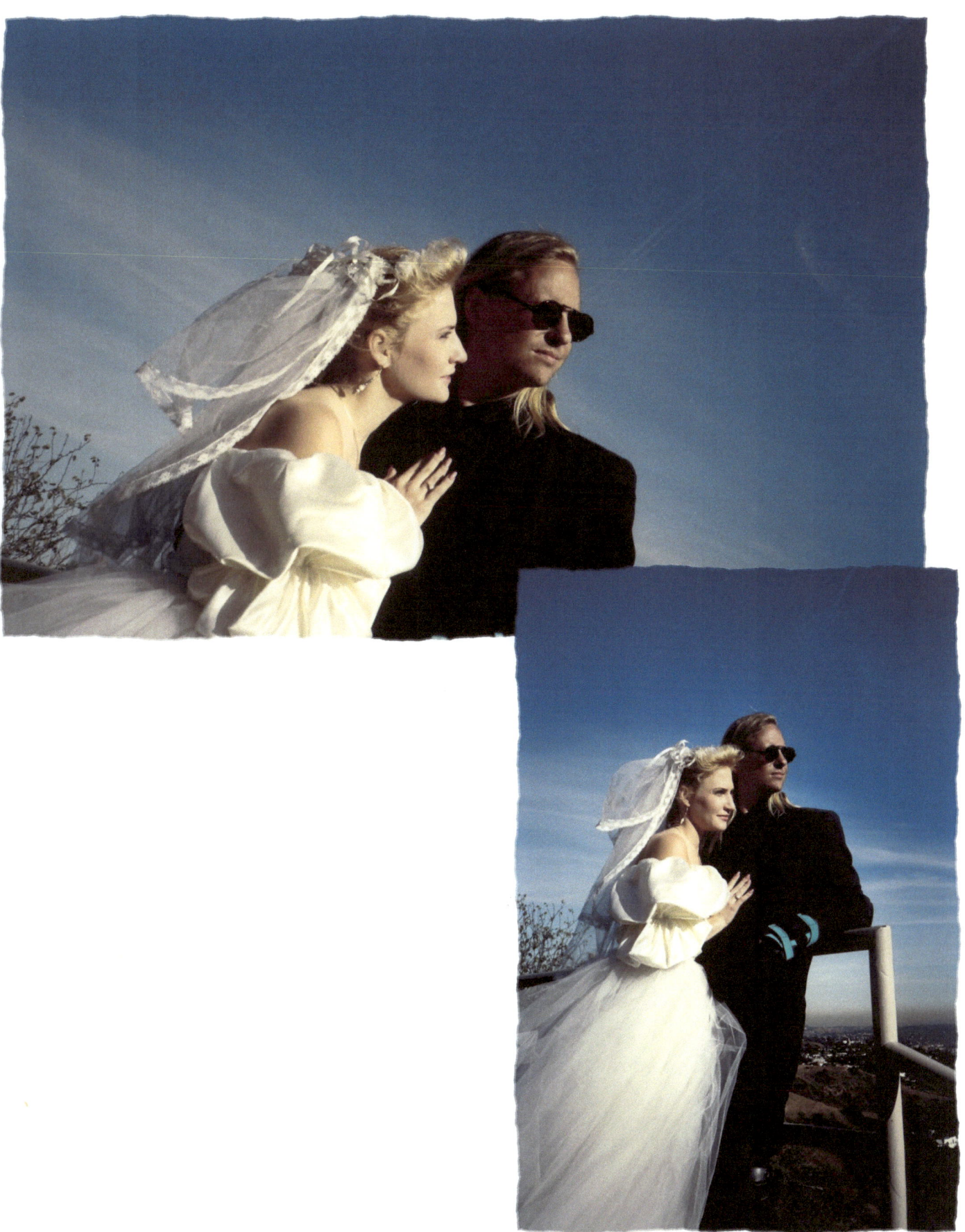

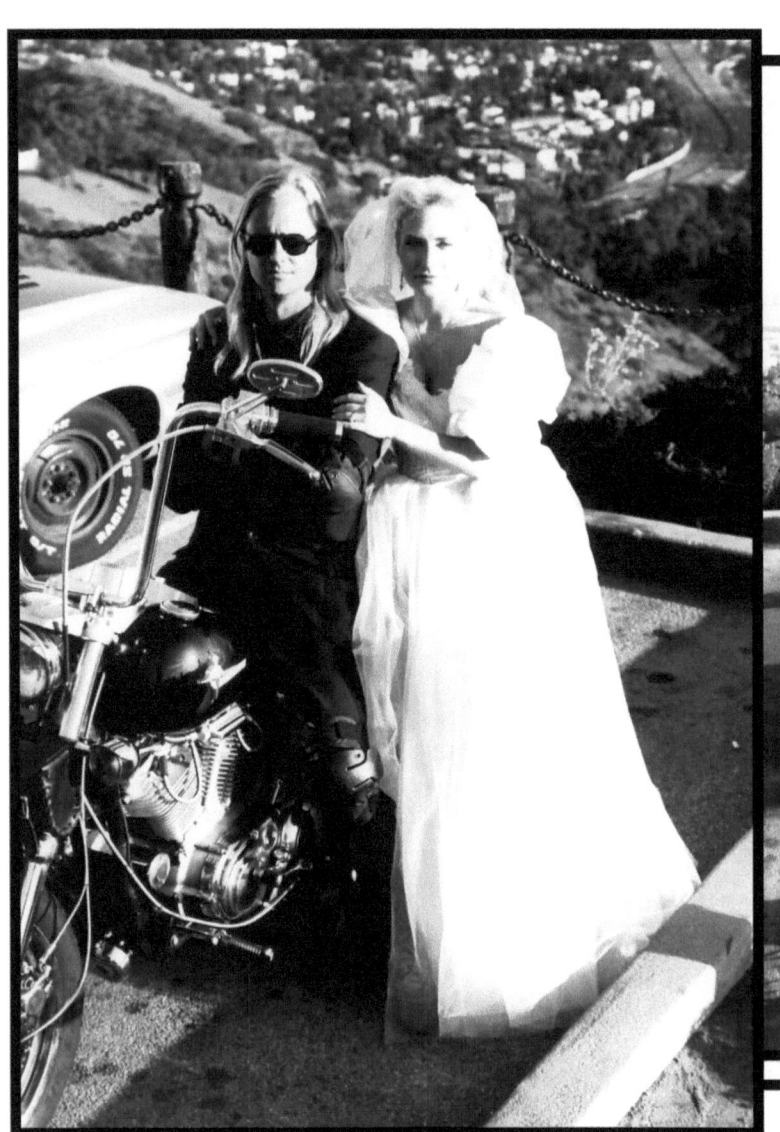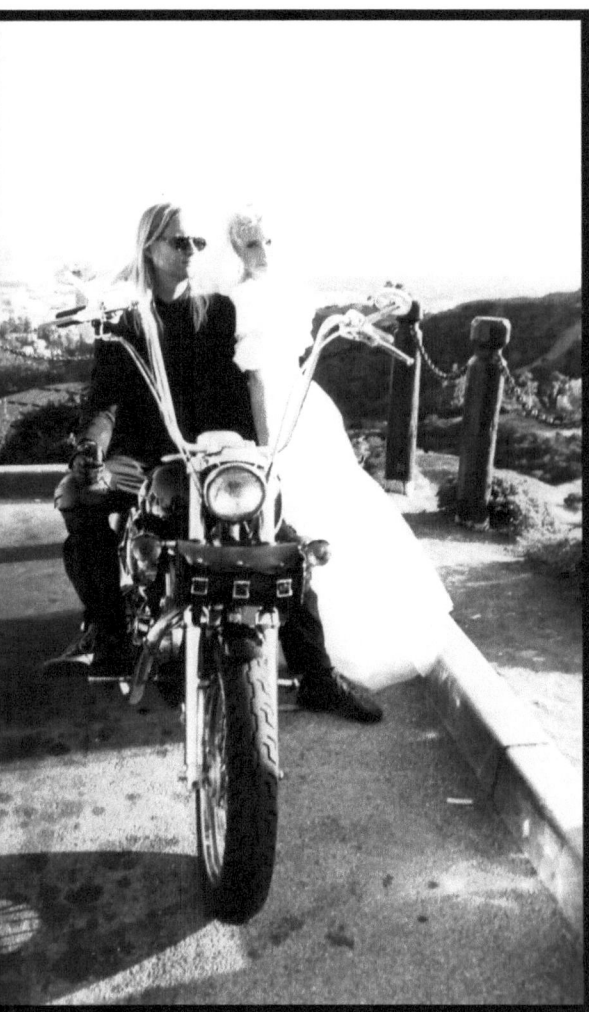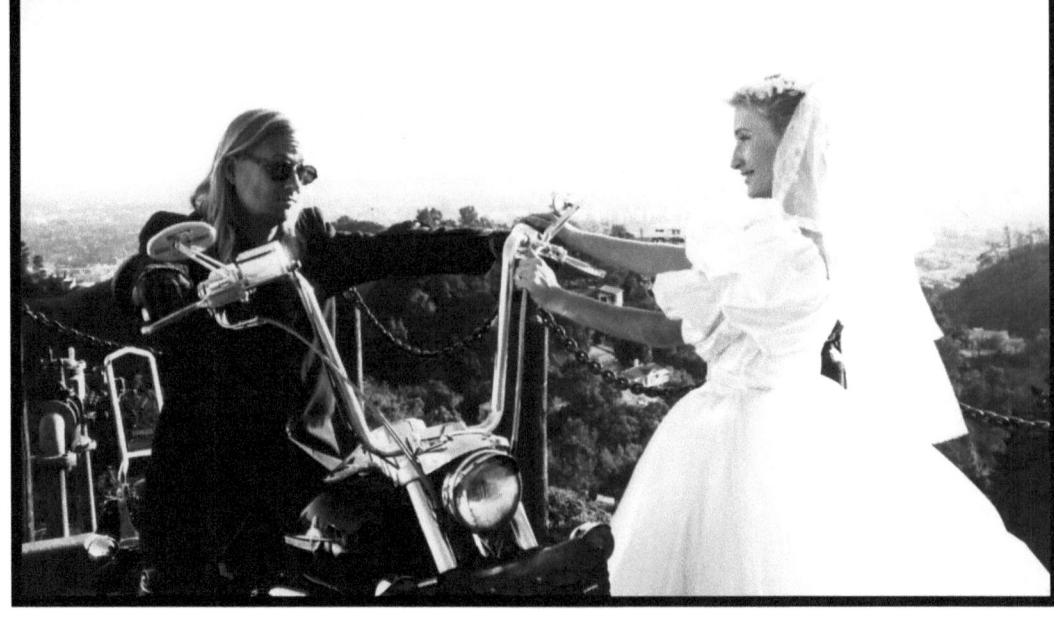

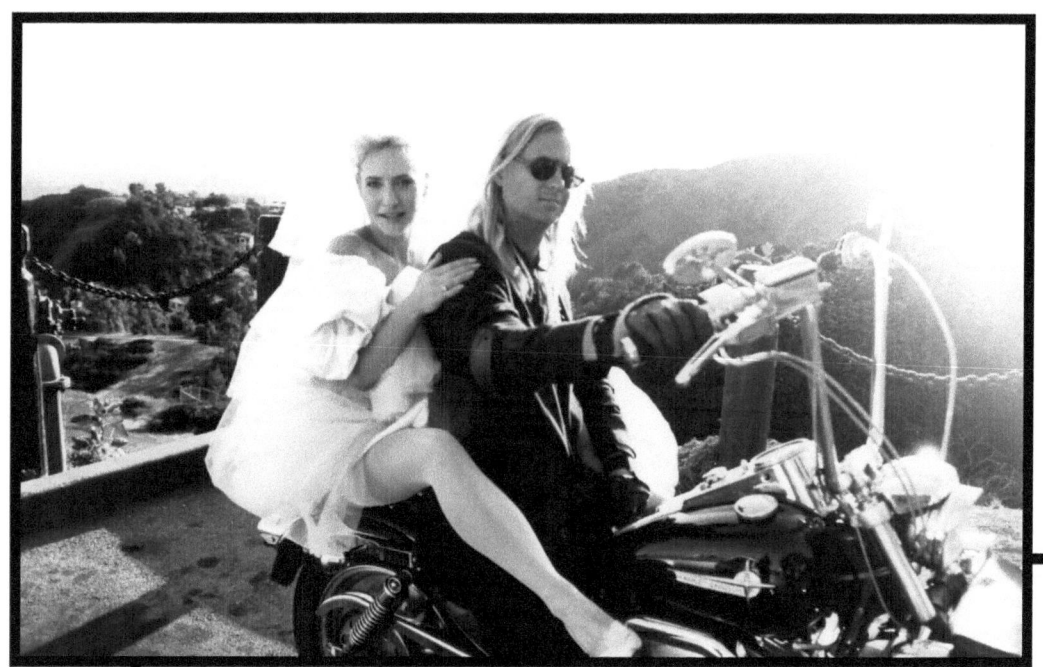
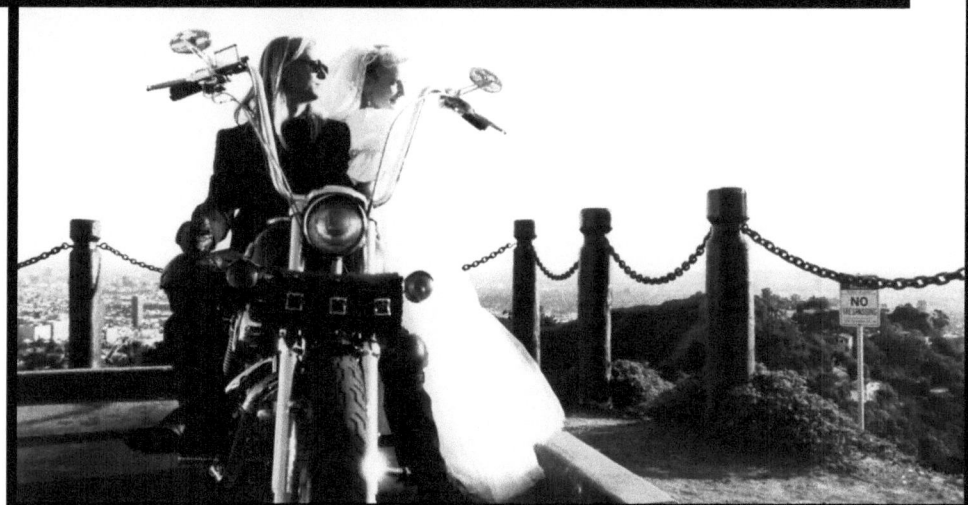
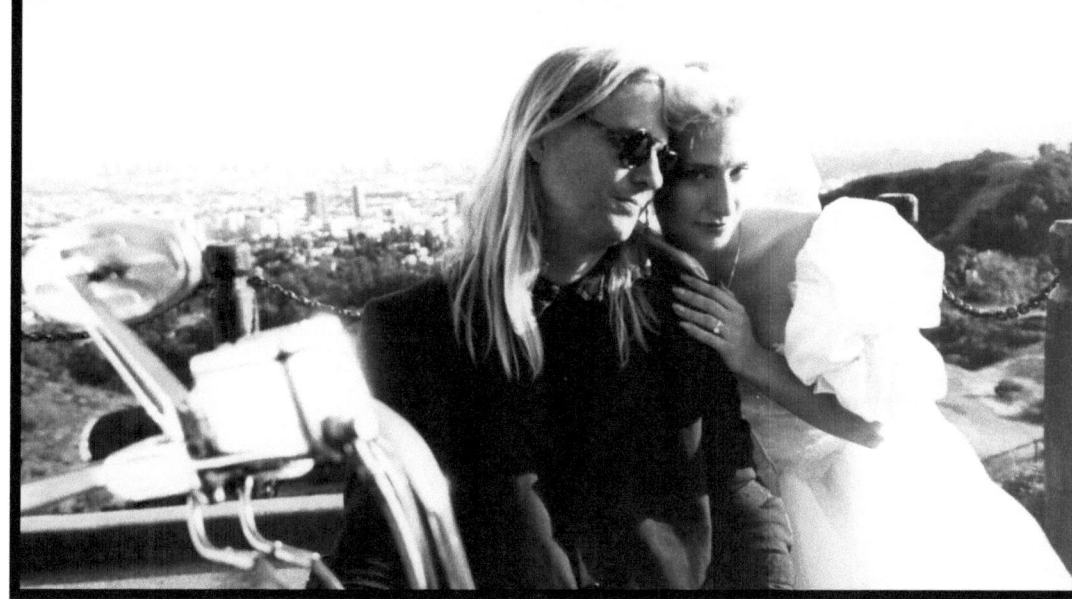

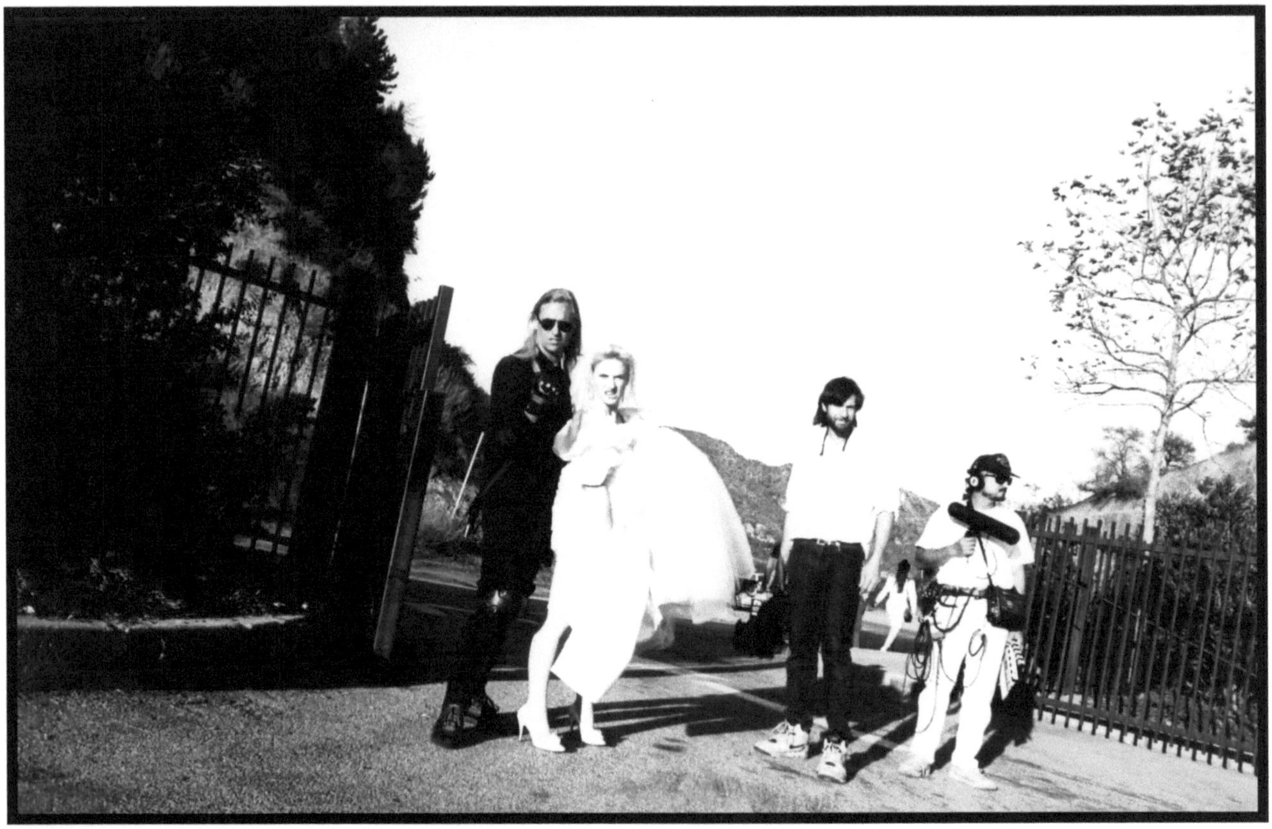

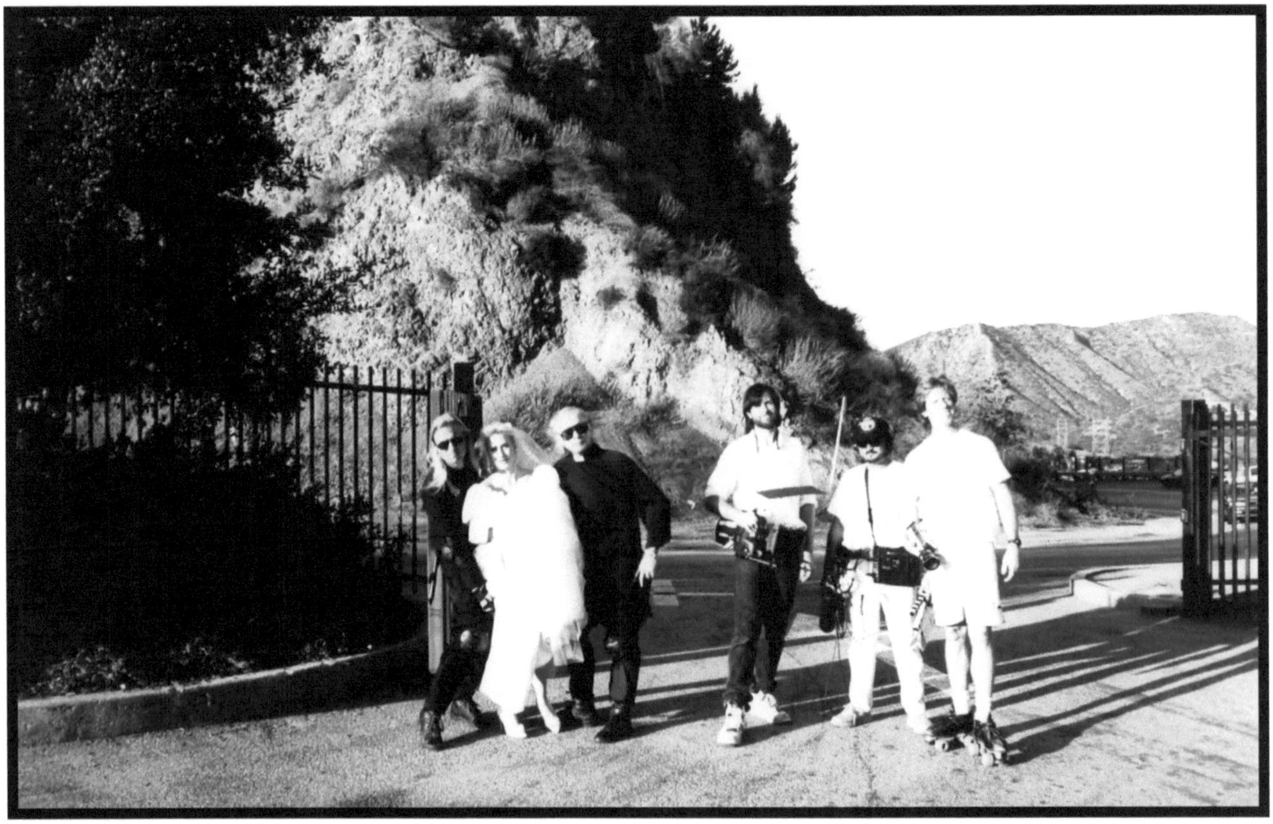

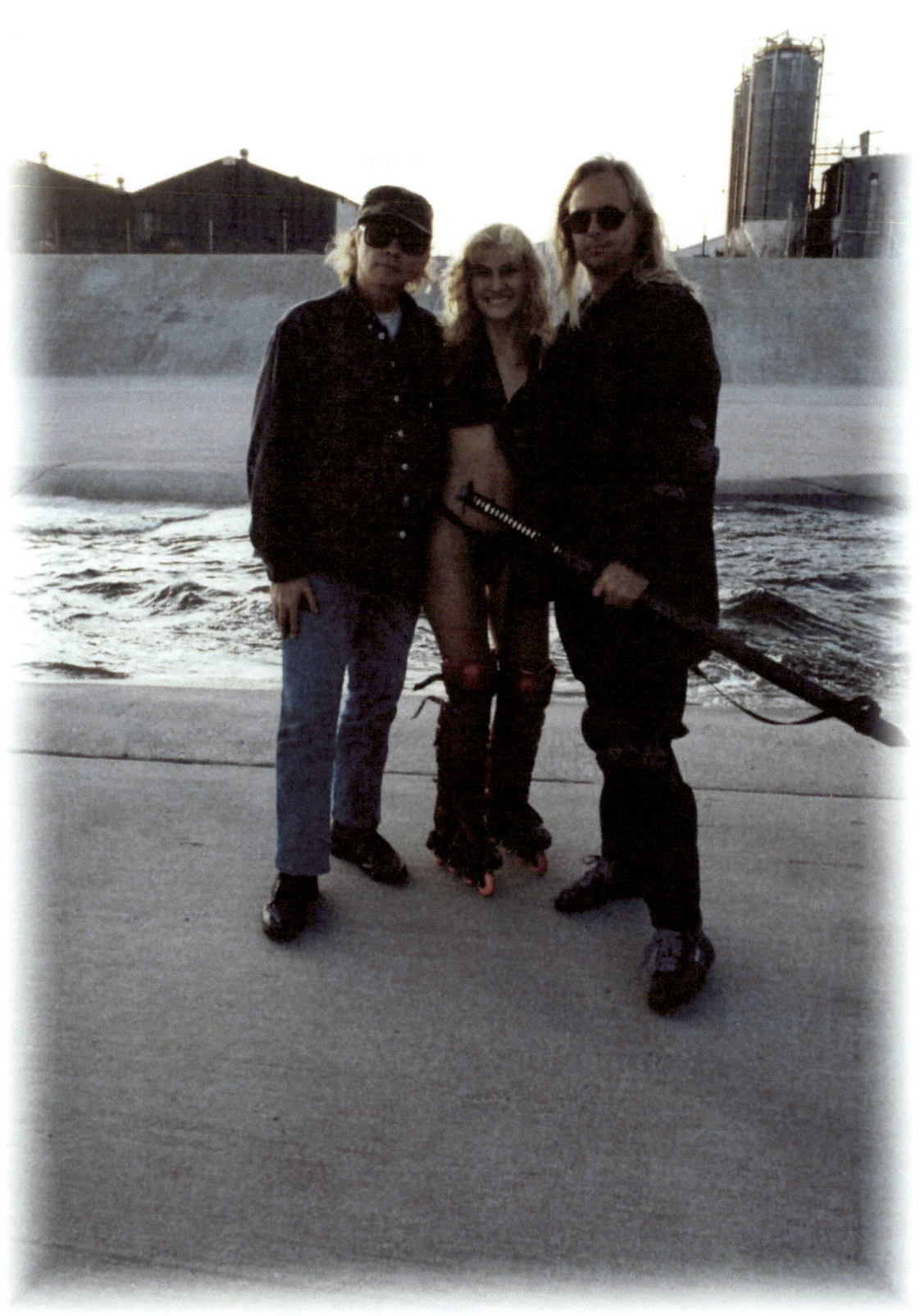

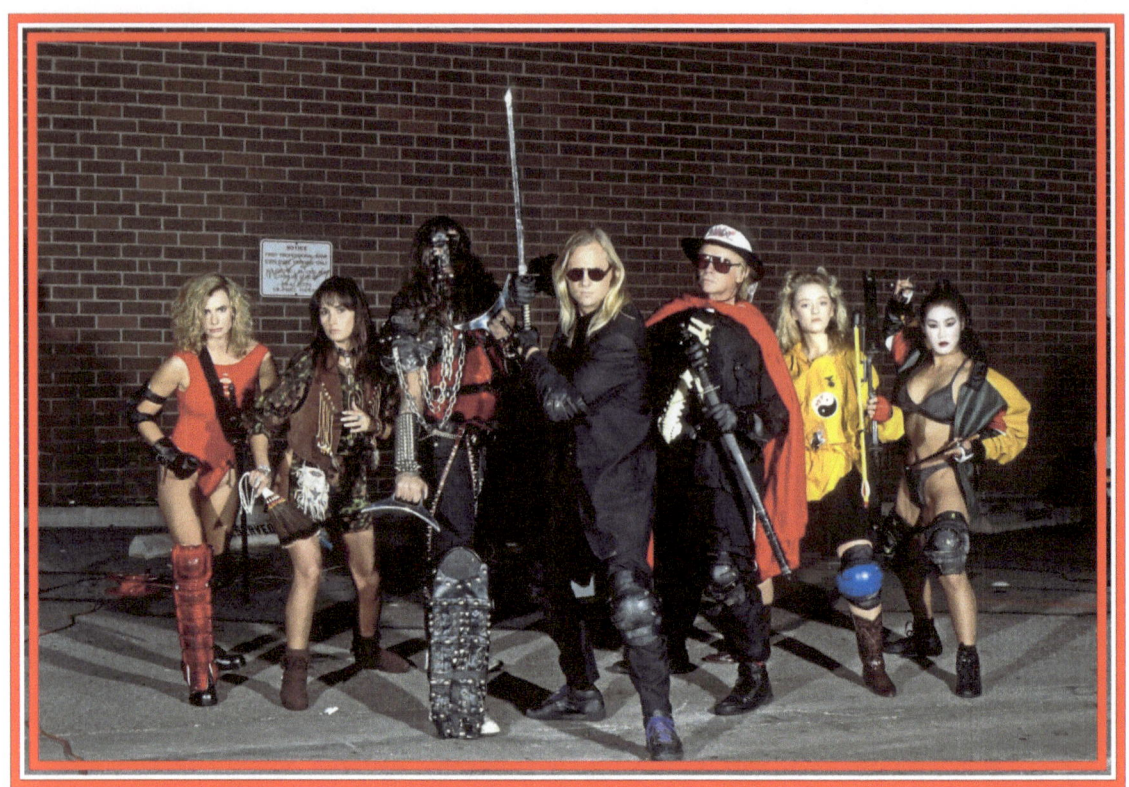

THE ROLLER BLADE SEVEN

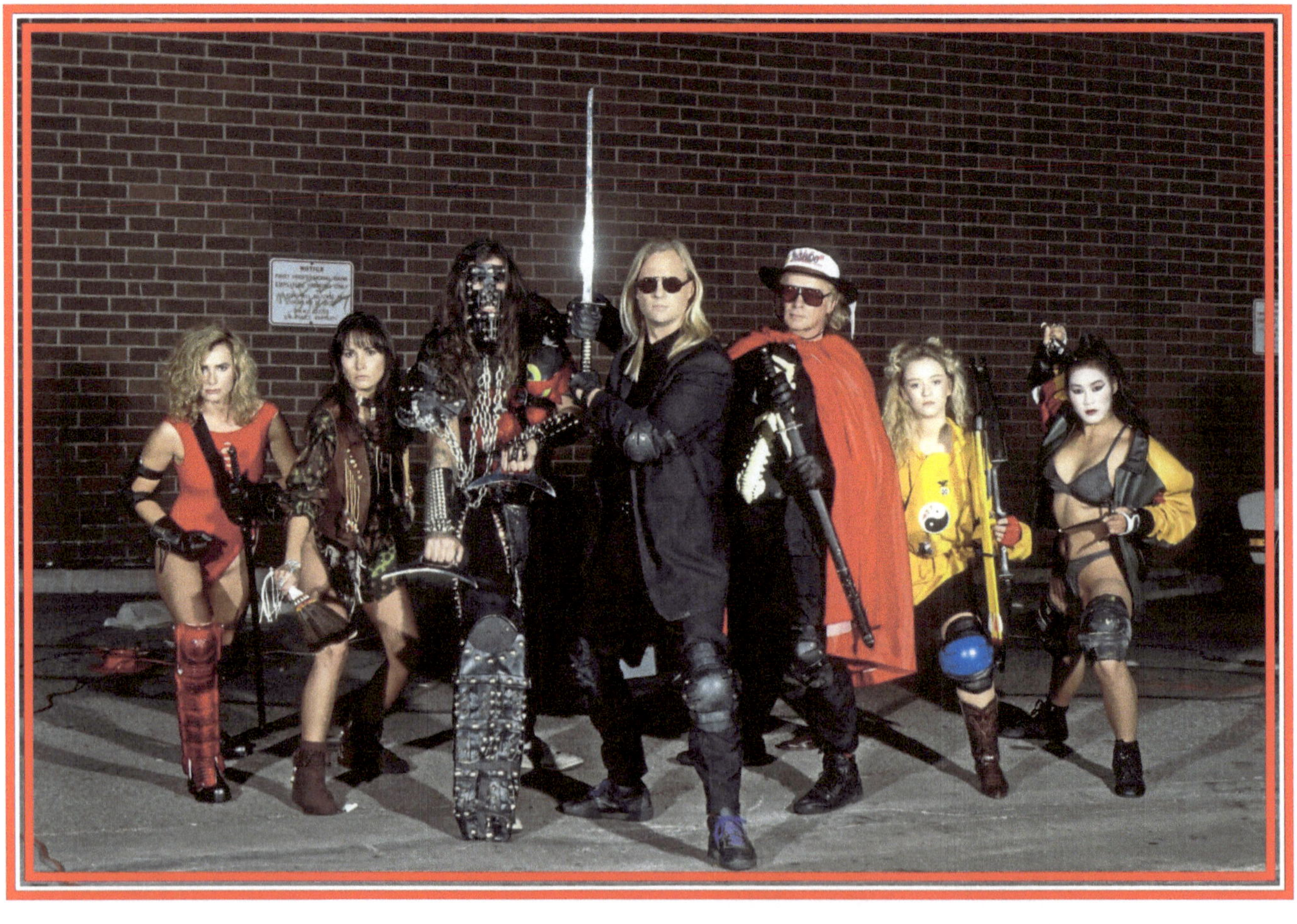

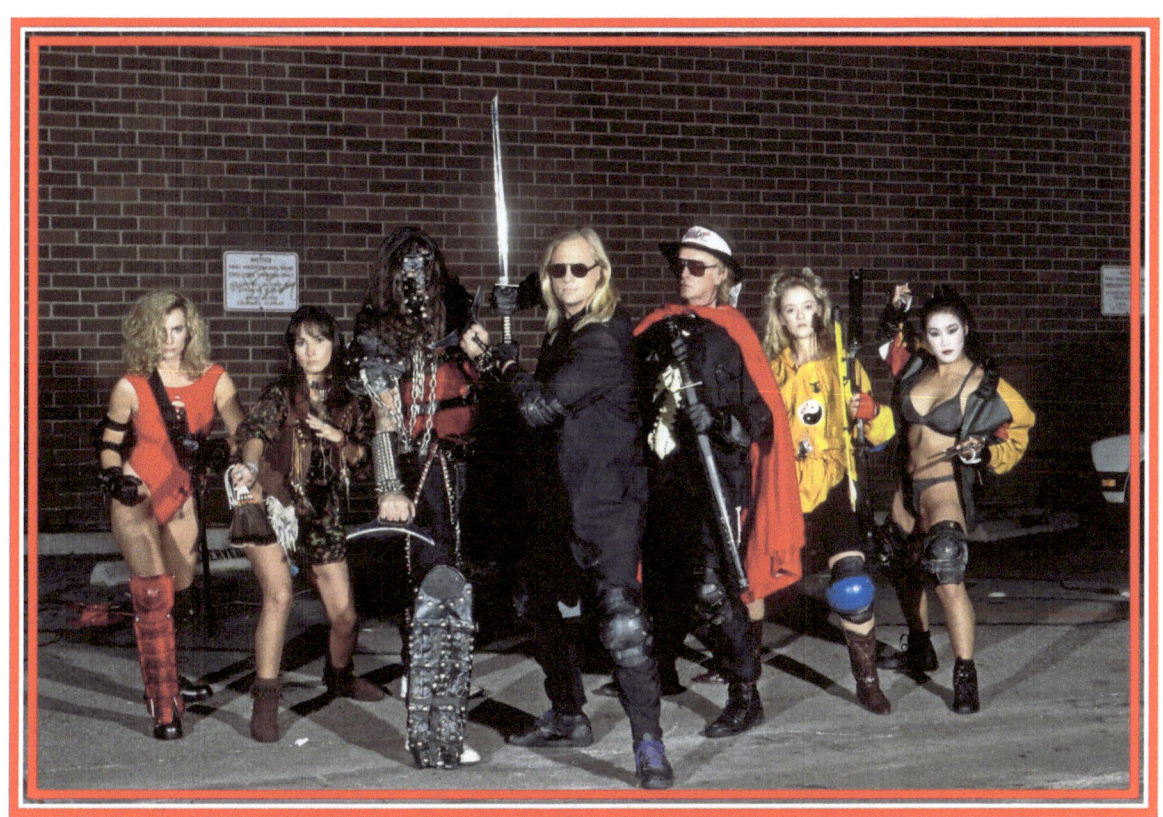

POSTER SHOOT

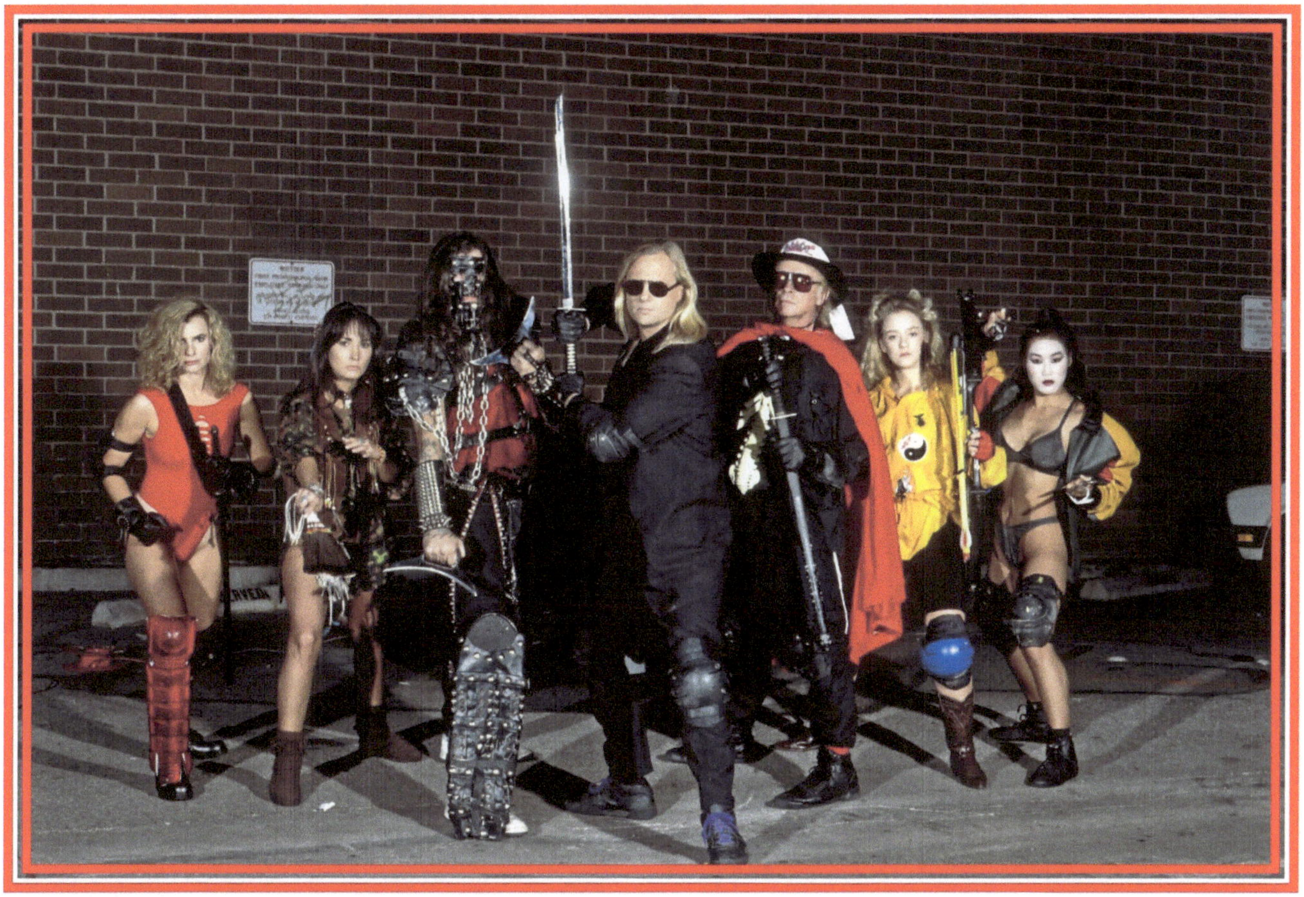

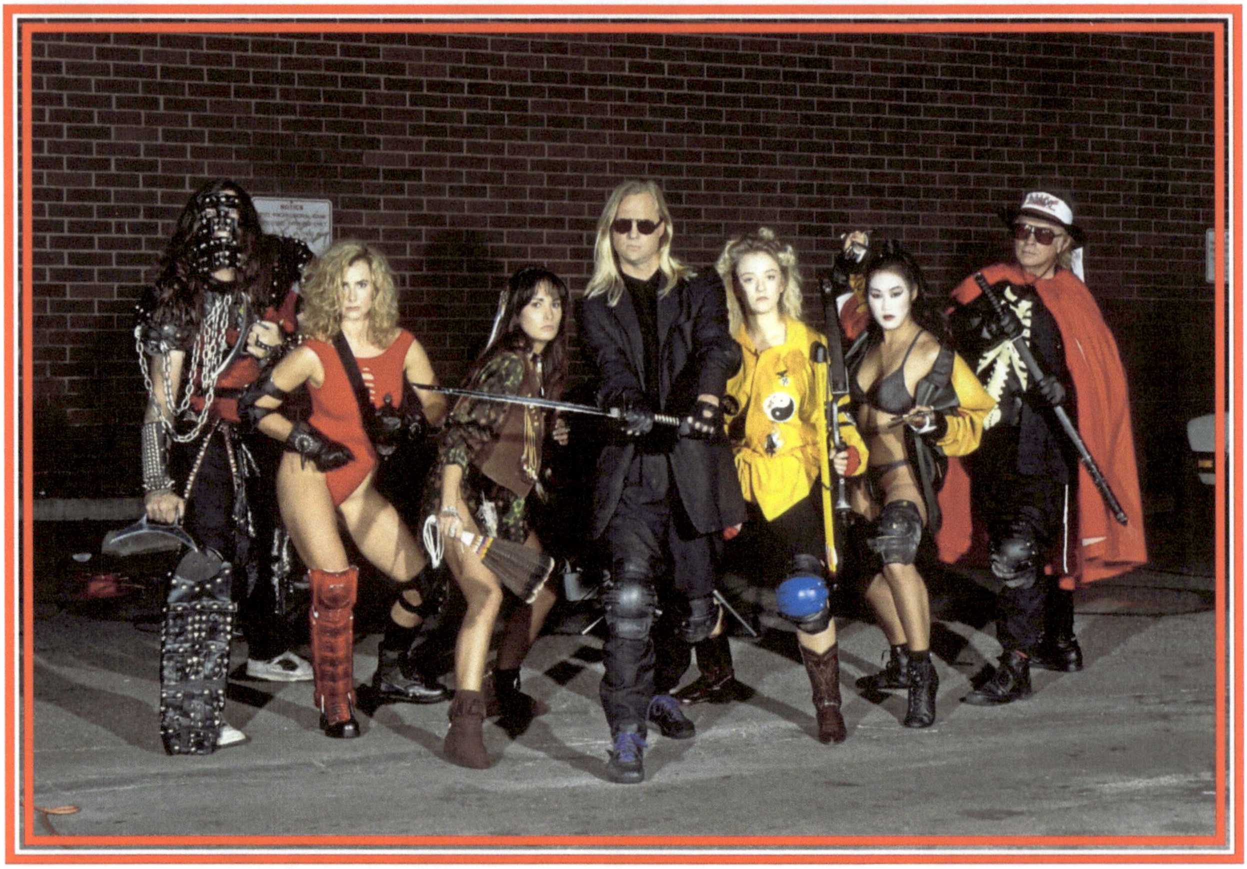

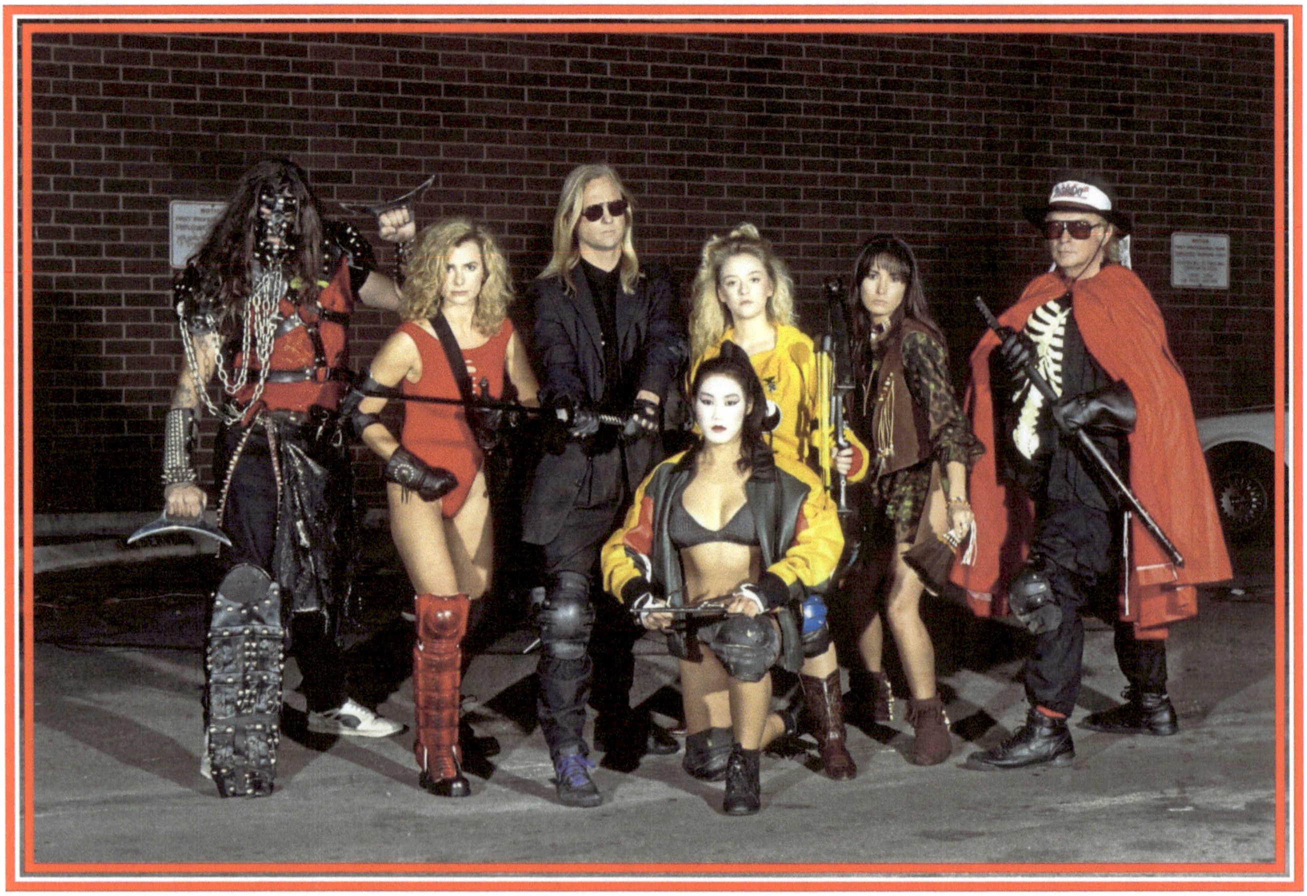

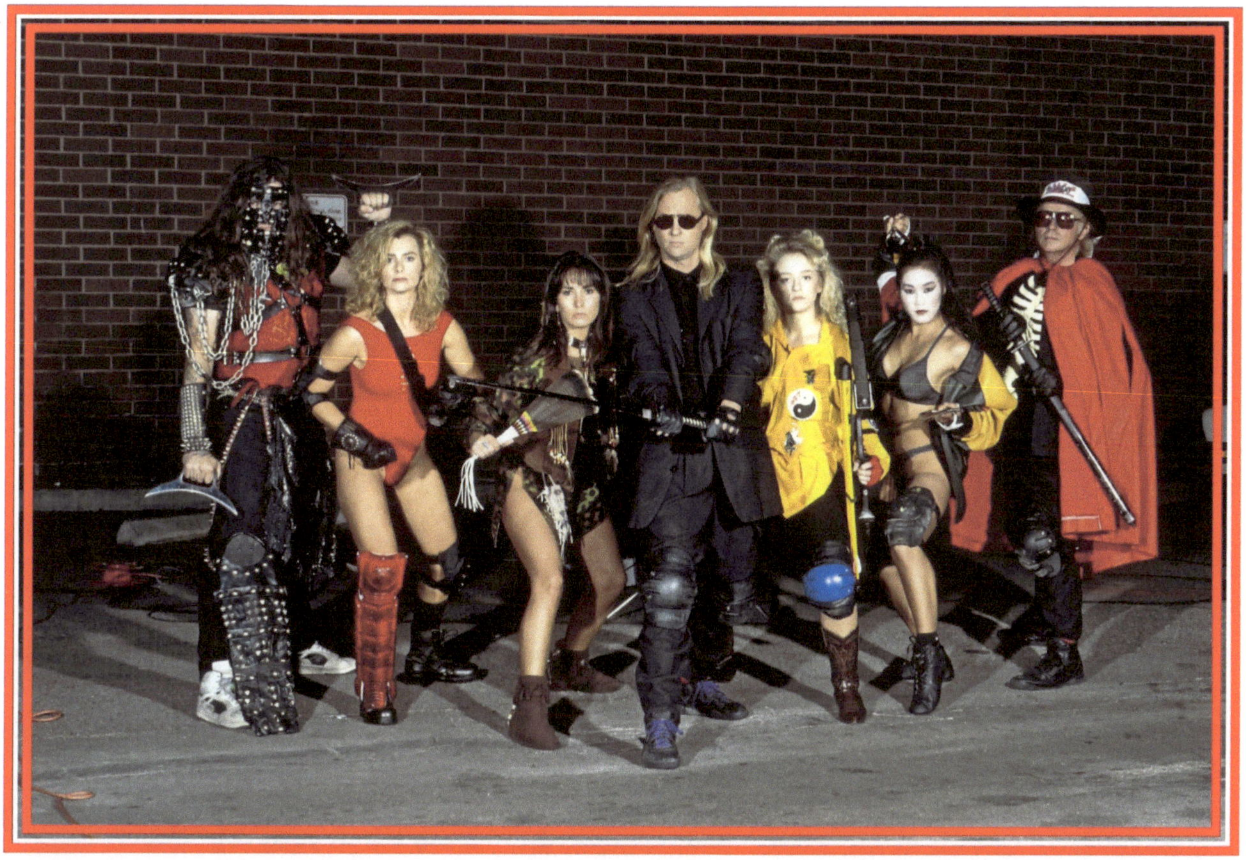

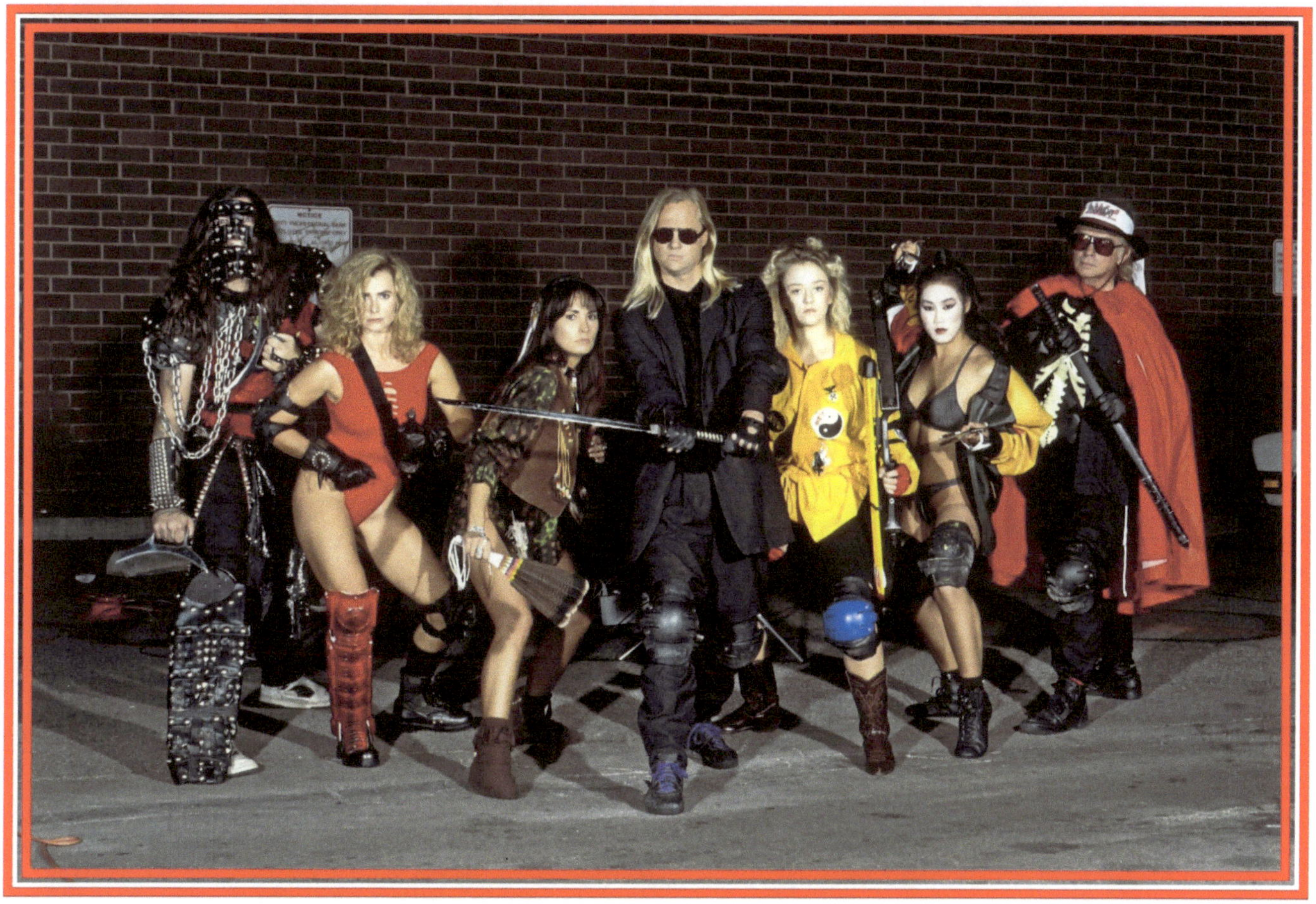

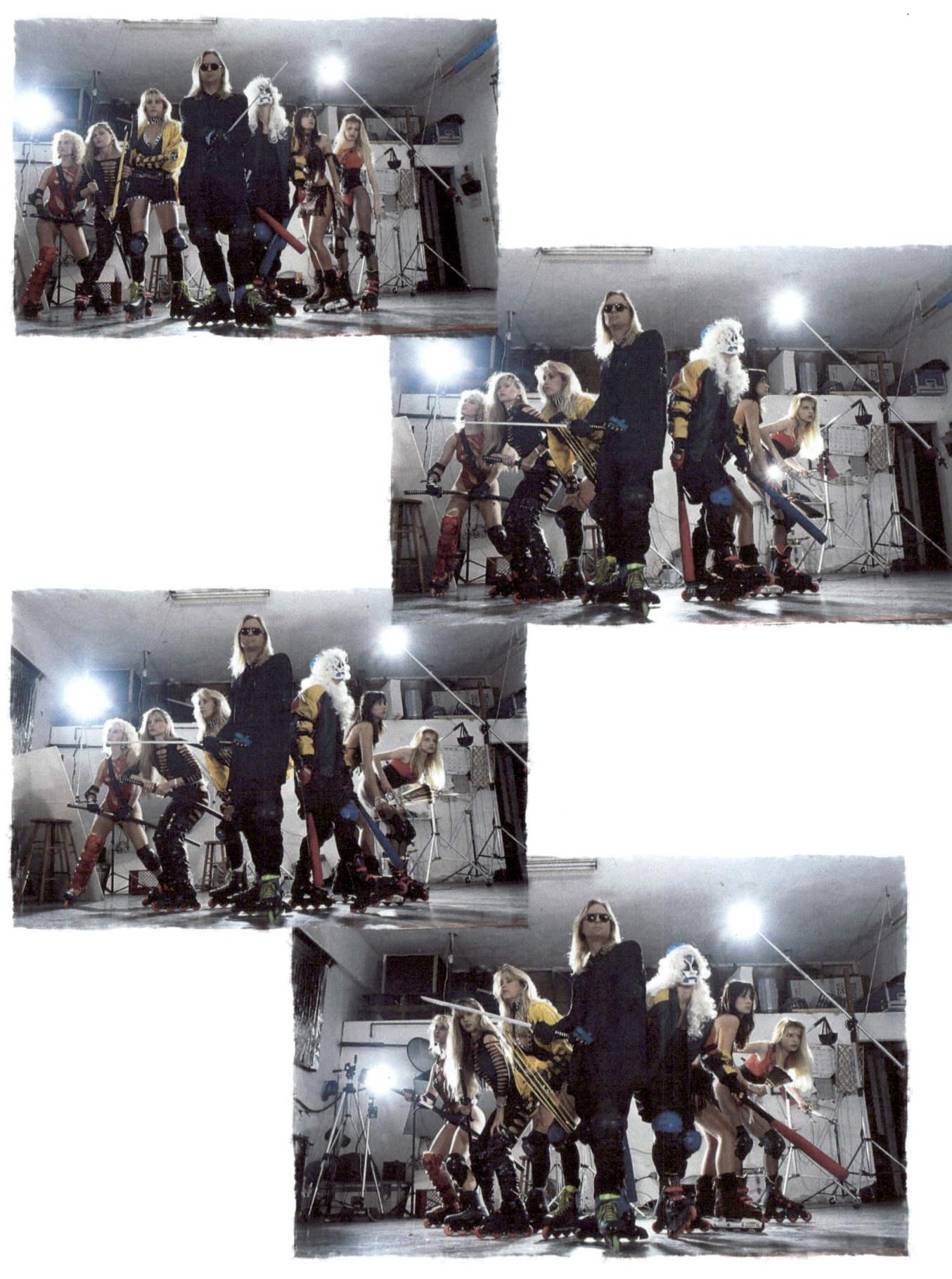

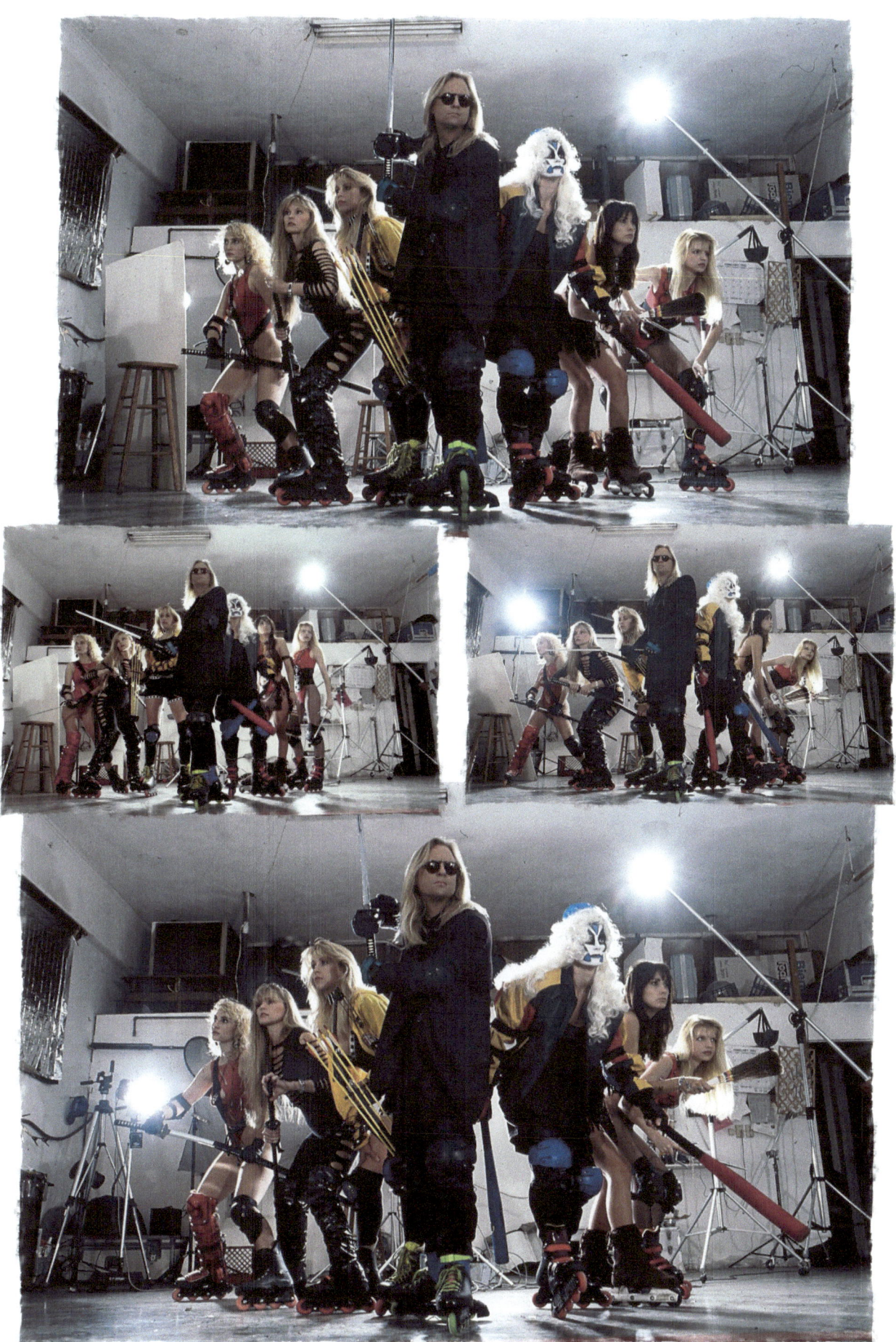

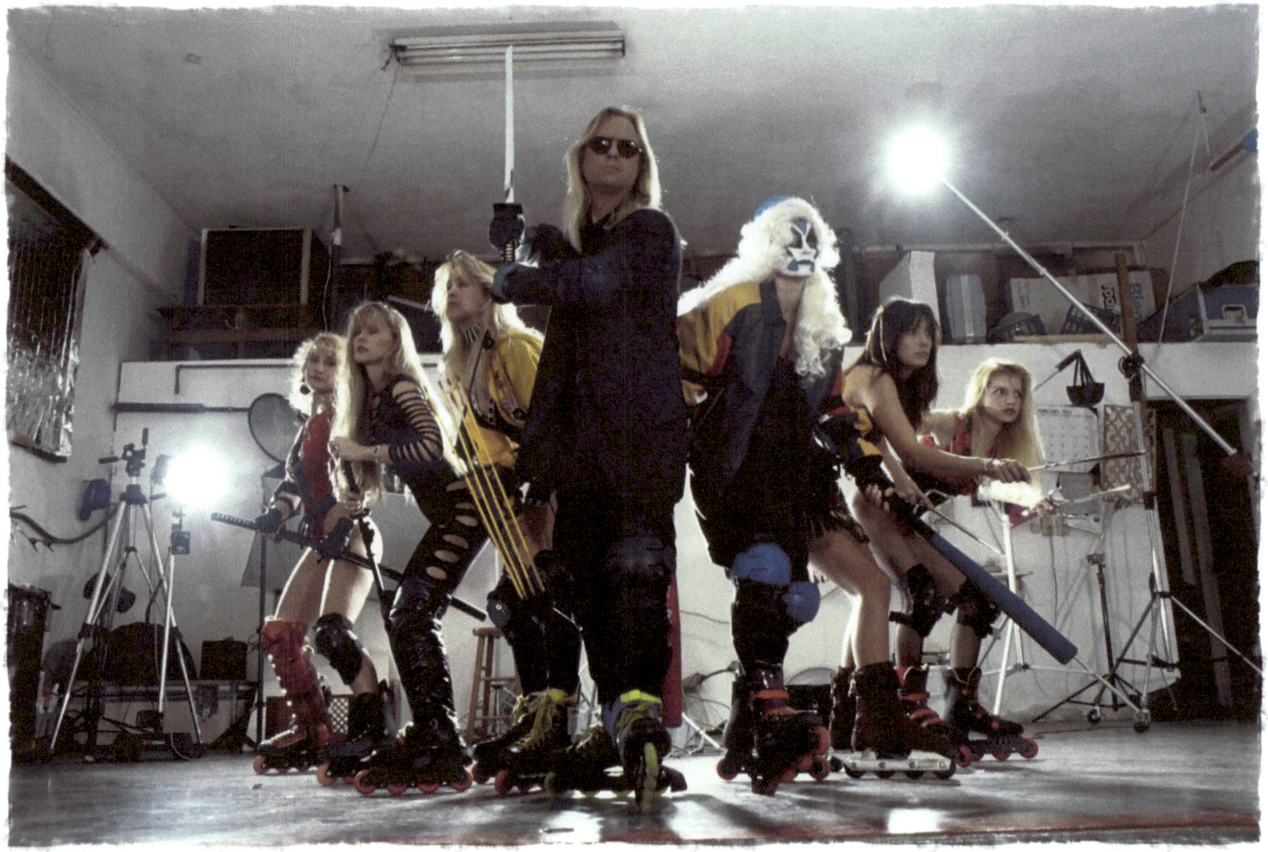

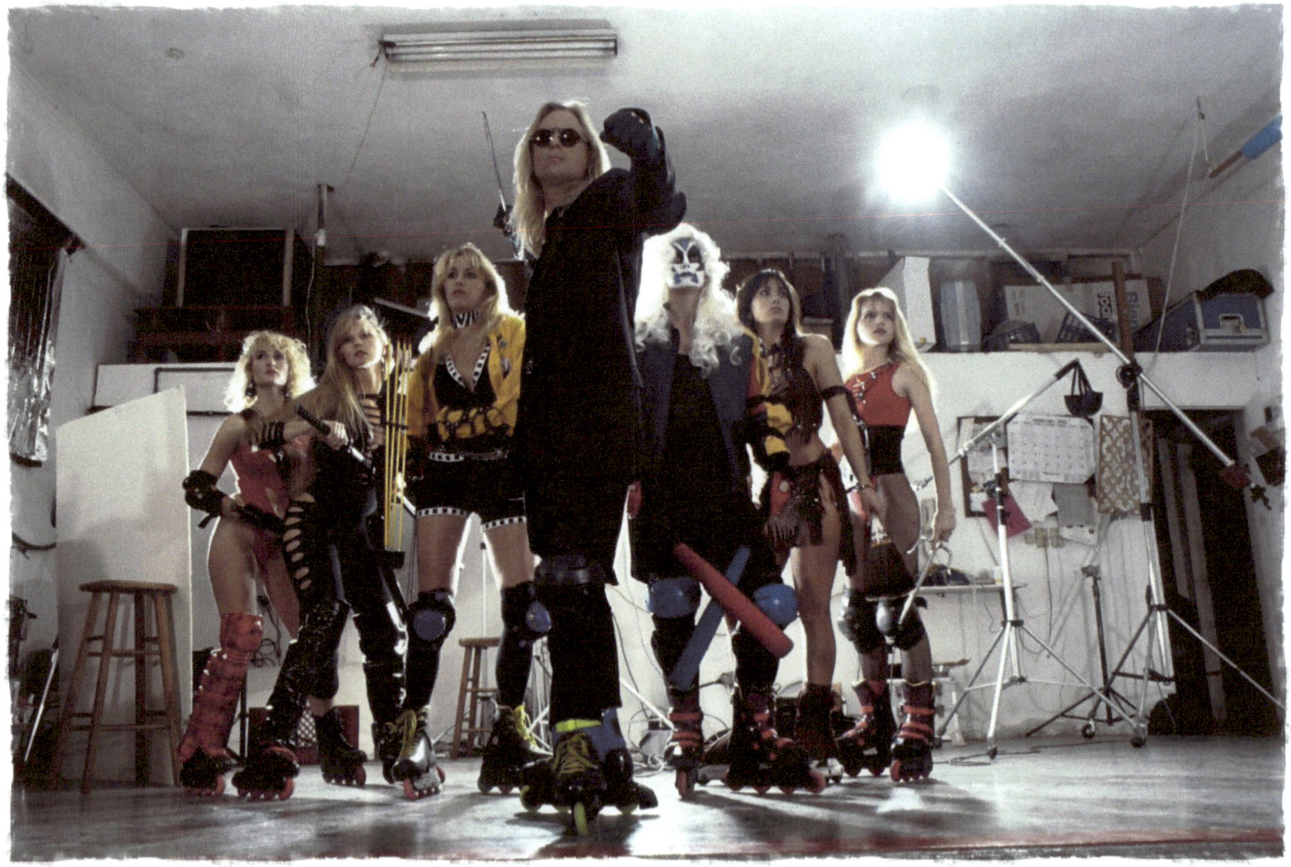

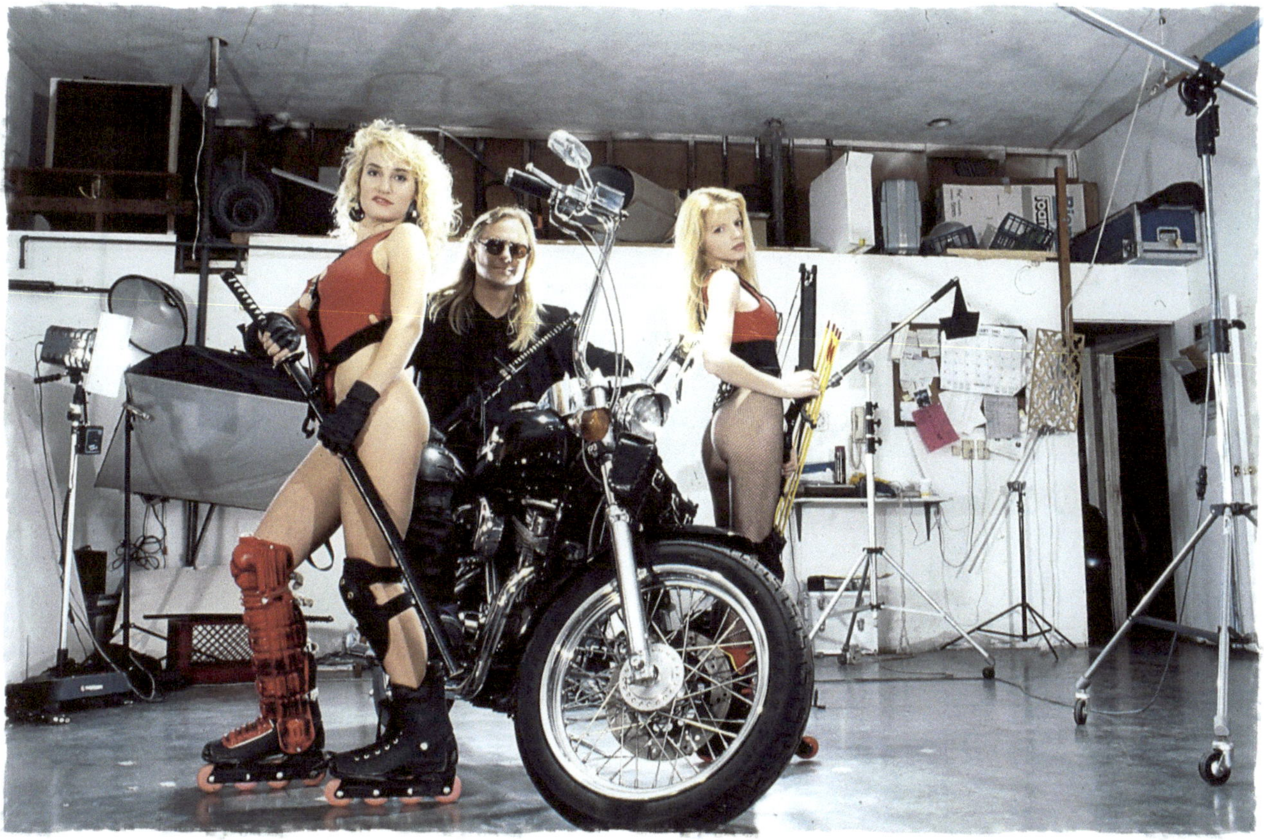

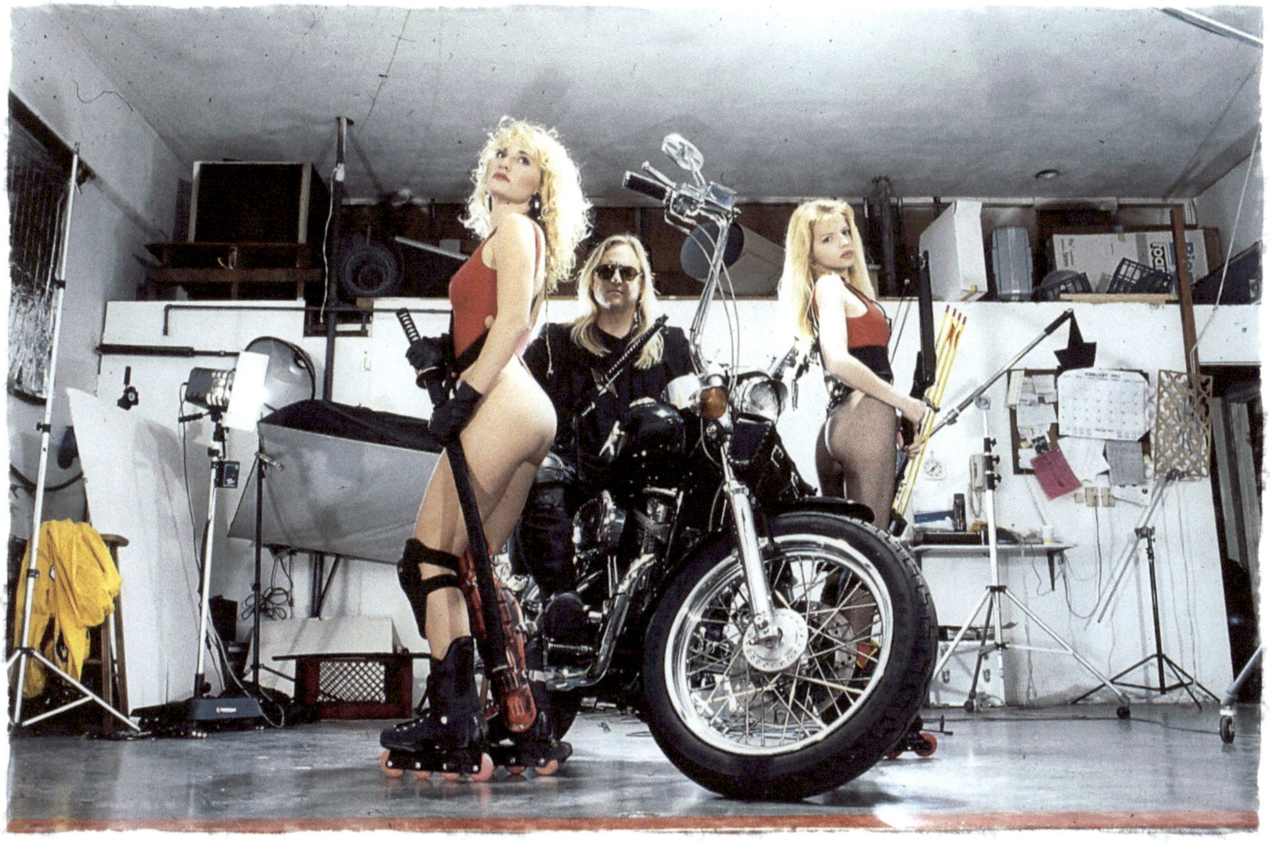

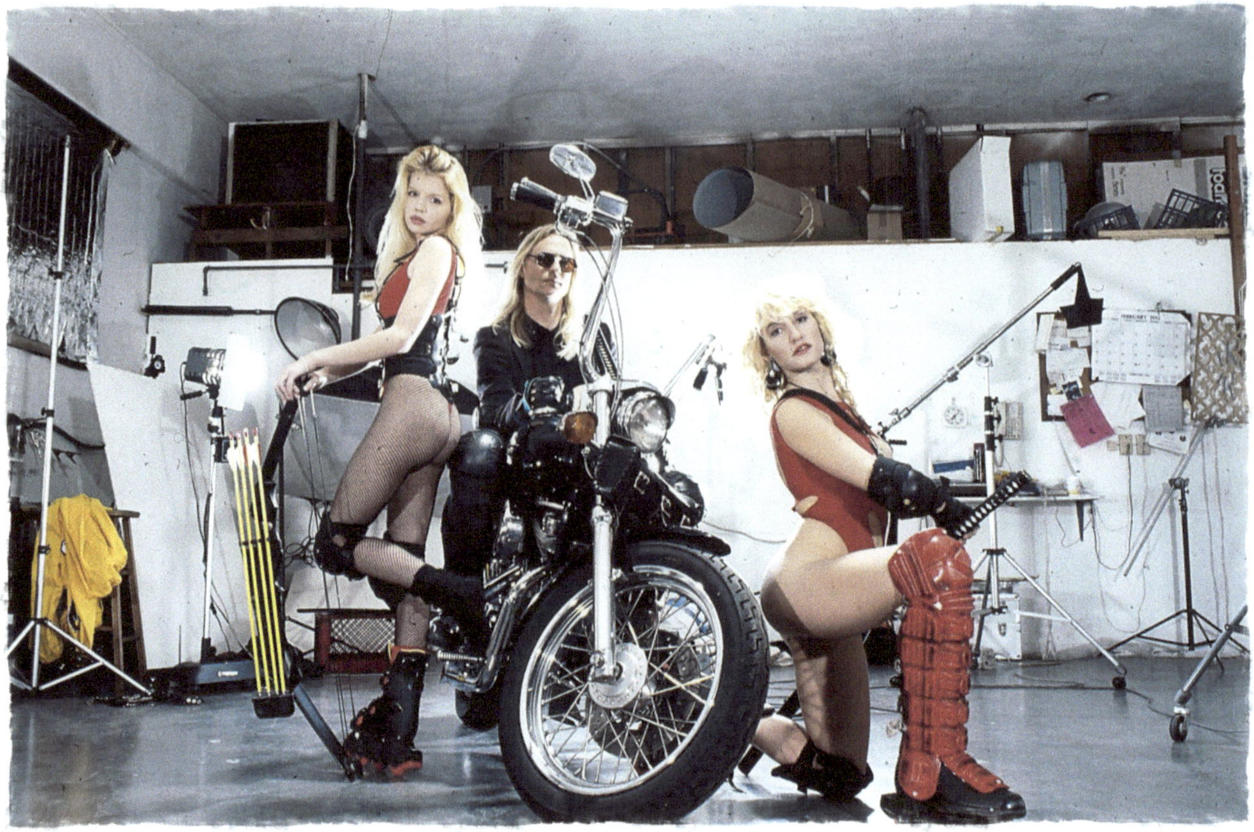

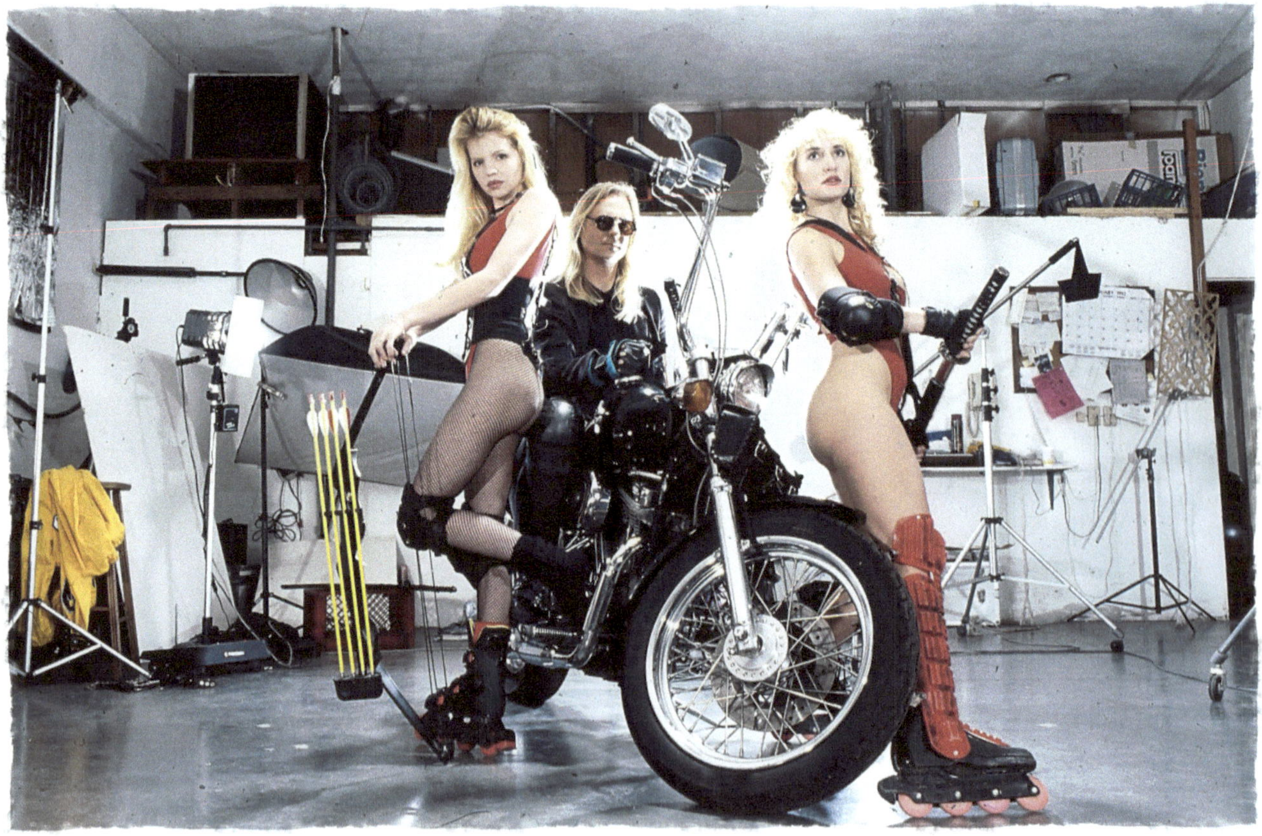

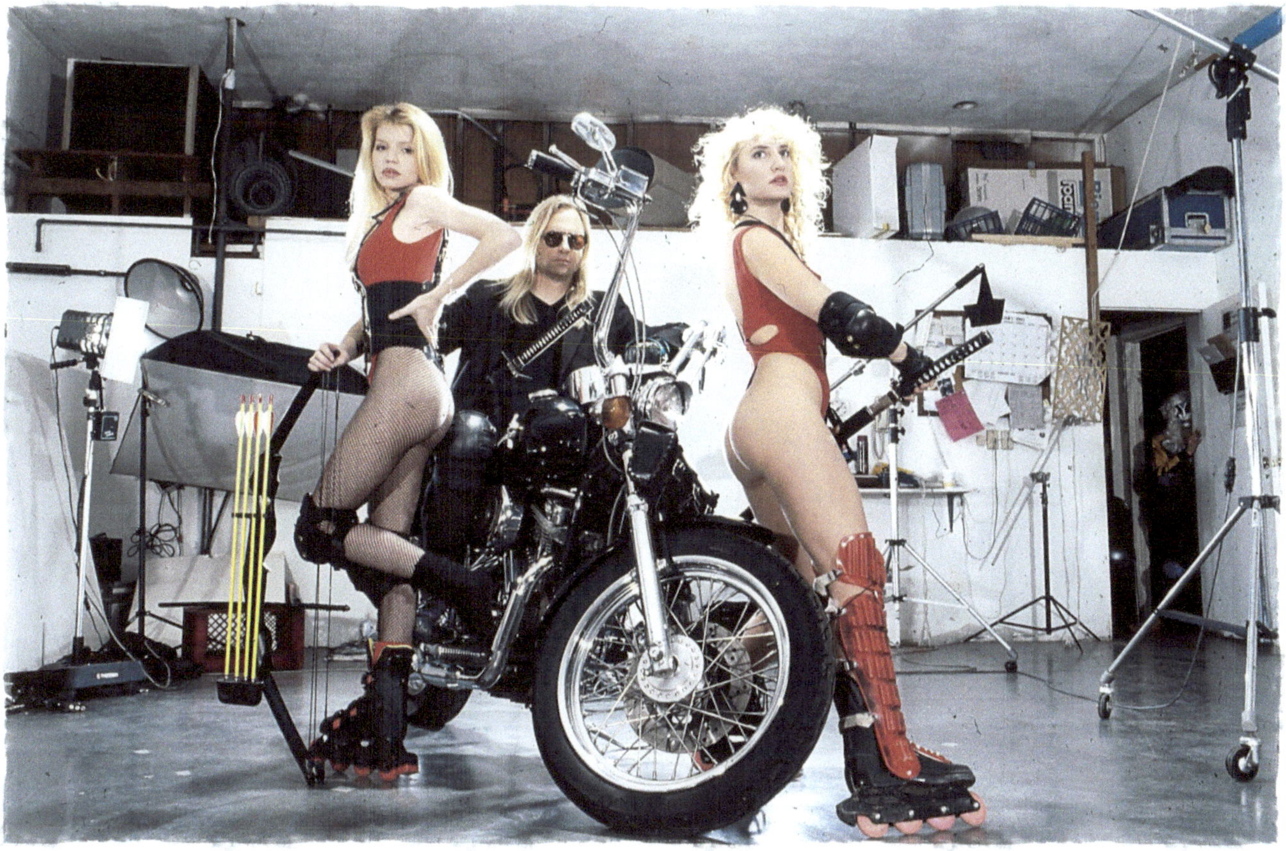

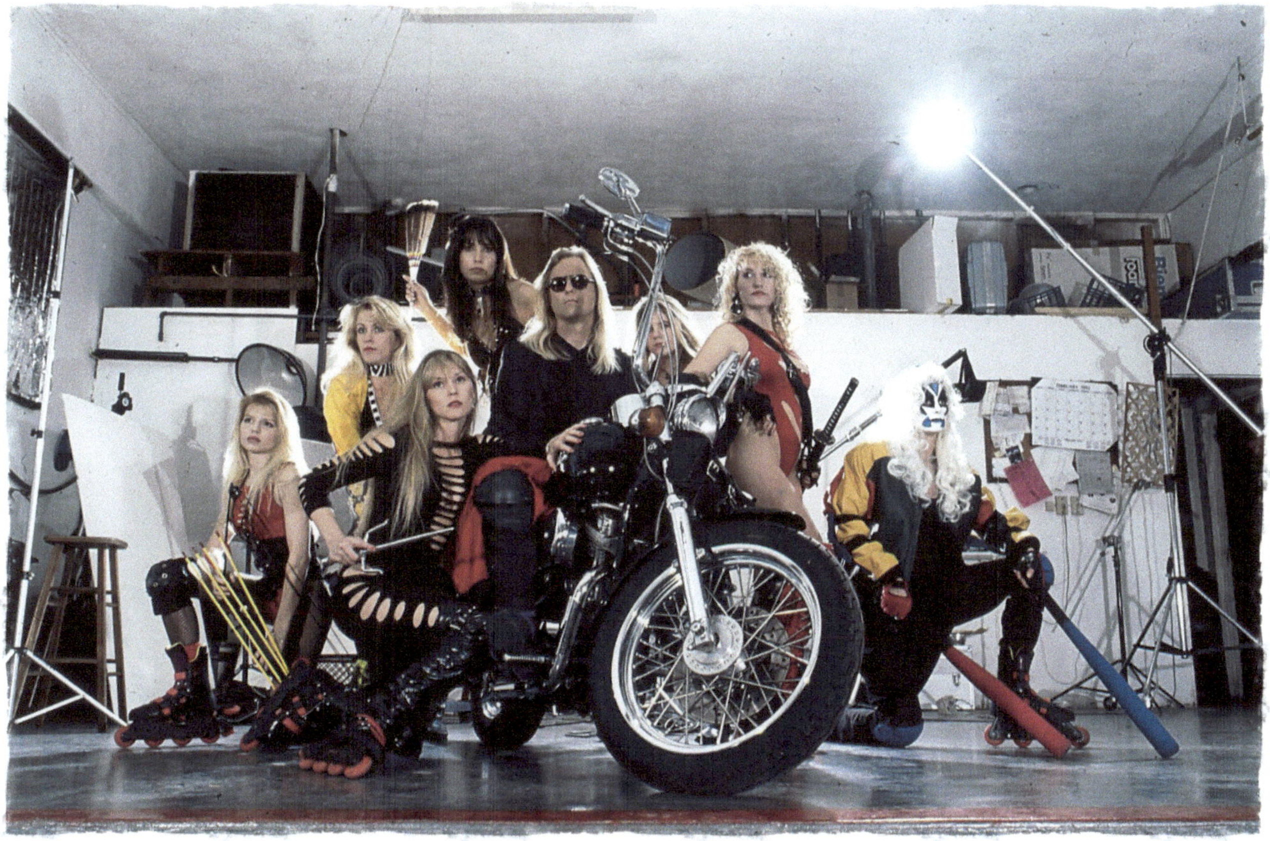

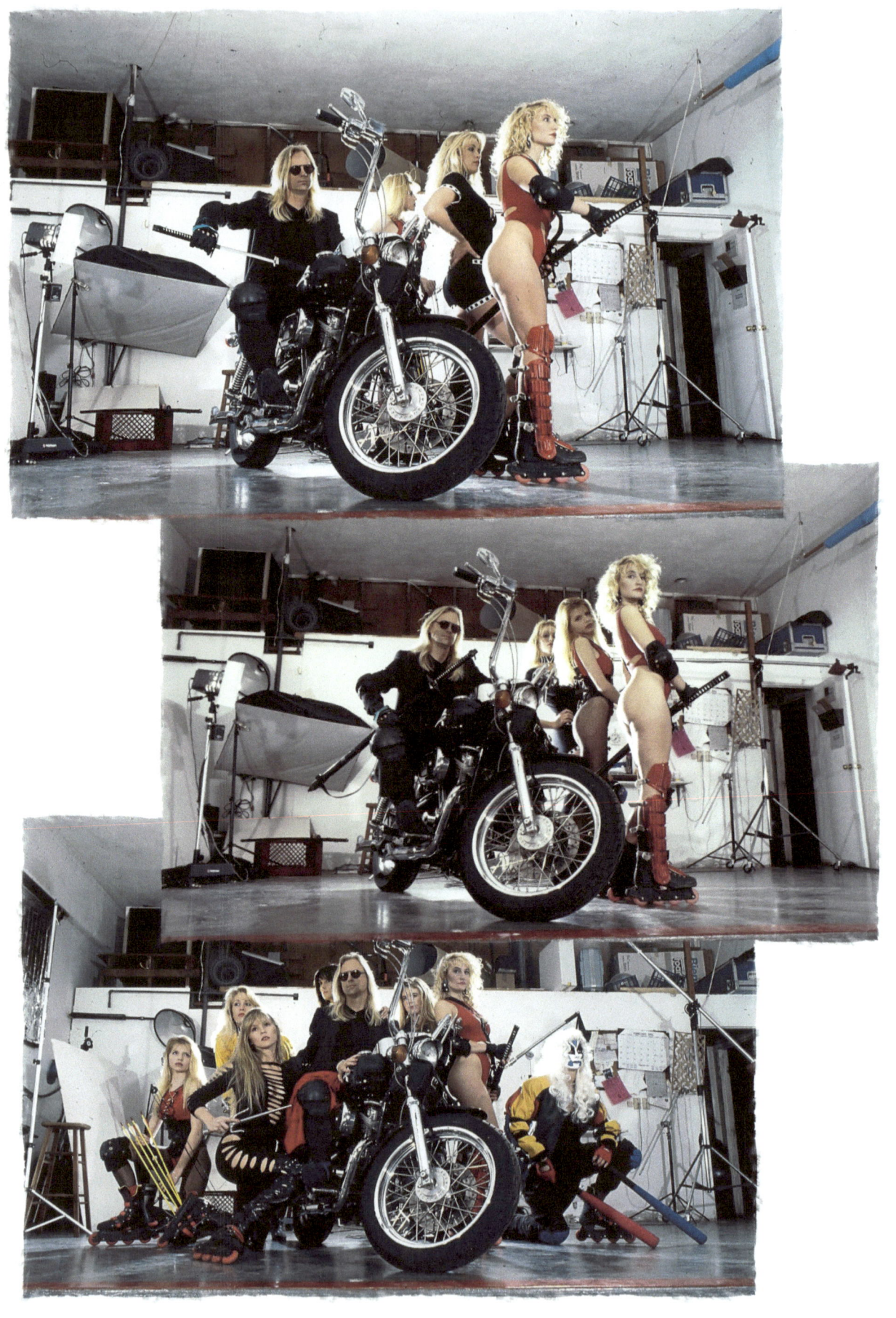

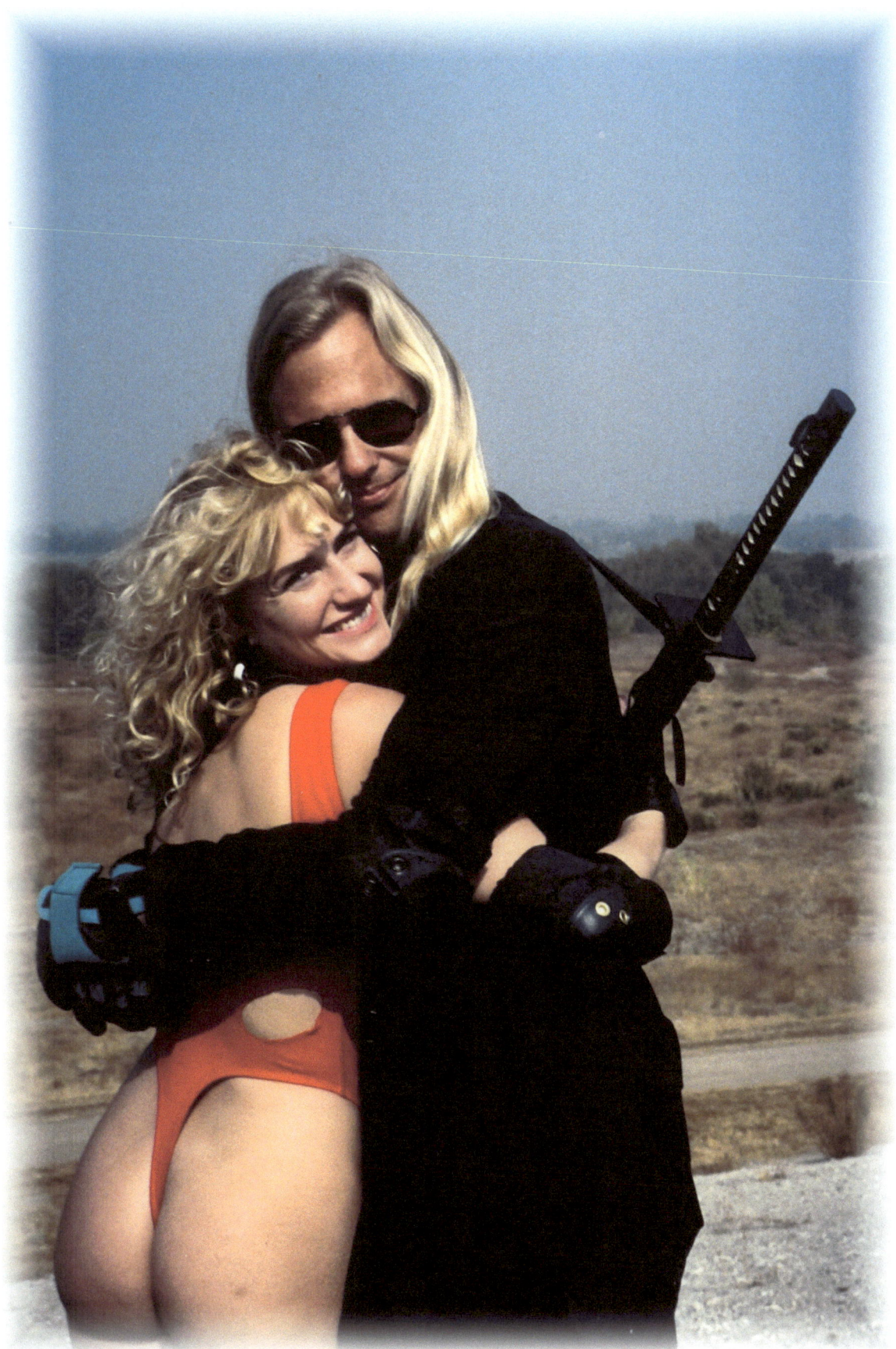

www.ingramcontent.com/pod-product-compliance
Lightning Source LLC
Chambersburg PA
CBHW051144220526
45473CB00003B/657